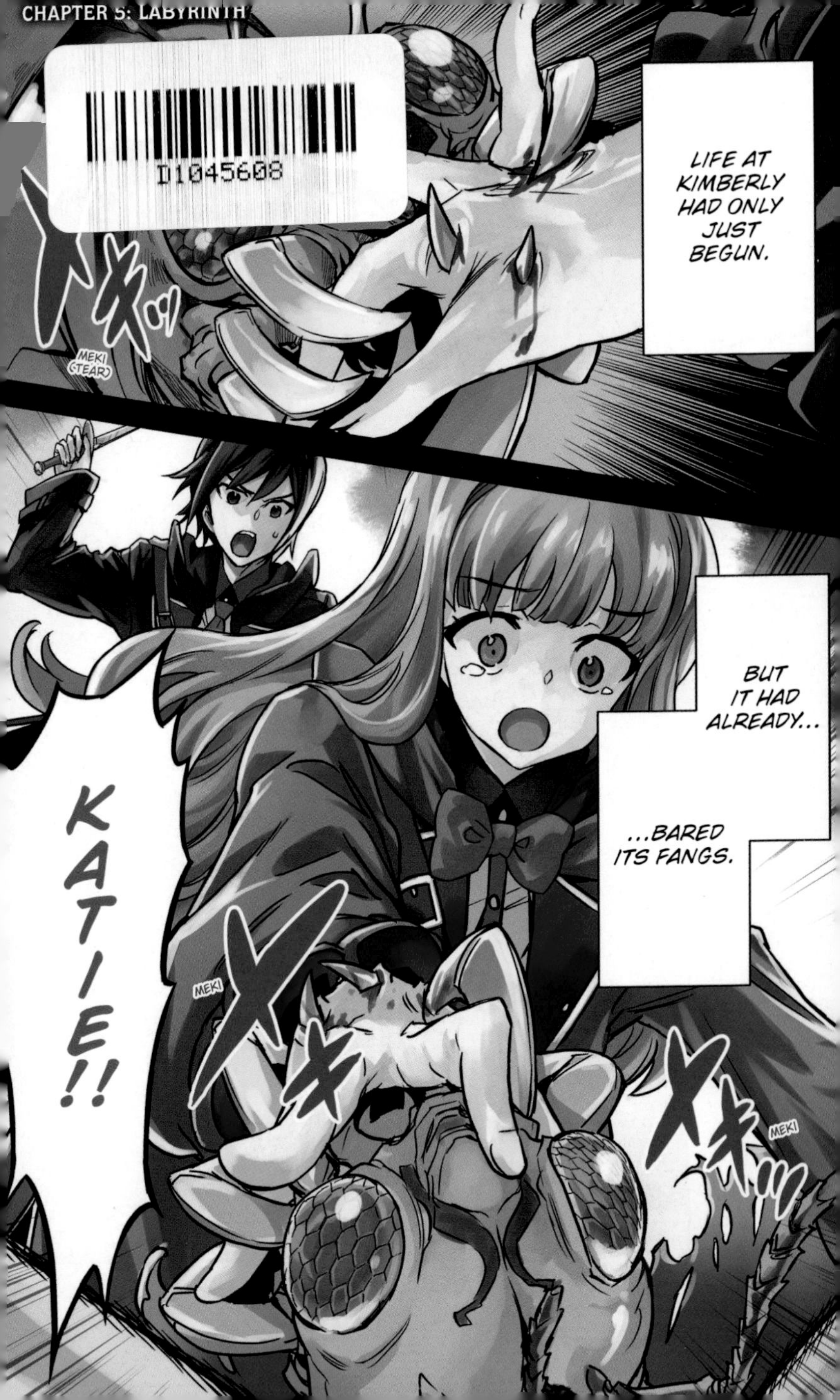
LIFE AT KIMBERLY HAD ONLY JUST BEGUN.
MEKI (TEAR)
BUT IT HAD ALREADY...
...BARED ITS FANGS.
MEKI
KATIE!!
MEKI

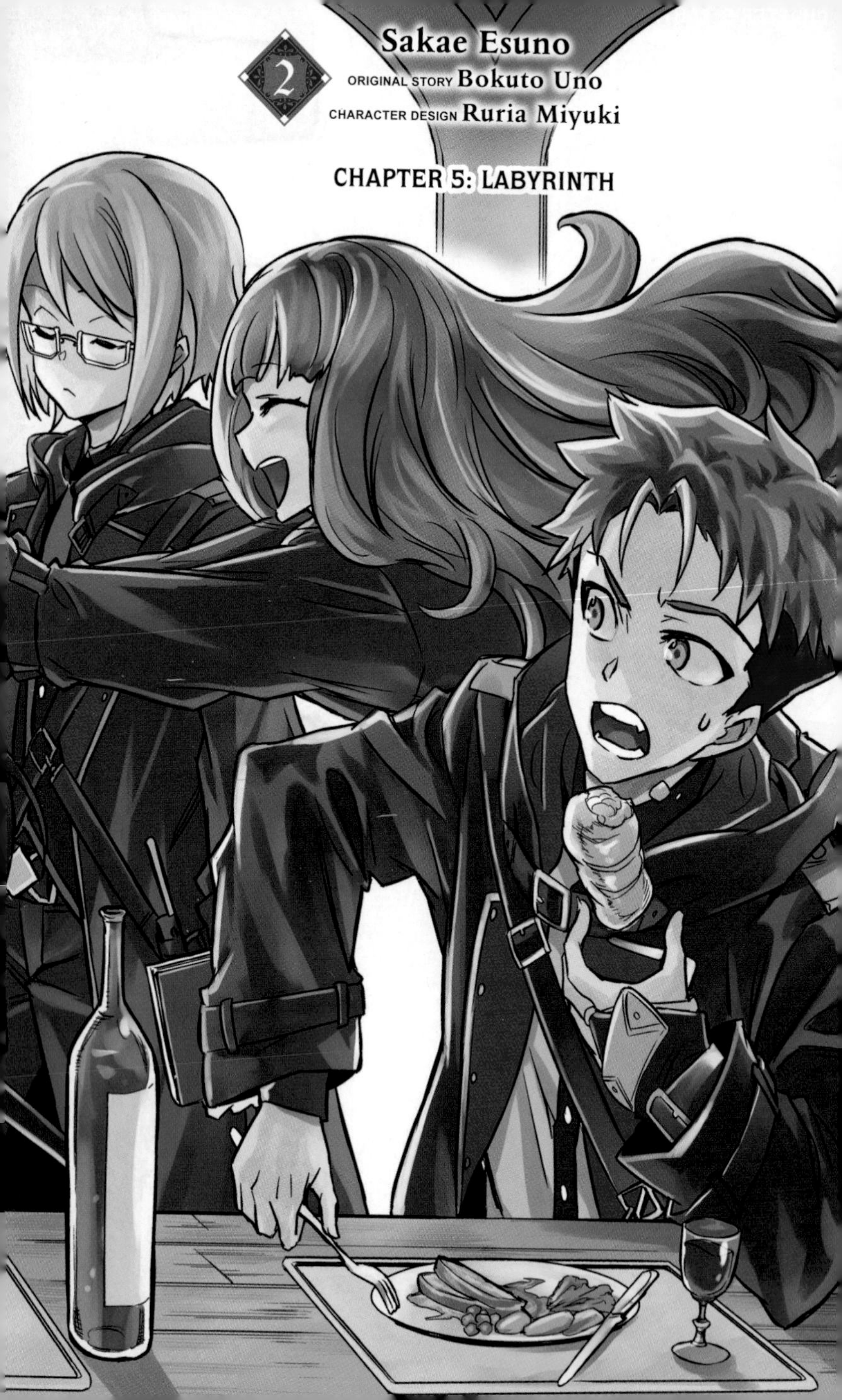

2
Sakae Esuno
ORIGINAL STORY Bokuto Uno
CHARACTER DESIGN Ruria Miyuki
CHAPTER 5: LABYRINTH

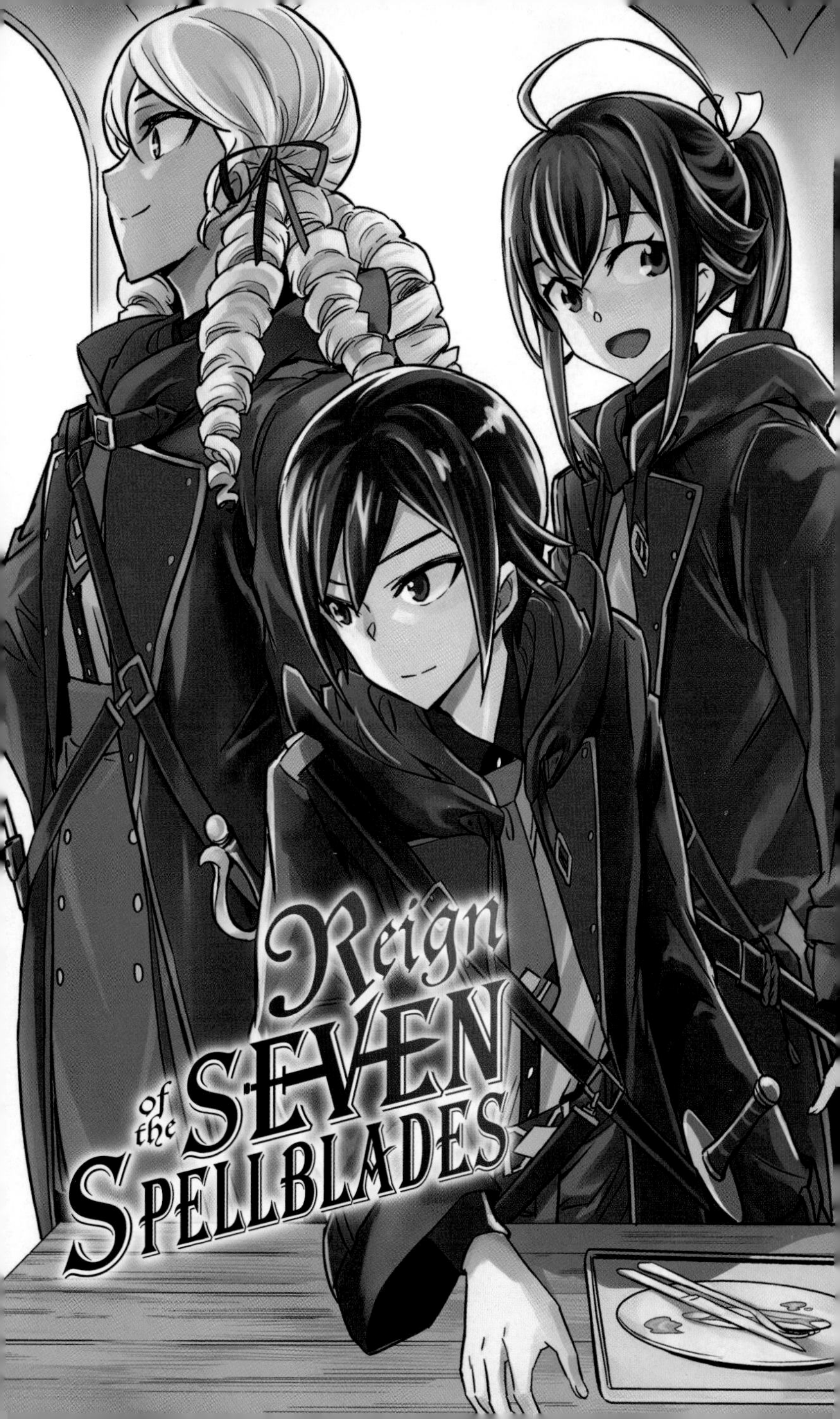
Reign of the Seven Spellblades

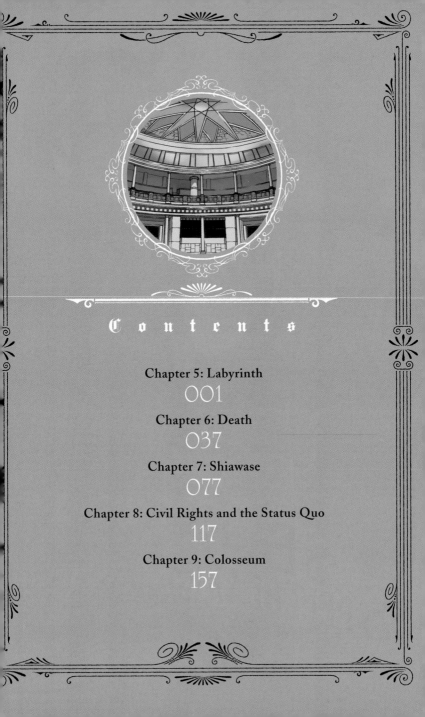

Contents

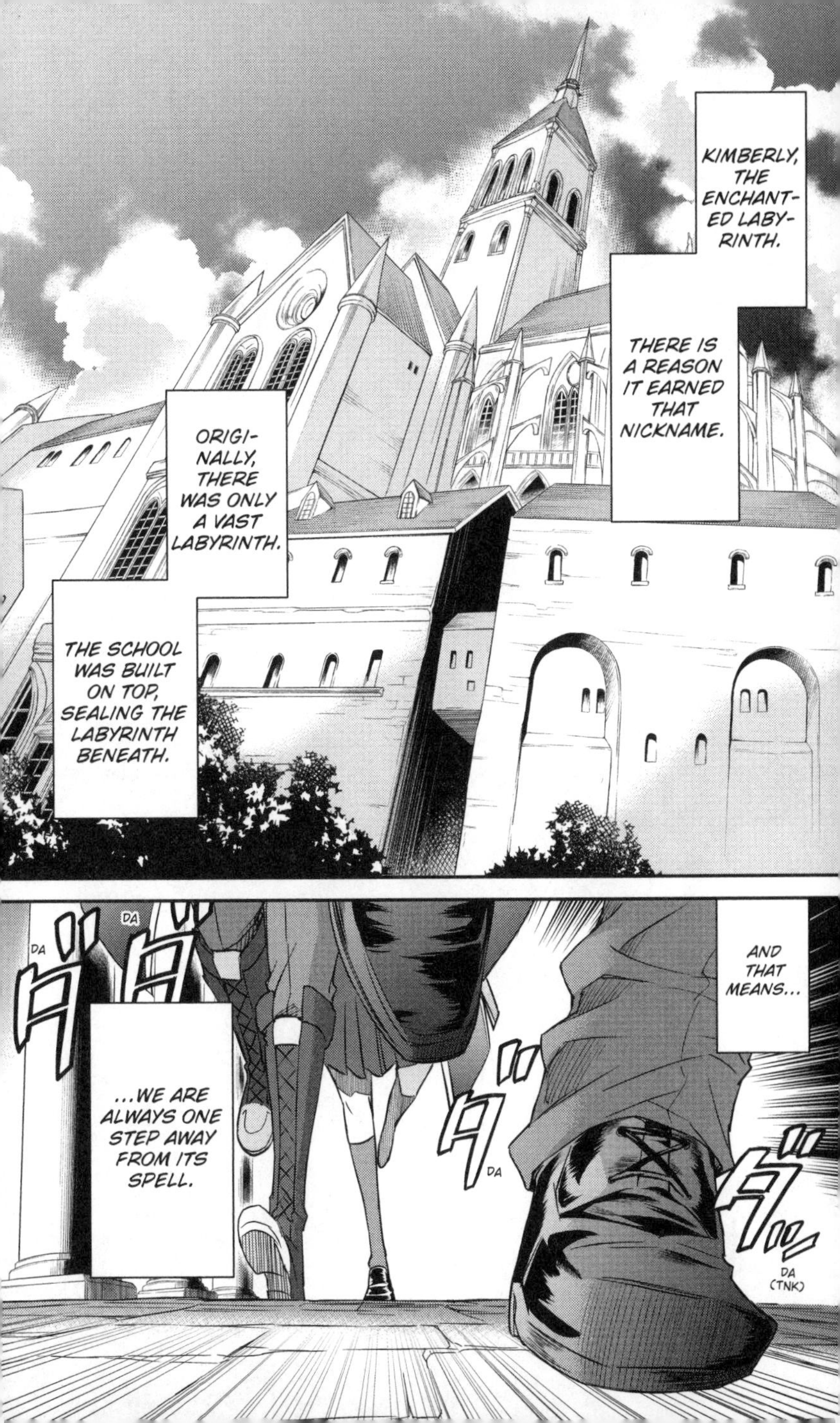
KIMBERLY, THE ENCHANTED LABYRINTH.
THERE IS A REASON IT EARNED THAT NICKNAME.
ORIGINALLY, THERE WAS ONLY A VAST LABYRINTH.
THE SCHOOL WAS BUILT ON TOP, SEALING THE LABYRINTH BENEATH.
AND THAT MEANS...
DA (TNK)
DA
...WE ARE ALWAYS ONE STEP AWAY FROM ITS SPELL.
DA
DA

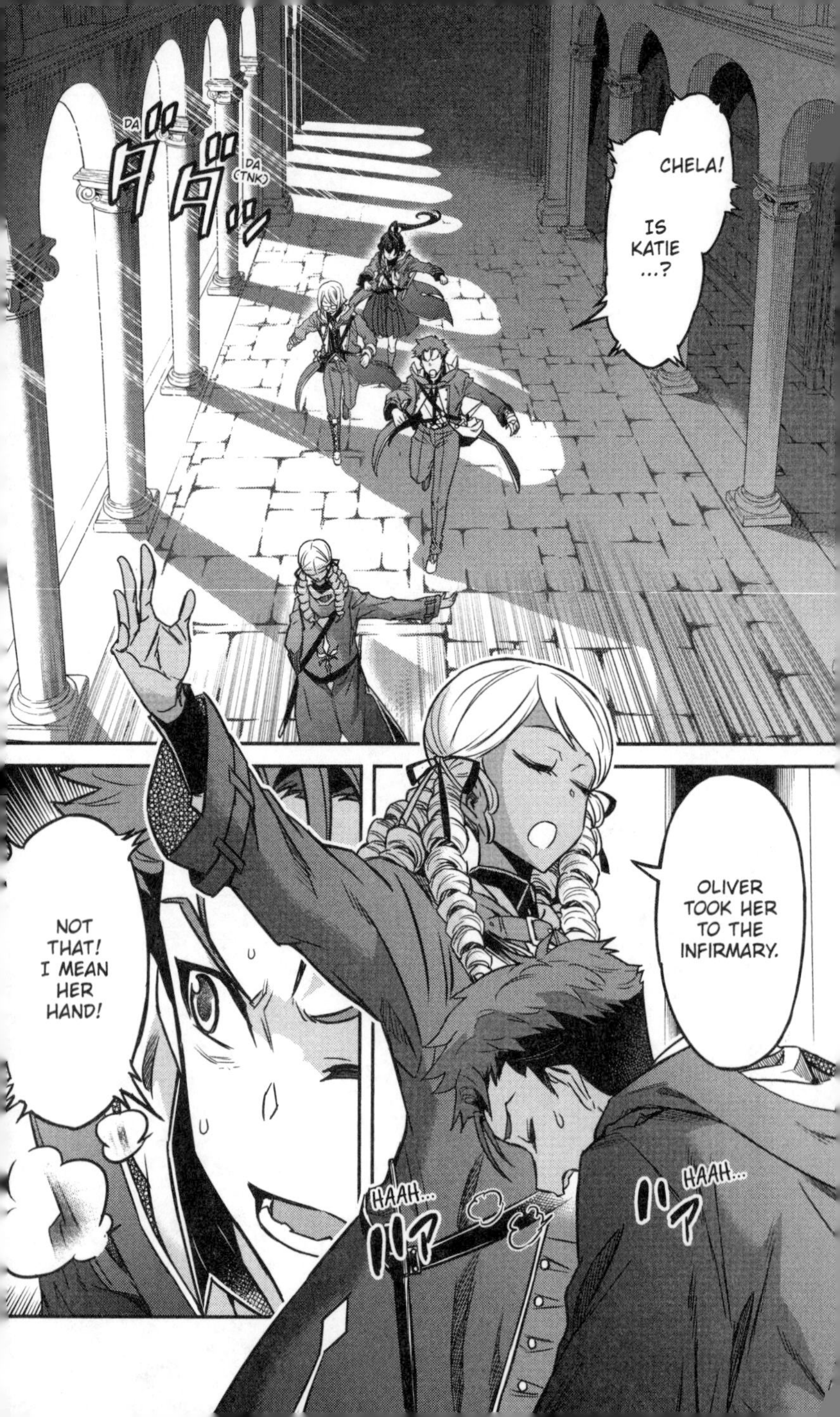
CHELA!
IS KATIE ...?
DA
DA (TNK)
OLIVER TOOK HER TO THE INFIRMARY.
NOT THAT! I MEAN HER HAND!
HAAH...
HAAH...

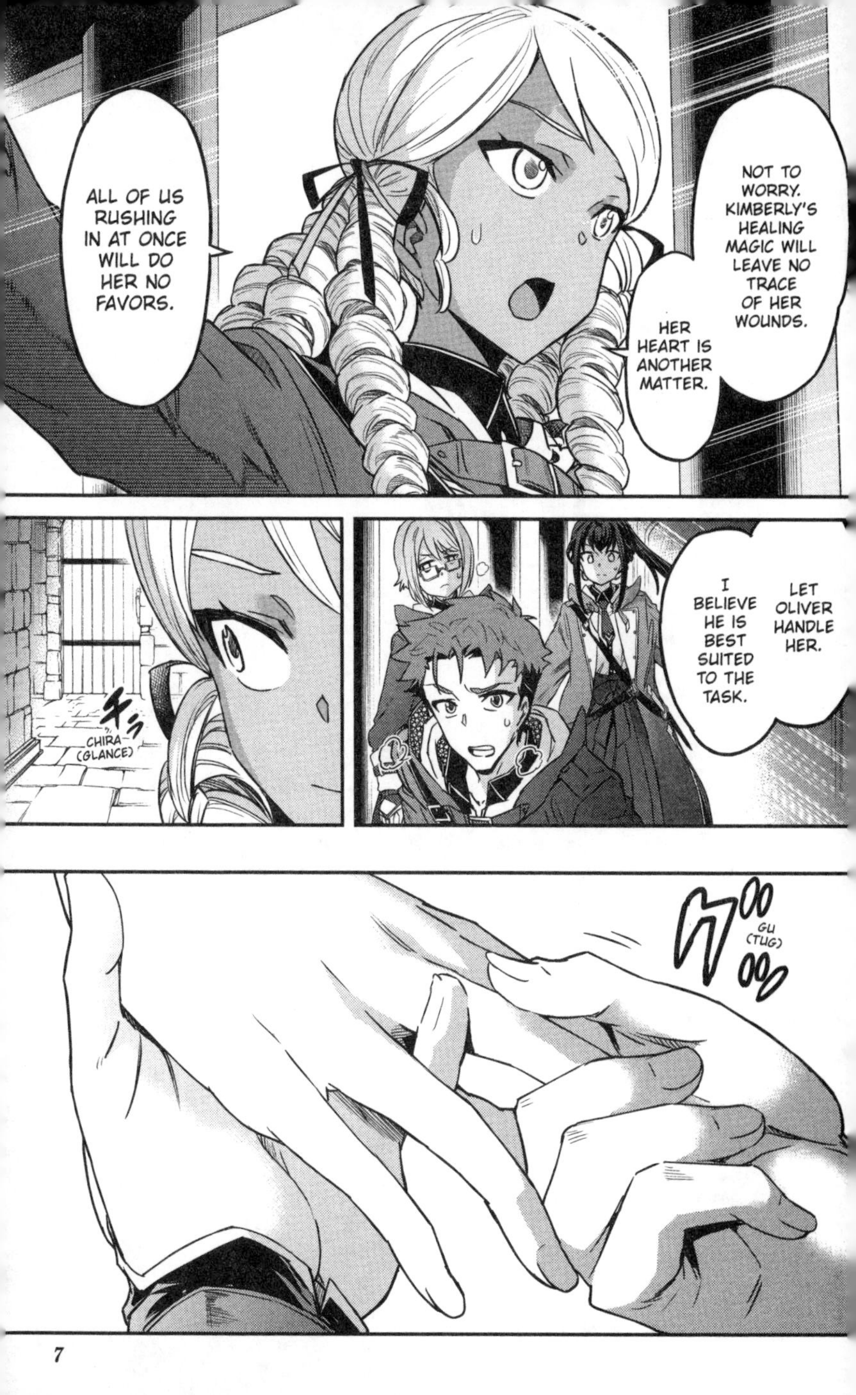
NOT TO WORRY. KIMBERLY'S HEALING MAGIC WILL LEAVE NO TRACE OF HER WOUNDS.
HER HEART IS ANOTHER MATTER.
ALL OF US RUSHING IN AT ONCE WILL DO HER NO FAVORS.
LET OLIVER HANDLE HER.
I BELIEVE HE IS BEST SUITED TO THE TASK.
CHIRA (GLANCE)
GU (TUG)

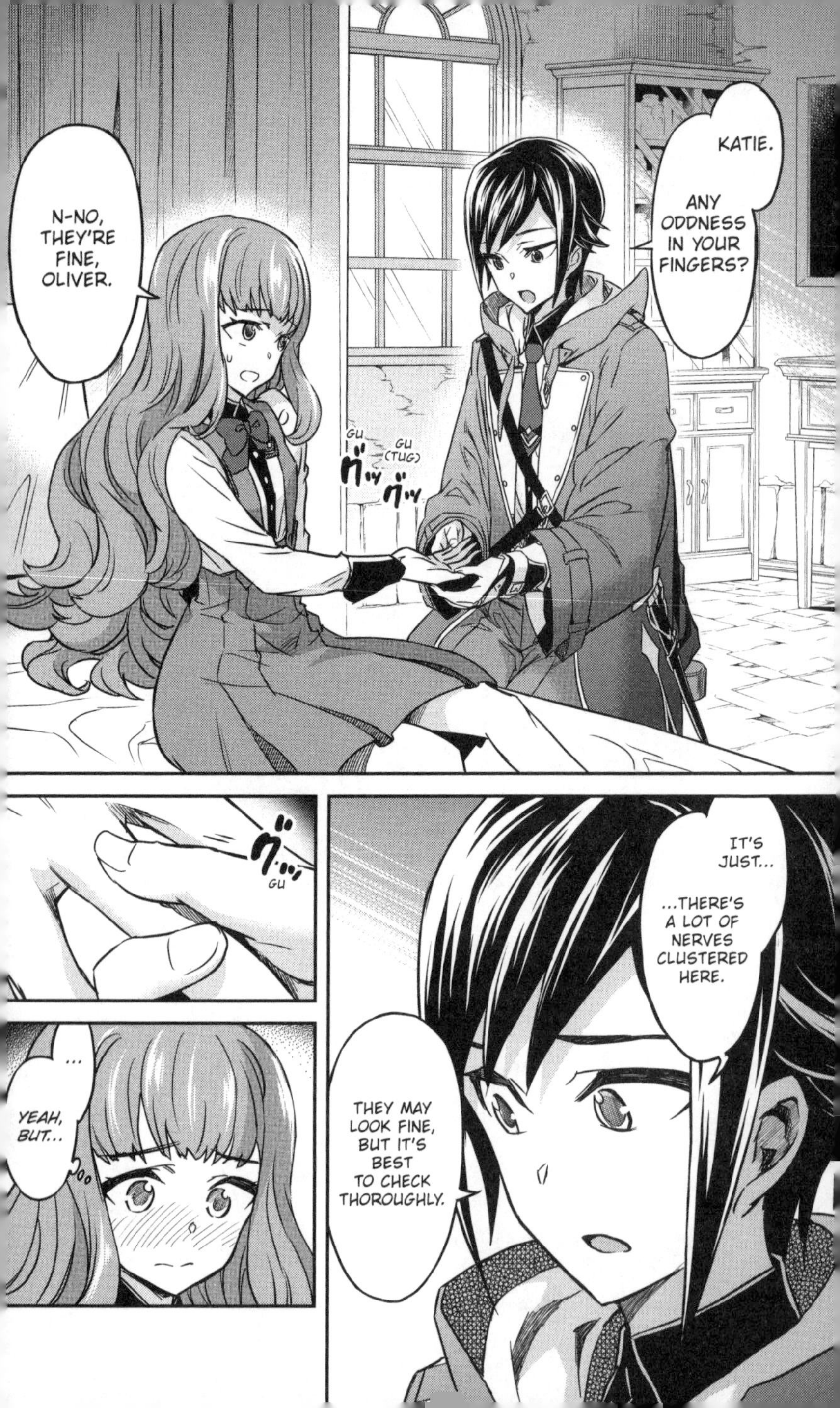
KATIE.
ANY ODDNESS IN YOUR FINGERS?
N-NO, THEY'RE FINE, OLIVER.
GU
GU (TUG)
IT'S JUST...
...THERE'S A LOT OF NERVES CLUSTERED HERE.
THEY MAY LOOK FINE, BUT IT'S BEST TO CHECK THOROUGHLY.
GU
...
YEAH, BUT...

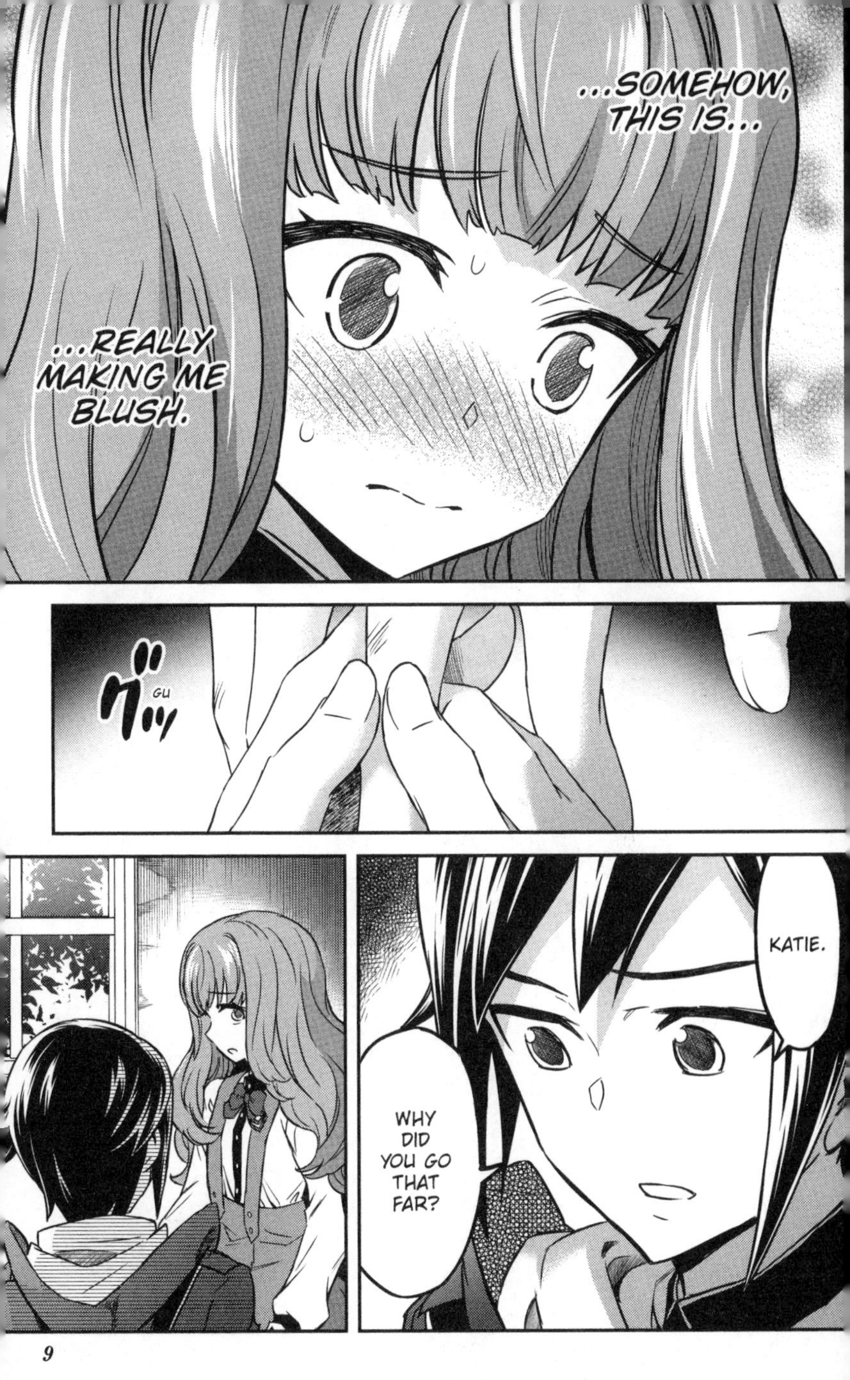
...SOMEHOW, THIS IS...
...REALLY MAKING ME BLUSH.
グッ
GU
KATIE.
WHY DID YOU GO THAT FAR?

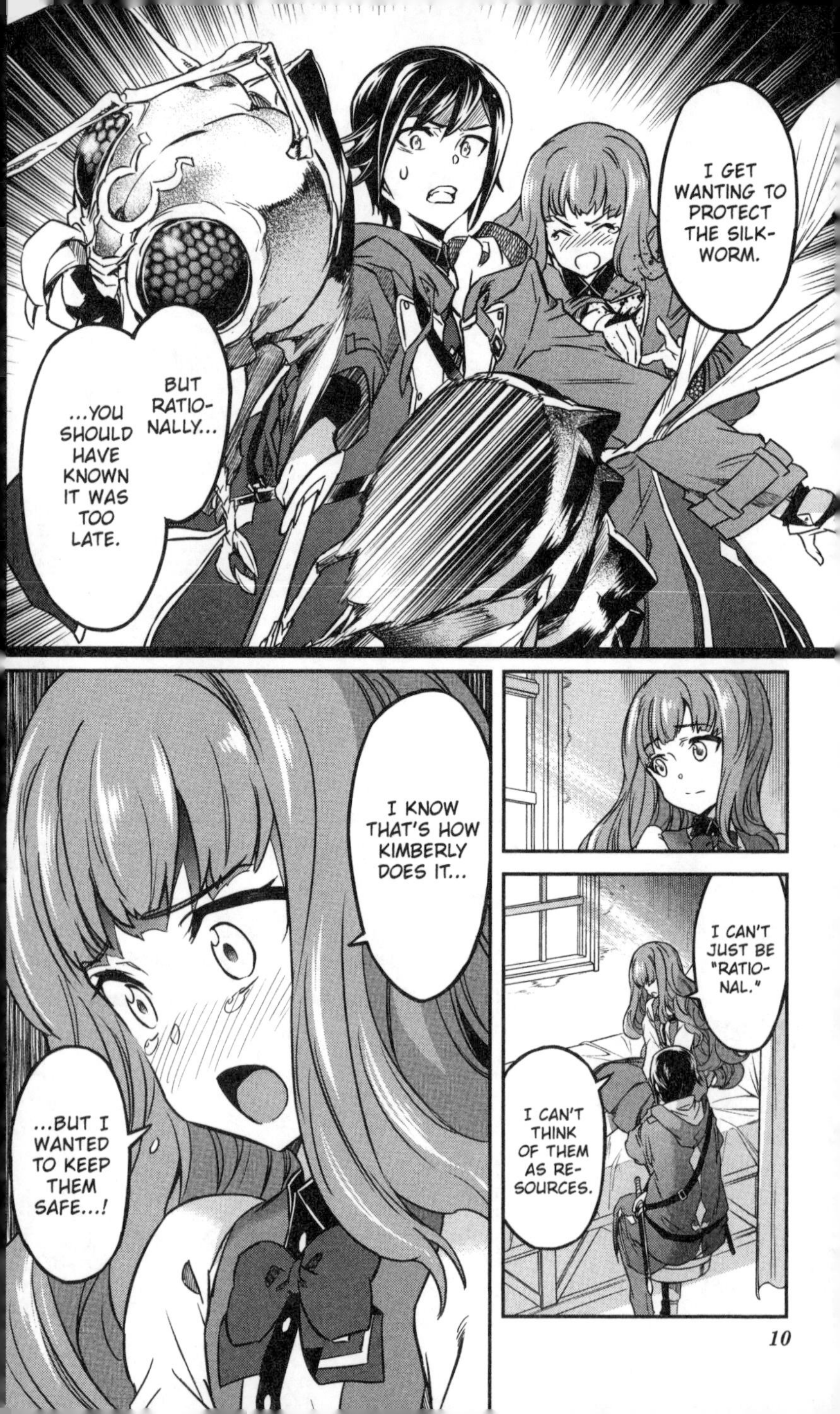
I GET WANTING TO PROTECT THE SILKWORM.
BUT RATIONALLY...
...YOU SHOULD HAVE KNOWN IT WAS TOO LATE.
I CAN'T JUST BE "RATIONAL."
I CAN'T THINK OF THEM AS RESOURCES.
I KNOW THAT'S HOW KIMBERLY DOES IT...
...BUT I WANTED TO KEEP THEM SAFE...!

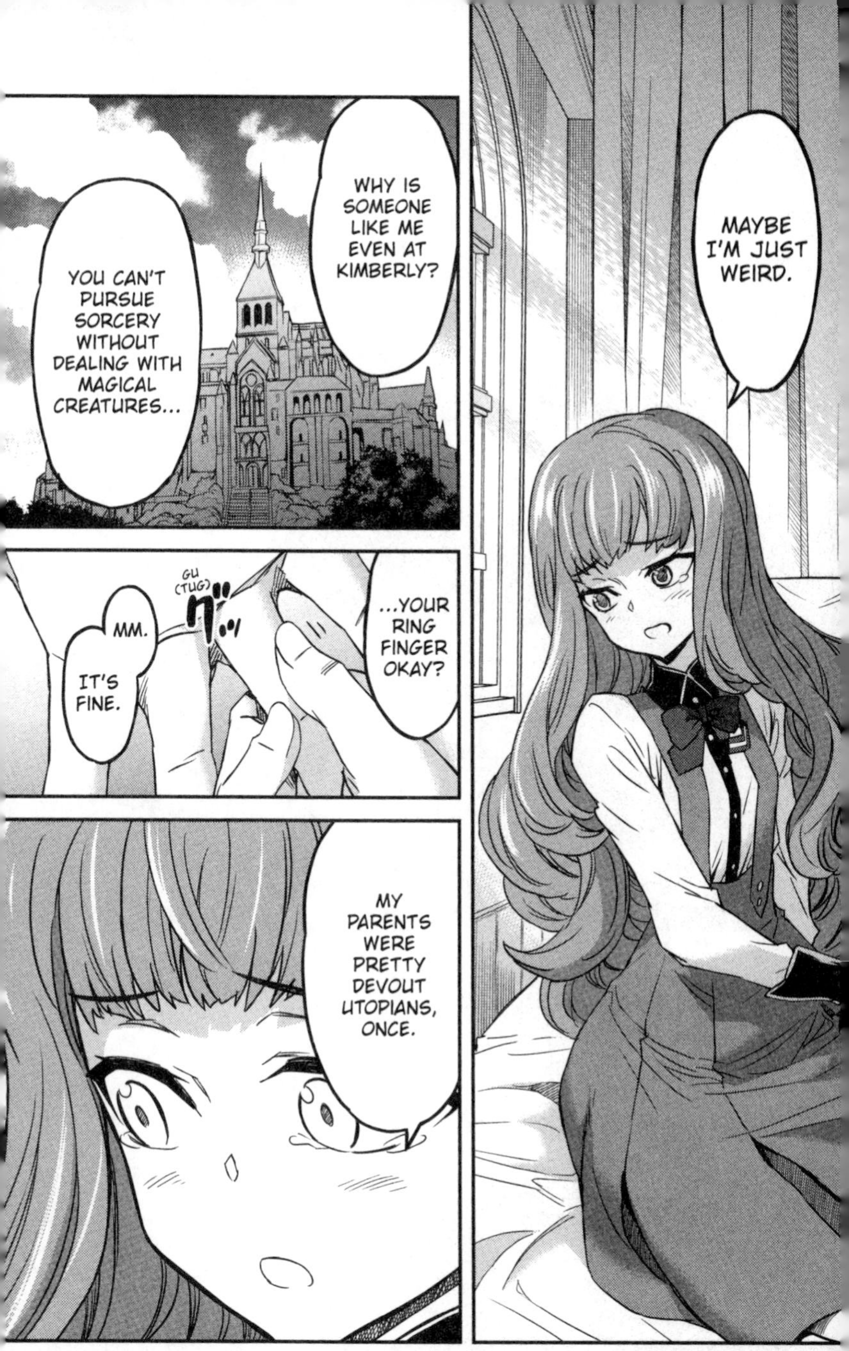
MAYBE I'M JUST WEIRD.
WHY IS SOMEONE LIKE ME EVEN AT KIMBERLY?
YOU CAN'T PURSUE SORCERY WITHOUT DEALING WITH MAGICAL CREATURES...
...YOUR RING FINGER OKAY?
GU (TUG)
MM.
IT'S FINE.
MY PARENTS WERE PRETTY DEVOUT UTOPIANS, ONCE.

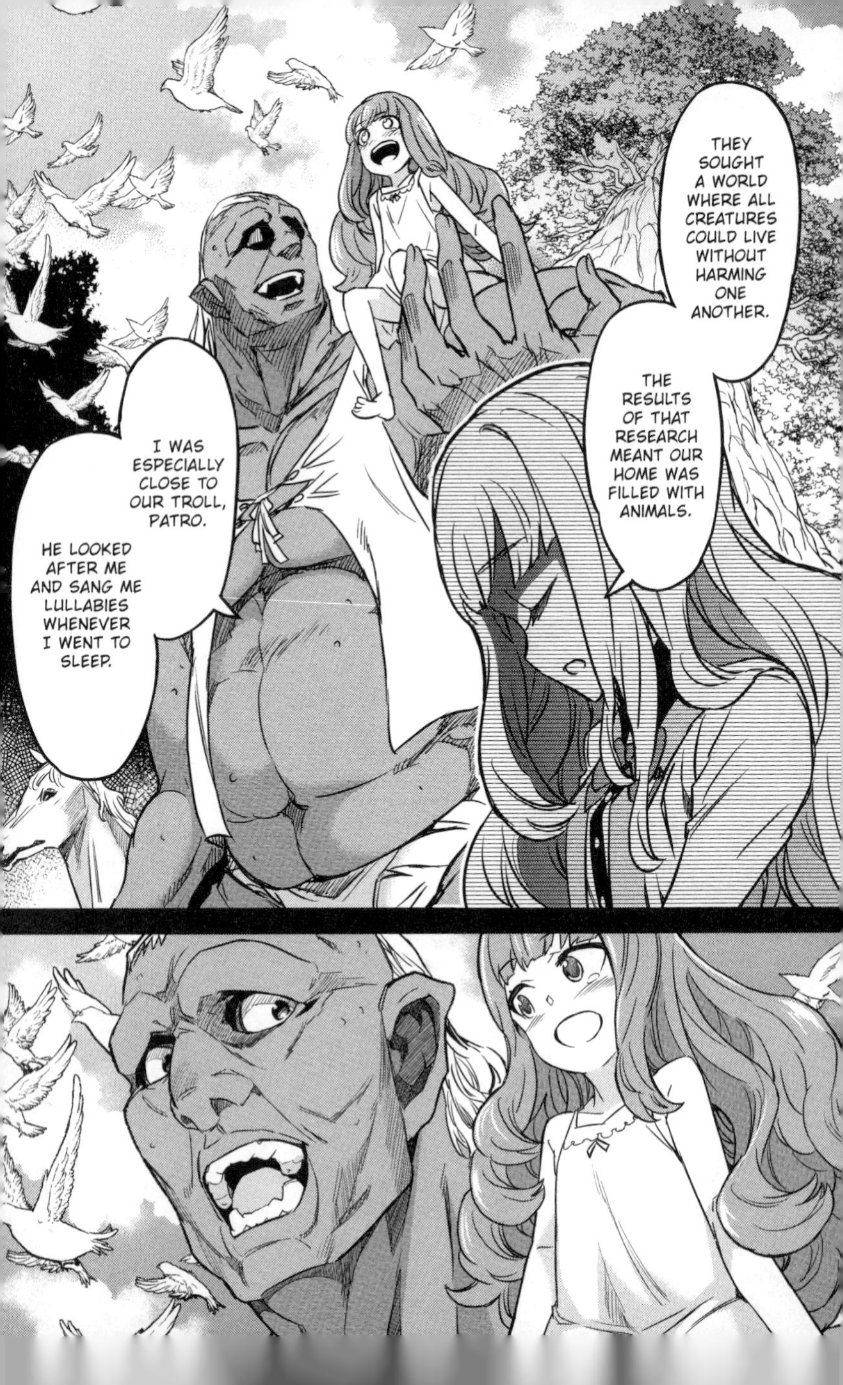
THEY SOUGHT A WORLD WHERE ALL CREATURES COULD LIVE WITHOUT HARMING ONE ANOTHER.
THE RESULTS OF THAT RESEARCH MEANT OUR HOME WAS FILLED WITH ANIMALS.
I WAS ESPECIALLY CLOSE TO OUR TROLL, PATRO.
HE LOOKED AFTER ME AND SANG ME LULLABIES WHENEVER I WENT TO SLEEP.

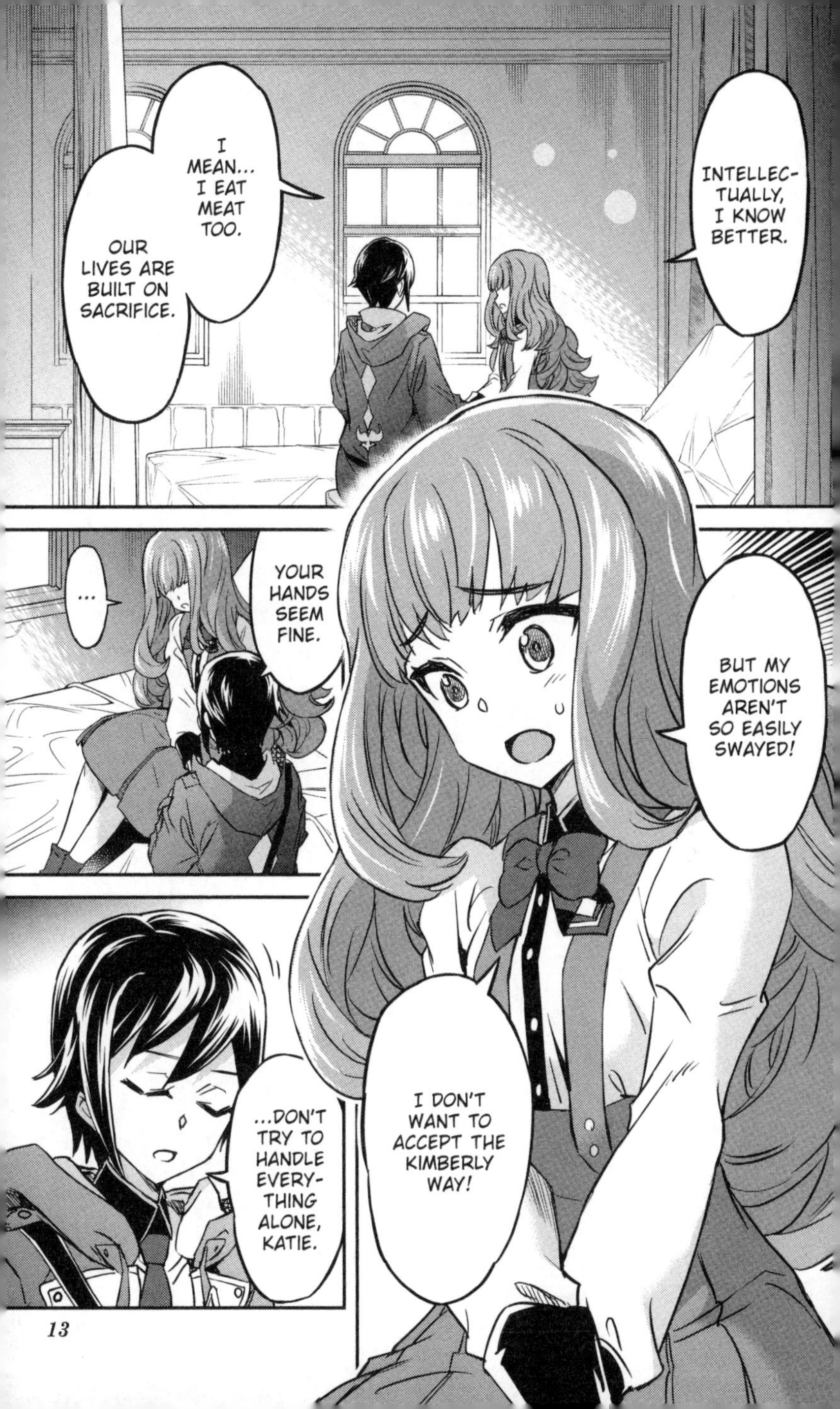
I MEAN... I EAT MEAT TOO.
OUR LIVES ARE BUILT ON SACRIFICE.
INTELLECTUALLY, I KNOW BETTER.
BUT MY EMOTIONS AREN'T SO EASILY SWAYED!
I DON'T WANT TO ACCEPT THE KIMBERLY WAY!
YOUR HANDS SEEM FINE.
...
...DON'T TRY TO HANDLE EVERYTHING ALONE, KATIE.

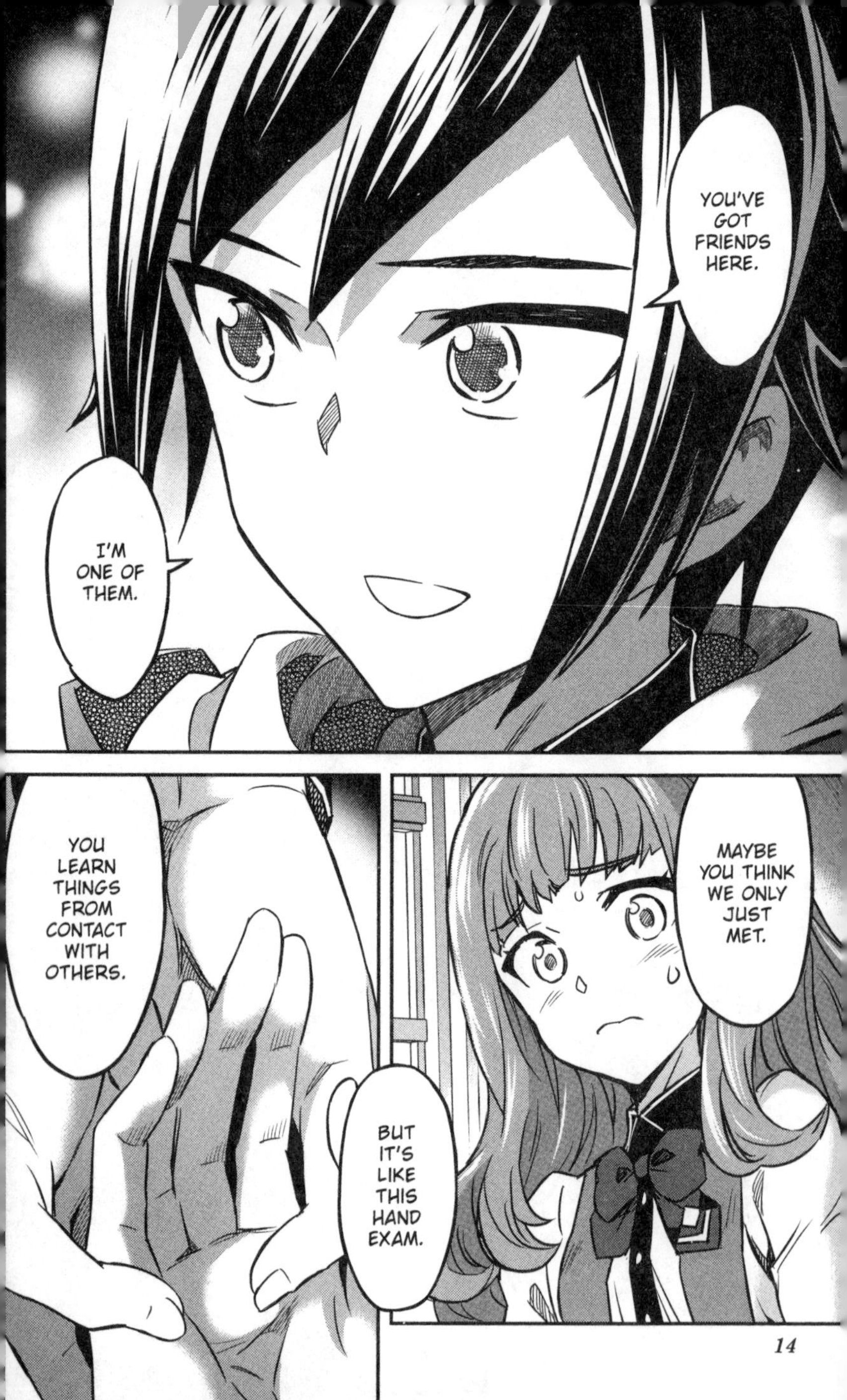
YOU'VE GOT FRIENDS HERE.
I'M ONE OF THEM.
MAYBE YOU THINK WE ONLY JUST MET.
BUT IT'S LIKE THIS HAND EXAM.
YOU LEARN THINGS FROM CONTACT WITH OTHERS.

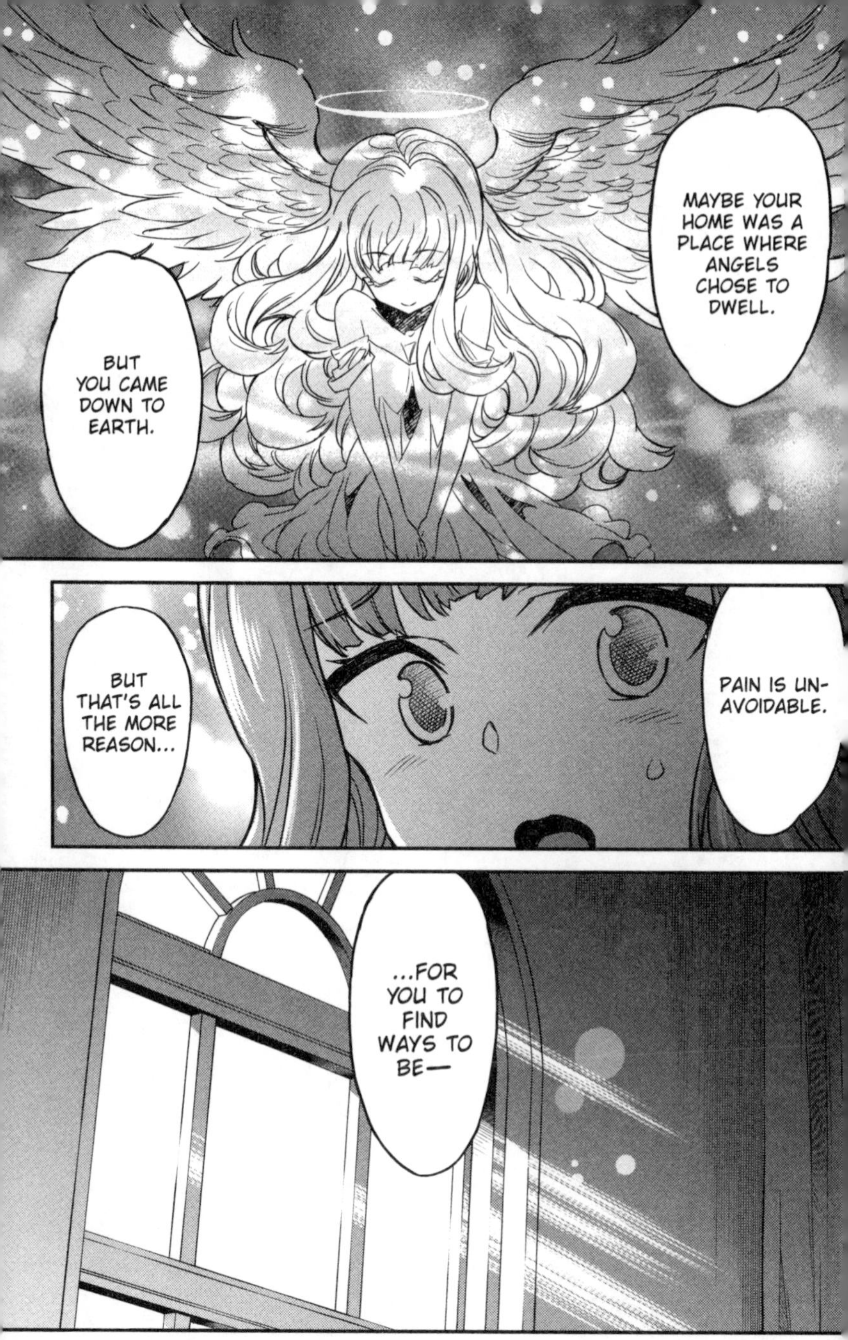
MAYBE YOUR HOME WAS A PLACE WHERE ANGELS CHOSE TO DWELL.
BUT YOU CAME DOWN TO EARTH.
PAIN IS UN-AVOIDABLE.
BUT THAT'S ALL THE MORE REASON...
...FOR YOU TO FIND WAYS TO BE—

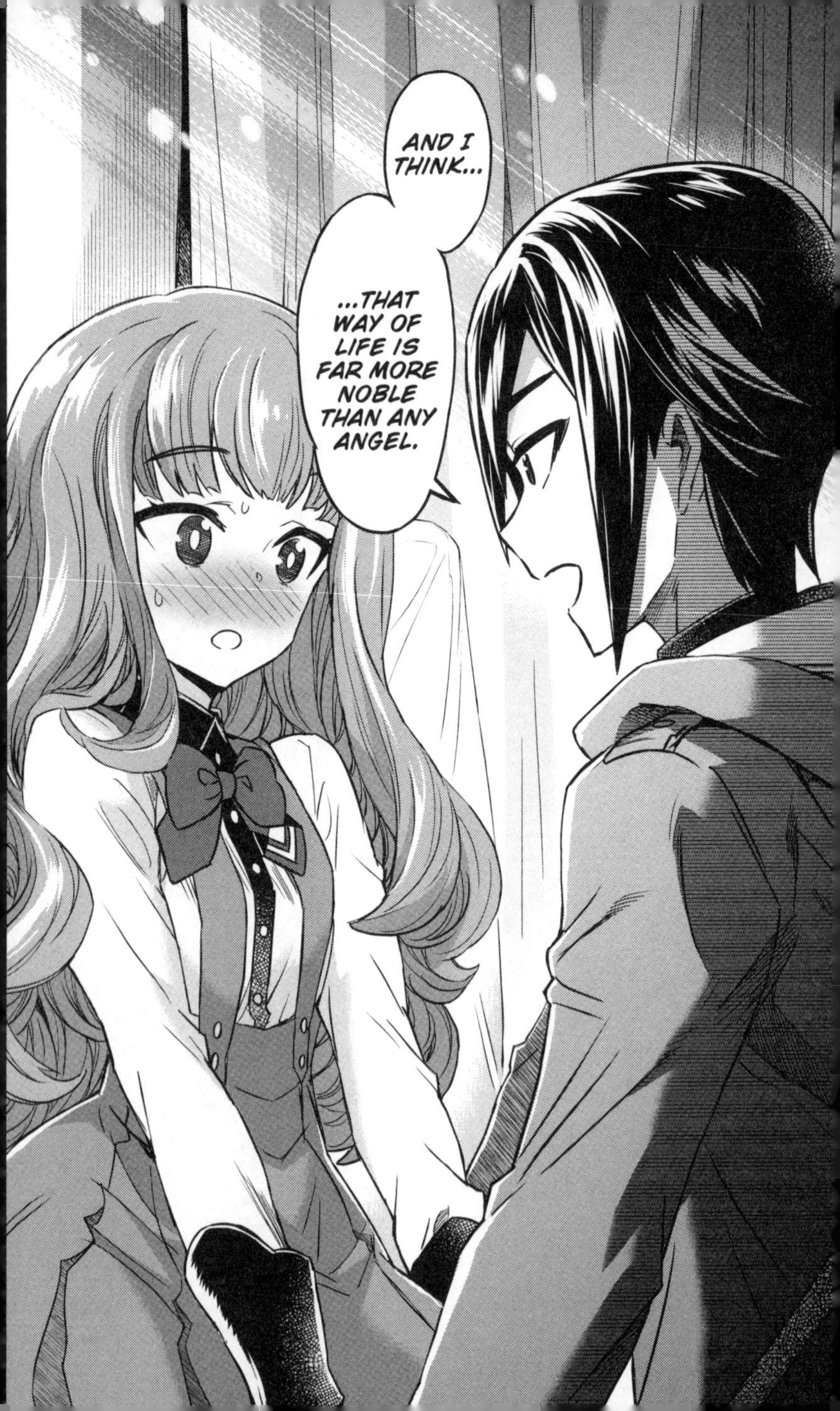
AND I THINK...
...THAT WAY OF LIFE IS FAR MORE NOBLE THAN ANY ANGEL.

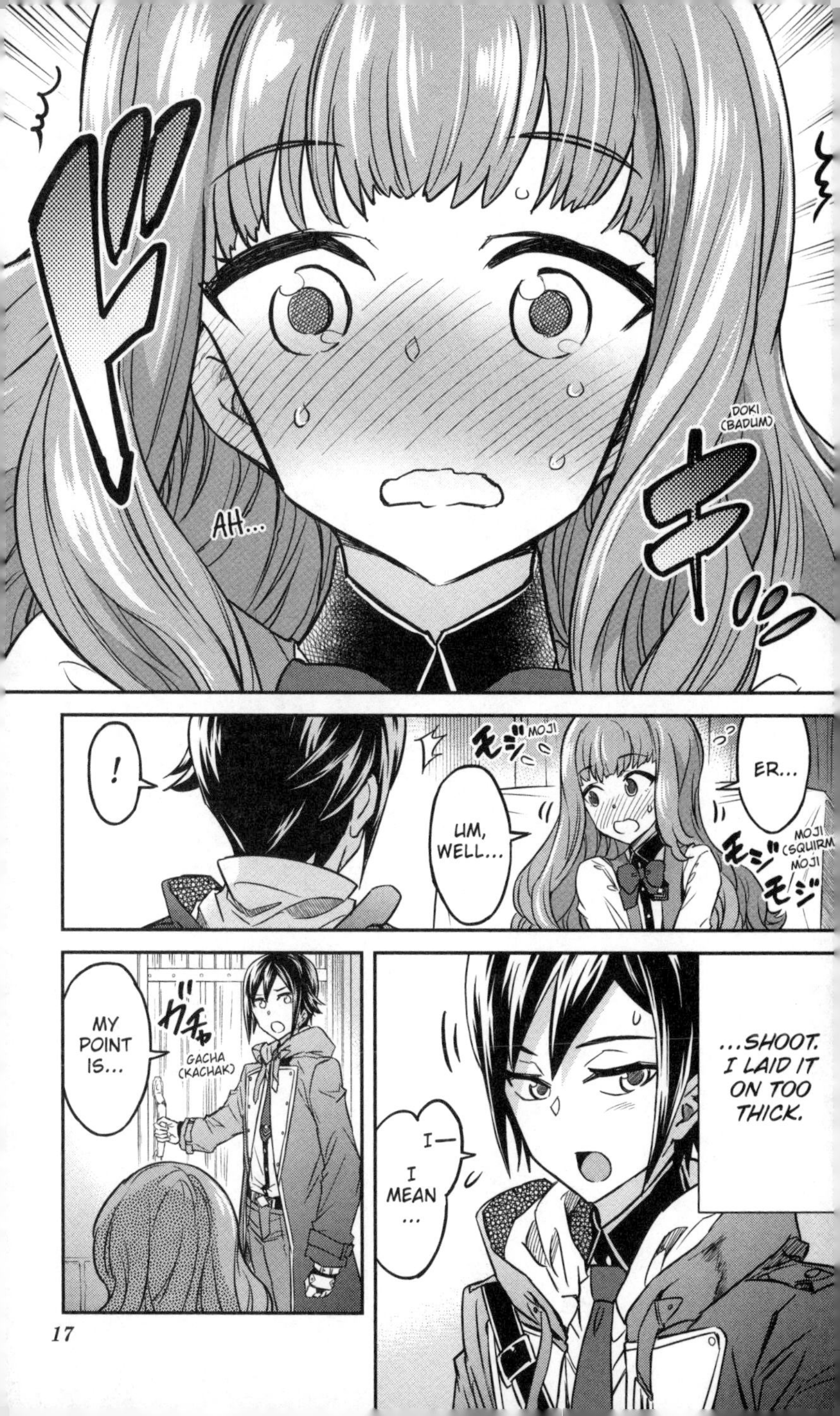
DOKI (BADUM)
AH...
ER...
MOJI (SQUIRM) MOJI
MOJI
UM, WELL...
!
...SHOOT. I LAID IT ON TOO THICK.
I— I MEAN ...
MY POINT IS...
GACHA (KACHAK)

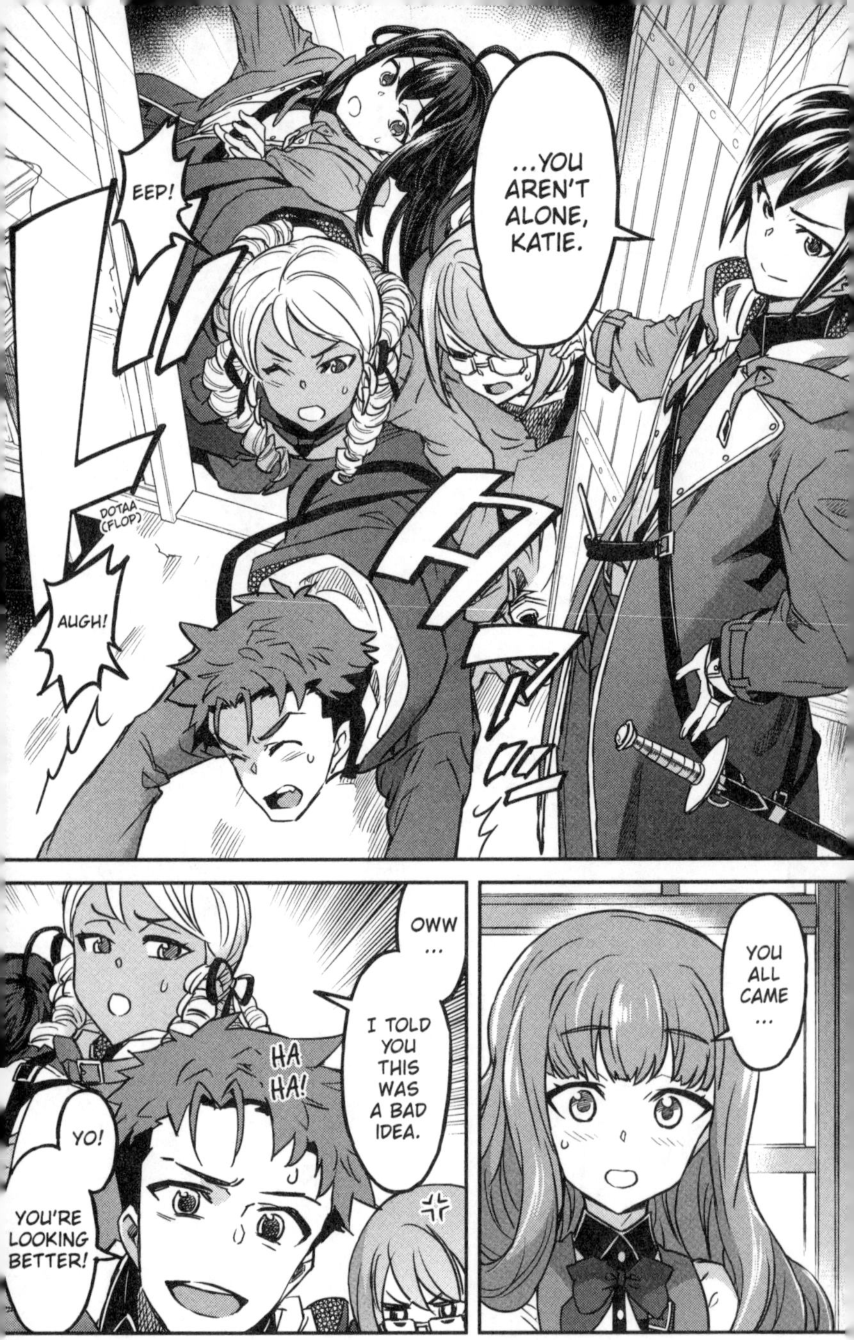
...YOU AREN'T ALONE, KATIE.
EEP!
DOTAA (FLOP)
AUGH!
YOU ALL CAME ...
OWW ...
I TOLD YOU THIS WAS A BAD IDEA.
HA HA!
YO!
YOU'RE LOOKING BETTER!

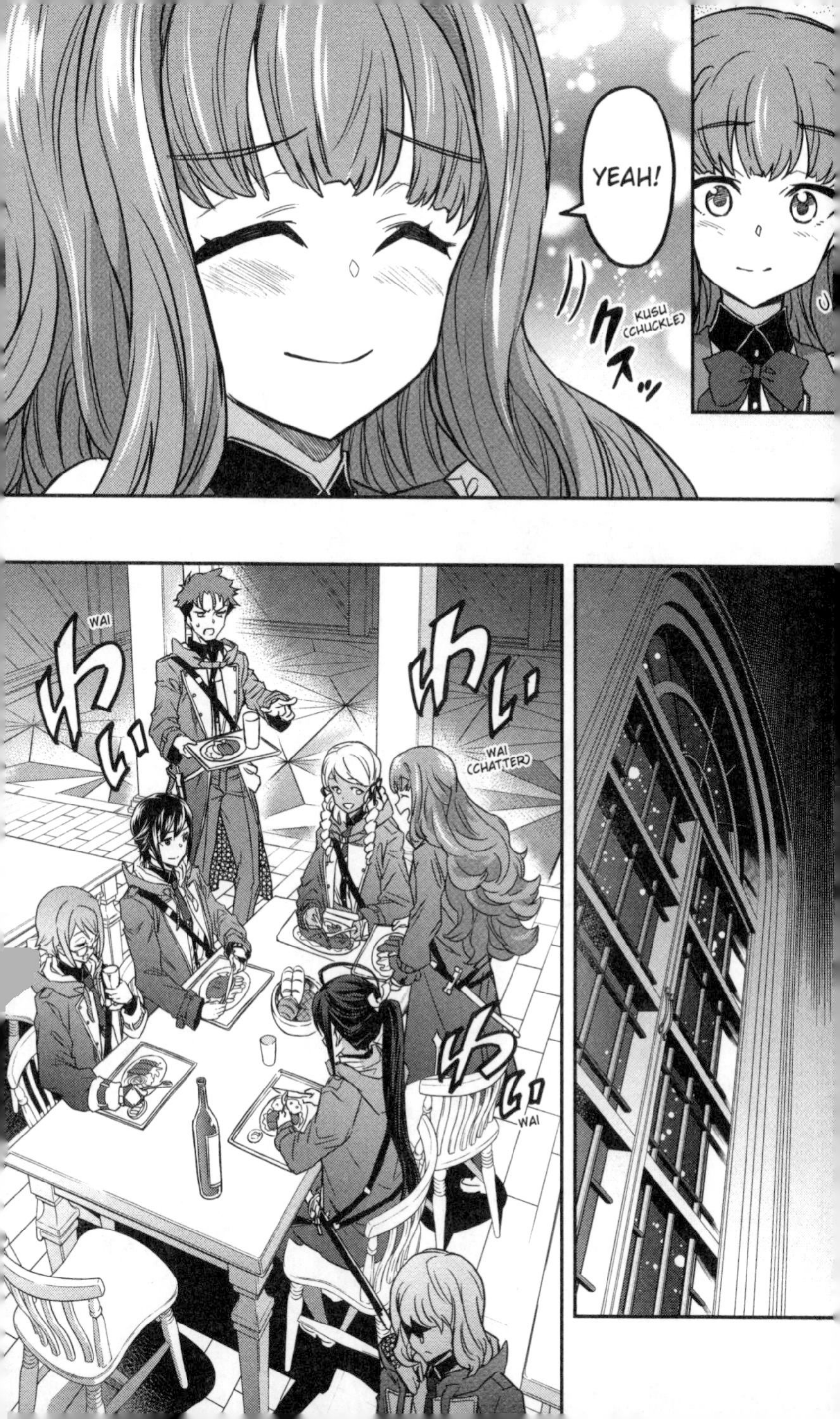
YEAH!
KUSU (CHUCKLE)
WAI (CHATTER)
WAI
WAI

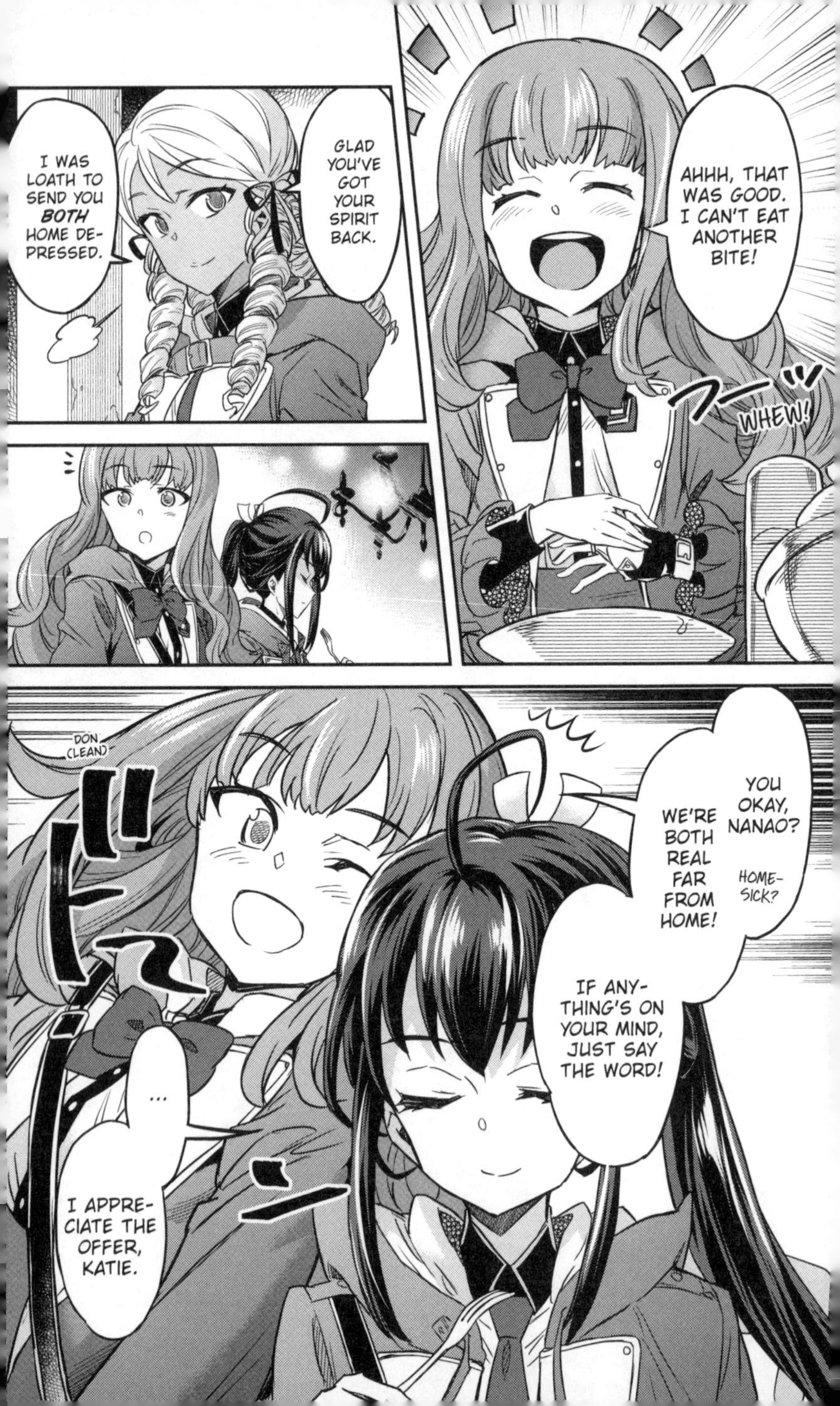

AHHH, THAT WAS GOOD. I CAN'T EAT ANOTHER BITE!
WHEW!
GLAD YOU'VE GOT YOUR SPIRIT BACK.
I WAS LOATH TO SEND YOU *BOTH* HOME DE-PRESSED.
DON CLEAN
YOU OKAY, NANAO?
HOME-SICK?
WE'RE BOTH REAL FAR FROM HOME!
IF ANY-THING'S ON YOUR MIND, JUST SAY THE WORD!
...
I APPRE-CIATE THE OFFER, KATIE.

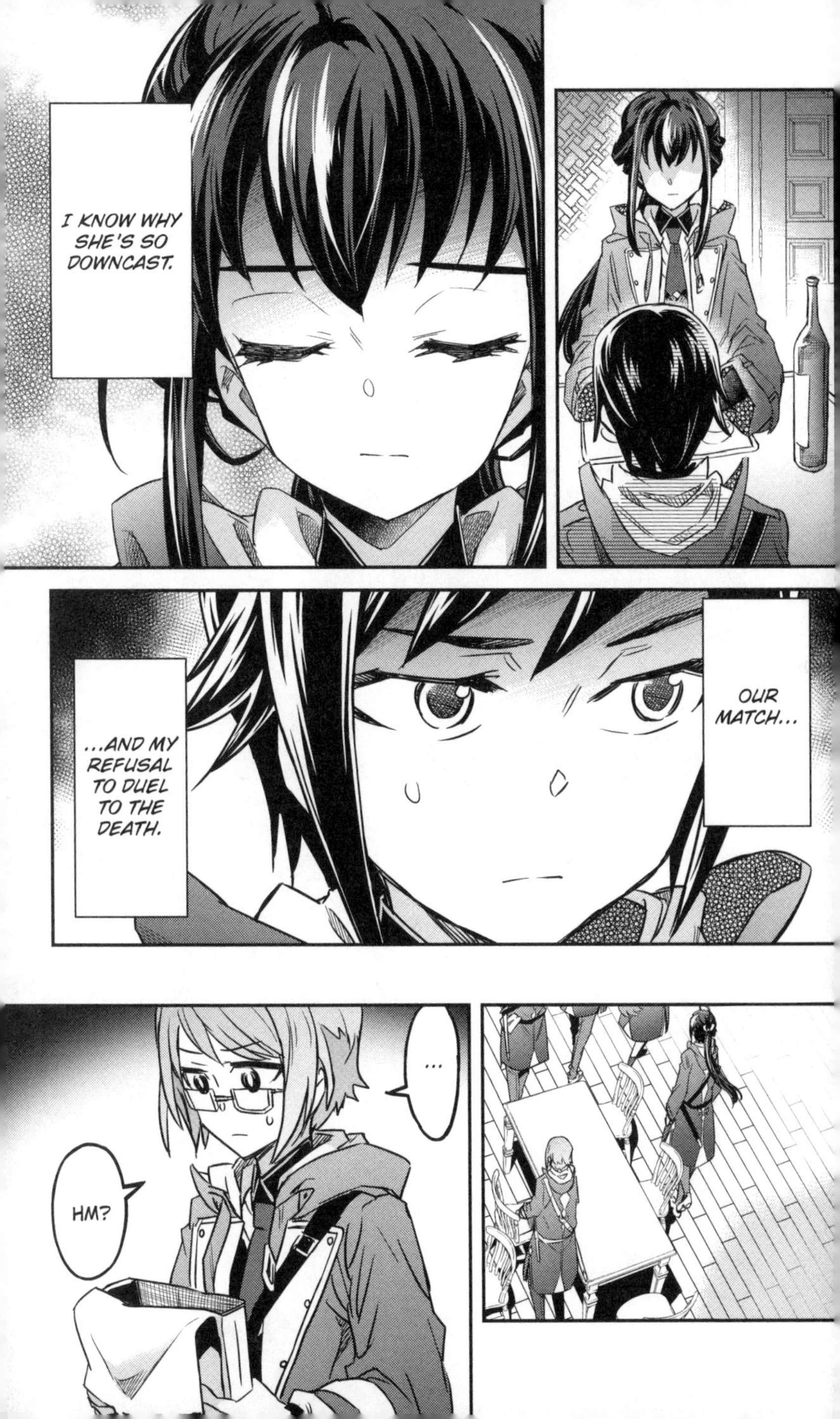
I KNOW WHY SHE'S SO DOWNCAST.
OUR MATCH...
...AND MY REFUSAL TO DUEL TO THE DEATH.
...
HM?

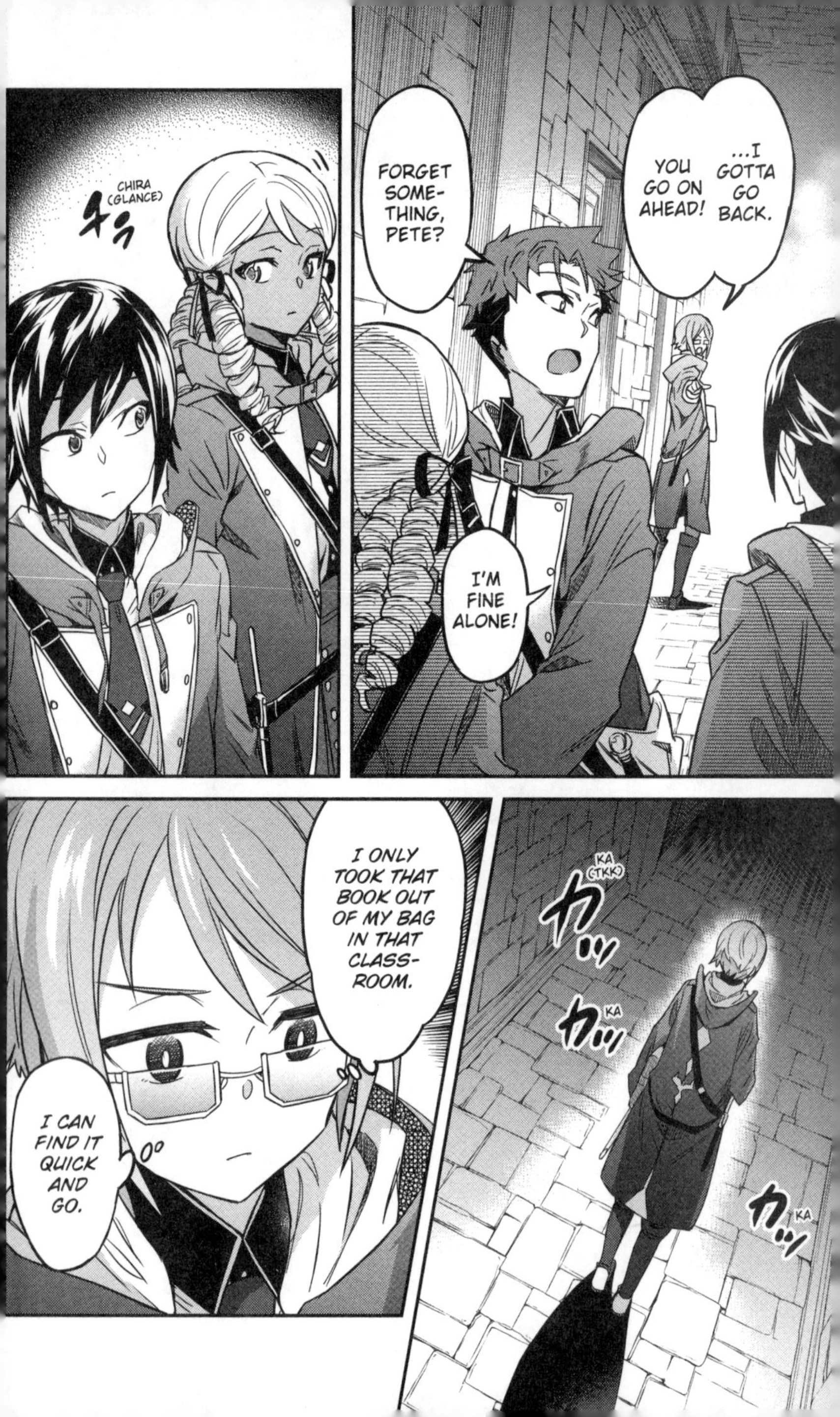

...I GOTTA GO BACK.
YOU GO ON AHEAD!
FORGET SOME-THING, PETE?
I'M FINE ALONE!
CHIRA (GLANCE)
KA (TKK)
KA
KA
I ONLY TOOK THAT BOOK OUT OF MY BAG IN THAT CLASS-ROOM.
I CAN FIND IT QUICK AND GO.

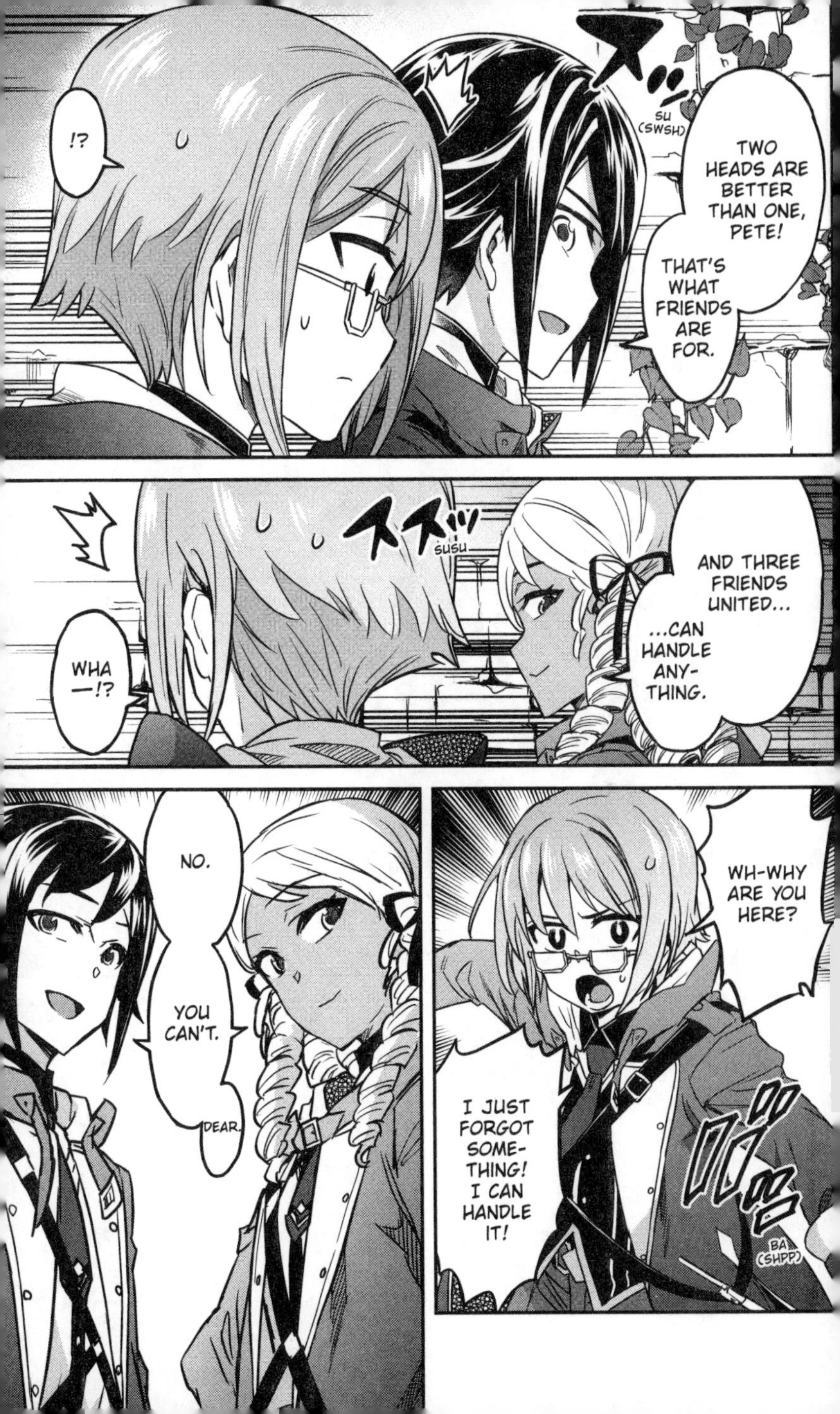
SU (SWSH)
TWO HEADS ARE BETTER THAN ONE, PETE!
THAT'S WHAT FRIENDS ARE FOR.
!?
SUSU
AND THREE FRIENDS UNITED...
...CAN HANDLE ANY-THING.
WHA—!?
WH-WHY ARE YOU HERE?
I JUST FORGOT SOME-THING! I CAN HANDLE IT!
BA (SHPP)
NO.
YOU CAN'T.
DEAR.

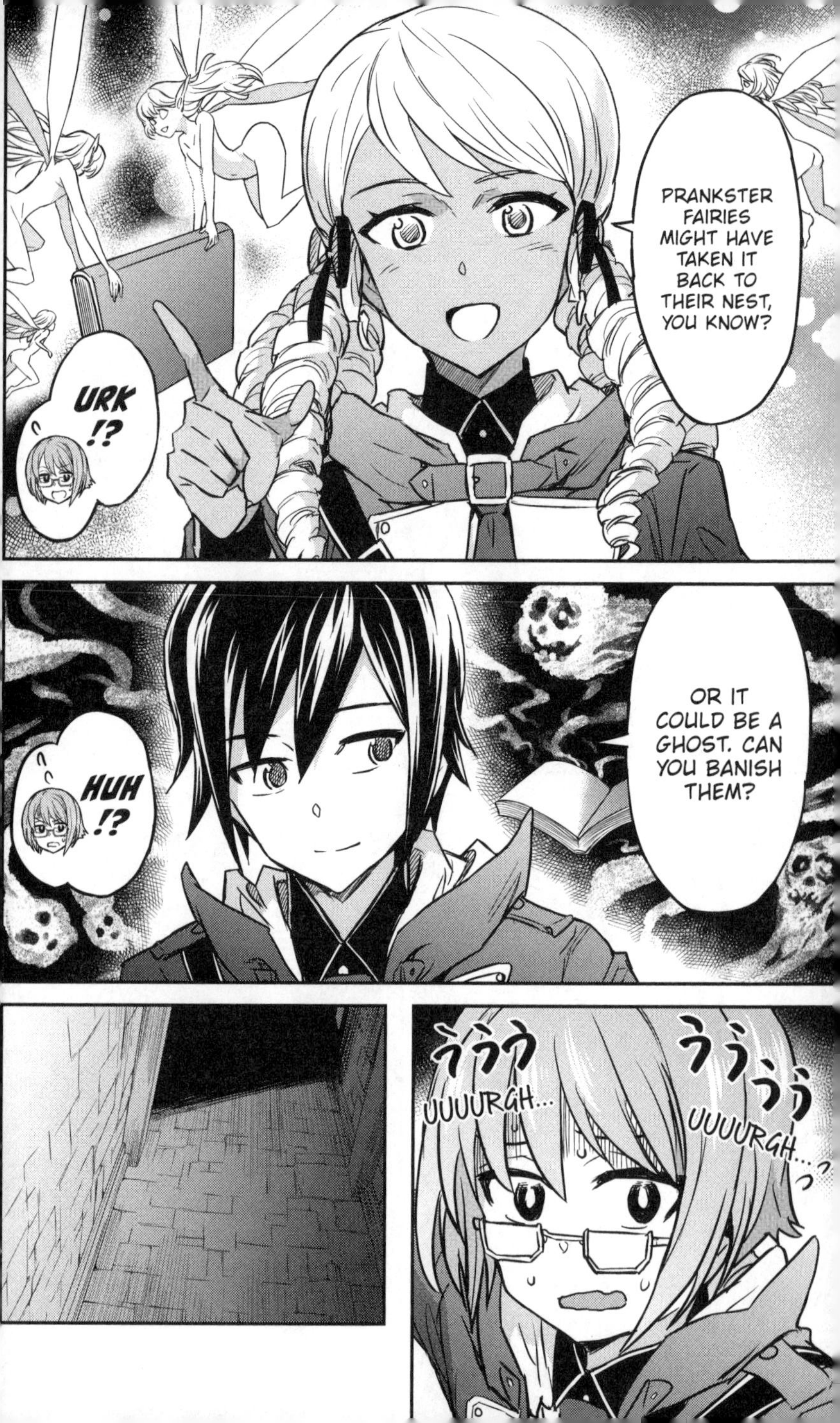
PRANKSTER FAIRIES MIGHT HAVE TAKEN IT BACK TO THEIR NEST, YOU KNOW?
URK !?
OR IT COULD BE A GHOST. CAN YOU BANISH THEM?
HUH !?
UUUURGH...
UUUURGH...?

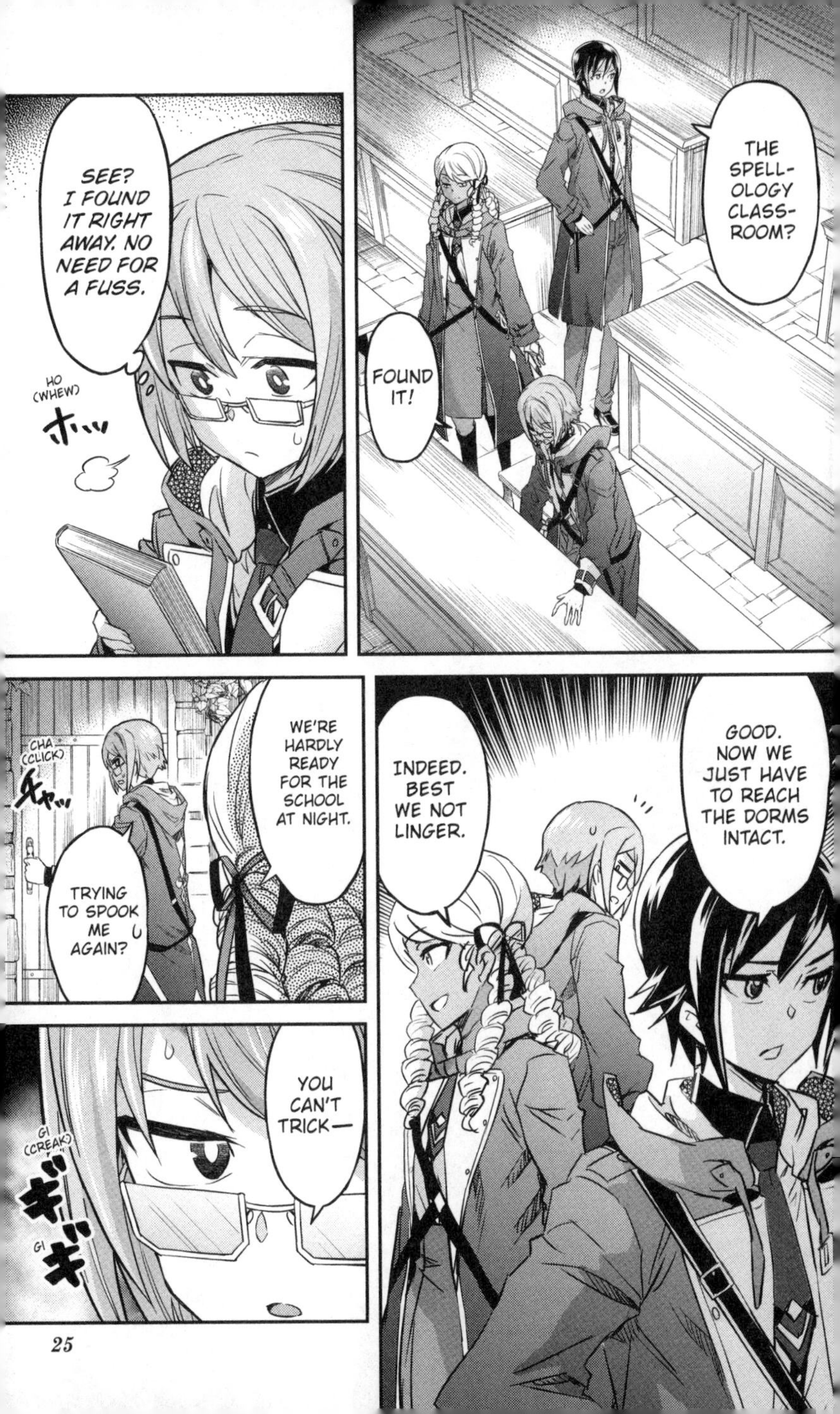
THE SPELL-OLOGY CLASSROOM?
FOUND IT!
SEE? I FOUND IT RIGHT AWAY. NO NEED FOR A FUSS.
HO (WHEW)
GOOD. NOW WE JUST HAVE TO REACH THE DORMS INTACT.
INDEED. BEST WE NOT LINGER.
WE'RE HARDLY READY FOR THE SCHOOL AT NIGHT.
CHA (CLICK)
TRYING TO SPOOK ME AGAIN?
YOU CAN'T TRICK—
GI (CREAK)
GI

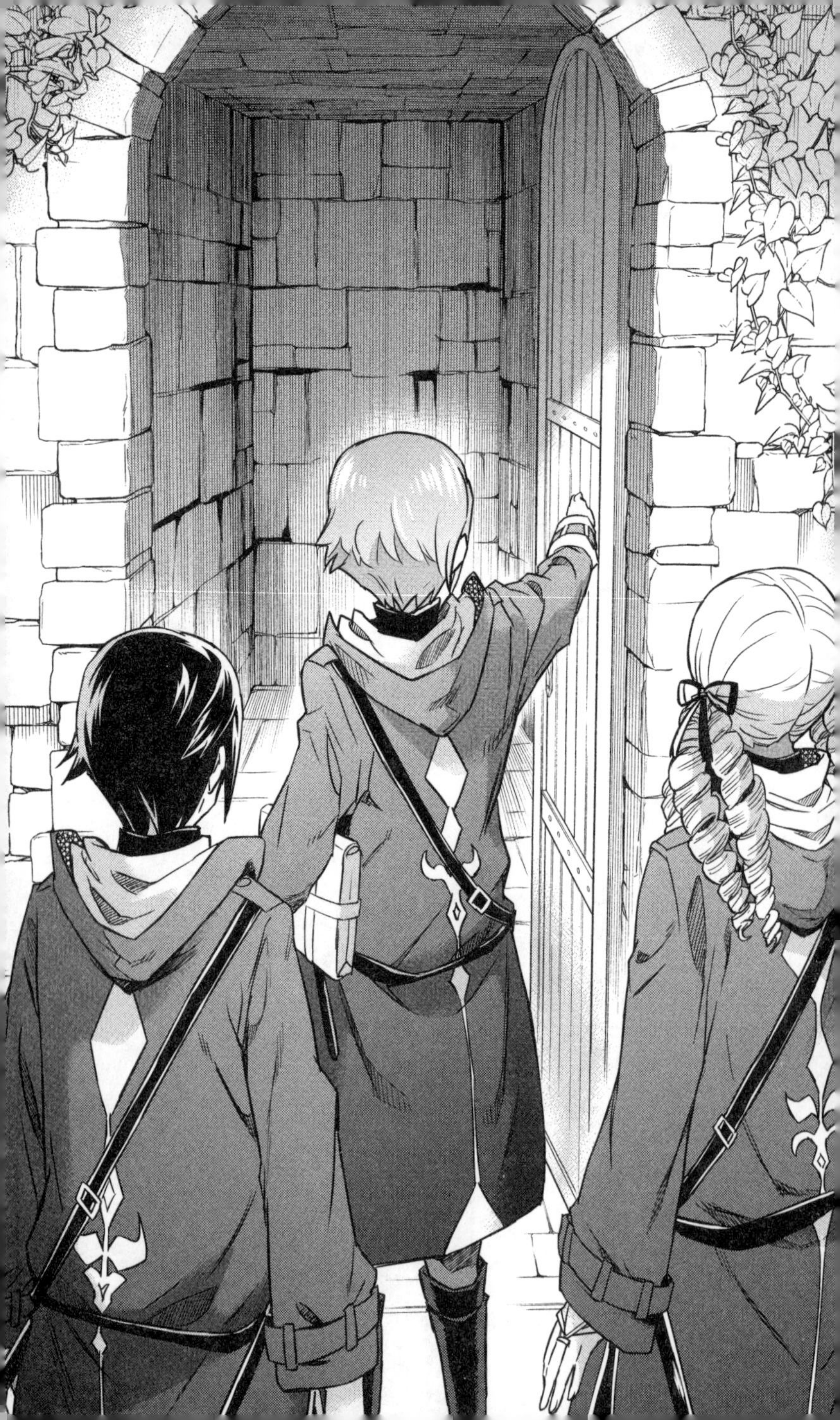

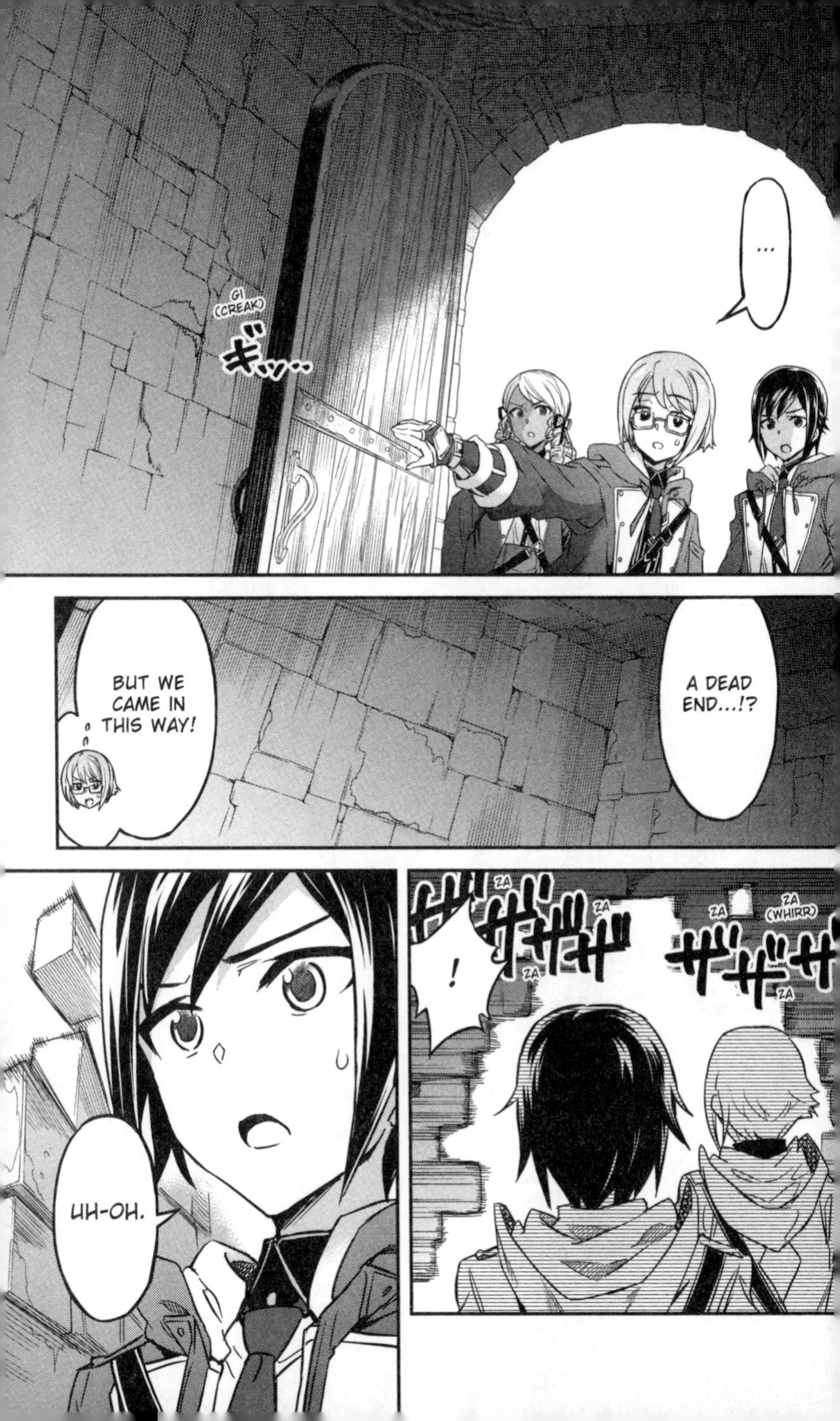
...
GI (CREAK)
ギッ‥
A DEAD END...!?
BUT WE CAME IN THIS WAY!
ZA (WHIRR)
ZA
ZA
ZA
ZA
ZA
!
UH-OH.

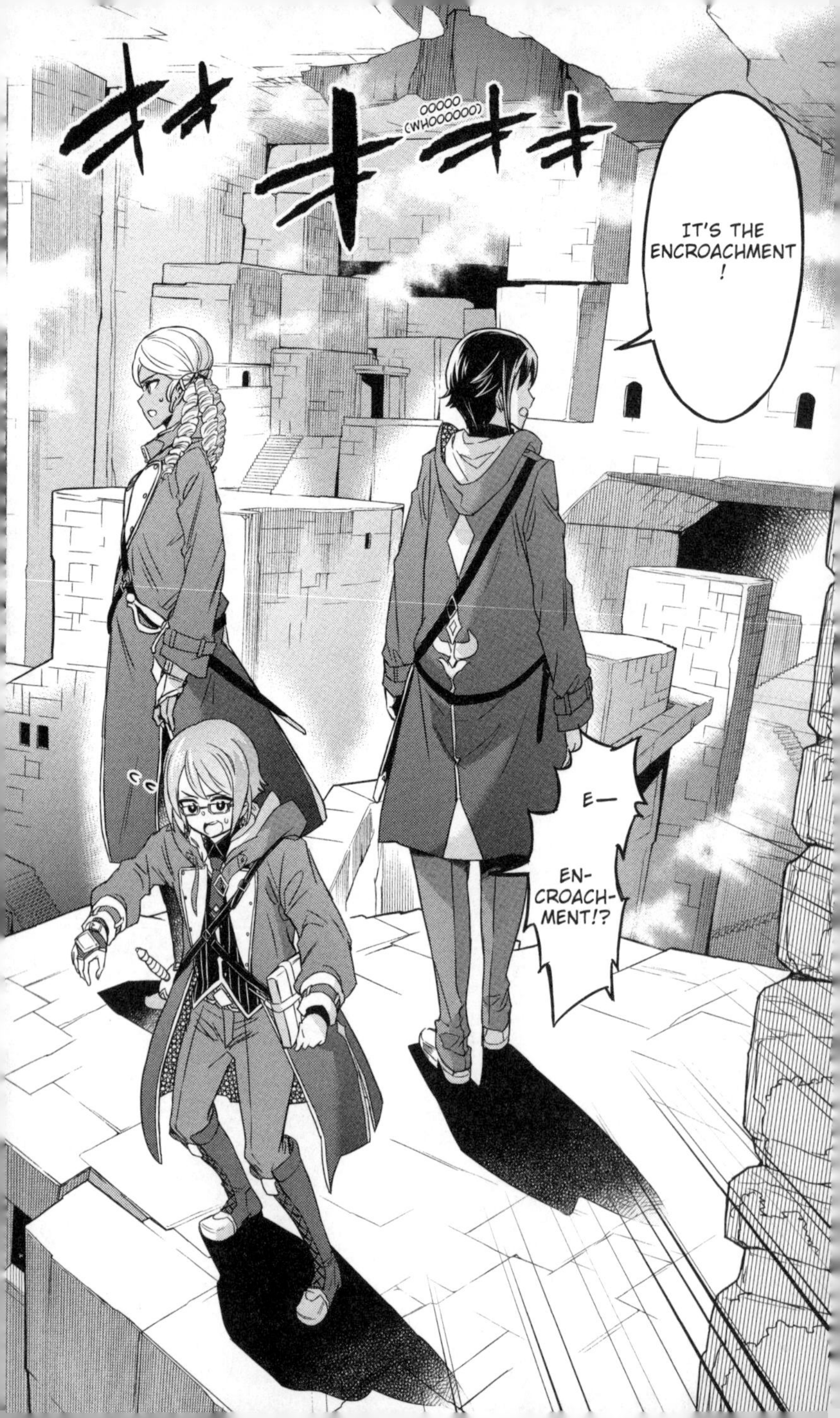
OOOOO (WHOOOOOO)
IT'S THE ENCROACHMENT!
E—
EN-CROACHMENT!?

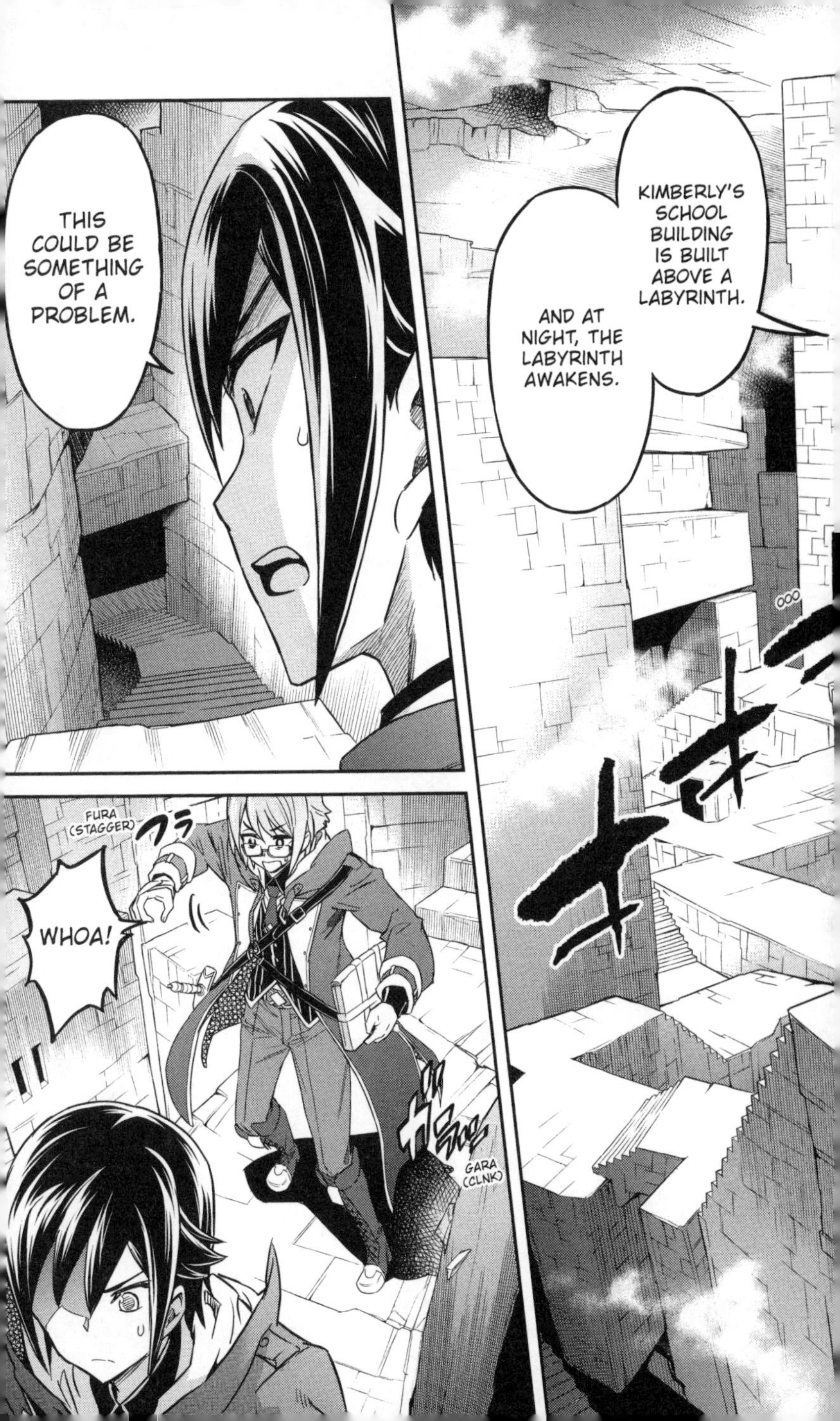
KIMBERLY'S SCHOOL BUILDING IS BUILT ABOVE A LABYRINTH.
AND AT NIGHT, THE LABYRINTH AWAKENS.
ooo
THIS COULD BE SOMETHING OF A PROBLEM.
FURA (STAGGER)
フラ
WHOA!
GARA (CLNK)

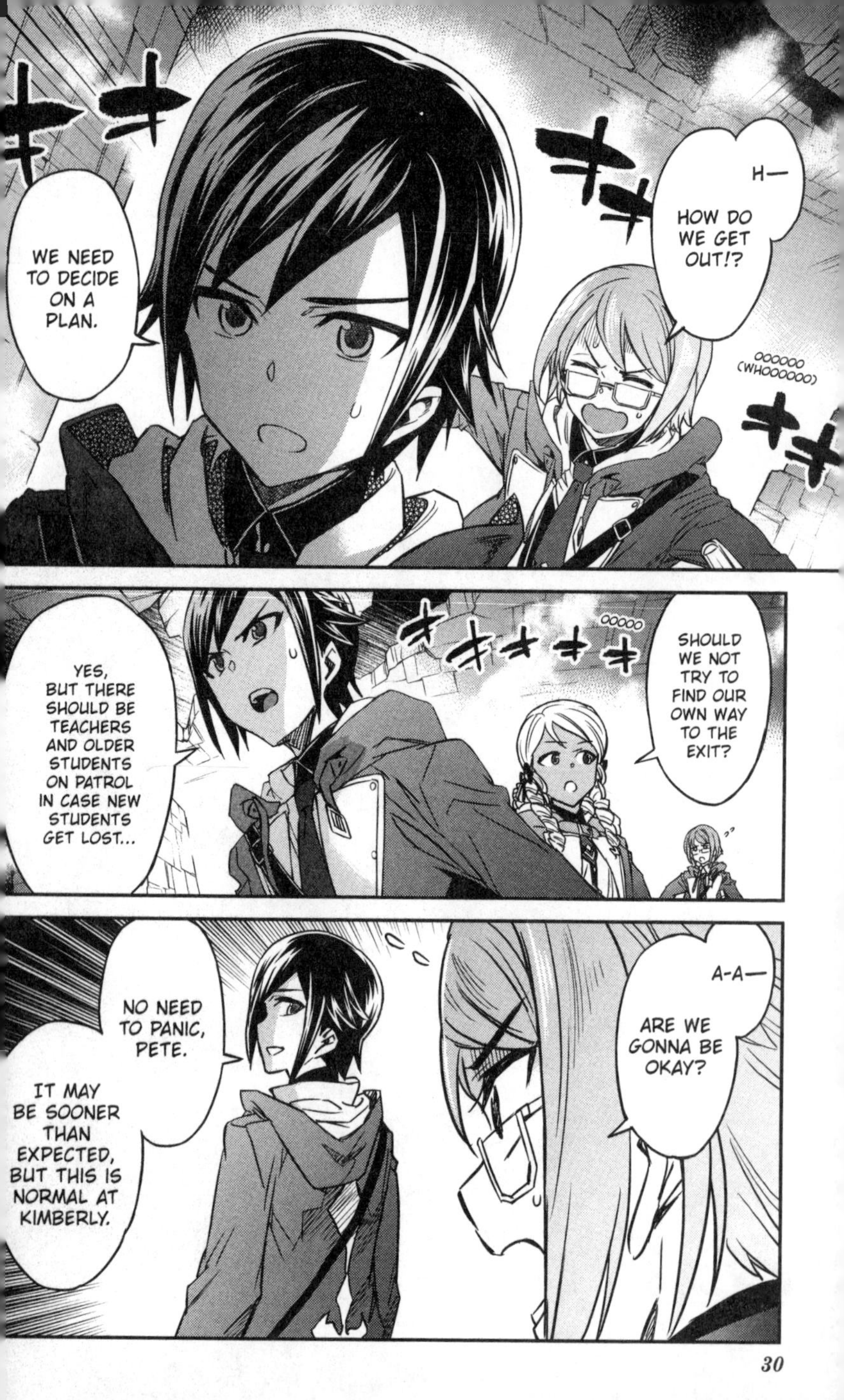
H—
HOW DO WE GET OUT!?
OOOOOO (WHOOOOOOO)
WE NEED TO DECIDE ON A PLAN.
SHOULD WE NOT TRY TO FIND OUR OWN WAY TO THE EXIT?
OOOOO
YES, BUT THERE SHOULD BE TEACHERS AND OLDER STUDENTS ON PATROL IN CASE NEW STUDENTS GET LOST...
A-A—
ARE WE GONNA BE OKAY?
NO NEED TO PANIC, PETE.
IT MAY BE SOONER THAN EXPECTED, BUT THIS IS NORMAL AT KIMBERLY.

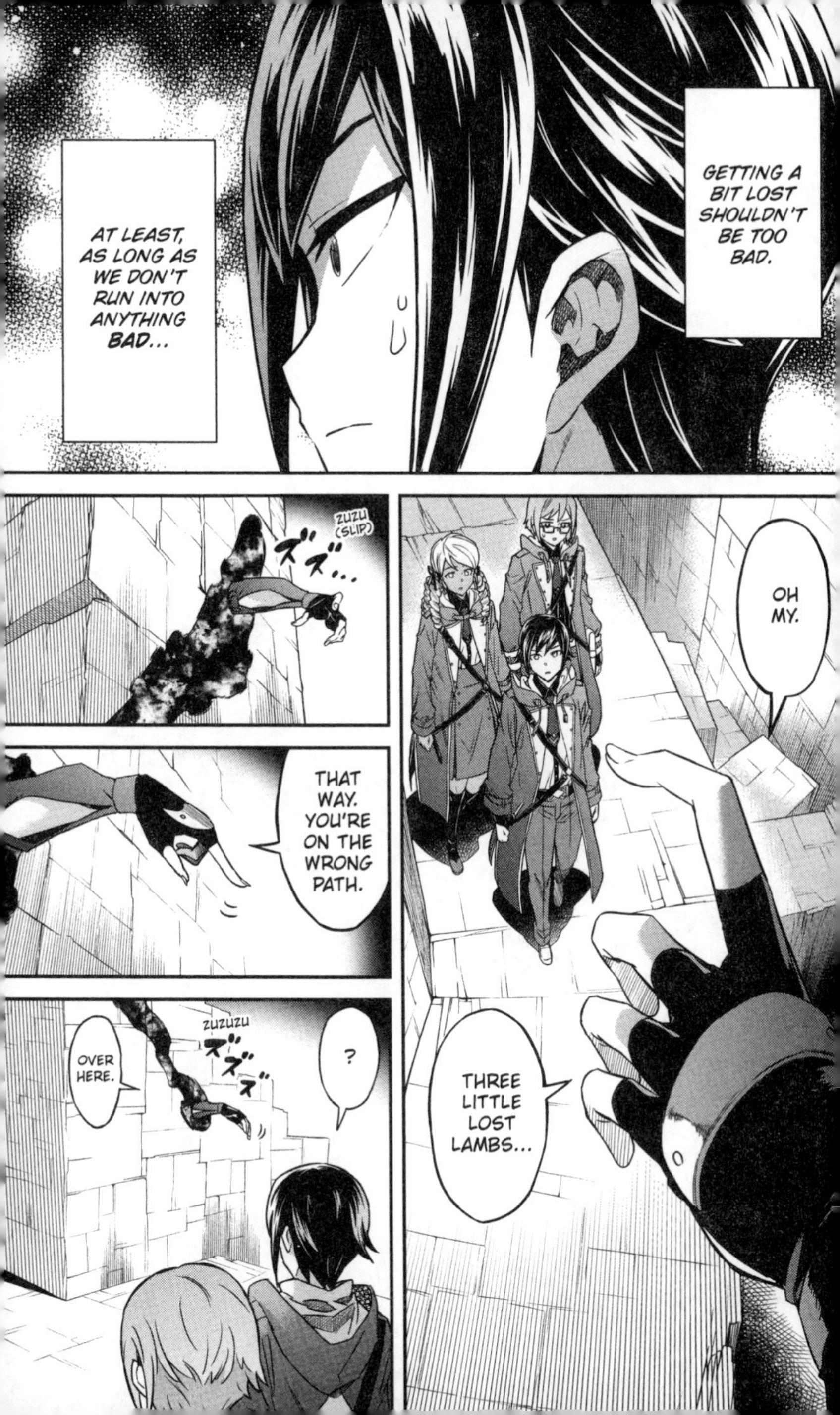
GETTING A BIT LOST SHOULDN'T BE TOO BAD.
AT LEAST, AS LONG AS WE DON'T RUN INTO ANYTHING BAD...
OH MY.
THREE LITTLE LOST LAMBS...
ZUZU (SLIP)
ズズ...
THAT WAY. YOU'RE ON THE WRONG PATH.
?
ZUZUZU
ズズズ
OVER HERE.

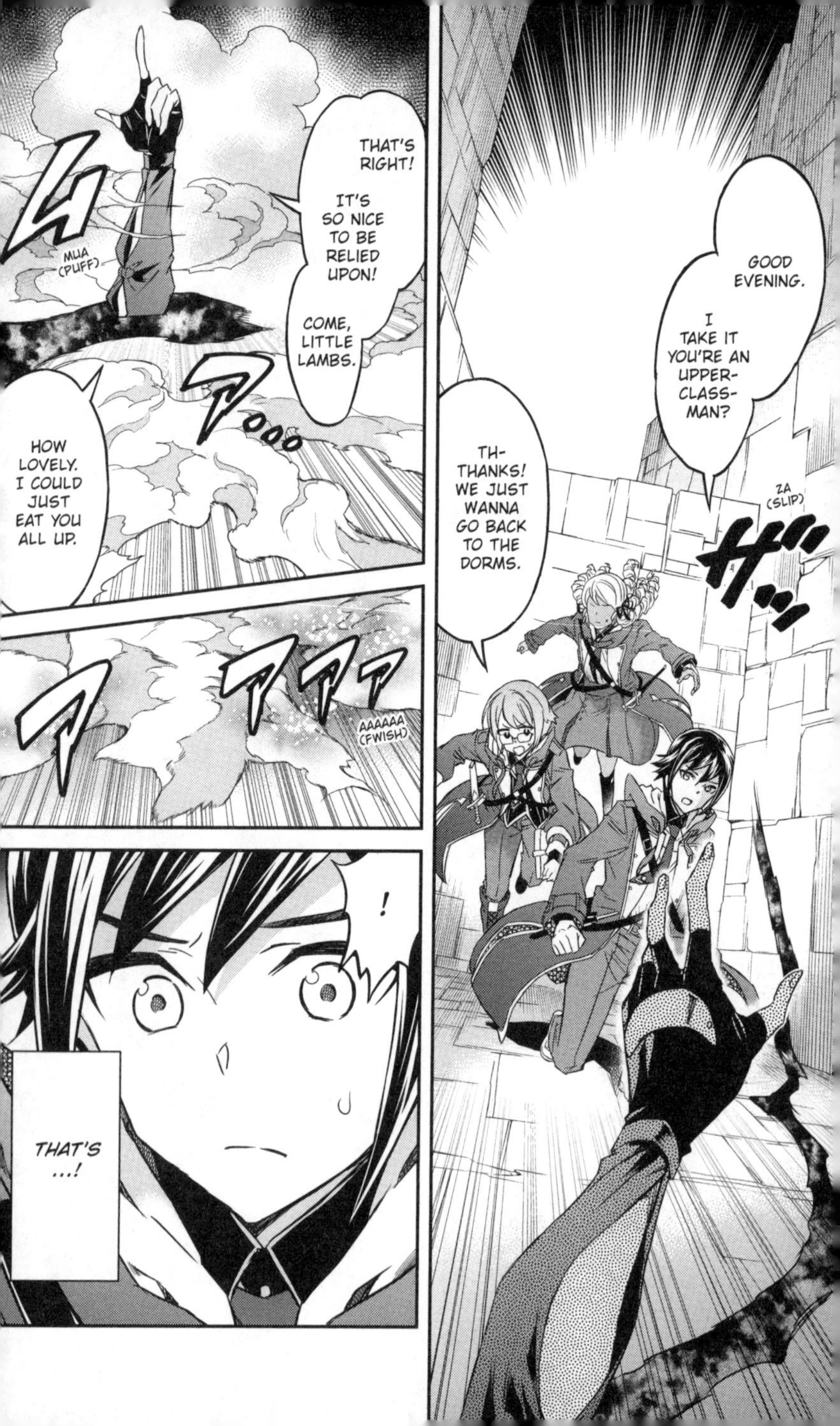
GOOD EVENING.
I TAKE IT YOU'RE AN UPPER-CLASS-MAN?
ZA (SLIP)
TH-THANKS! WE JUST WANNA GO BACK TO THE DORMS.
THAT'S RIGHT!
IT'S SO NICE TO BE RELIED UPON!
COME, LITTLE LAMBS.
MUA (PUFF)
HOW LOVELY. I COULD JUST EAT YOU ALL UP.
AAAAAA (FWISH)
!
THAT'S ...!

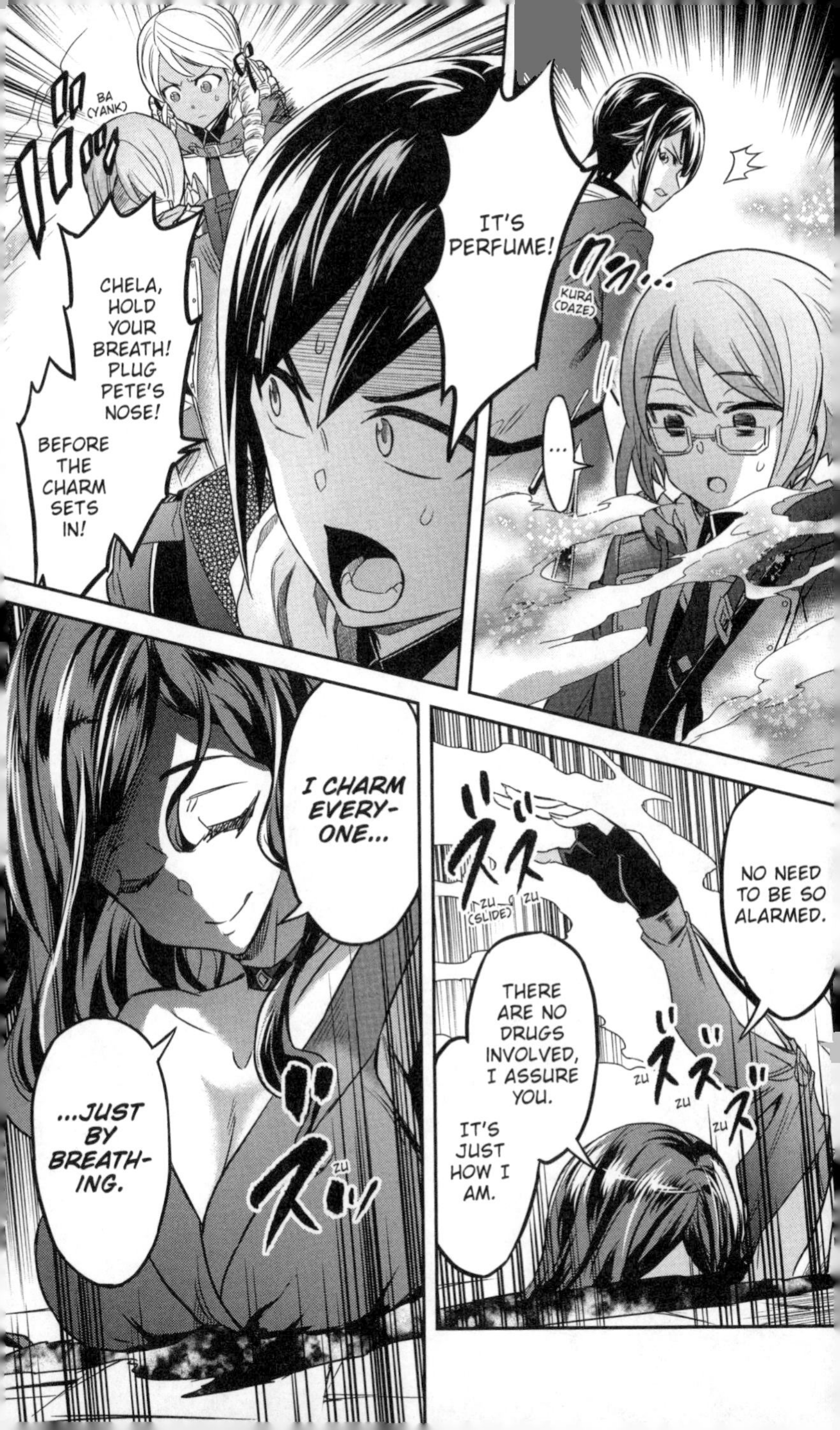
KURA (DAZE)
...
IT'S PERFUME!
BA (YANK)
CHELA, HOLD YOUR BREATH! PLUG PETE'S NOSE!
BEFORE THE CHARM SETS IN!
NO NEED TO BE SO ALARMED.
ZU (SLIDE) ZU
THERE ARE NO DRUGS INVOLVED, I ASSURE YOU.
IT'S JUST HOW I AM.
ZU ZU ZU
I CHARM EVERY-ONE...
...JUST BY BREATH-ING.
ZU

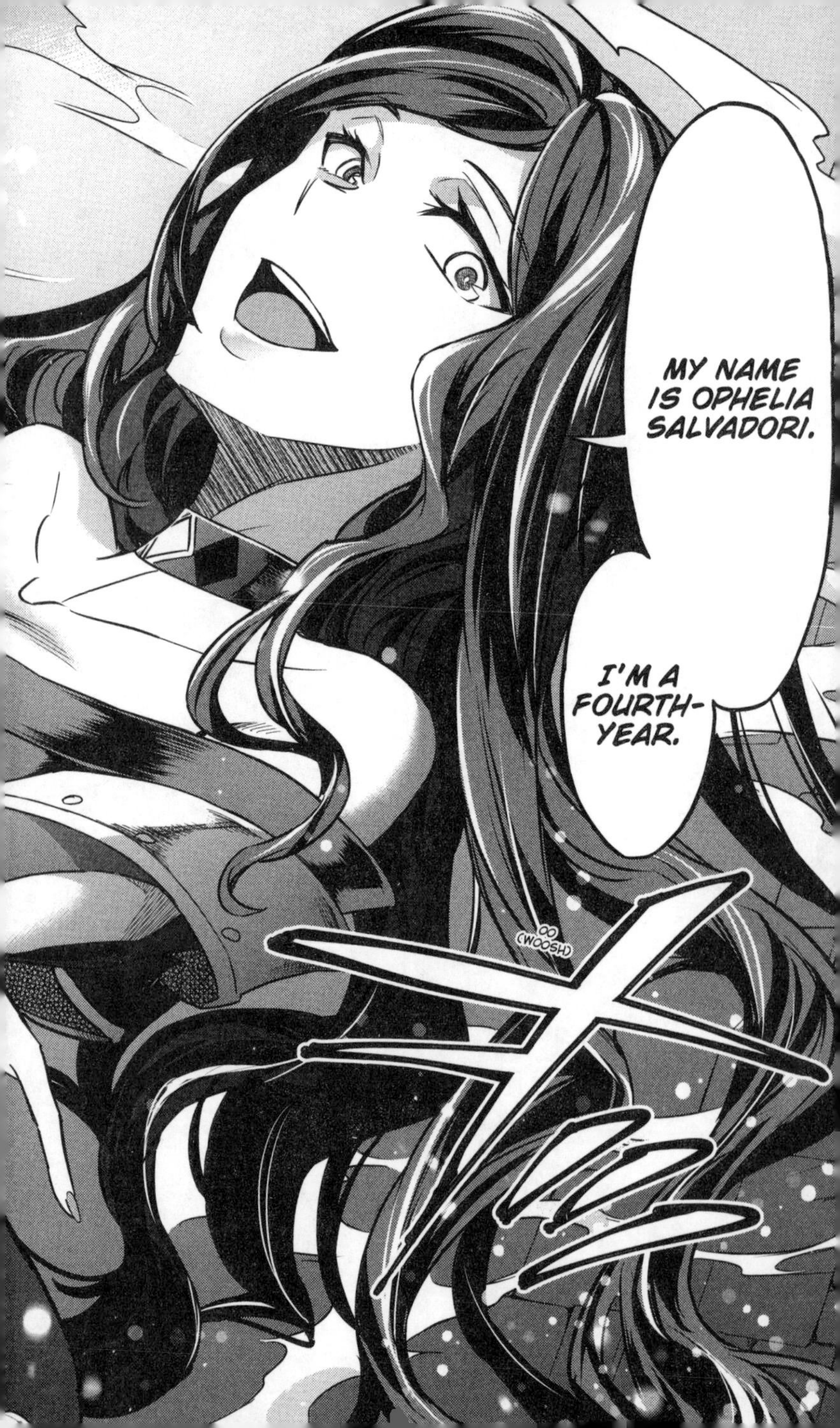
MY NAME IS OPHELIA SALVADORI.
I'M A FOURTH-YEAR.
OO (WOOSH)

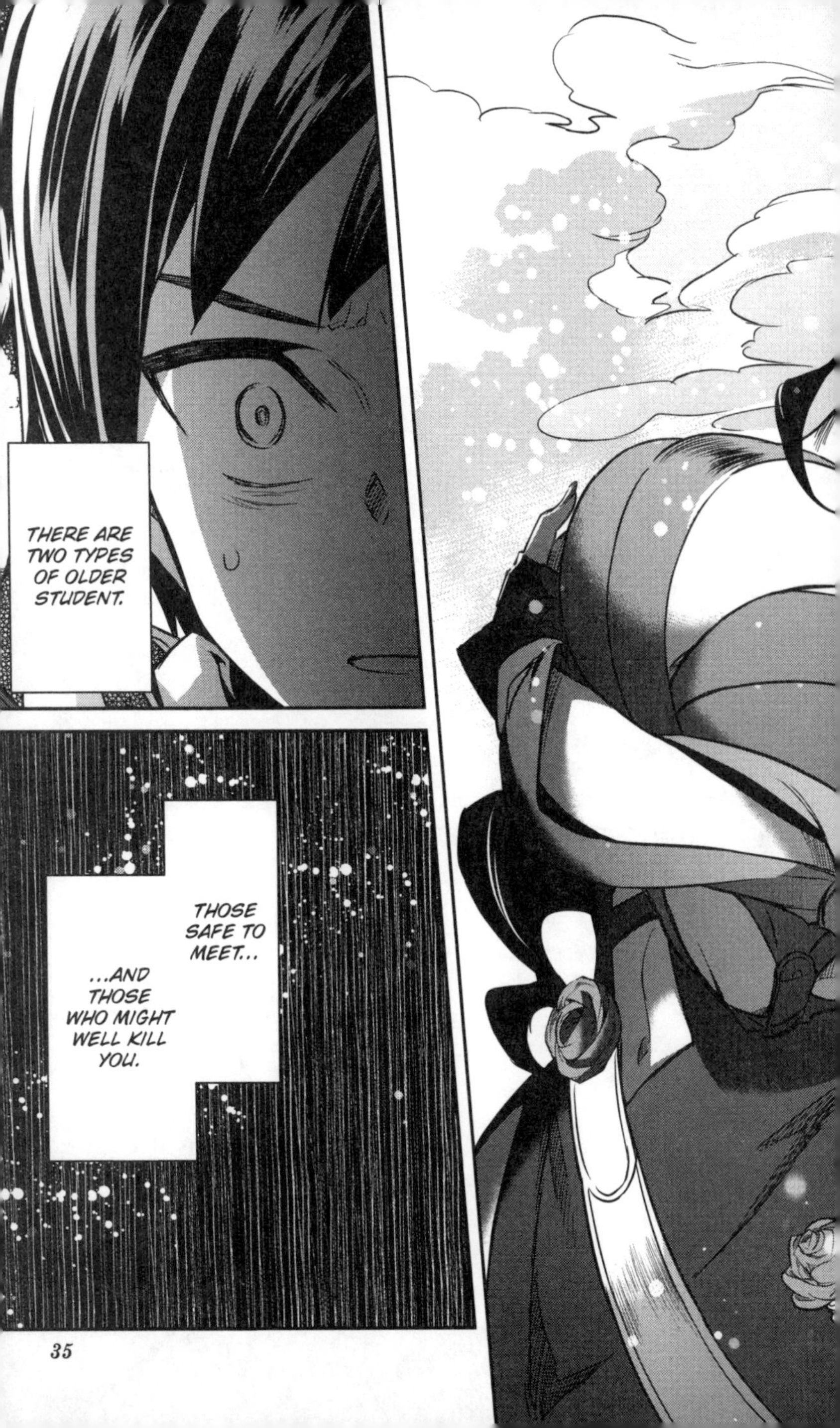
THERE ARE TWO TYPES OF OLDER STUDENT.
THOSE SAFE TO MEET...
...AND THOSE WHO MIGHT WELL KILL YOU.

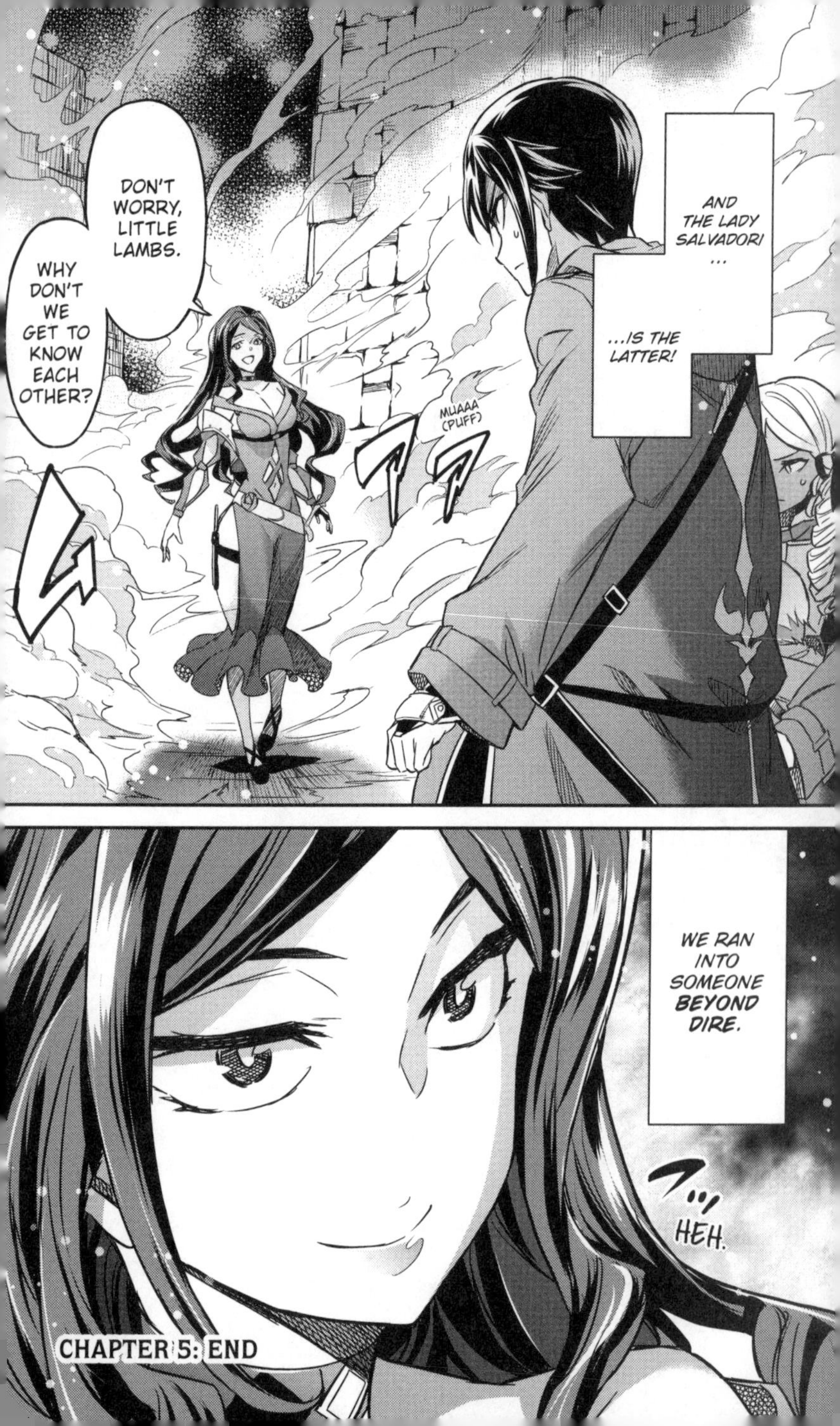
AND THE LADY SALVADORI ...
...IS THE LATTER!
MUAAA (PUFF)
DON'T WORRY, LITTLE LAMBS.
WHY DON'T WE GET TO KNOW EACH OTHER?
WE RAN INTO SOMEONE BEYOND DIRE.
HEH.
CHAPTER 5: END

CHAPTER 6: DEATH

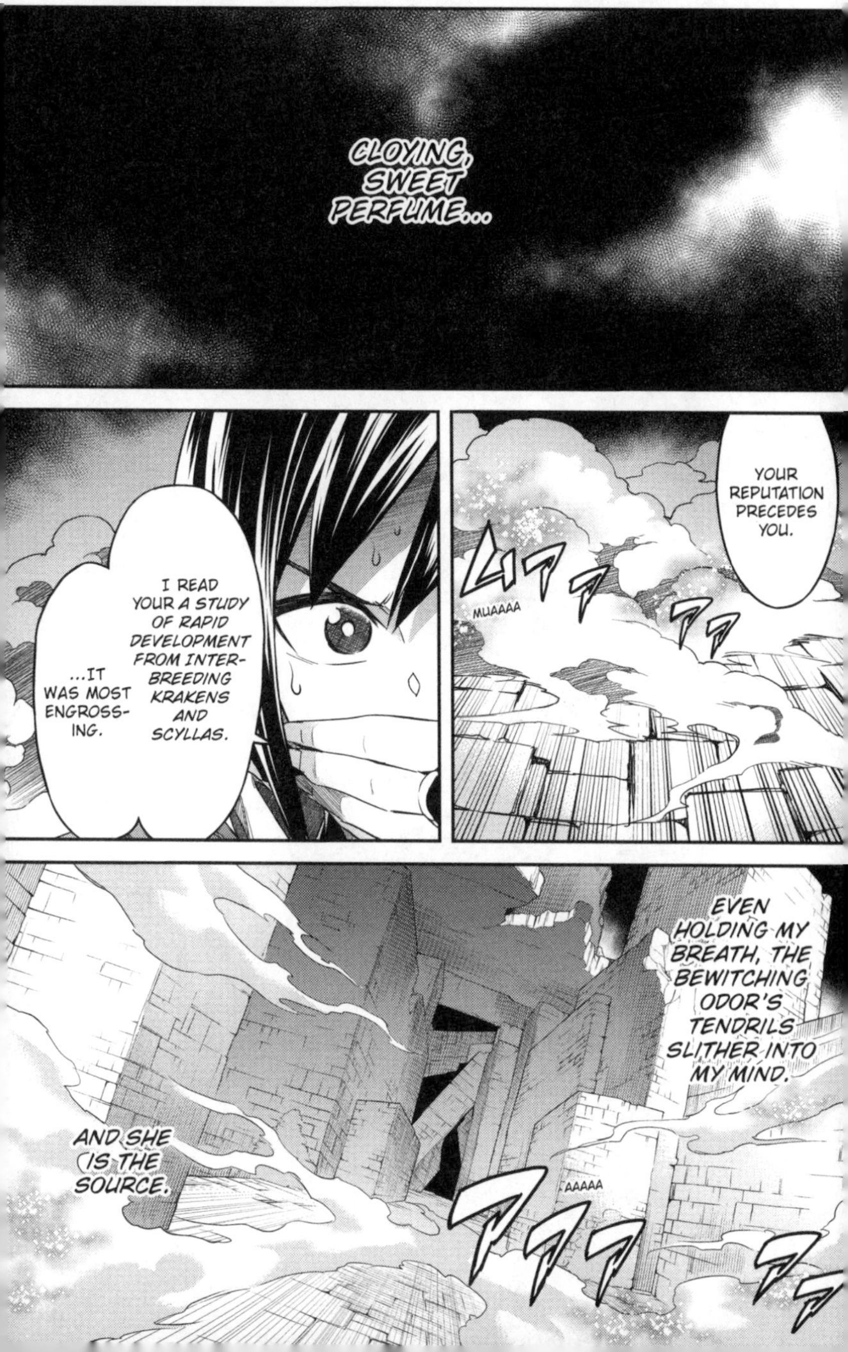
CLOYING, SWEET PERFUME...
YOUR REPUTATION PRECEDES YOU.
MUAAAA
I READ YOUR A STUDY OF RAPID DEVELOPMENT FROM INTER-BREEDING KRAKENS AND SCYLLAS.
...IT WAS MOST ENGROSS-ING.
EVEN HOLDING MY BREATH, THE BEWITCHING ODOR'S TENDRILS SLITHER INTO MY MIND.
AND SHE IS THE SOURCE.
AAAAA

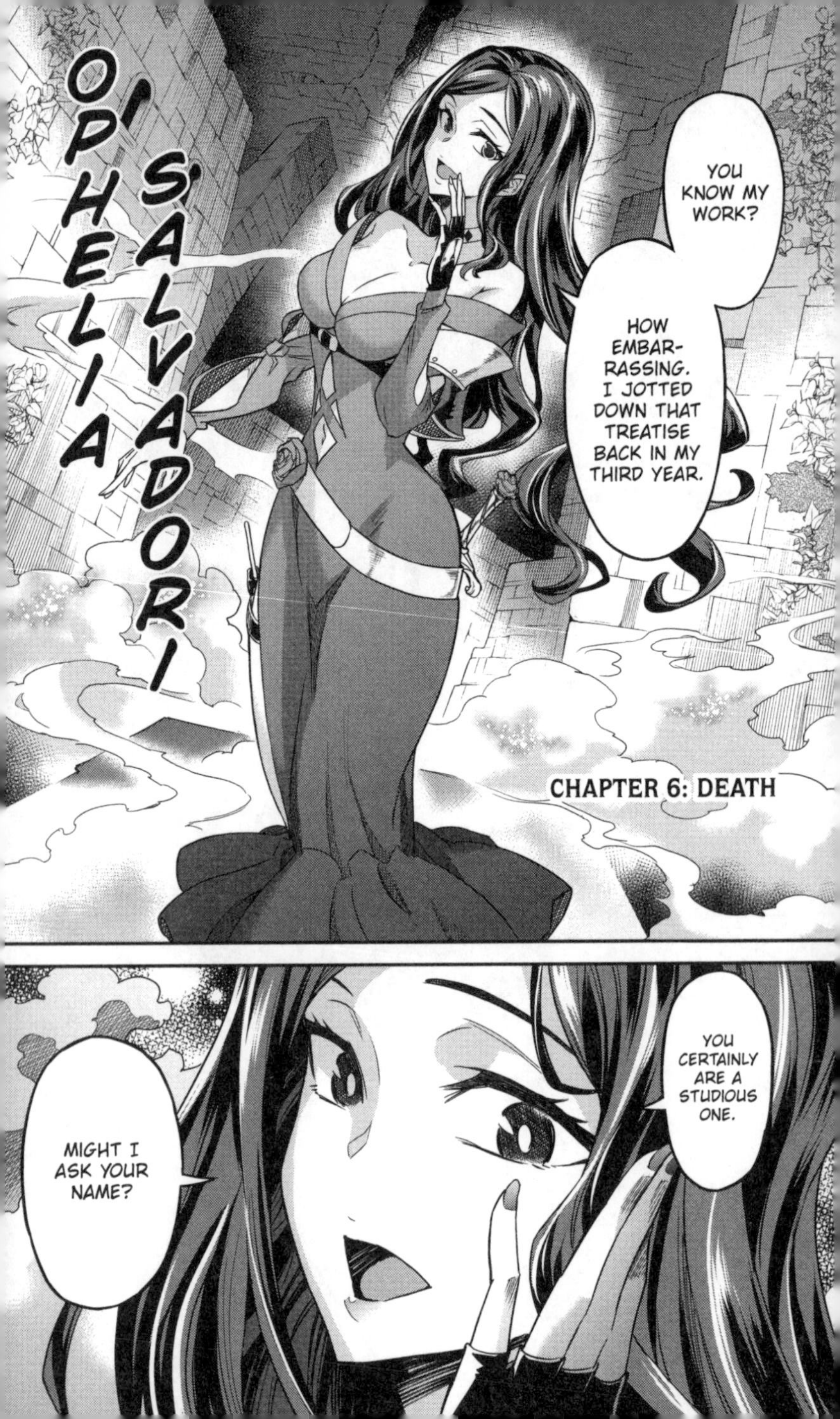
YOU KNOW MY WORK?
HOW EMBAR-RASSING. I JOTTED DOWN THAT TREATISE BACK IN MY THIRD YEAR.
OPHELIA SALVADORI
CHAPTER 6: DEATH
YOU CERTAINLY ARE A STUDIOUS ONE.
MIGHT I ASK YOUR NAME?

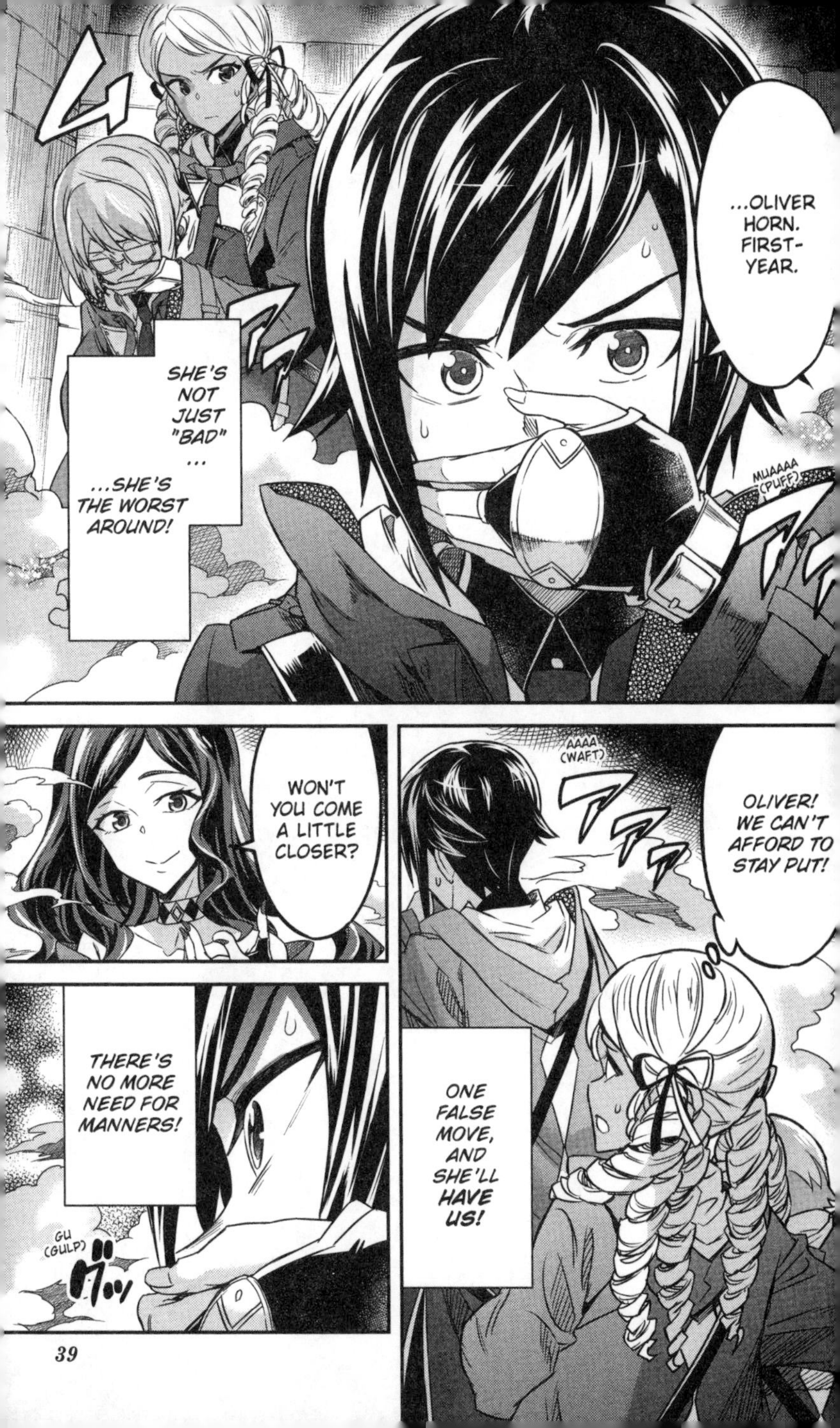
...OLIVER HORN. FIRST-YEAR.
MUAAAA (PUFF)
SHE'S NOT JUST "BAD" ...
...SHE'S THE WORST AROUND!
OLIVER! WE CAN'T AFFORD TO STAY PUT!
AAAA (WAFT)
ONE FALSE MOVE, AND SHE'LL HAVE US!
WON'T YOU COME A LITTLE CLOSER?
THERE'S NO MORE NEED FOR MANNERS!
GU (GULP)

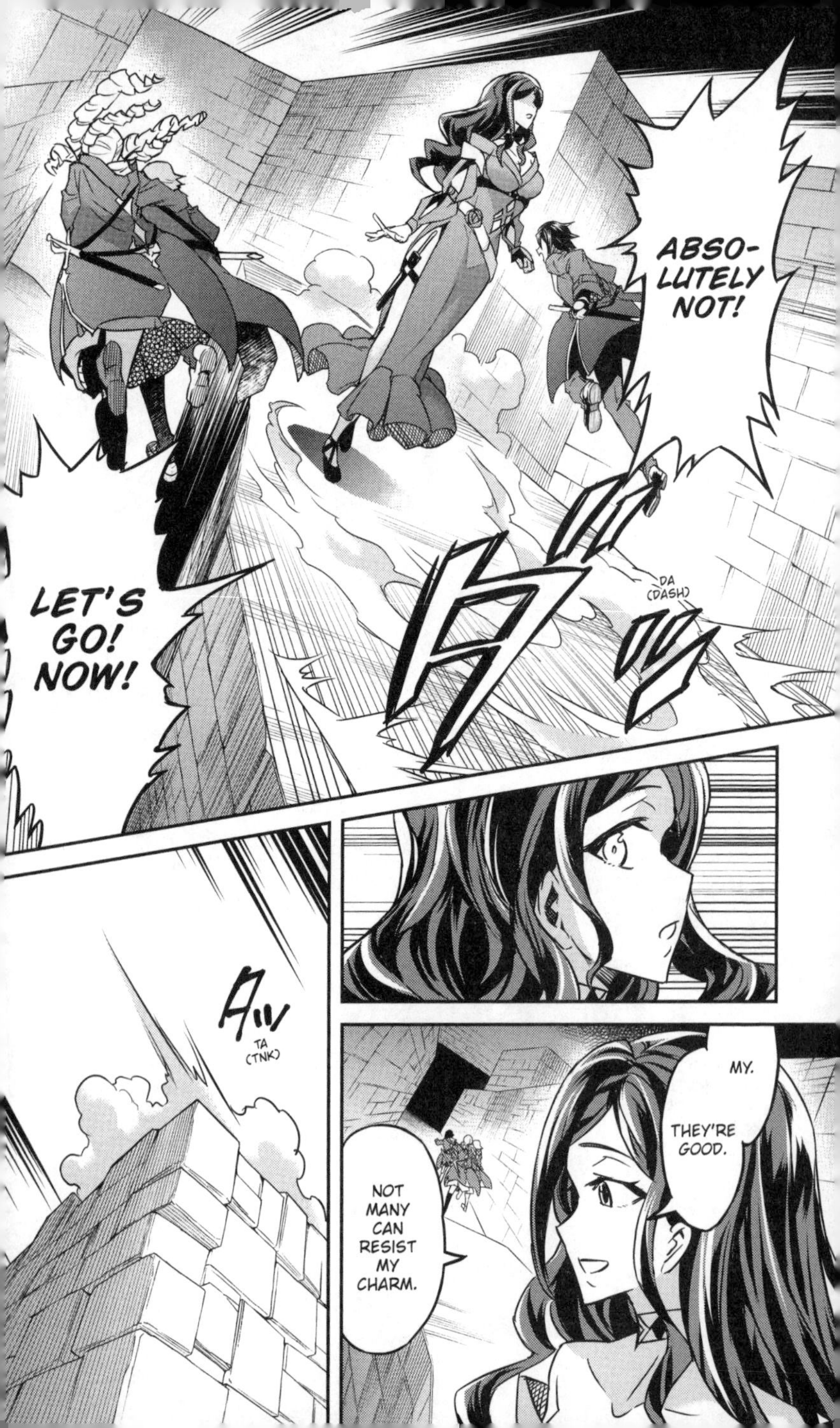
ABSO-LUTELY NOT!
DA (DASH)
LET'S GO! NOW!
MY.
THEY'RE GOOD.
NOT MANY CAN RESIST MY CHARM.
TA (TNK)

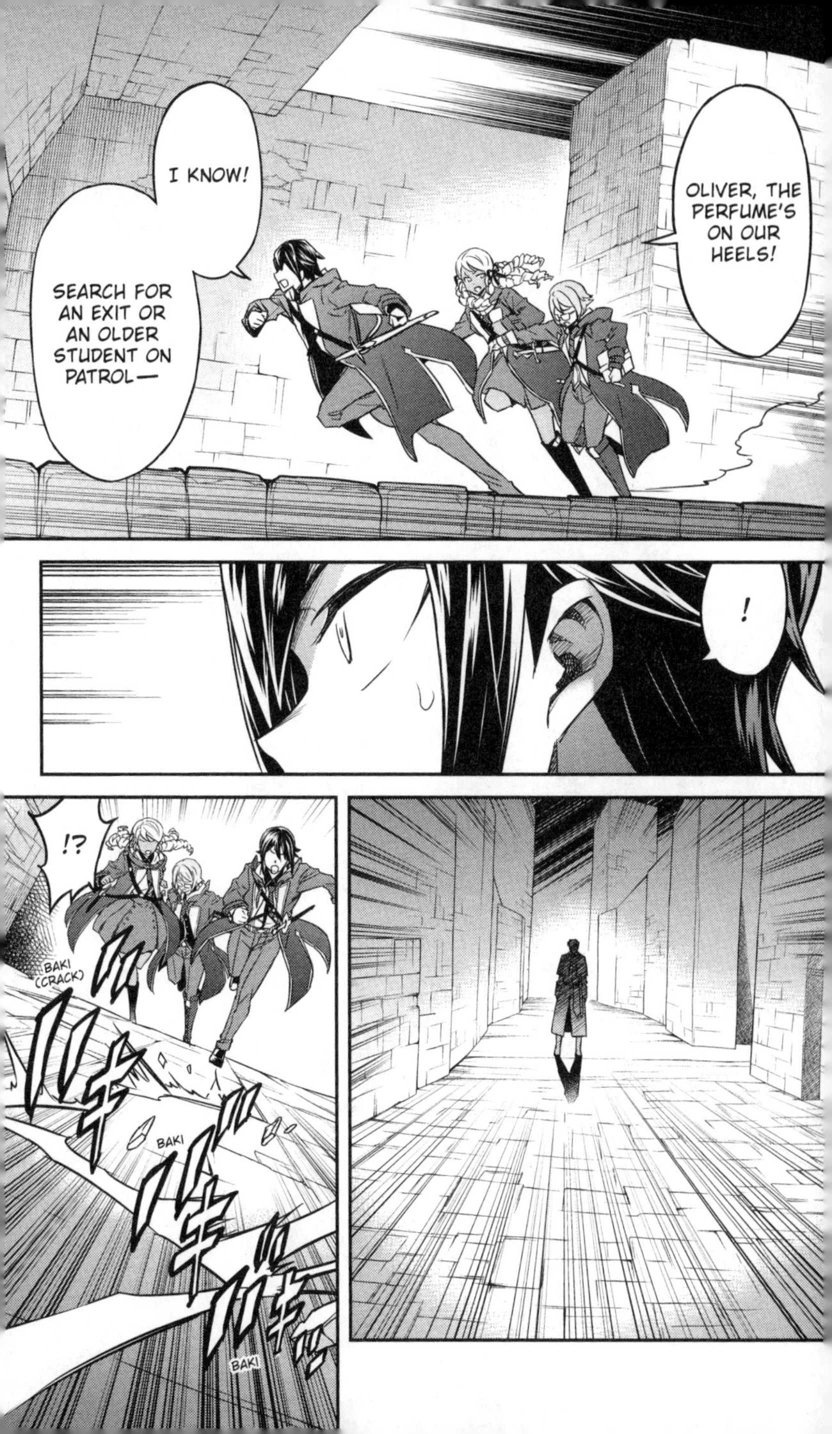
OLIVER, THE PERFUME'S ON OUR HEELS!
I KNOW!
SEARCH FOR AN EXIT OR AN OLDER STUDENT ON PATROL—
!
!?
BAKI (CRACK)
BAKI
BAKI

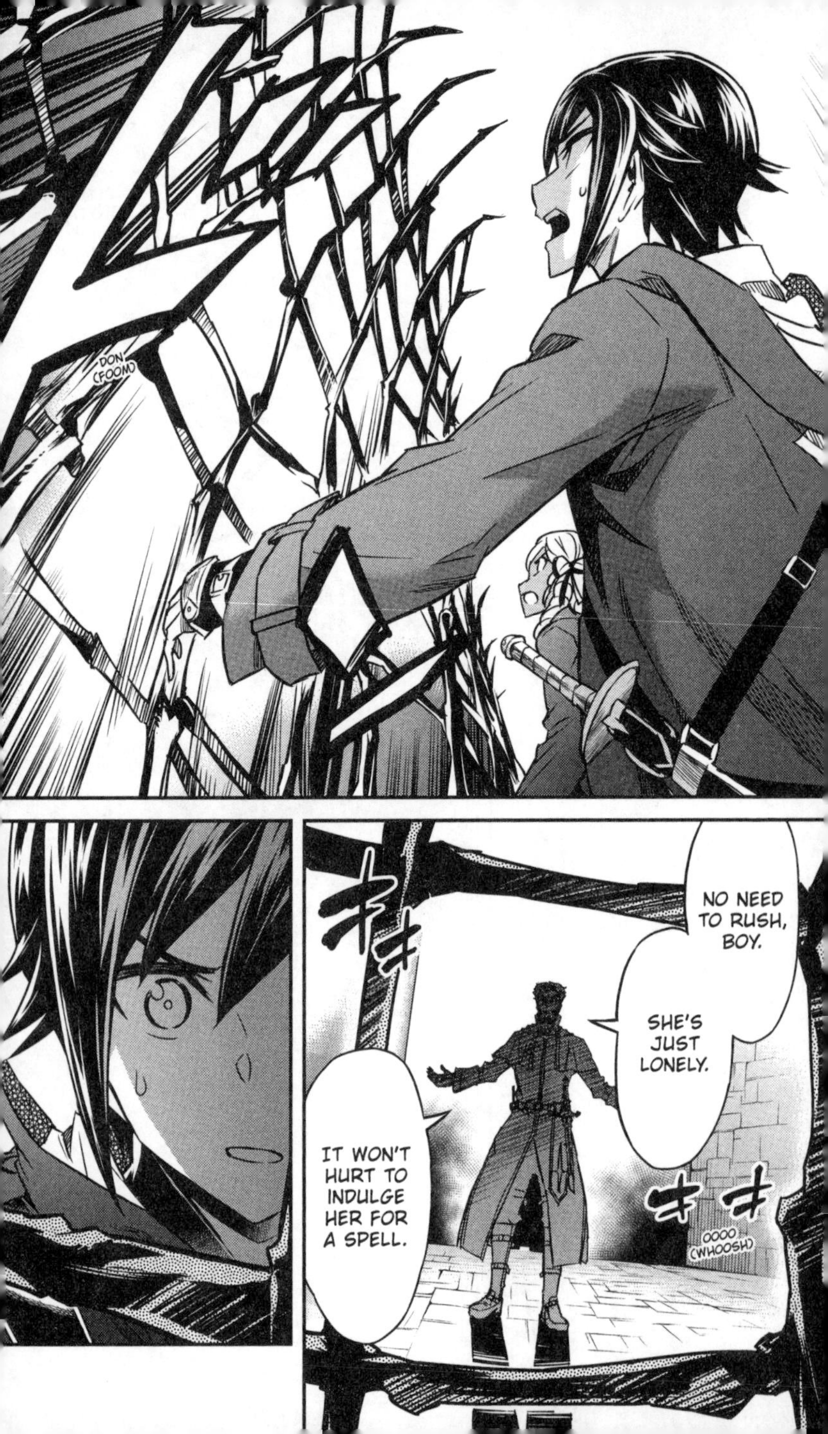
DON (FOOM)
NO NEED TO RUSH, BOY.
SHE'S JUST LONELY.
IT WON'T HURT TO INDULGE HER FOR A SPELL.
OOOO (WHOOSH)

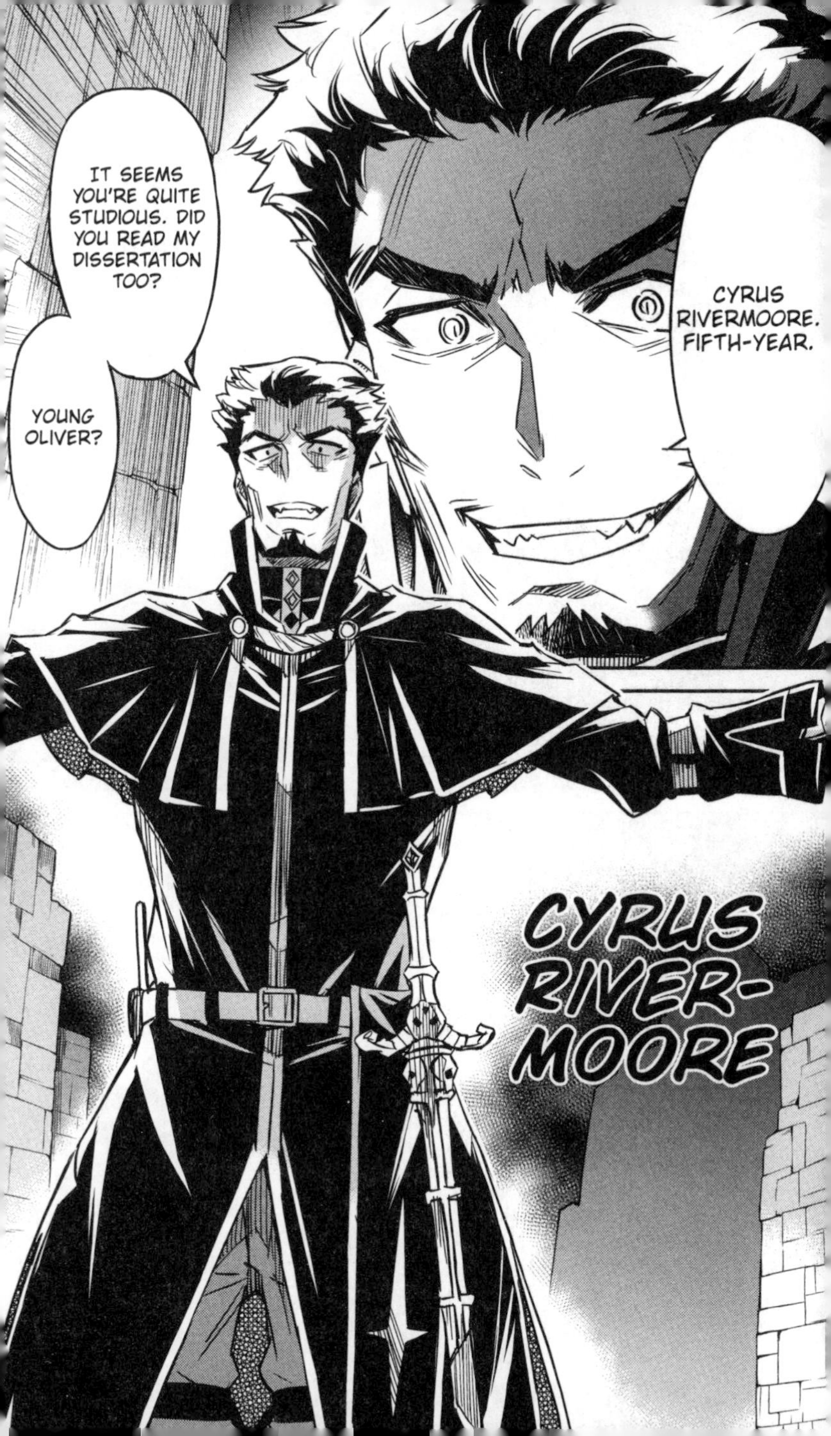
CYRUS RIVERMOORE. FIFTH-YEAR.
IT SEEMS YOU'RE QUITE STUDIOUS. DID YOU READ MY DISSERTATION TOO?
YOUNG OLIVER?
CYRUS RIVER-MOORE

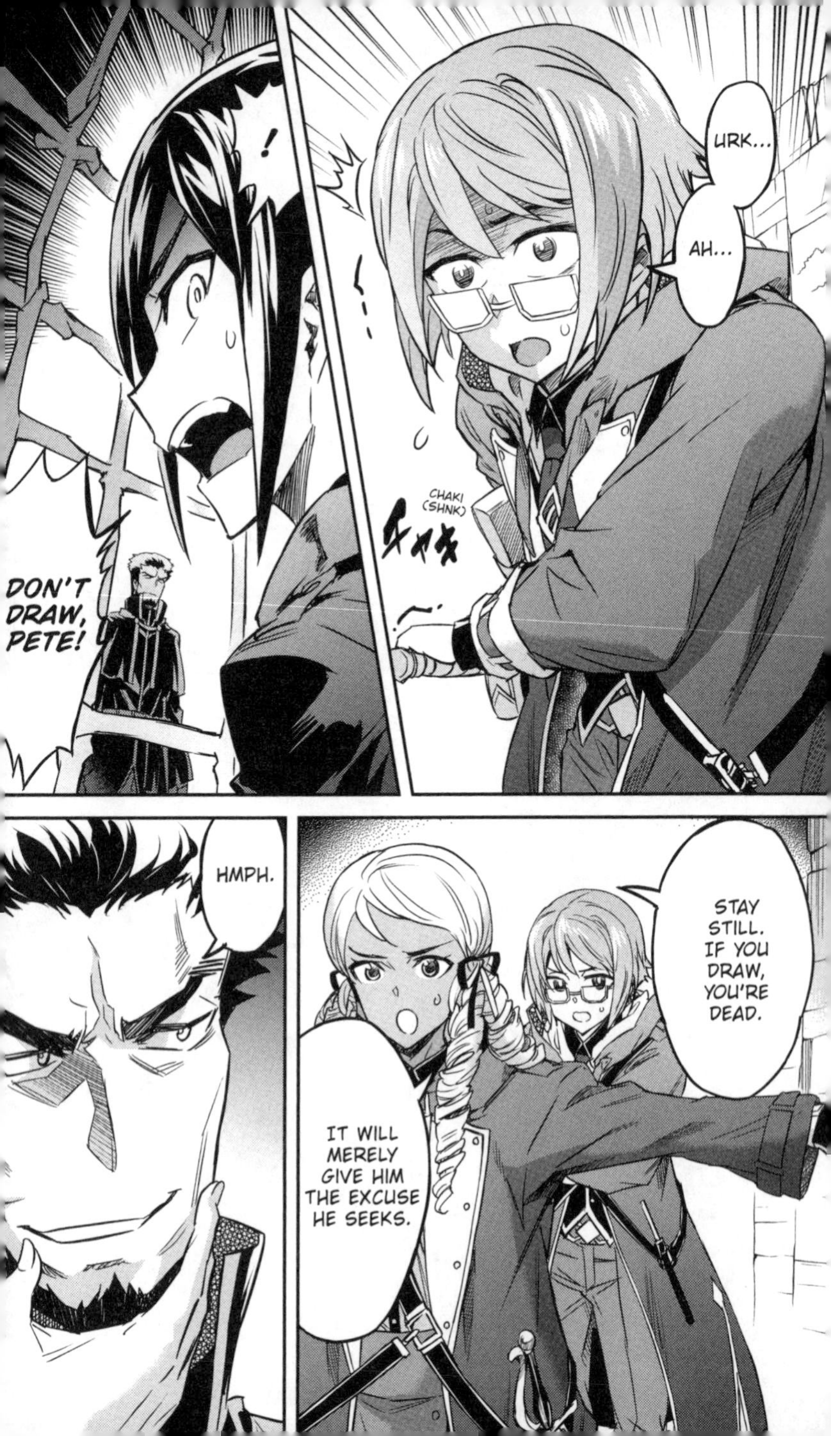
URK...
AH...
CHAKI (SHNK)
チャキ
DON'T DRAW, PETE!
STAY STILL. IF YOU DRAW, YOU'RE DEAD.
IT WILL MERELY GIVE HIM THE EXCUSE HE SEEKS.
HMPH.

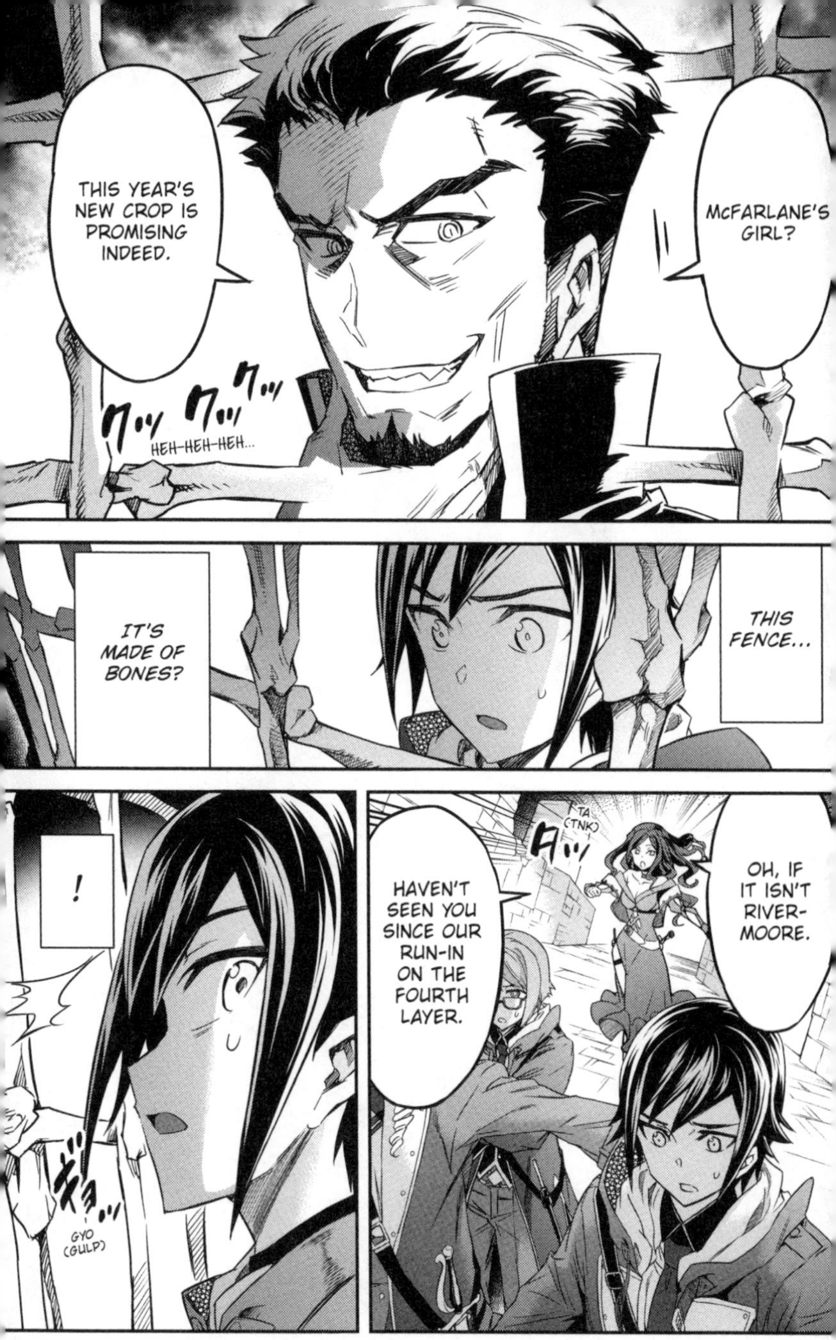
McFARLANE'S GIRL?
THIS YEAR'S NEW CROP IS PROMISING INDEED.
HEH-HEH-HEH...
THIS FENCE...
IT'S MADE OF BONES?
OH, IF IT ISN'T RIVER-MOORE.
TA (TNK)
HAVEN'T SEEN YOU SINCE OUR RUN-IN ON THE FOURTH LAYER.
!
GYO (GULP)

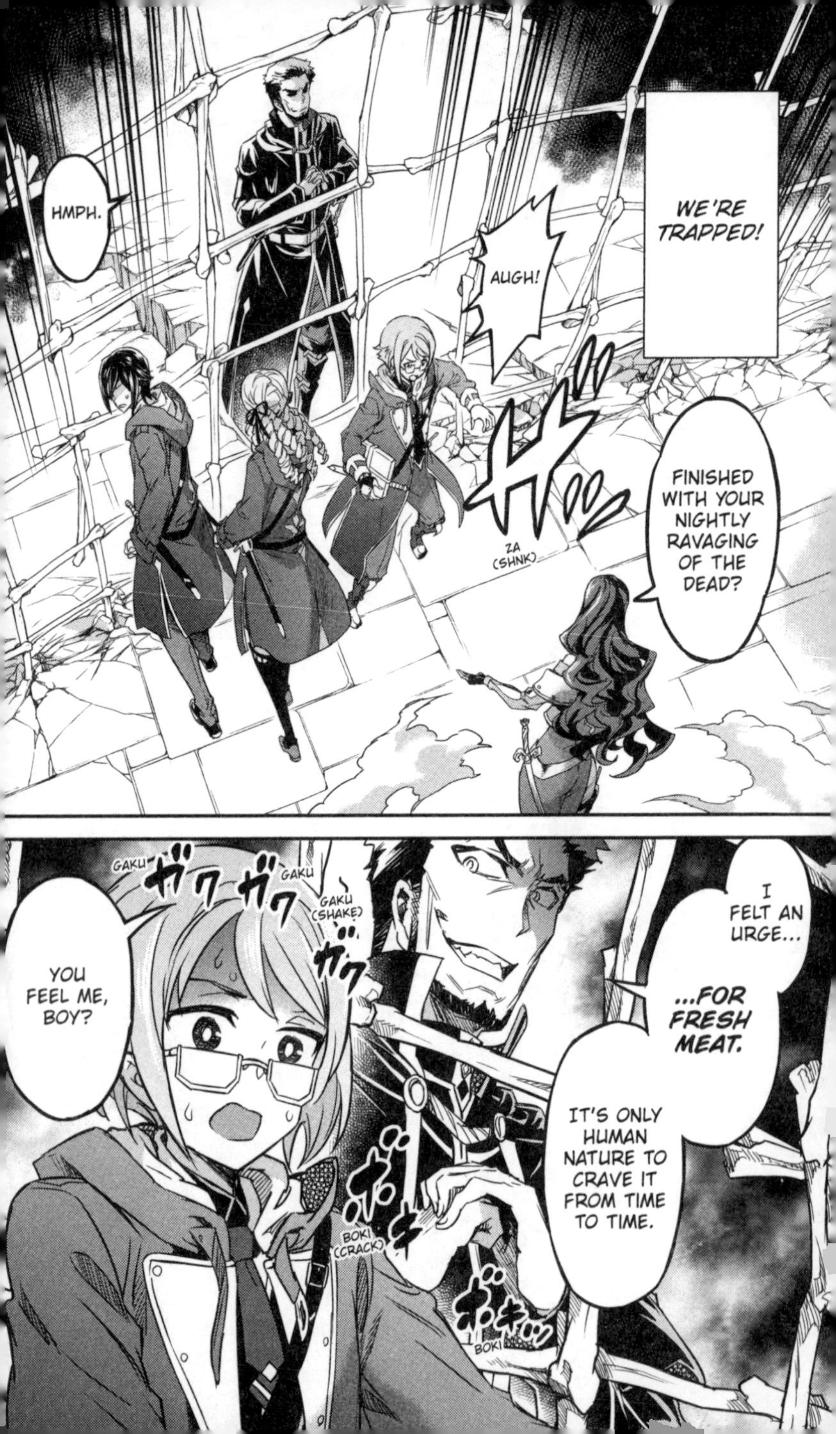
WE'RE TRAPPED!
AUGH!
HMPH.
FINISHED WITH YOUR NIGHTLY RAVAGING OF THE DEAD?
ZA (SHNK)
I FELT AN URGE...
...FOR FRESH MEAT.
IT'S ONLY HUMAN NATURE TO CRAVE IT FROM TIME TO TIME.
GAKU (SHAKE)
GAKU
GAKU
YOU FEEL ME, BOY?
BOKI (CRACK)
BOKI

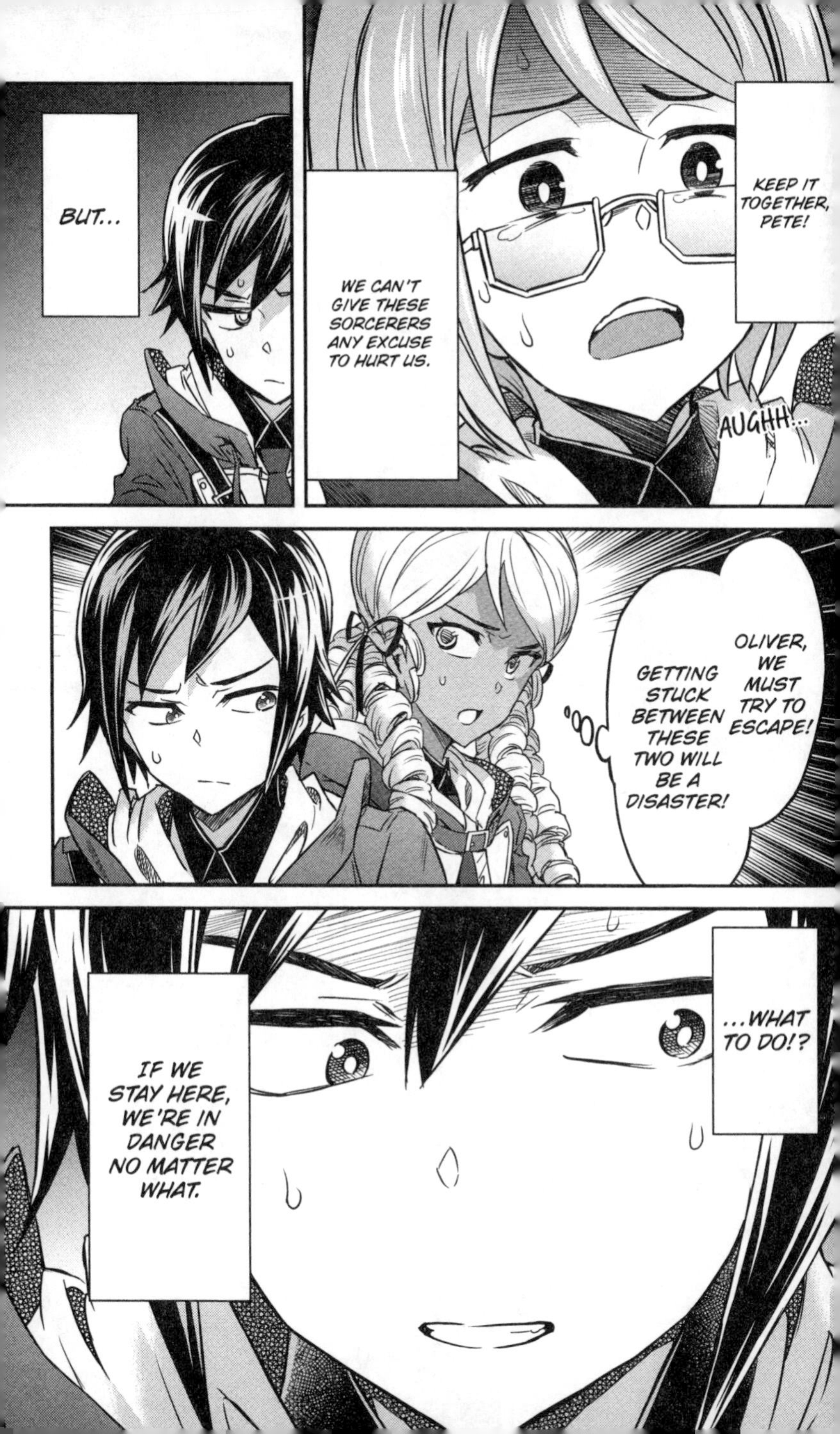
KEEP IT TOGETHER, PETE!
WE CAN'T GIVE THESE SORCERERS ANY EXCUSE TO HURT US.
AUGHH...
BUT...
OLIVER, WE MUST TRY TO ESCAPE!
GETTING STUCK BETWEEN THESE TWO WILL BE A DISASTER!
...WHAT TO DO!?
IF WE STAY HERE, WE'RE IN DANGER NO MATTER WHAT.

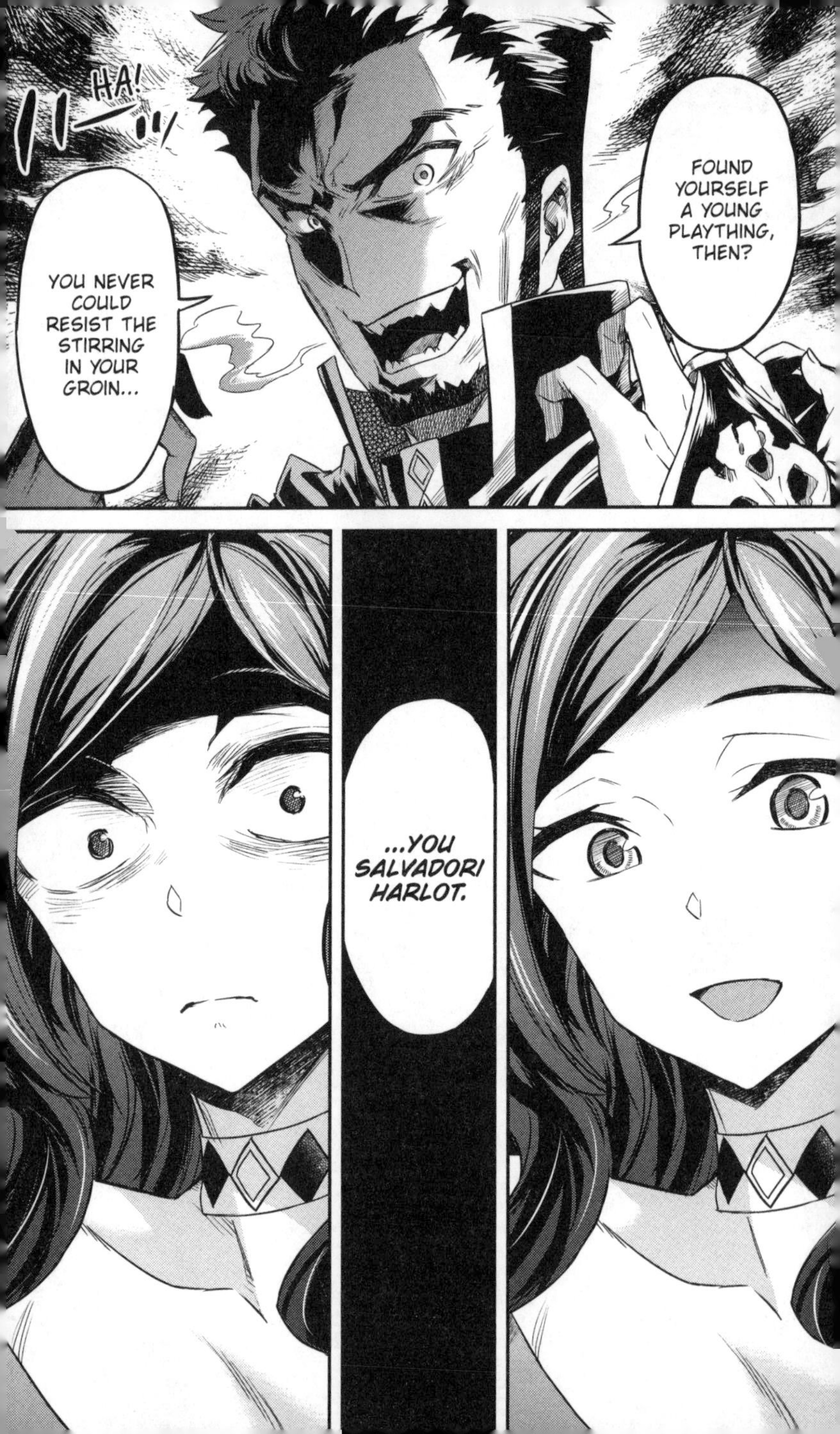
FOUND YOURSELF A YOUNG PLAYTHING, THEN?
HA!
YOU NEVER COULD RESIST THE STIRRING IN YOUR GROIN...
...YOU SALVADORI HARLOT.

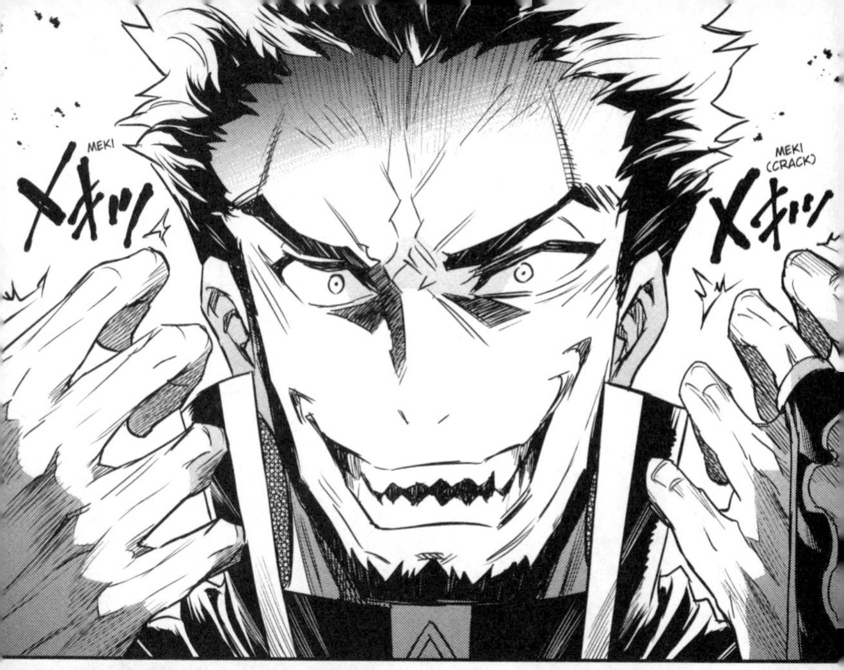
メキッ
MEKI (CRACK)
メキッ
MEKI

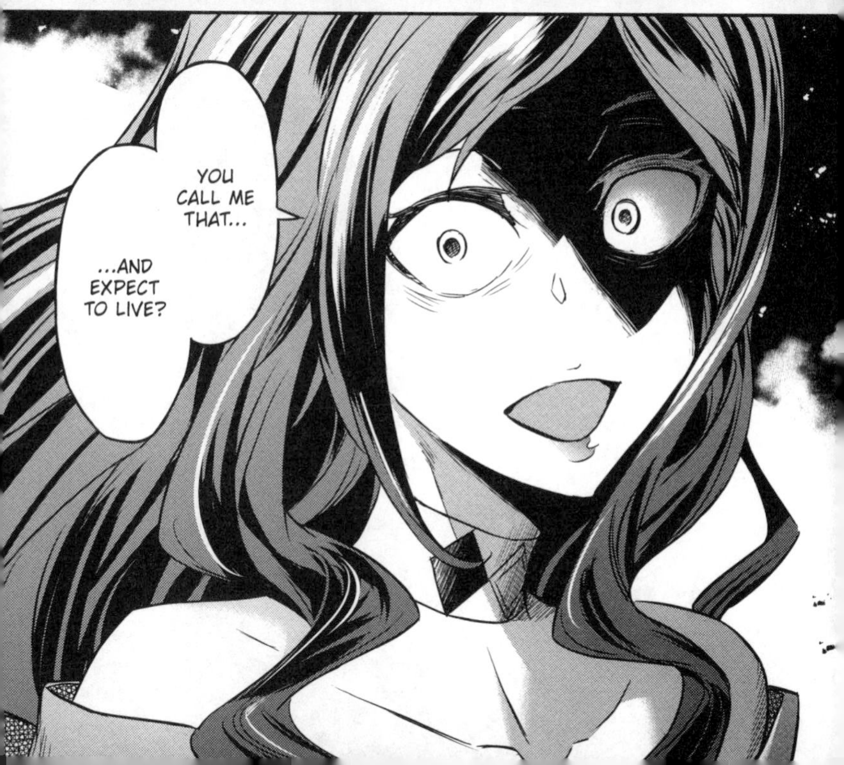
YOU CALL ME THAT...
...AND EXPECT TO LIVE?

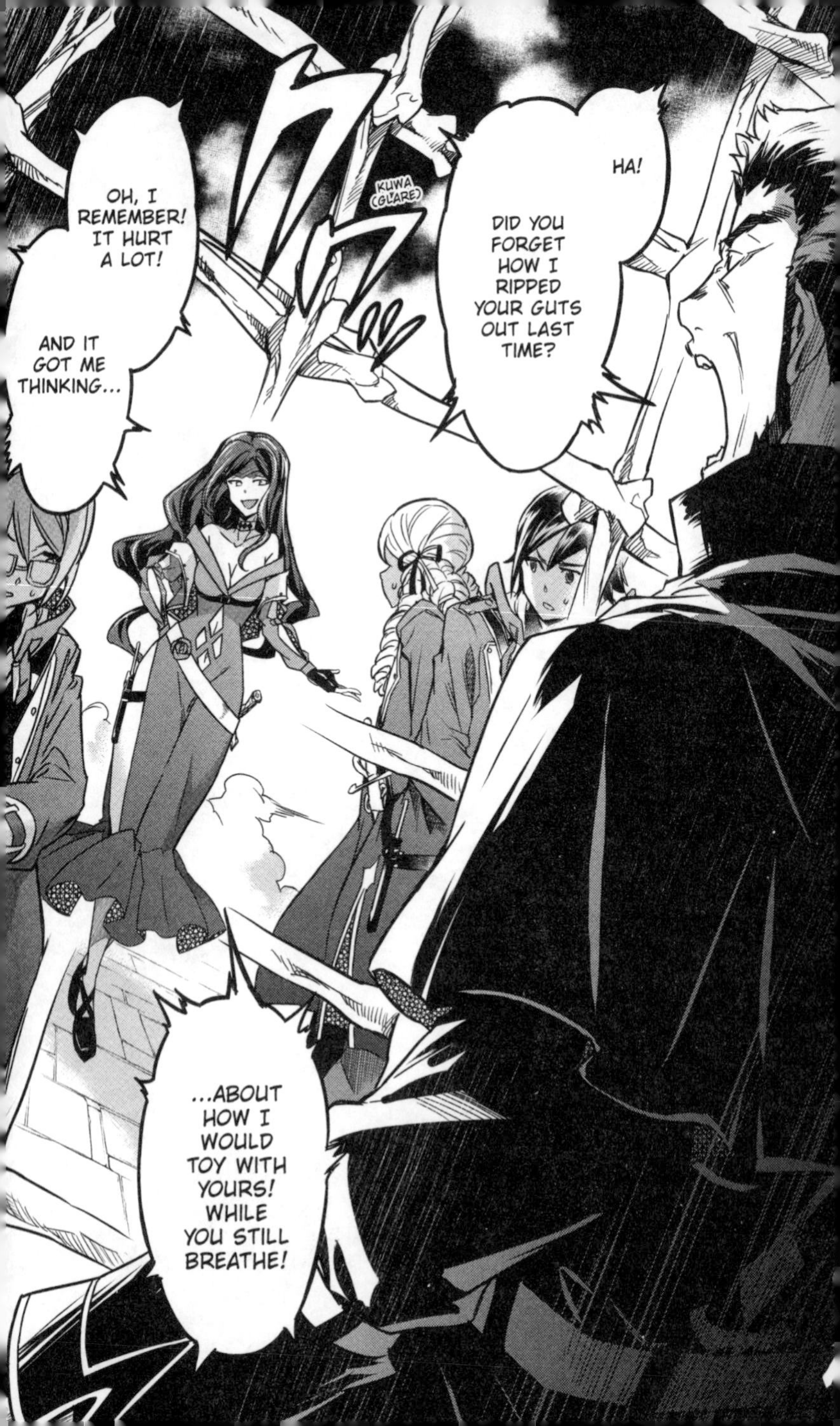
HA!
DID YOU FORGET HOW I RIPPED YOUR GUTS OUT LAST TIME?
KUWA (GLARE)
OH, I REMEMBER! IT HURT A LOT!
AND IT GOT ME THINKING...
...ABOUT HOW I WOULD TOY WITH YOURS! WHILE YOU STILL BREATHE!

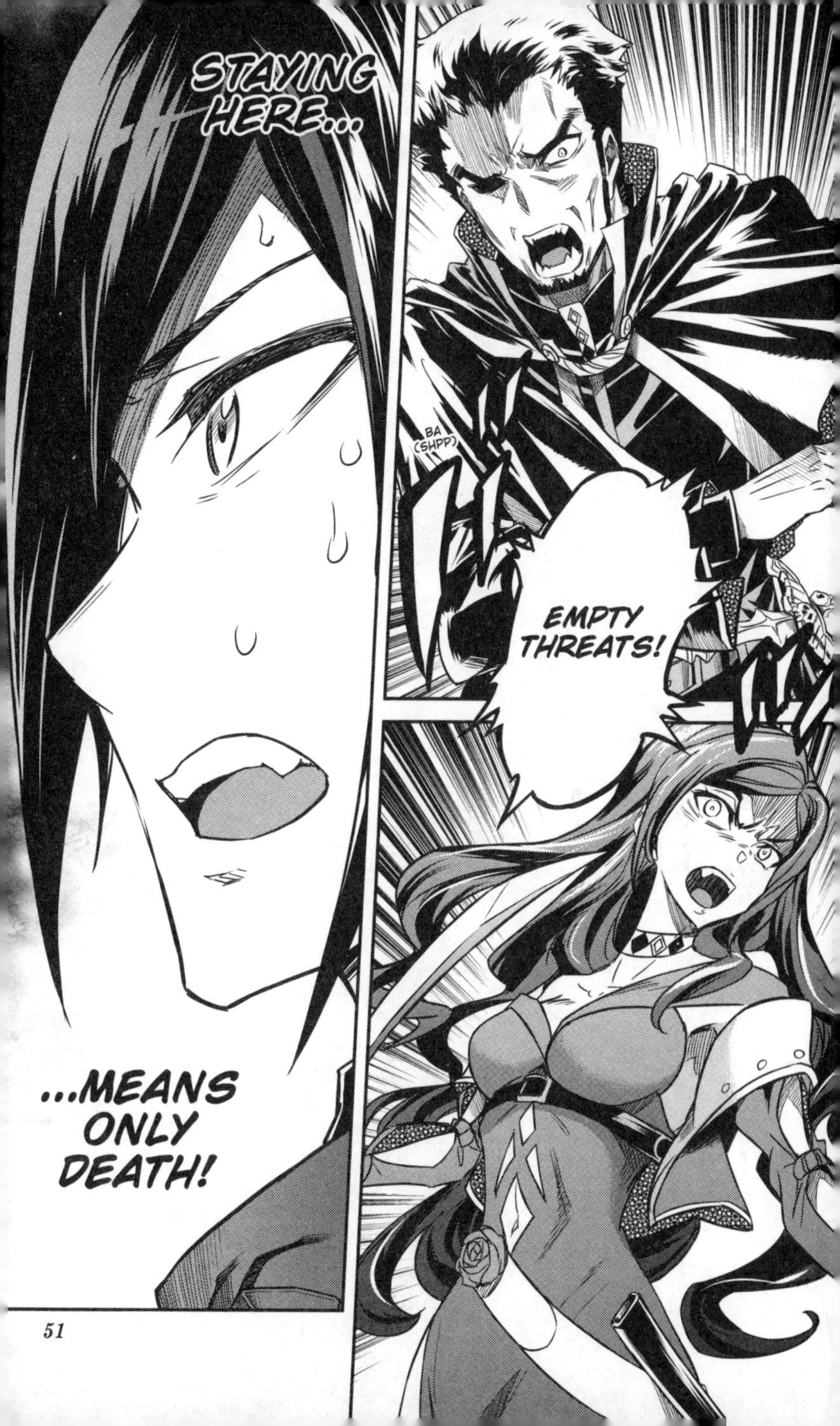

BA (SHPP)
EMPTY THREATS!
STAYING HERE...
...MEANS ONLY DEATH!

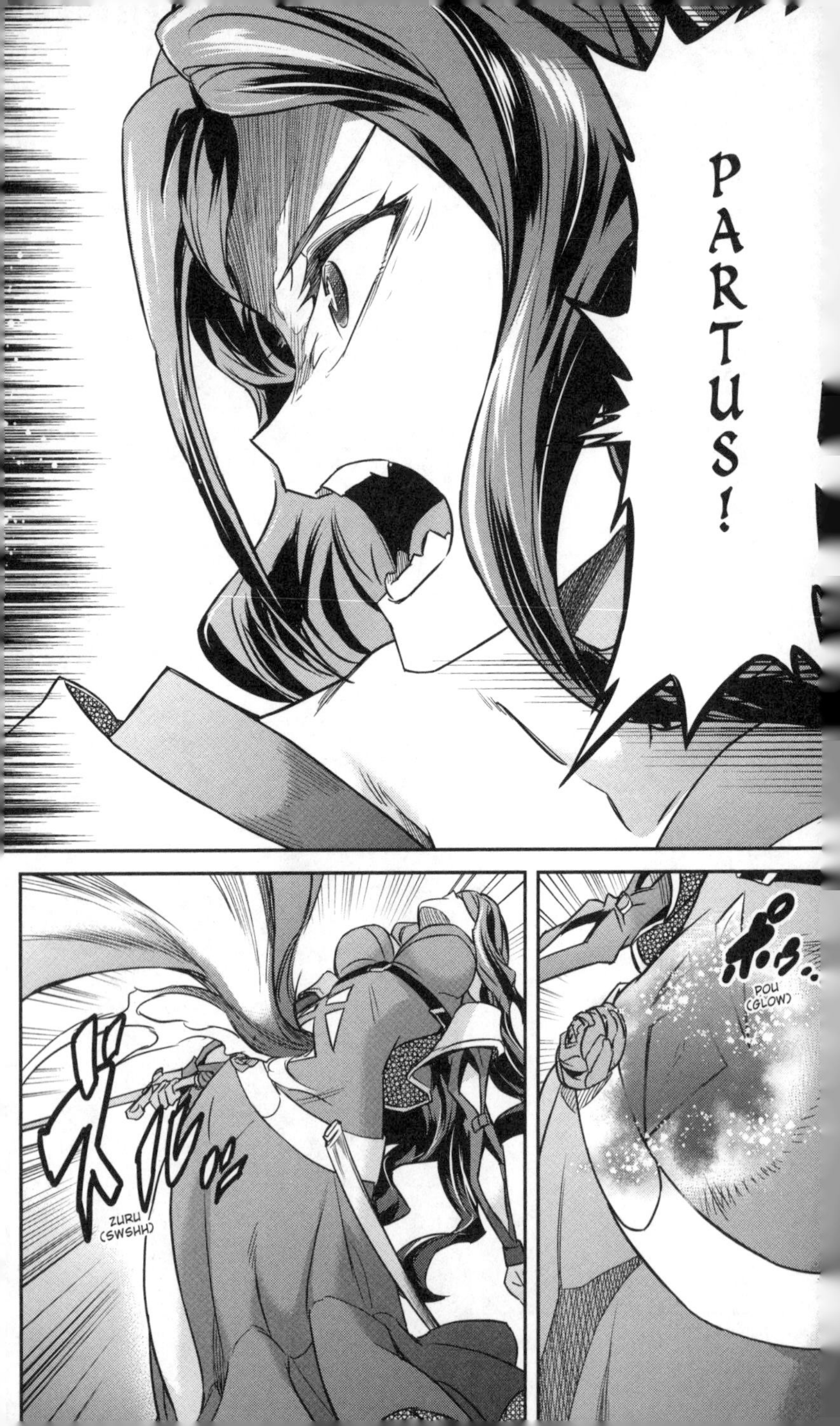
PARTUS!
POU (GLOW)
ZURU (SWSHH)

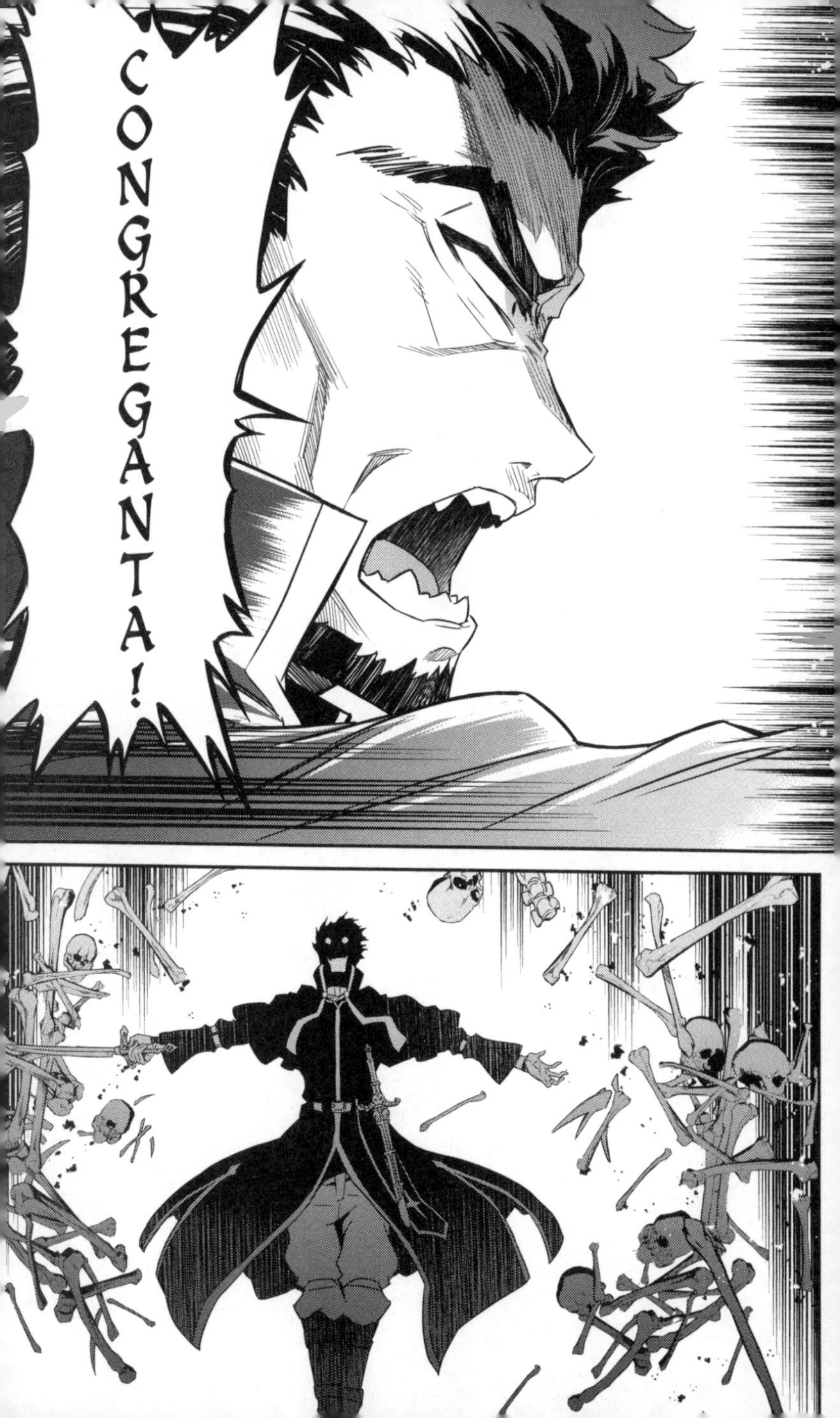
CONGREGANTA!

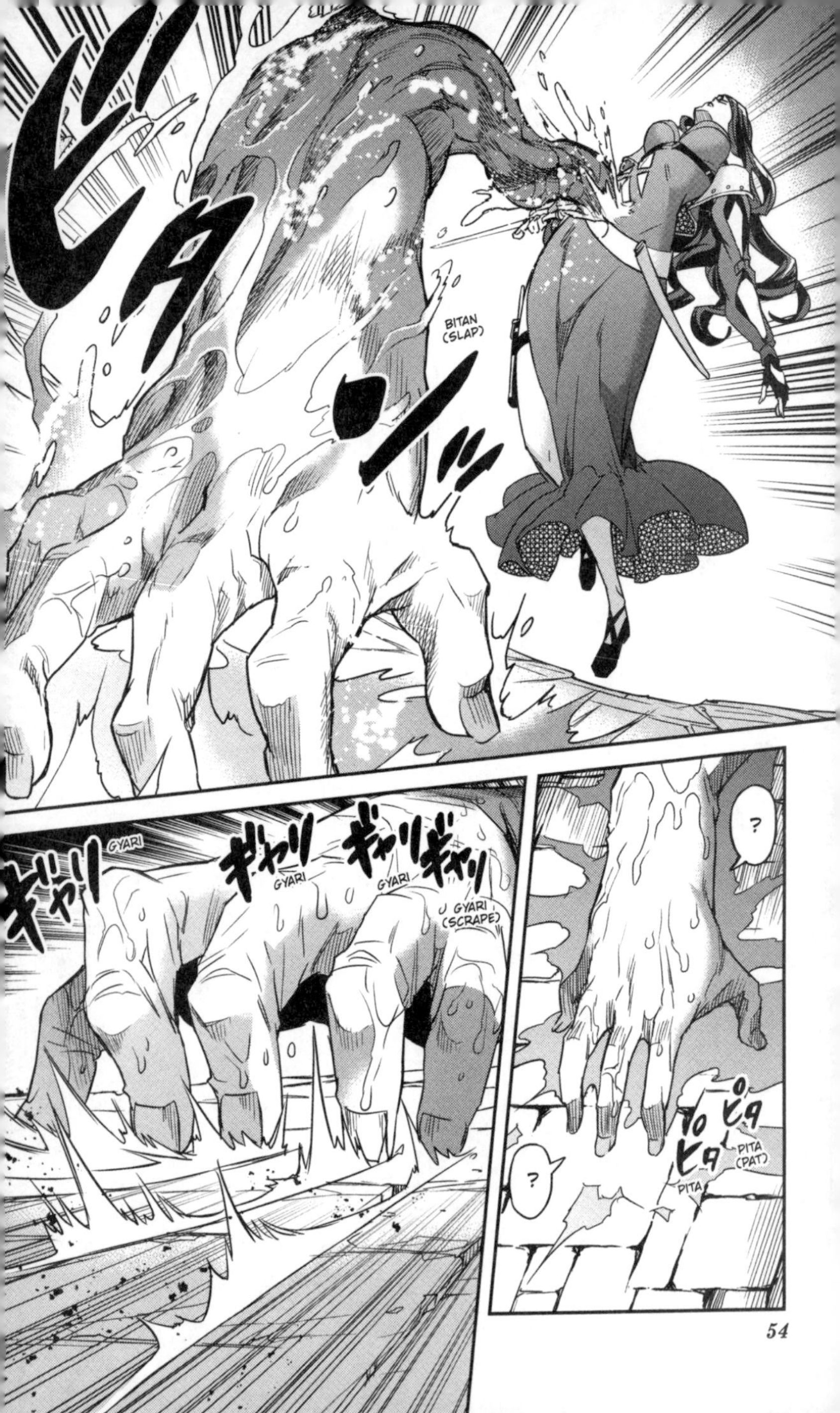

ビタン
BITAN (SLAP)
?
ピタ
PITA (PAT)
ピタ
PITA
?
ギャリ
GYARI
GYARI (SCRAPE)
ギャリ
GYARI
ギャリ
GYARI

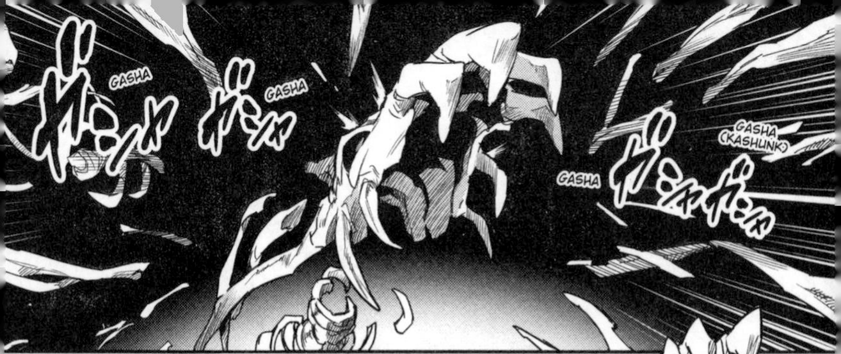
GASHA (KASHUNK)
GASHA
GASHA
GASHA
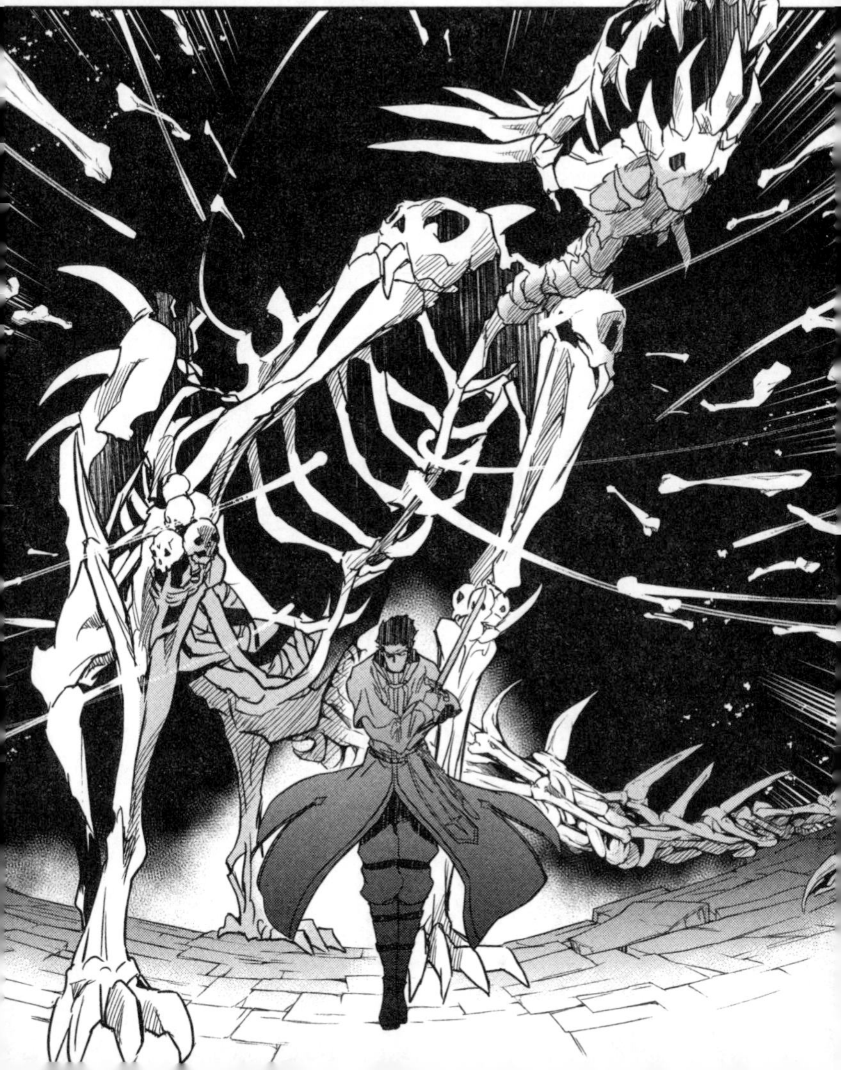

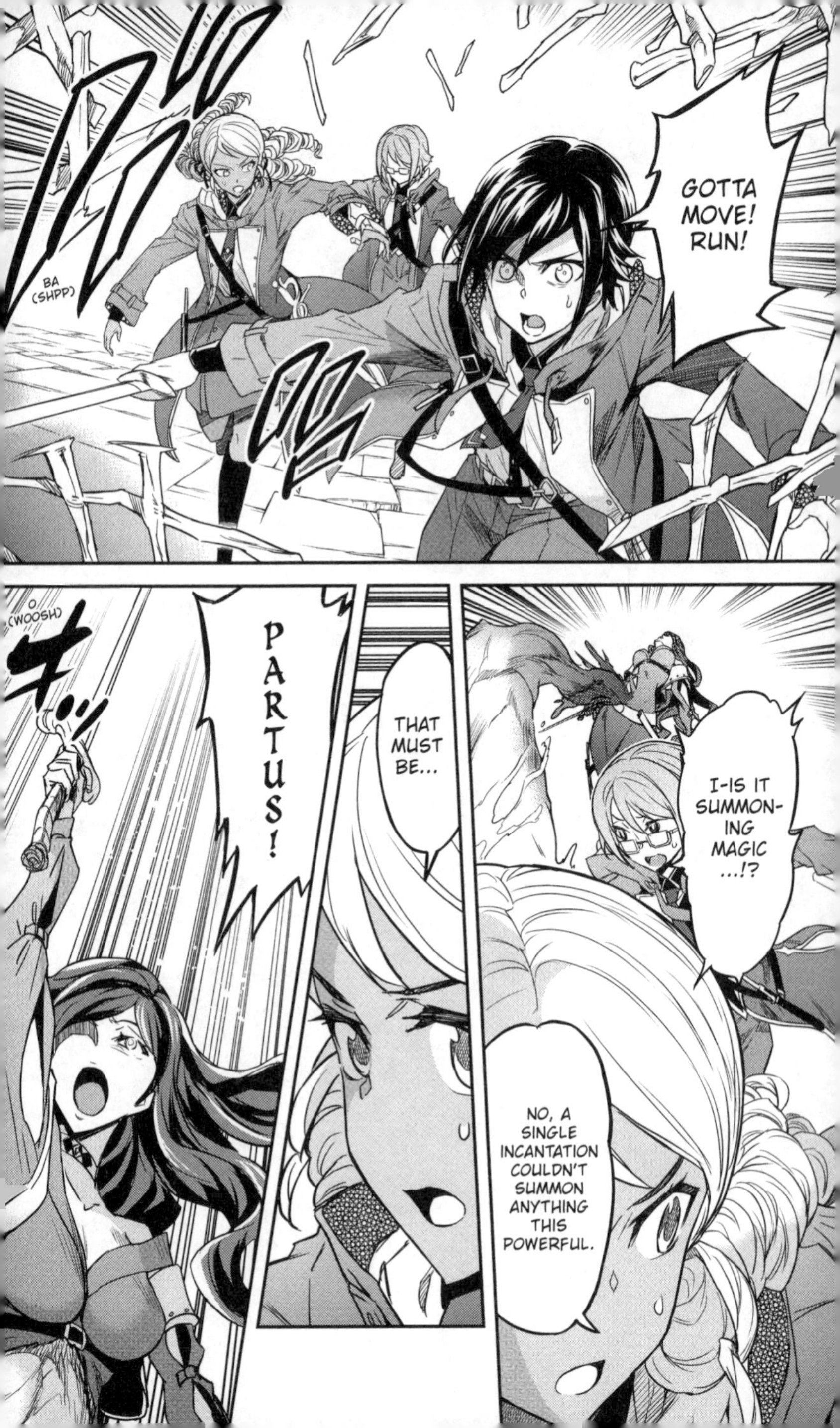
GOTTA MOVE! RUN!
BA (SHPP)
I-IS IT SUMMONING MAGIC ...!?
NO, A SINGLE INCANTATION COULDN'T SUMMON ANYTHING THIS POWERFUL.
THAT MUST BE...
PARTUS!
O (WOOSH)

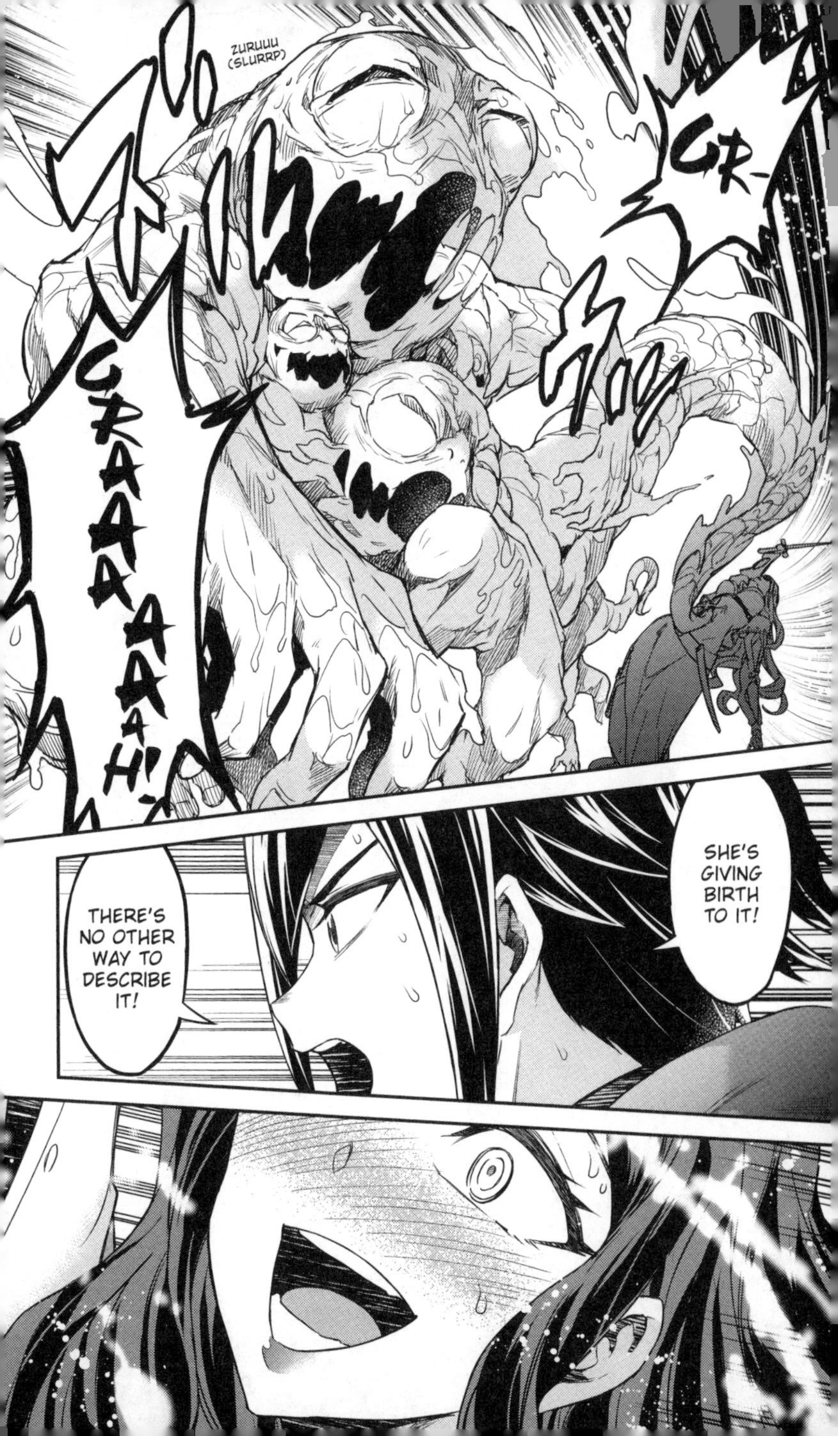
GR-
ZURUUU (SLURRP)
GRAAAAAAH!-
SHE'S GIVING BIRTH TO IT!
THERE'S NO OTHER WAY TO DESCRIBE IT!

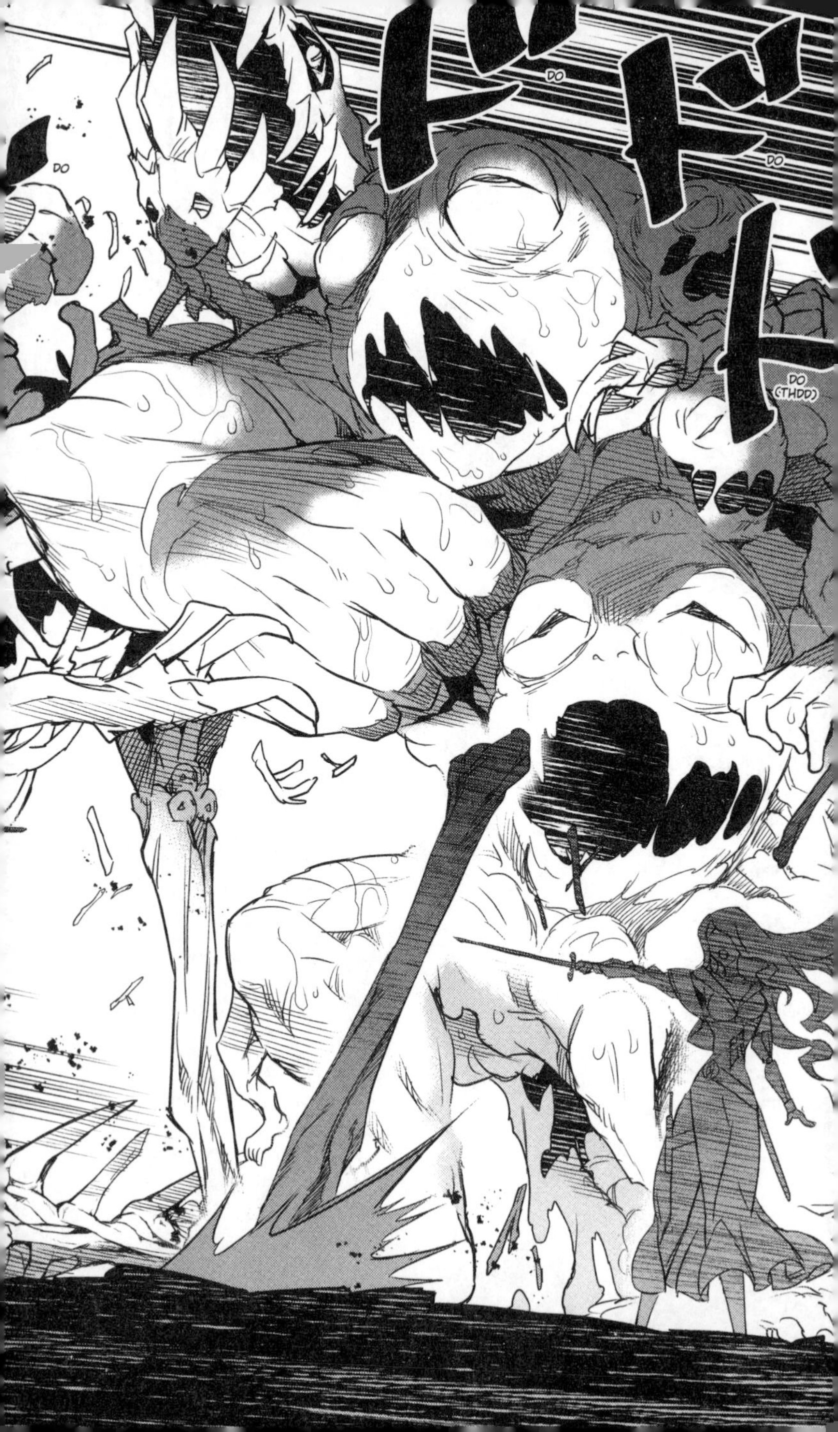
DO
DO
DO
(THDD)
DO

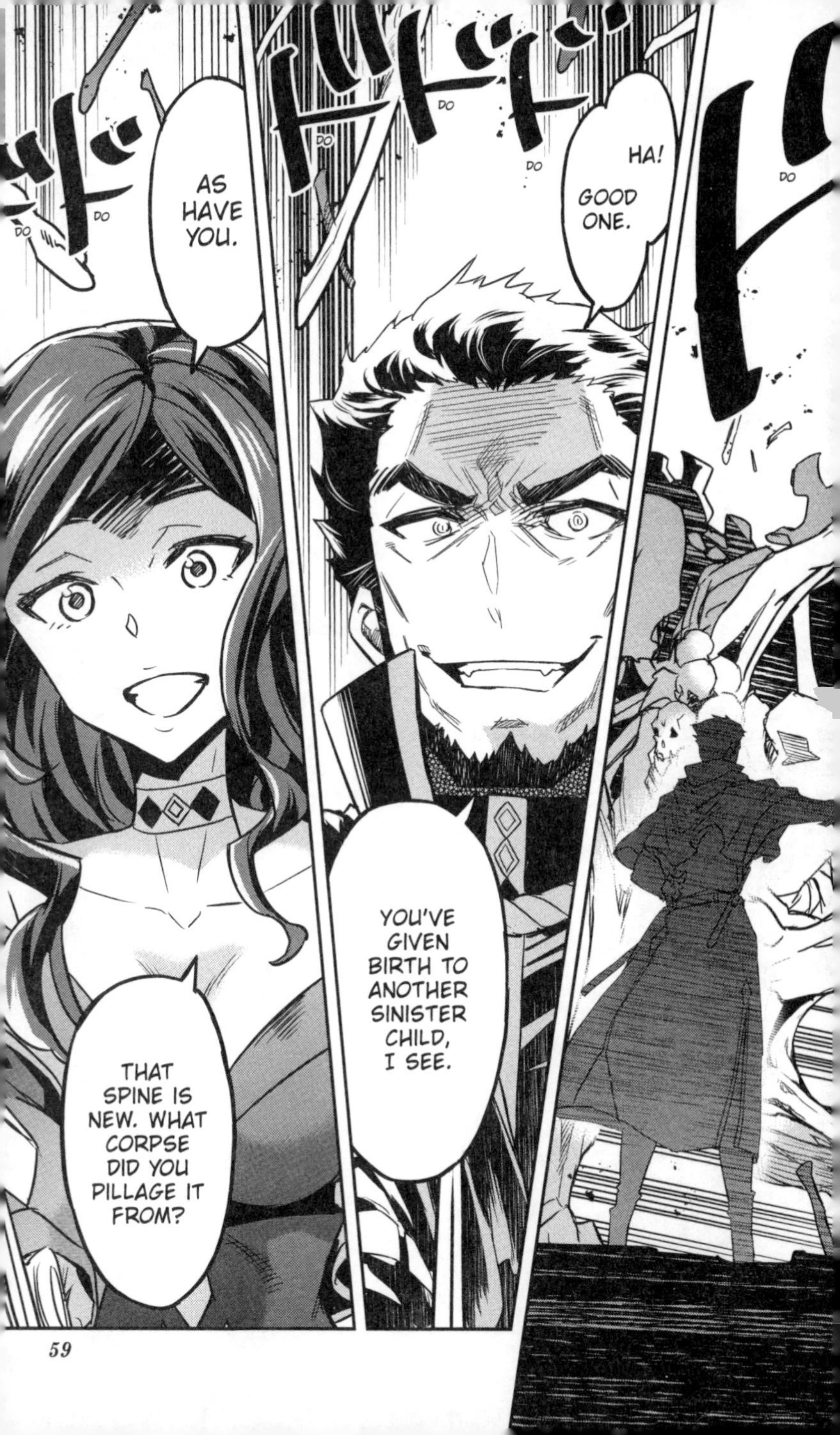
DO
DO
DO
HA! GOOD ONE.
YOU'VE GIVEN BIRTH TO ANOTHER SINISTER CHILD, I SEE.
DO
DO
AS HAVE YOU.
THAT SPINE IS NEW. WHAT CORPSE DID YOU PILLAGE IT FROM?

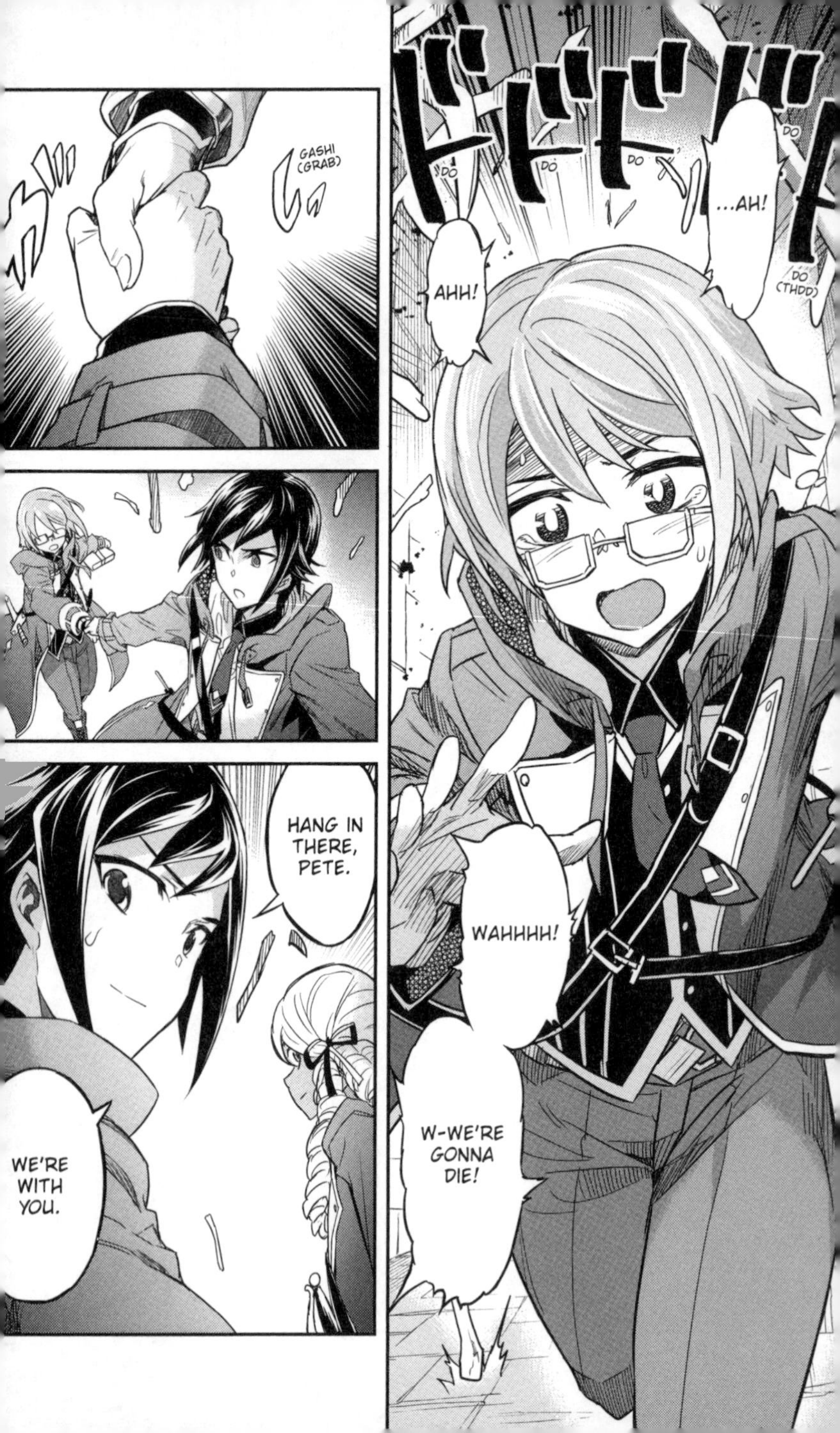
DO
DO
DO
DO
...AH!
DO (THDD)
AHH!
WAHHHH!
W-WE'RE GONNA DIE!
GASHI (GRAB)
HANG IN THERE, PETE.
WE'RE WITH YOU.

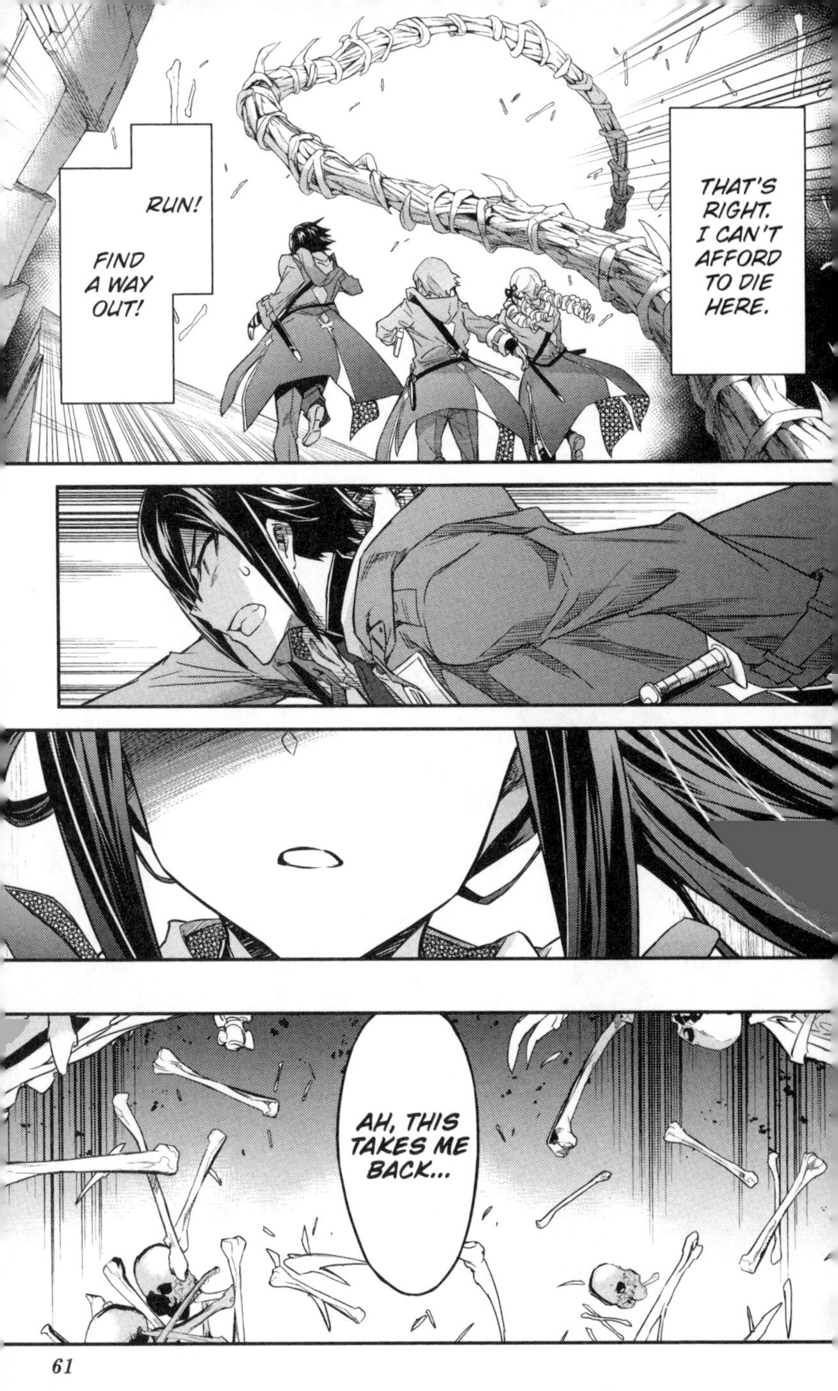
THAT'S RIGHT. I CAN'T AFFORD TO DIE HERE.
RUN!
FIND A WAY OUT!
AH, THIS TAKES ME BACK...

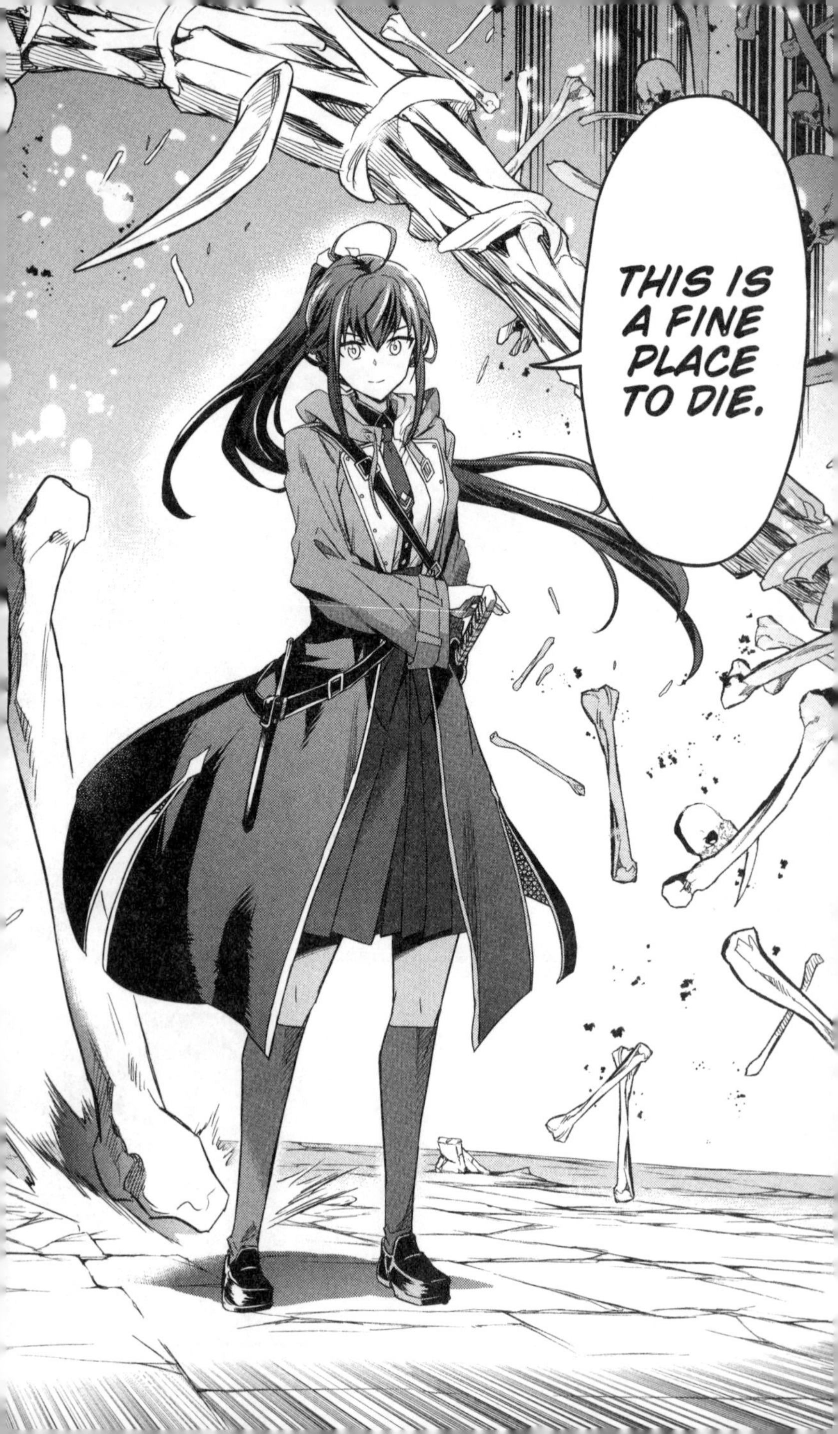
THIS IS A FINE PLACE TO DIE.

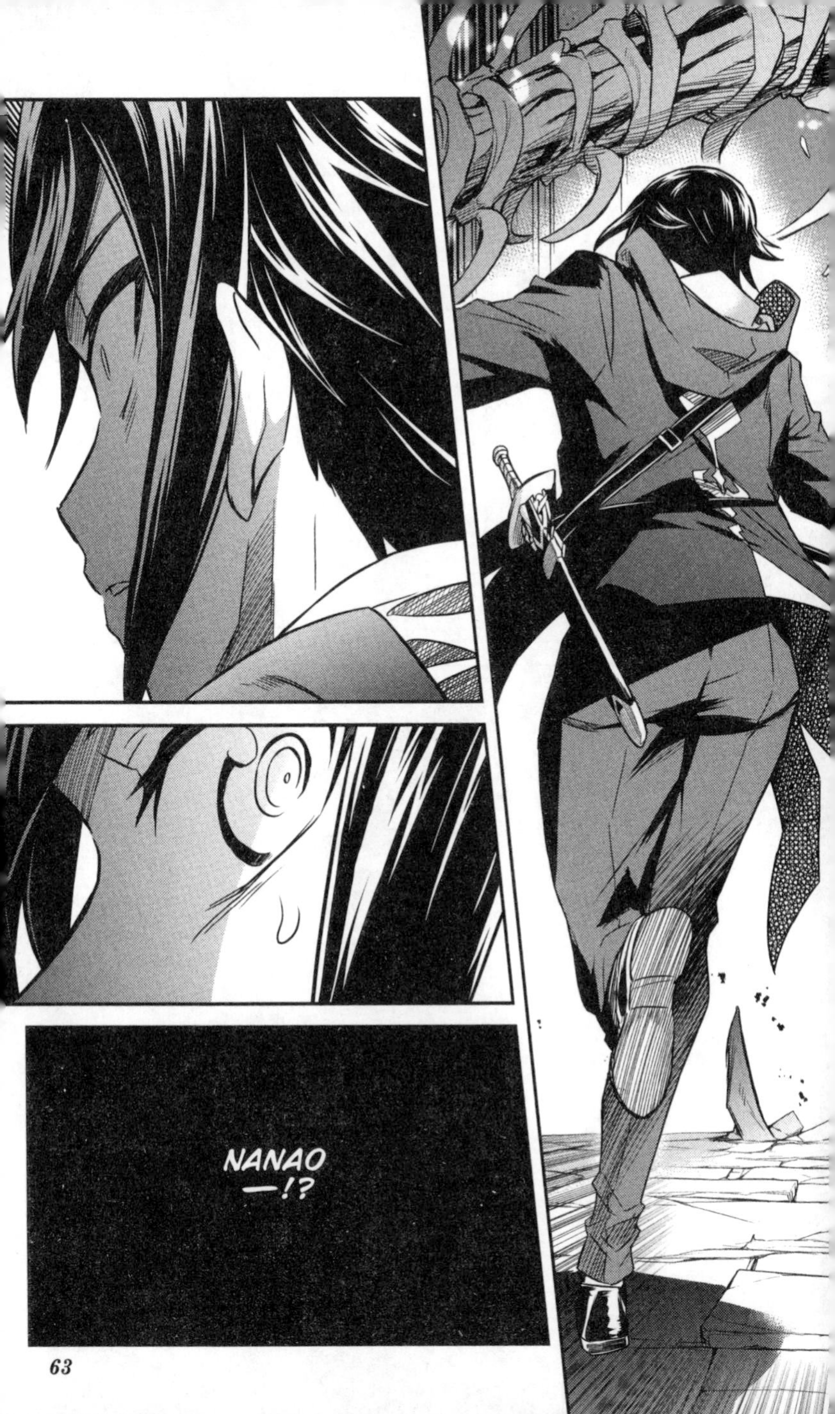
NANAO —!?

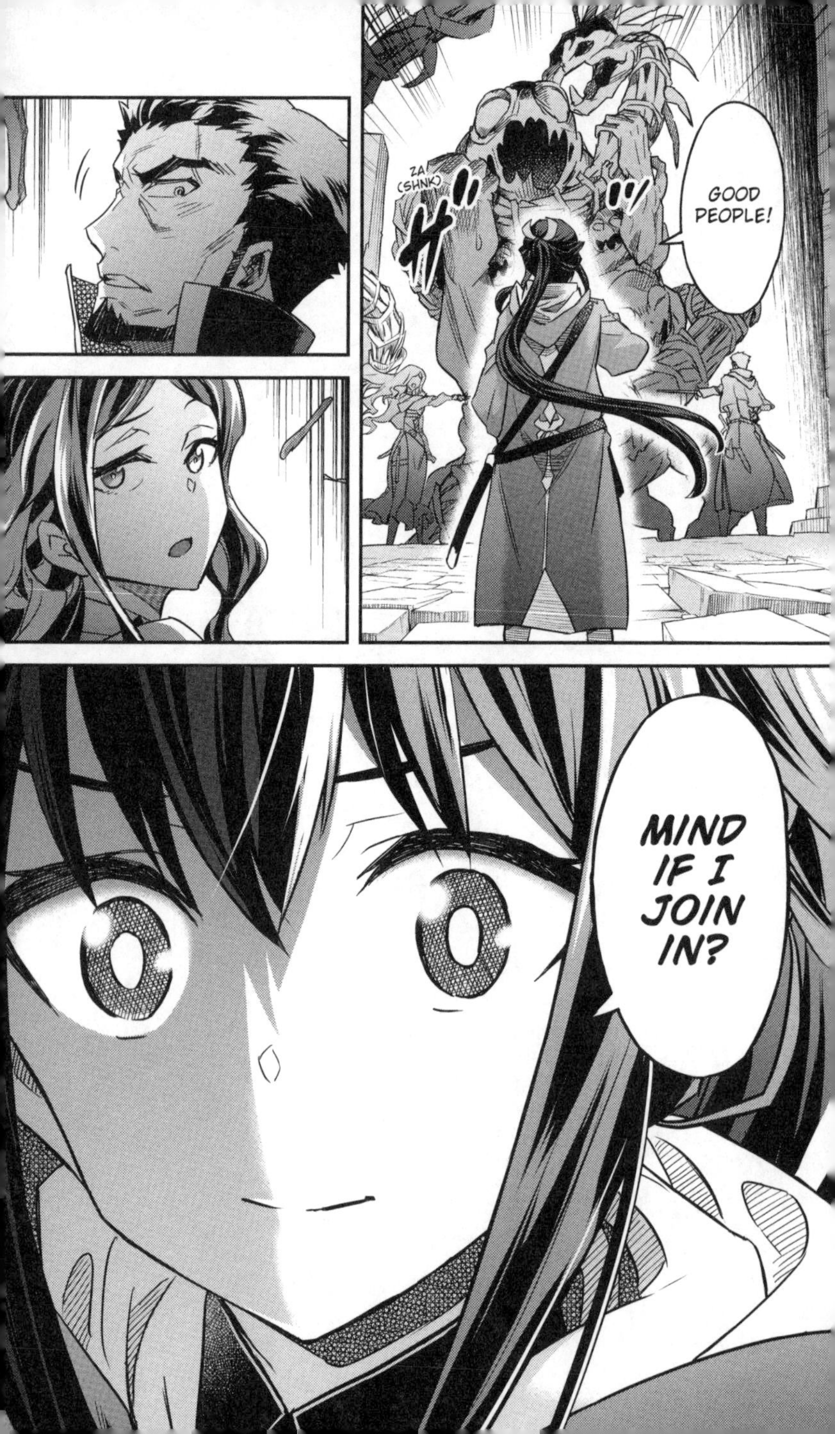
GOOD PEOPLE!
ZA (SHNK)
MIND IF I JOIN IN?

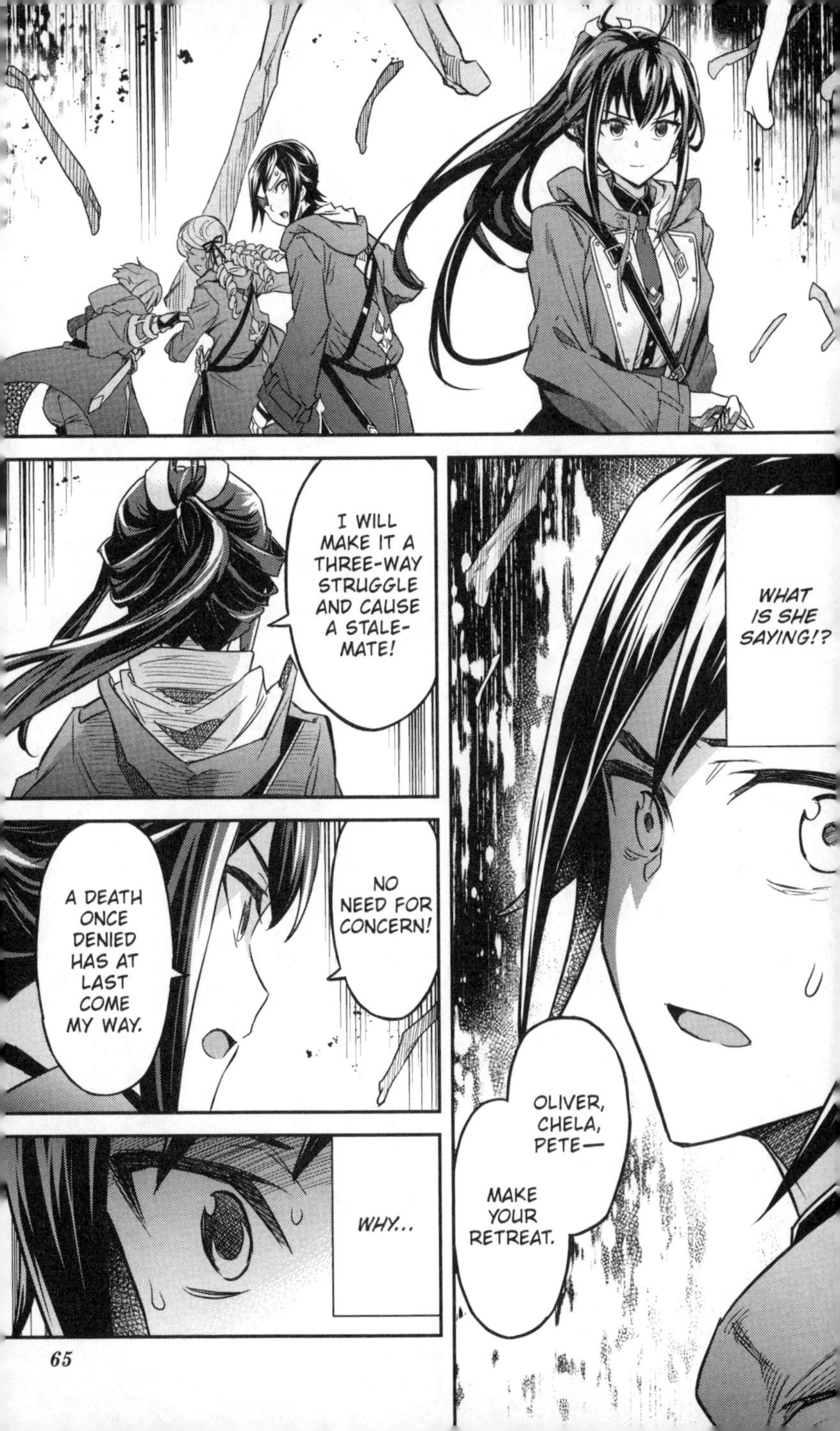
WHAT IS SHE SAYING!?
OLIVER, CHELA, PETE—
MAKE YOUR RETREAT.
I WILL MAKE IT A THREE-WAY STRUGGLE AND CAUSE A STALE-MATE!
NO NEED FOR CONCERN!
A DEATH ONCE DENIED HAS AT LAST COME MY WAY.
WHY...

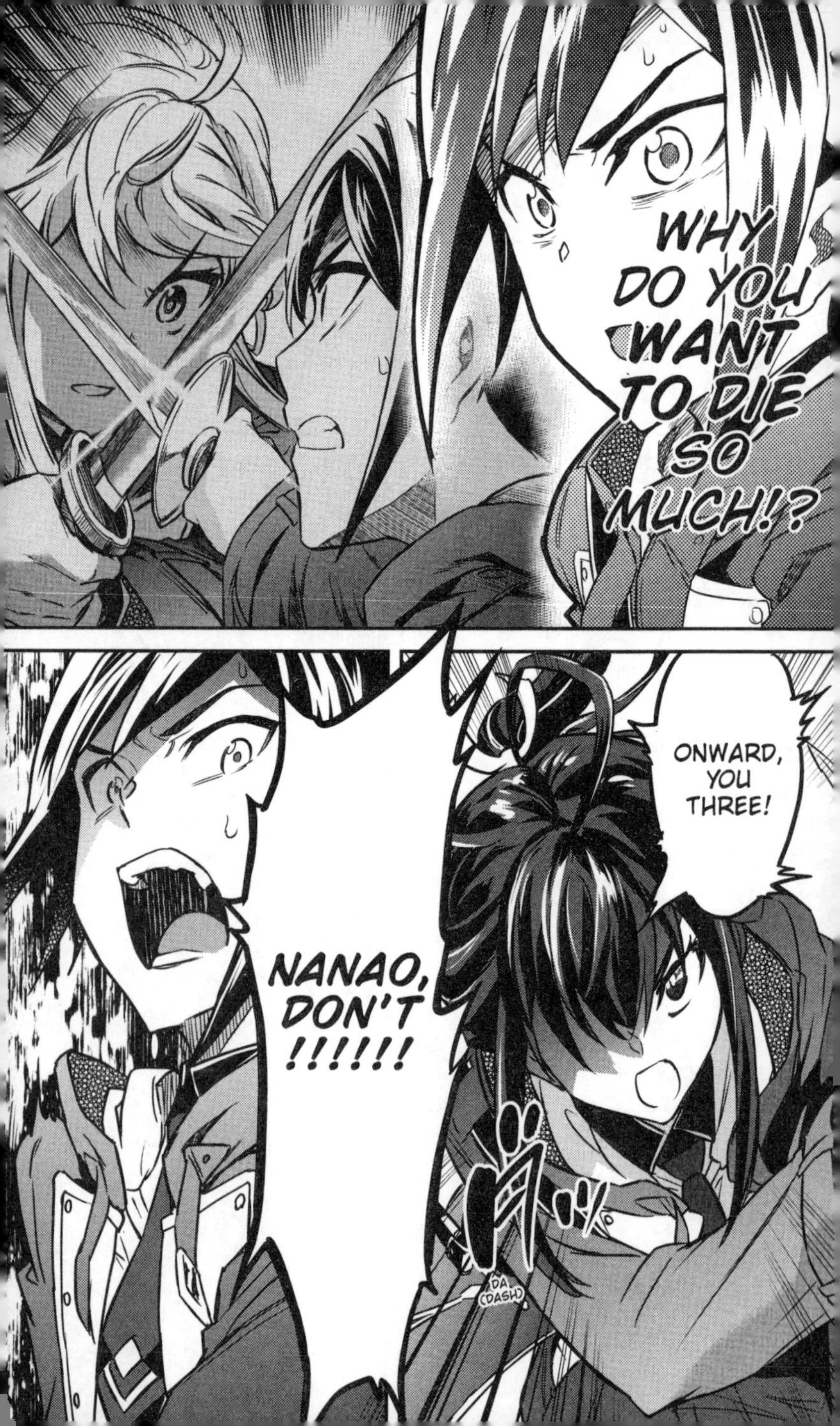
WHY DO YOU WANT TO DIE SO MUCH!?
ONWARD, YOU THREE!
DA (DASH)
NANAO, DON'T !!!!!!

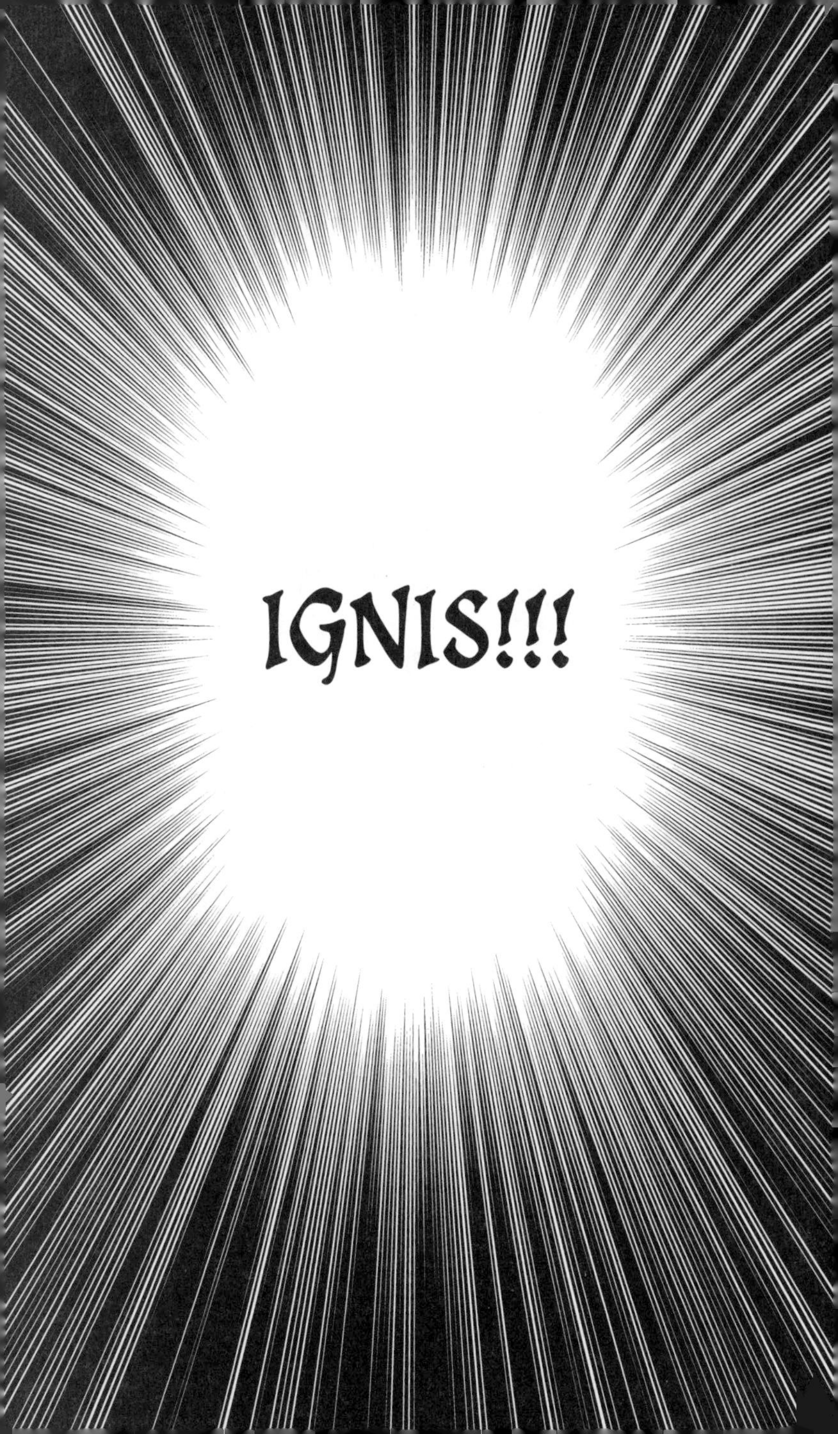
IGNIS!!!

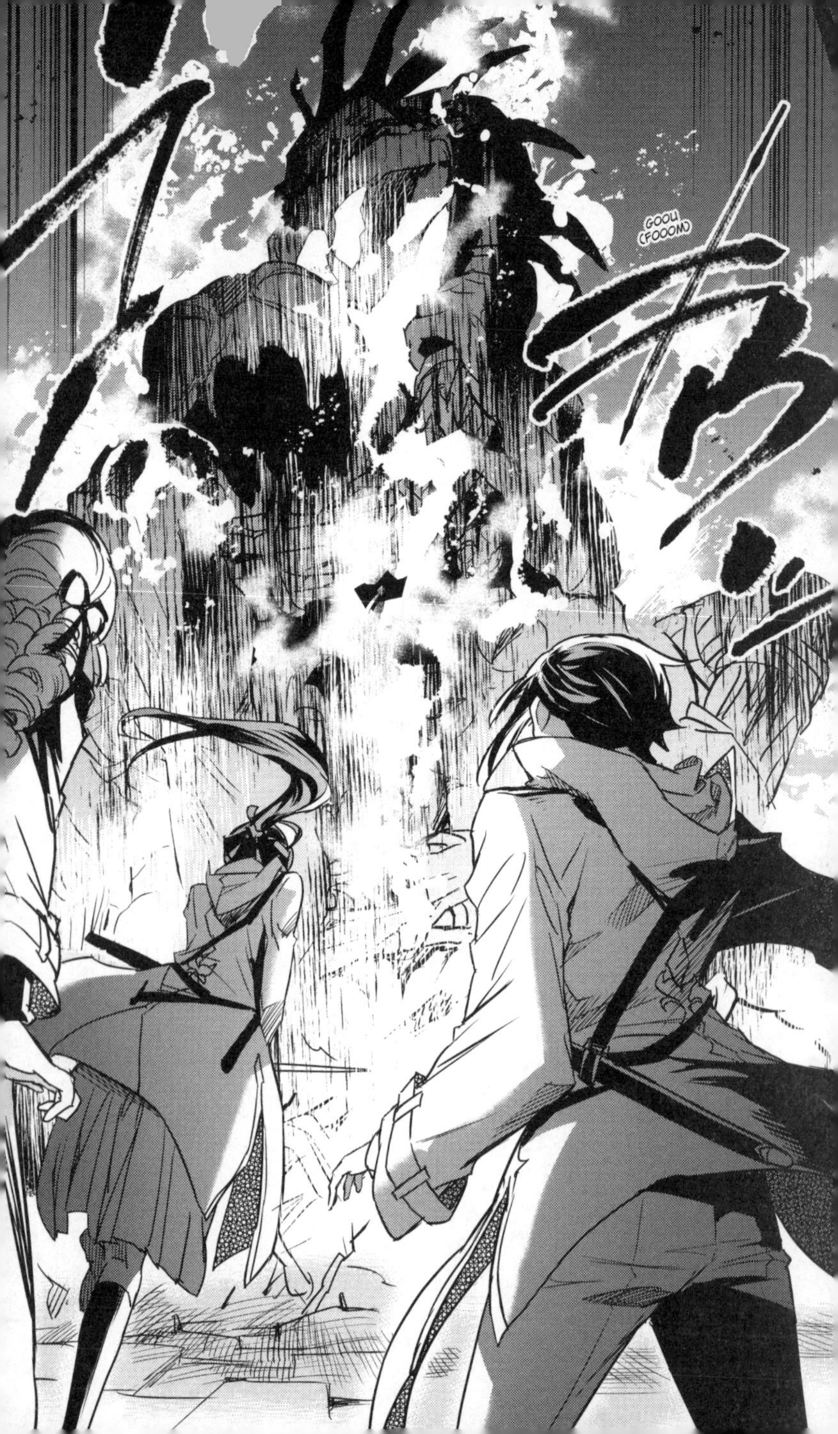
GOOU
(FOOOM)

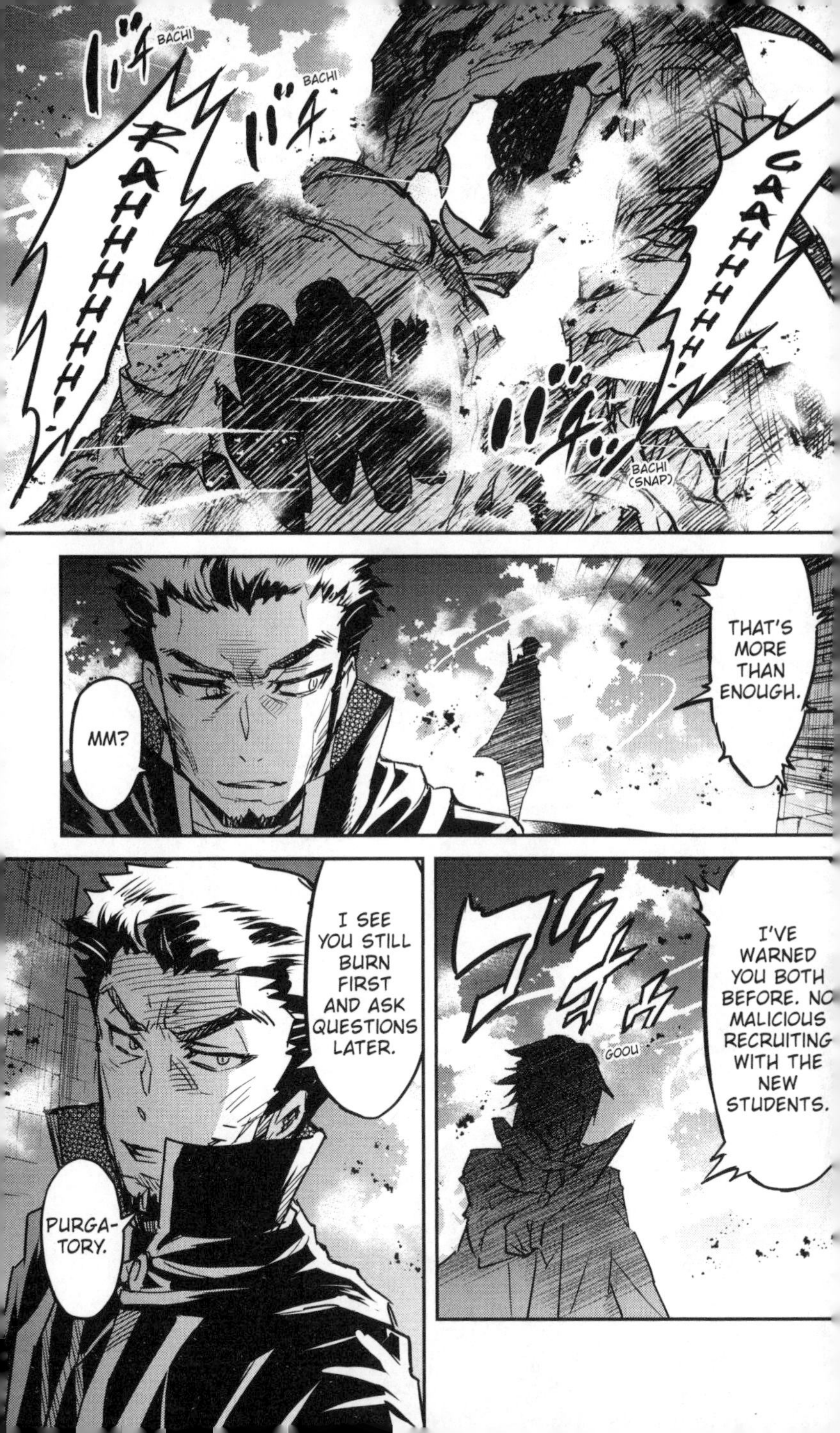
GAAHHHHHH!
BACHI
BACHI
RAHHHHHHH!
BACHI (SNAP)
THAT'S MORE THAN ENOUGH.
MM?
I'VE WARNED YOU BOTH BEFORE. NO MALICIOUS RECRUITING WITH THE NEW STUDENTS.
GOOU
I SEE YOU STILL BURN FIRST AND ASK QUESTIONS LATER.
PURGATORY.

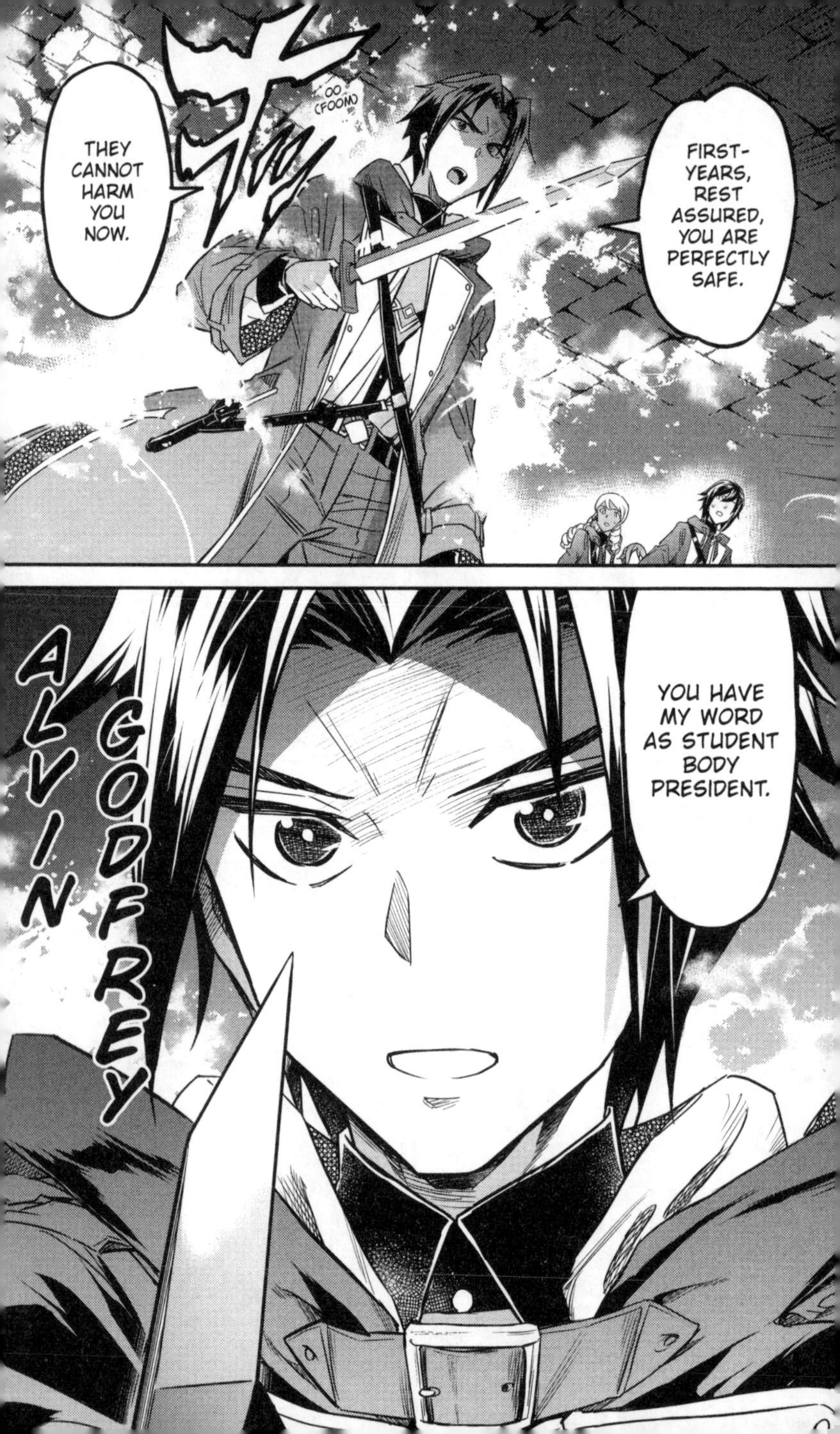
FIRST-YEARS, REST ASSURED, YOU ARE PERFECTLY SAFE.
OO (FOOM)
THEY CANNOT HARM YOU NOW.
YOU HAVE MY WORD AS STUDENT BODY PRESIDENT.
ALVIN GODFREY

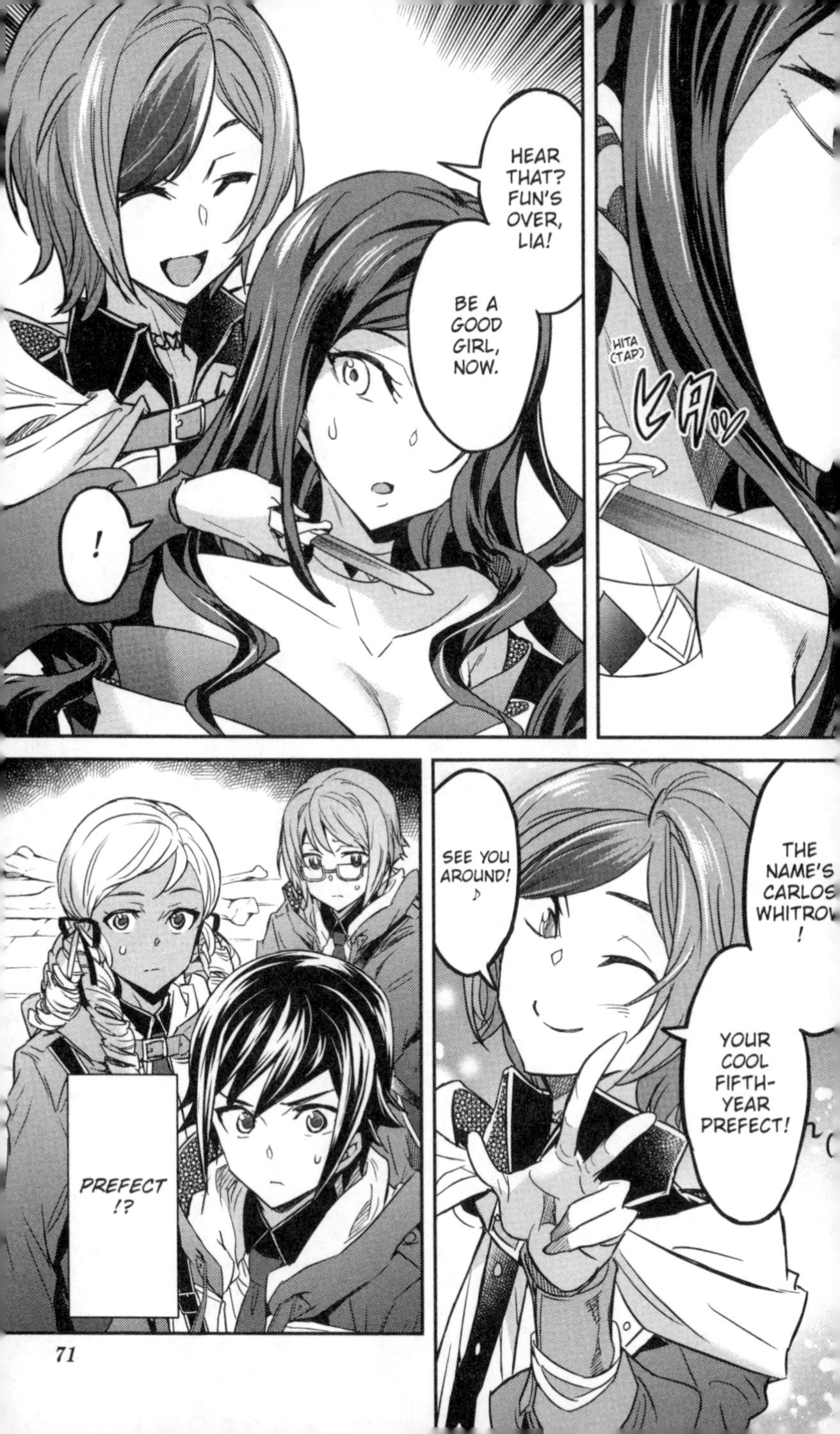
HITA (TAP)
HEAR THAT? FUN'S OVER, LIA!
BE A GOOD GIRL, NOW.
!
THE NAME'S CARLOS WHITROW!
YOUR COOL FIFTH-YEAR PREFECT!
SEE YOU AROUND! ♪
PREFECT!?

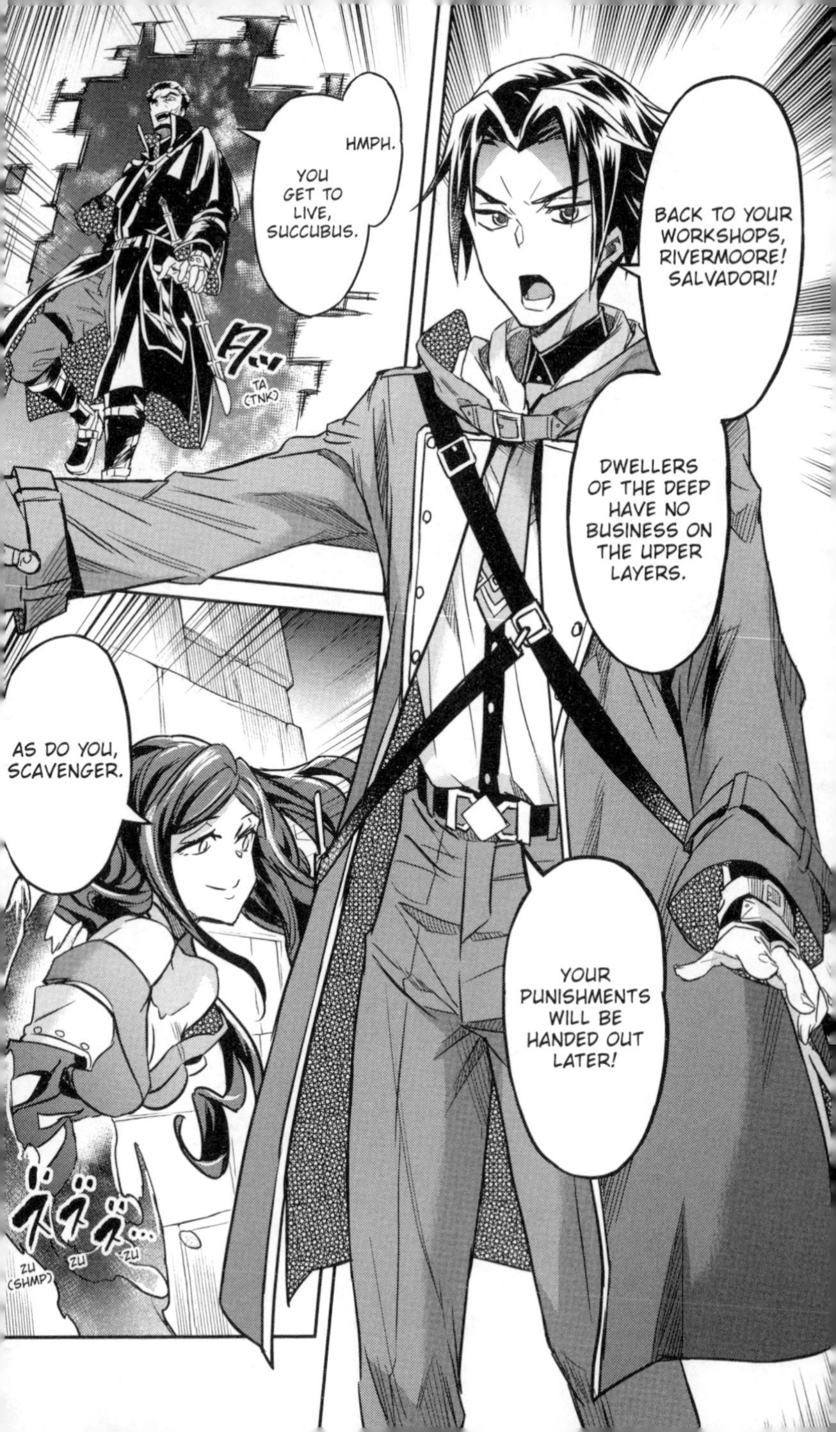
BACK TO YOUR WORKSHOPS, RIVERMOORE! SALVADORI!
DWELLERS OF THE DEEP HAVE NO BUSINESS ON THE UPPER LAYERS.
YOUR PUNISHMENTS WILL BE HANDED OUT LATER!
HMPH.
YOU GET TO LIVE, SUCCUBUS.
タッ
TA (TNK)
AS DO YOU, SCAVENGER.
ズズズ…
ZU ZU ZU (SHMP)

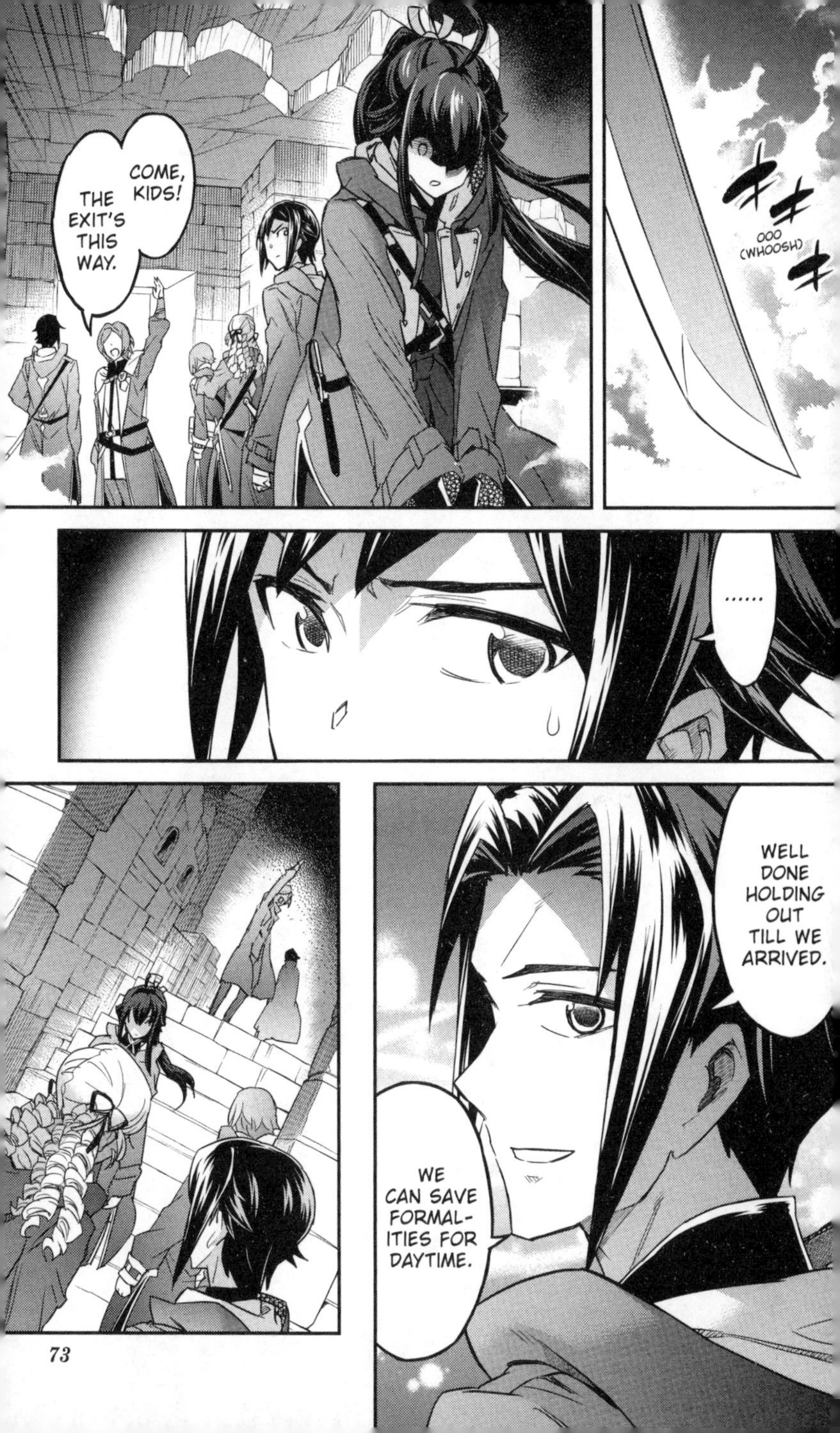
OOO (WHOOSH)
COME, KIDS! THE EXIT'S THIS WAY.
......
WELL DONE HOLDING OUT TILL WE ARRIVED.
WE CAN SAVE FORMAL-ITIES FOR DAYTIME.

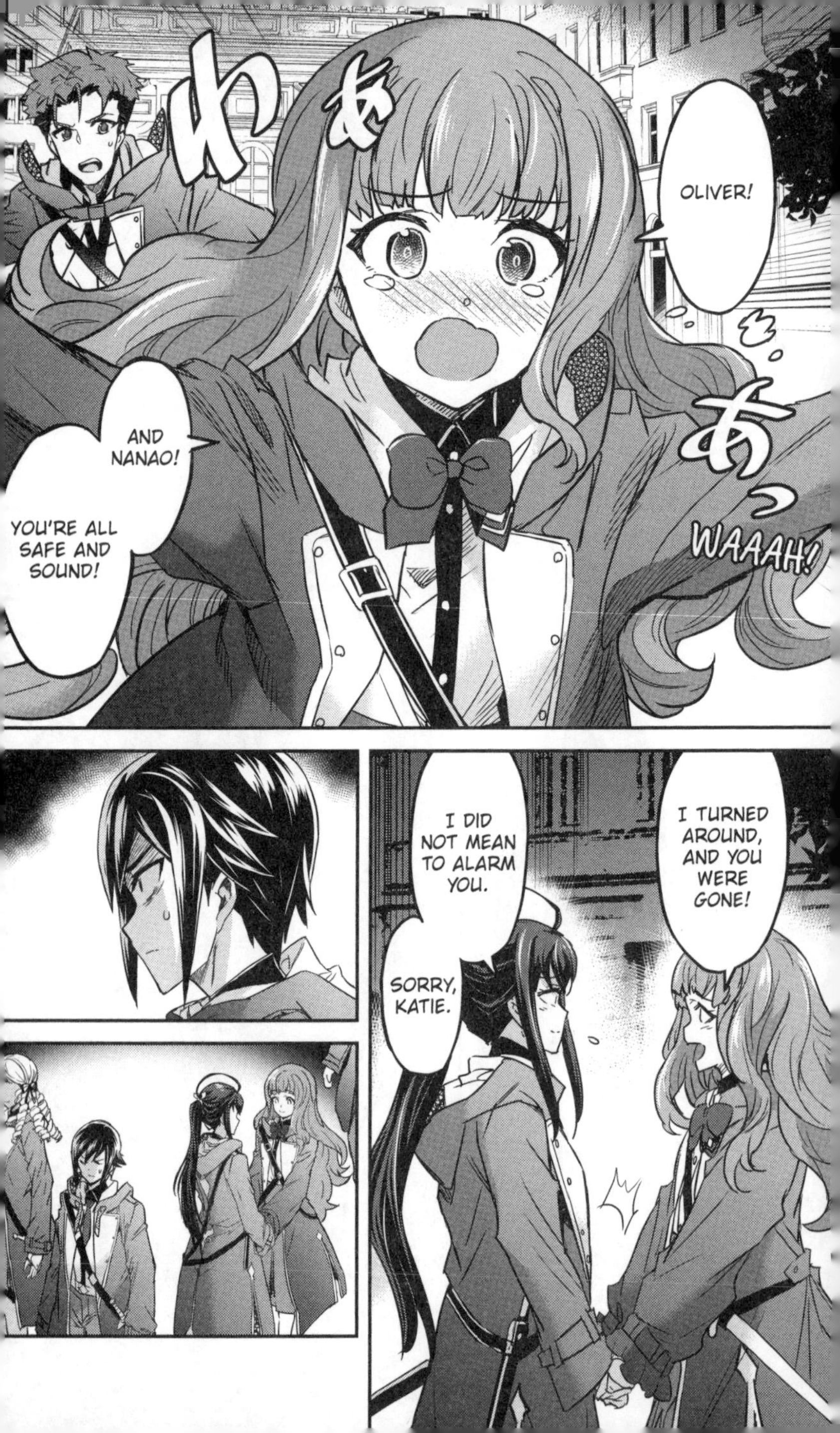
OLIVER!
あっ
WAAAH!
AND NANAO!
YOU'RE ALL SAFE AND SOUND!
I TURNED AROUND, AND YOU WERE GONE!
I DID NOT MEAN TO ALARM YOU.
SORRY, KATIE.

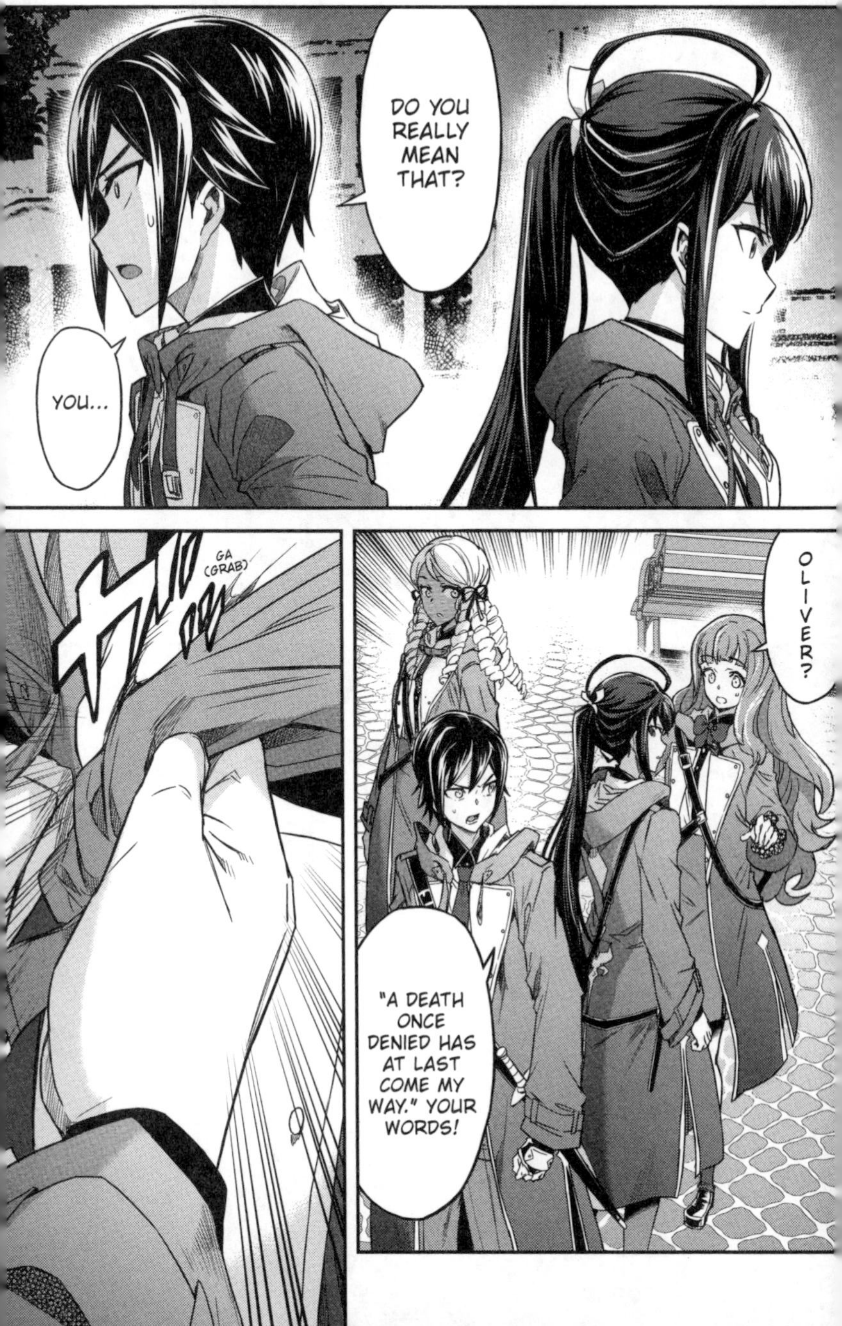
DO YOU REALLY MEAN THAT?
YOU...
OLIVER?
"A DEATH ONCE DENIED HAS AT LAST COME MY WAY." YOUR WORDS!
GA (GRAB)

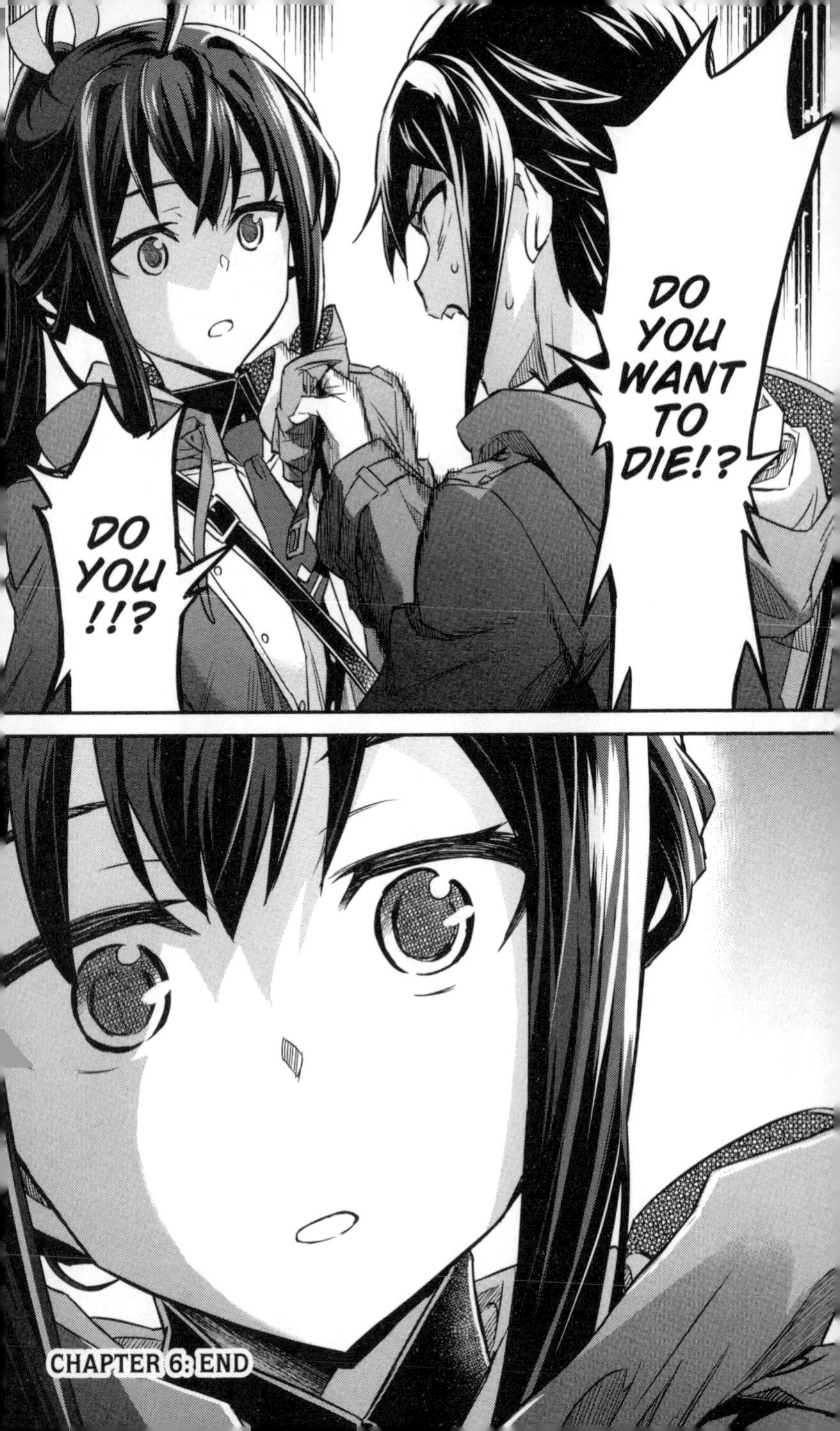
DO YOU WANT TO DIE!?
DO YOU!!?
CHAPTER 6: END

CHAPTER 7: SHIAWASE

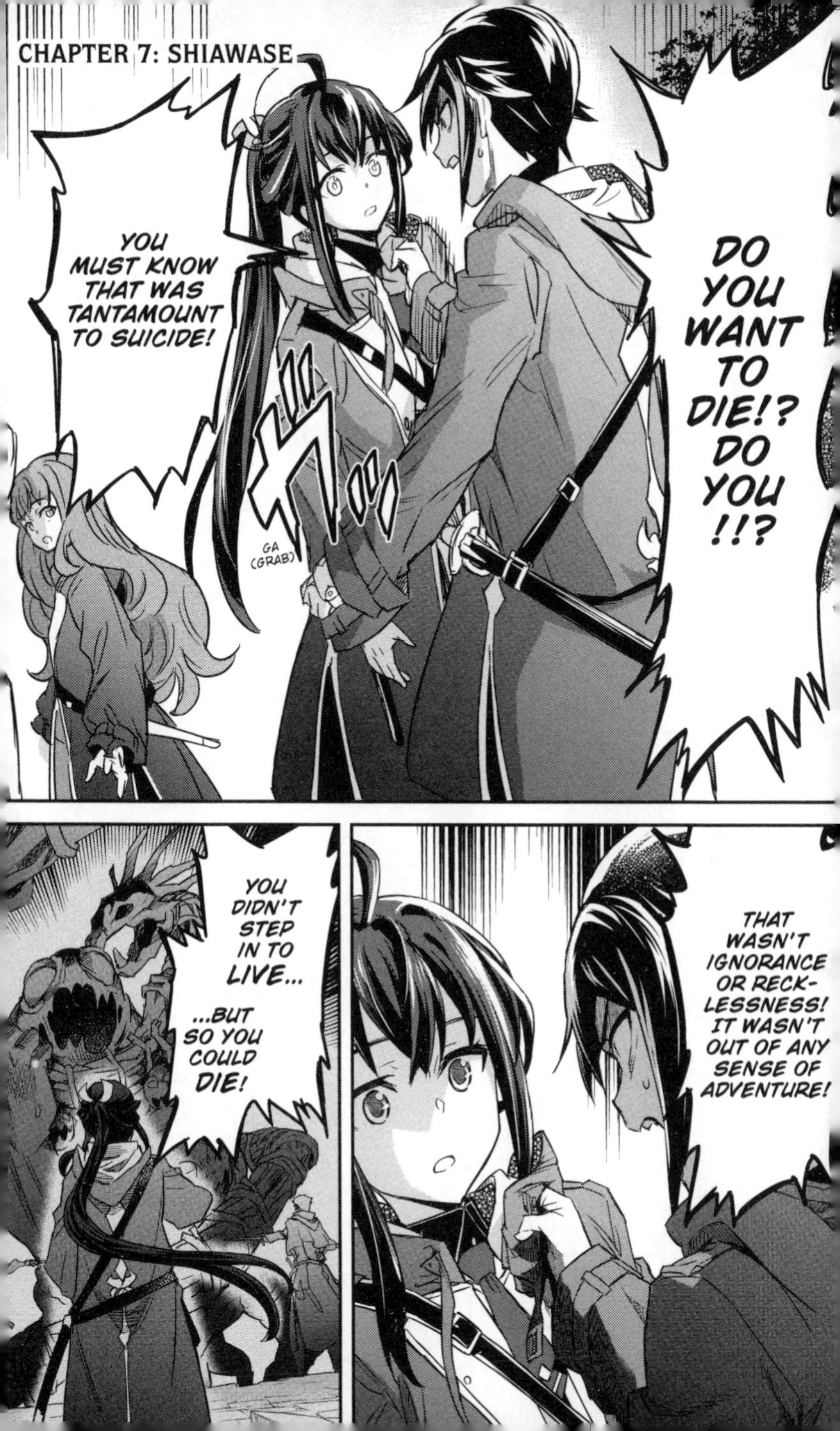
DO YOU WANT TO DIE!? DO YOU!!?
YOU MUST KNOW THAT WAS TANTAMOUNT TO SUICIDE!
GA (GRAB)
THAT WASN'T IGNORANCE OR RECK-LESSNESS! IT WASN'T OUT OF ANY SENSE OF ADVENTURE!
YOU DIDN'T STEP IN TO LIVE...
...BUT SO YOU COULD DIE!

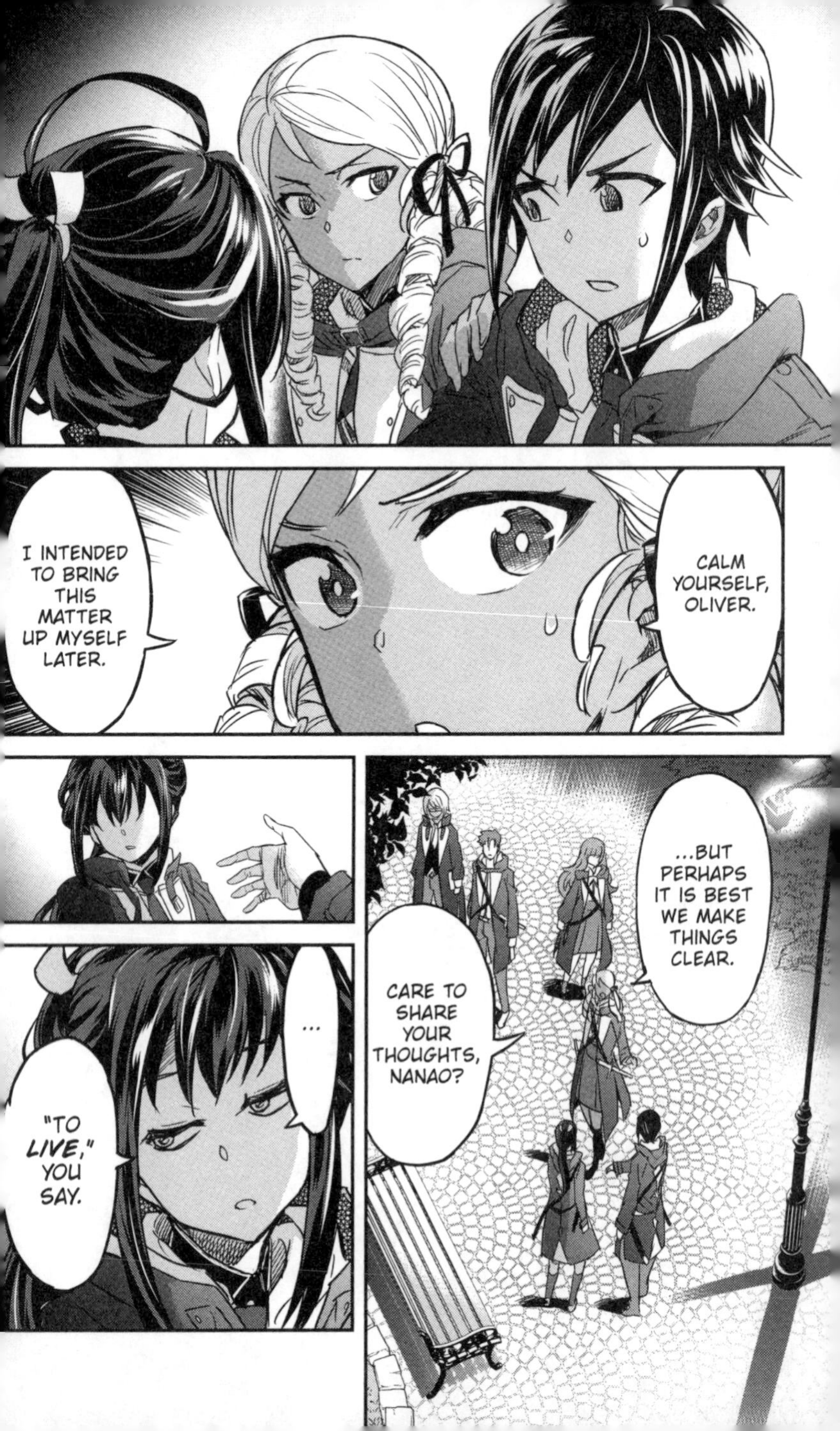
CALM YOURSELF, OLIVER.
I INTENDED TO BRING THIS MATTER UP MYSELF LATER.
...BUT PERHAPS IT IS BEST WE MAKE THINGS CLEAR.
CARE TO SHARE YOUR THOUGHTS, NANAO?
...
"TO *LIVE*," YOU SAY.

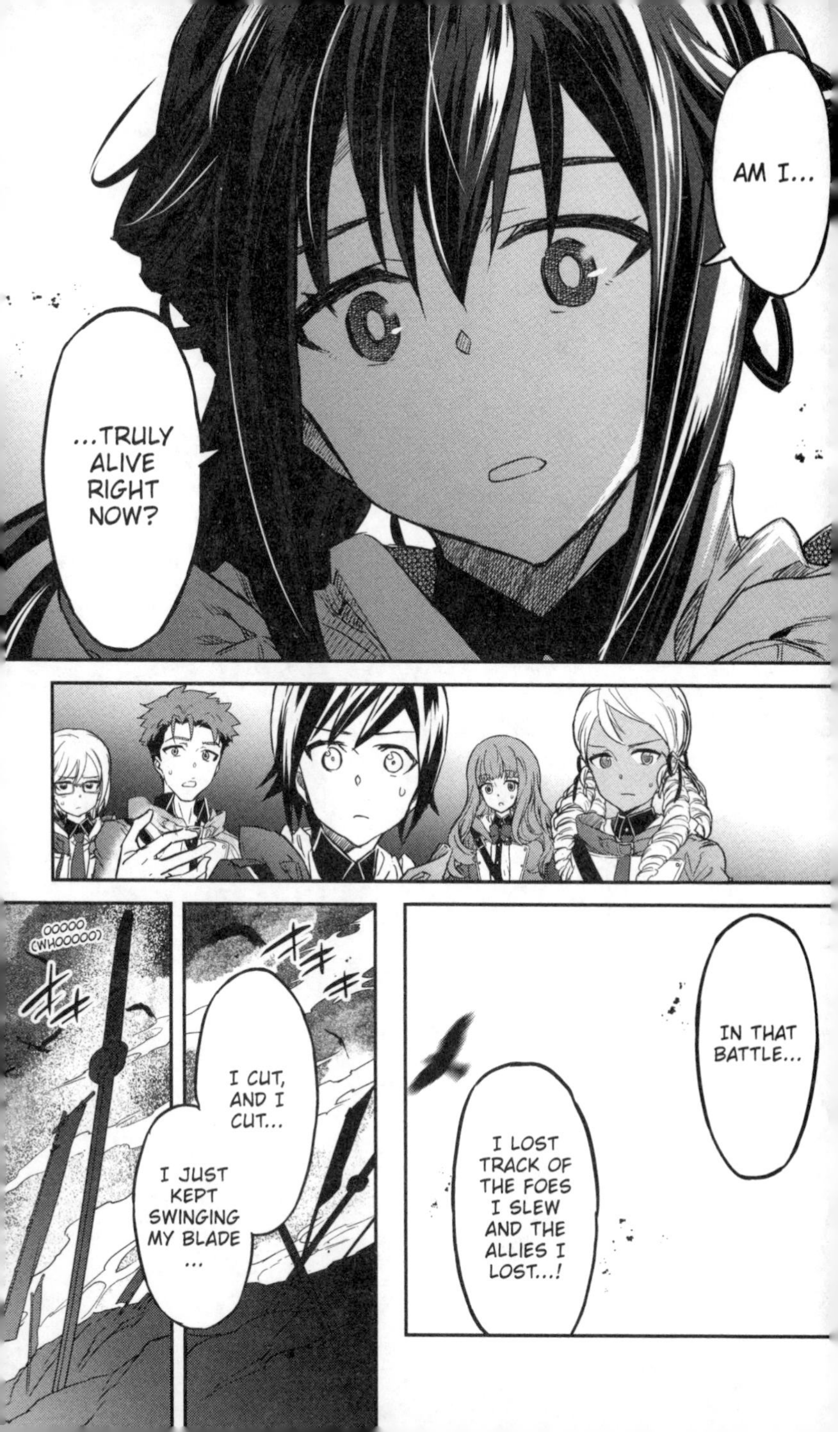
AM I...
...TRULY ALIVE RIGHT NOW?
IN THAT BATTLE...
I LOST TRACK OF THE FOES I SLEW AND THE ALLIES I LOST...!
I CUT, AND I CUT...
I JUST KEPT SWINGING MY BLADE ...
OOOOO (WHOOOOO)

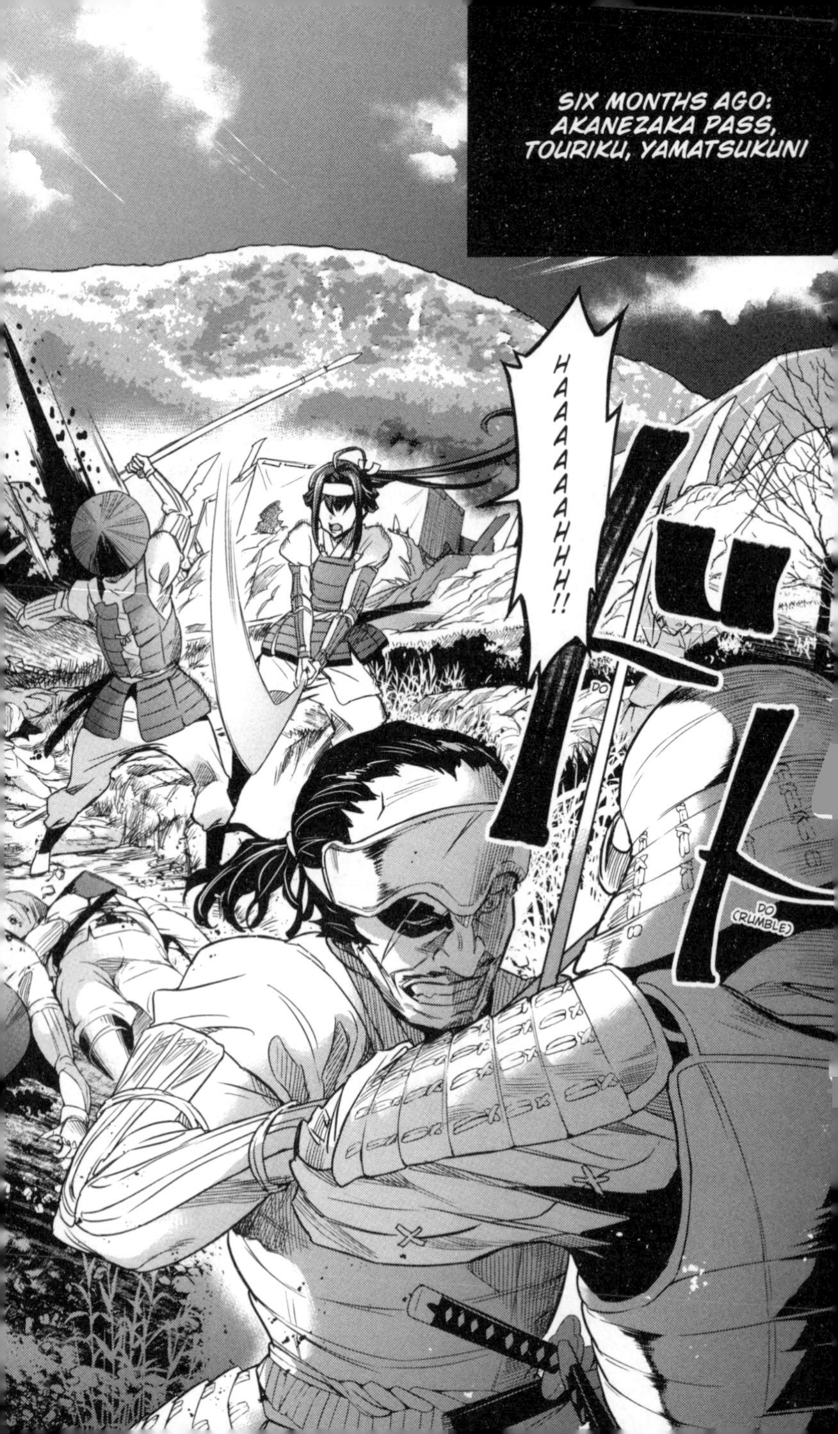
SIX MONTHS AGO:
AKANEZAKA PASS,
TOURIKU, YAMATSUKUNI
HAAAAAAAAHH!!
DO
DO
(RUMBLE)

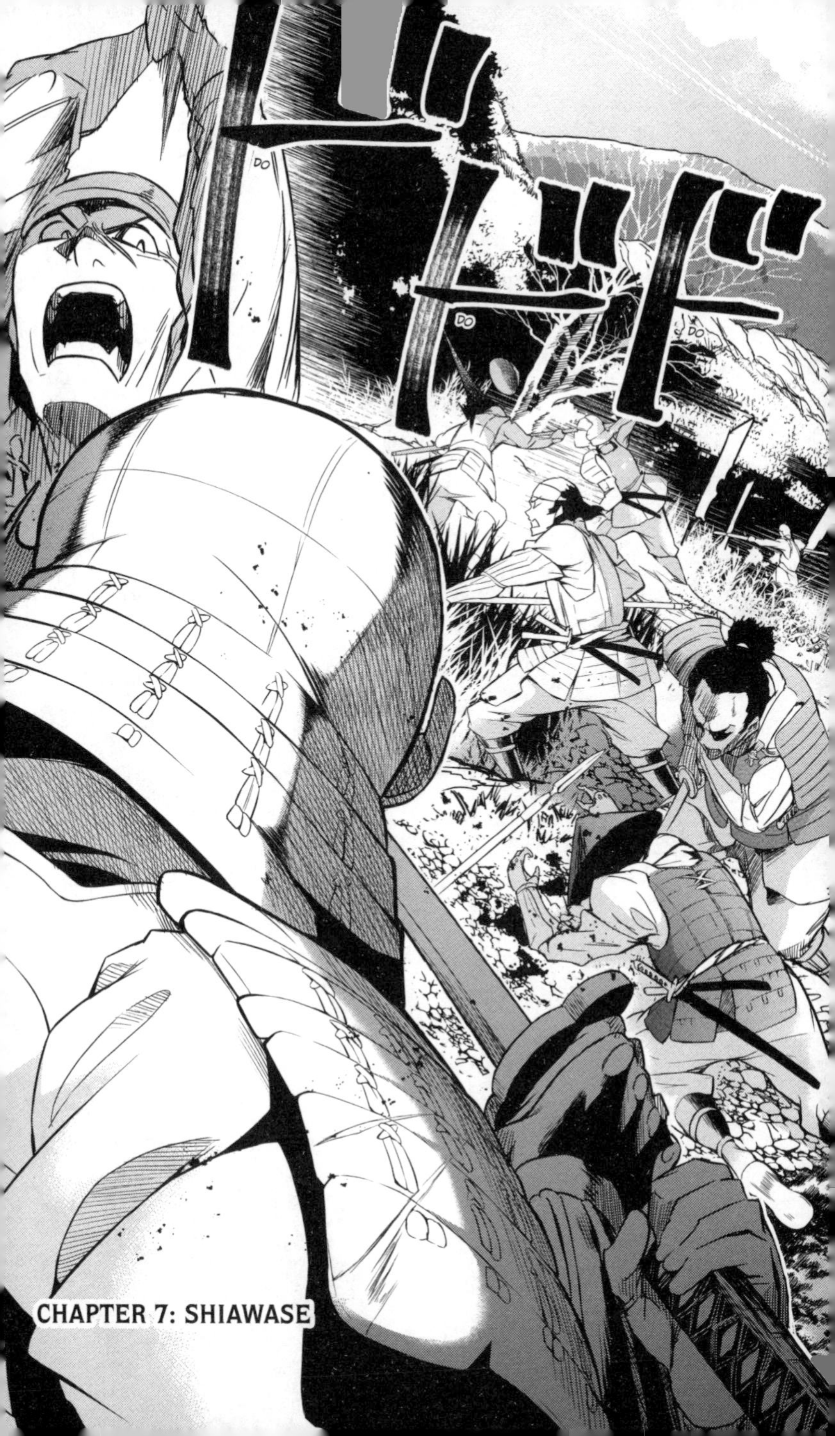
DO
DO
DO
CHAPTER 7: SHIAWASE

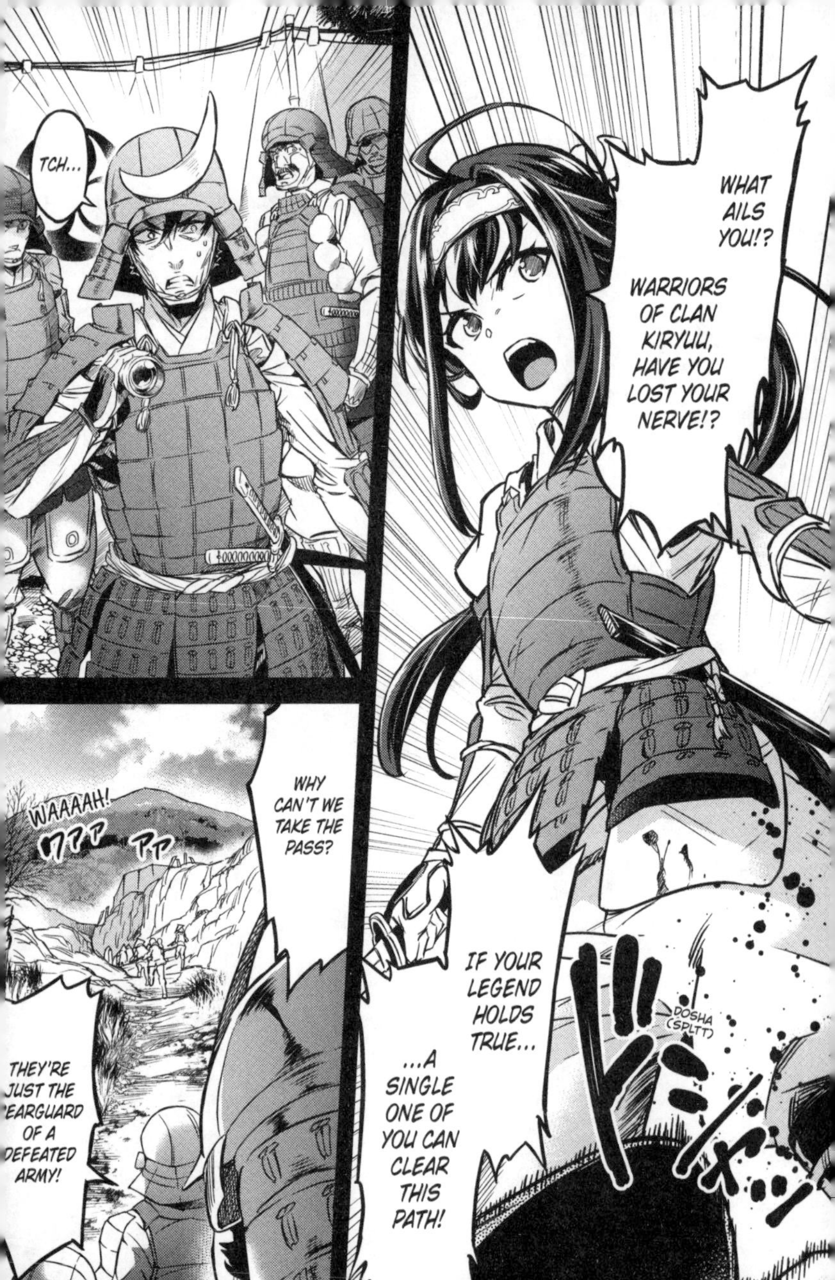
WHAT AILS YOU!?
WARRIORS OF CLAN KIRYUU, HAVE YOU LOST YOUR NERVE!?
IF YOUR LEGEND HOLDS TRUE...
...A SINGLE ONE OF YOU CAN CLEAR THIS PATH!
DOSHA (SPLTT)
TCH...
WHY CAN'T WE TAKE THE PASS?
WAAAAH!
THEY'RE JUST THE REARGUARD OF A DEFEATED ARMY!

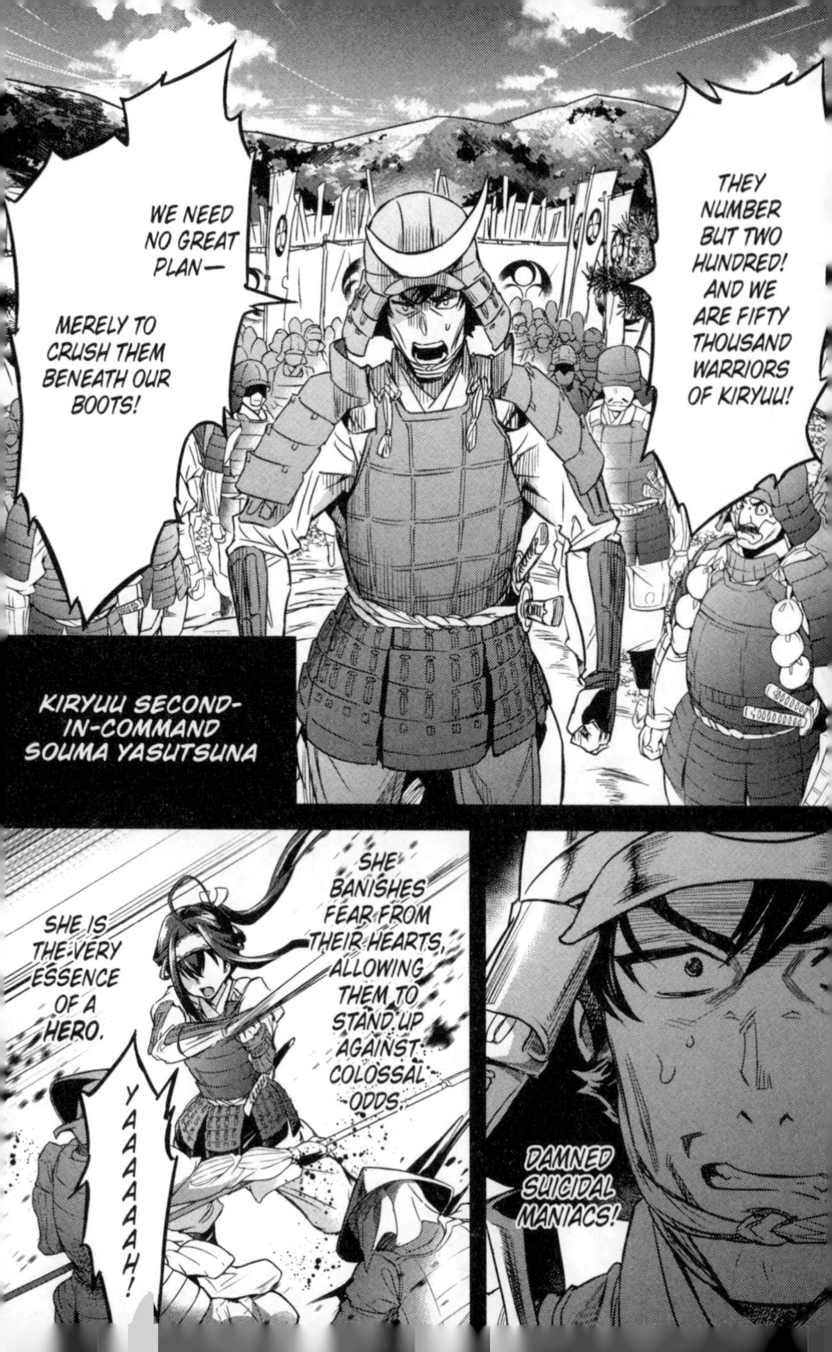
THEY NUMBER BUT TWO HUNDRED! AND WE ARE FIFTY THOUSAND WARRIORS OF KIRYUU!
WE NEED NO GREAT PLAN—
MERELY TO CRUSH THEM BENEATH OUR BOOTS!
KIRYUU SECOND-IN-COMMAND SOUMA YASUTSUNA
DAMNED SUICIDAL MANIACS!
SHE BANISHES FEAR FROM THEIR HEARTS, ALLOWING THEM TO STAND UP AGAINST COLOSSAL ODDS.
SHE IS THE VERY ESSENCE OF A HERO.
YAAAAAAAH!

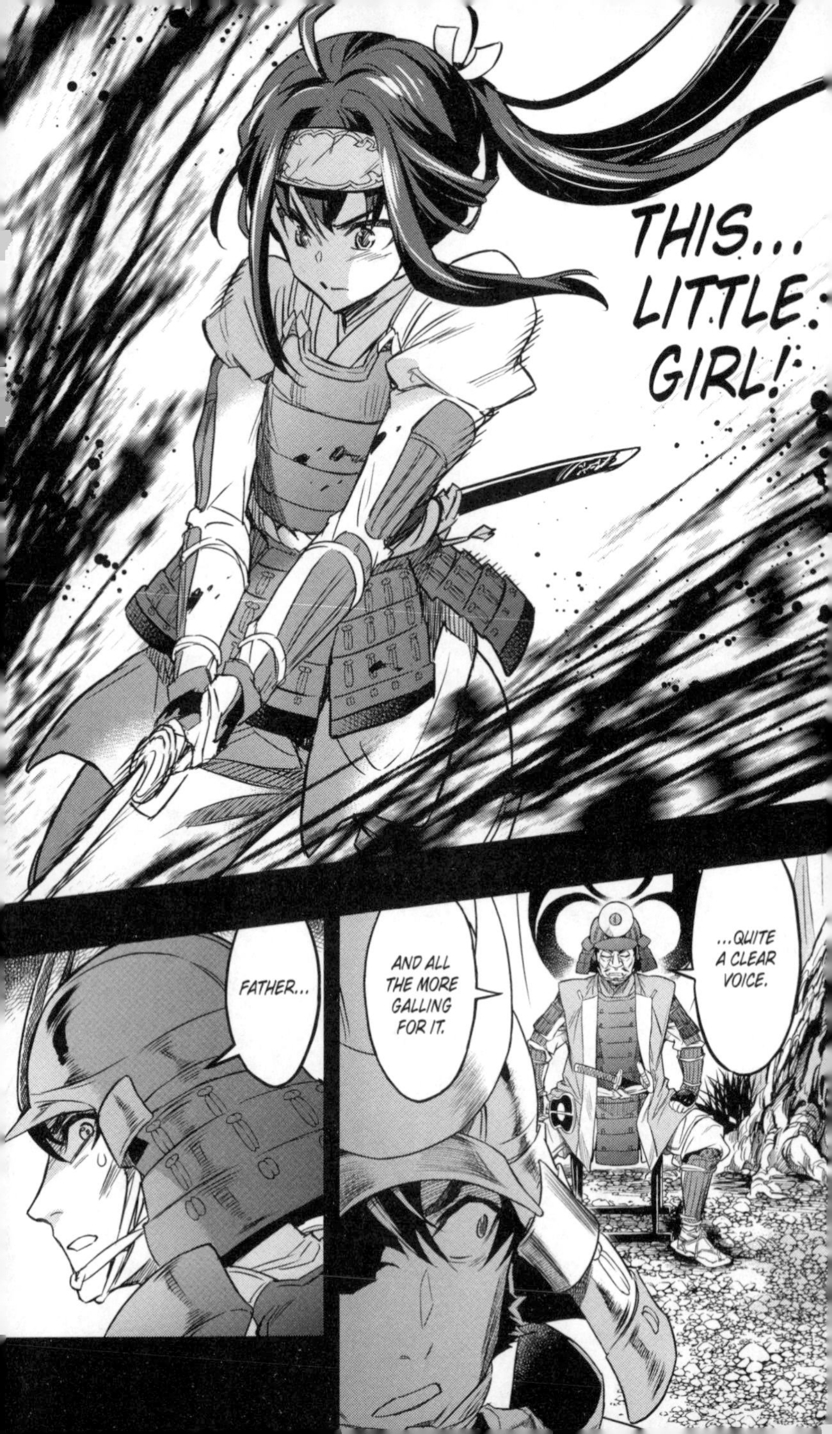
THIS... LITTLE GIRL!
...QUITE A CLEAR VOICE.
AND ALL THE MORE GALLING FOR IT.
FATHER...

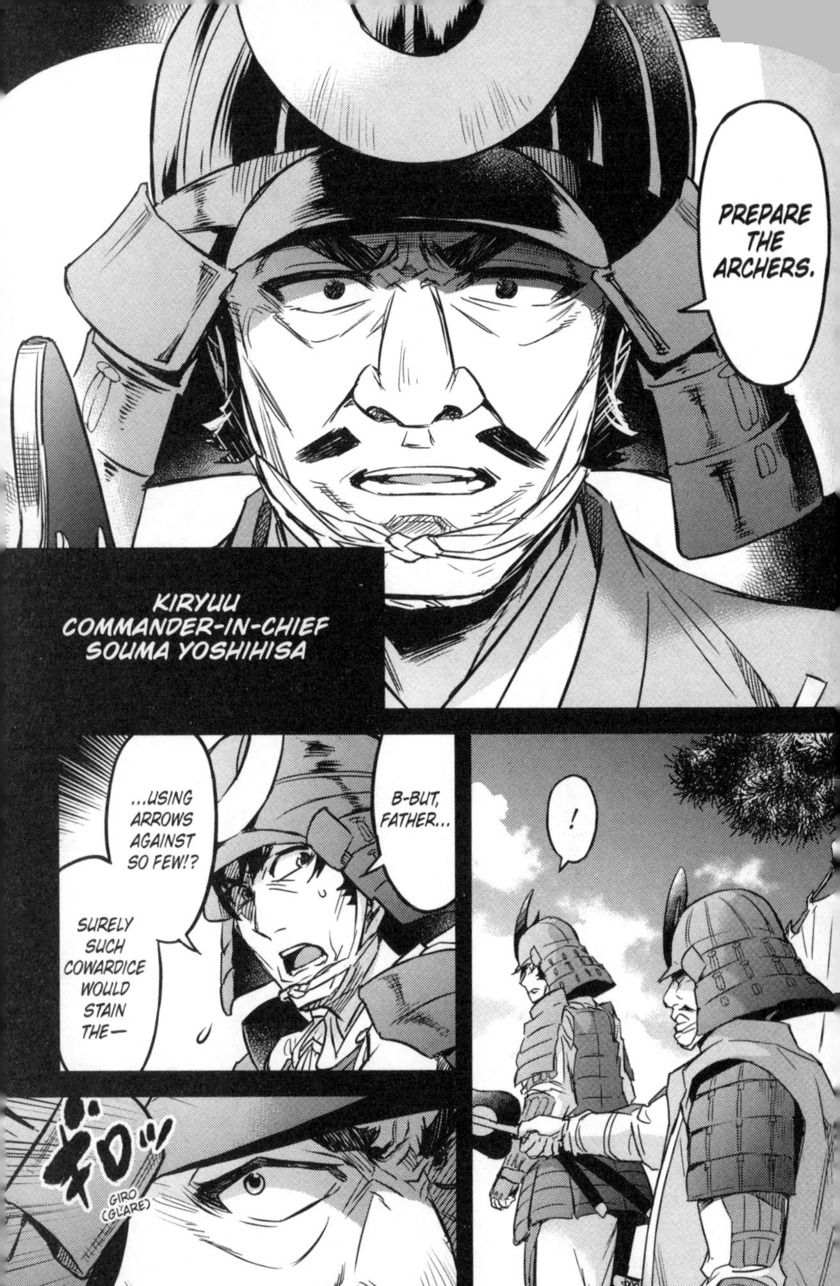
PREPARE THE ARCHERS.
KIRYUU COMMANDER-IN-CHIEF SOUMA YOSHIHISA
!
B-BUT, FATHER...
...USING ARROWS AGAINST SO FEW!?
SURELY SUCH COWARDICE WOULD STAIN THE—
ギロッ
GIRO (GLARE)

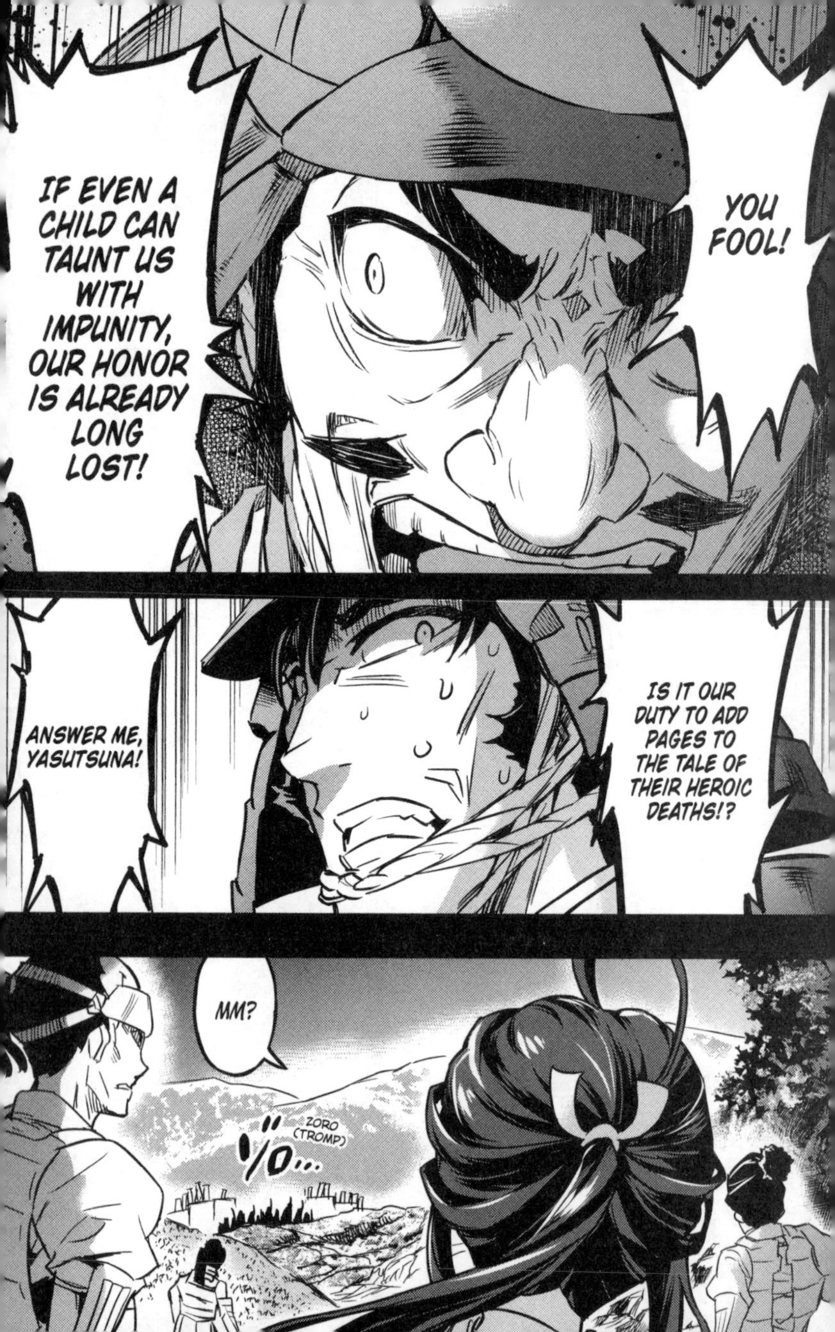
YOU FOOL!
IF EVEN A CHILD CAN TAUNT US WITH IMPUNITY, OUR HONOR IS ALREADY LONG LOST!
IS IT OUR DUTY TO ADD PAGES TO THE TALE OF THEIR HEROIC DEATHS!?
ANSWER ME, YASUTSUNA!
MM?
ZORO (TROMP)

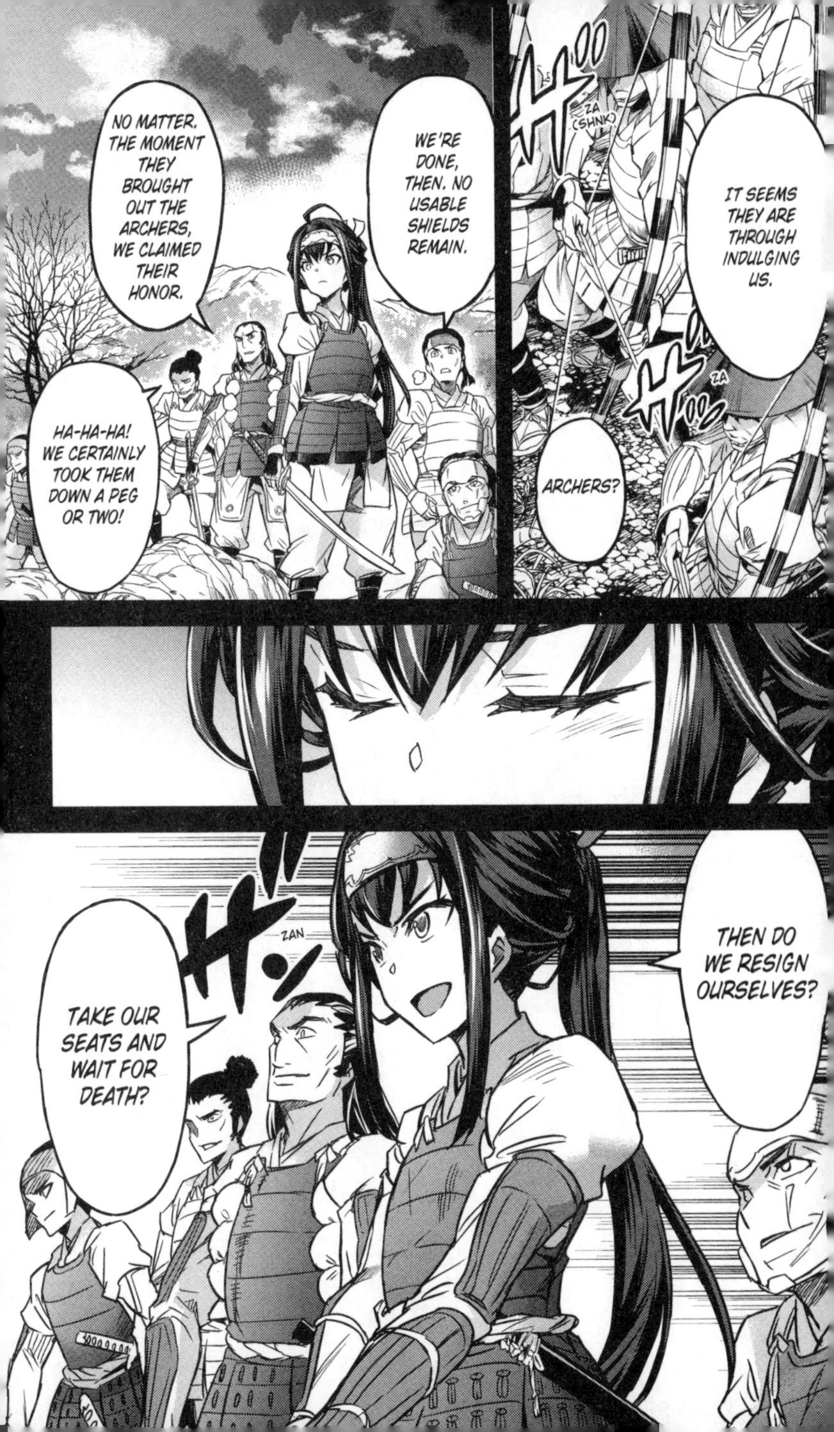
ZA
(SHNK)
IT SEEMS THEY ARE THROUGH INDULGING US.
ZA
ARCHERS?
WE'RE DONE, THEN. NO USABLE SHIELDS REMAIN.
NO MATTER. THE MOMENT THEY BROUGHT OUT THE ARCHERS, WE CLAIMED THEIR HONOR.
HA-HA-HA! WE CERTAINLY TOOK THEM DOWN A PEG OR TWO!
THEN DO WE RESIGN OURSELVES?
ZAN
TAKE OUR SEATS AND WAIT FOR DEATH?

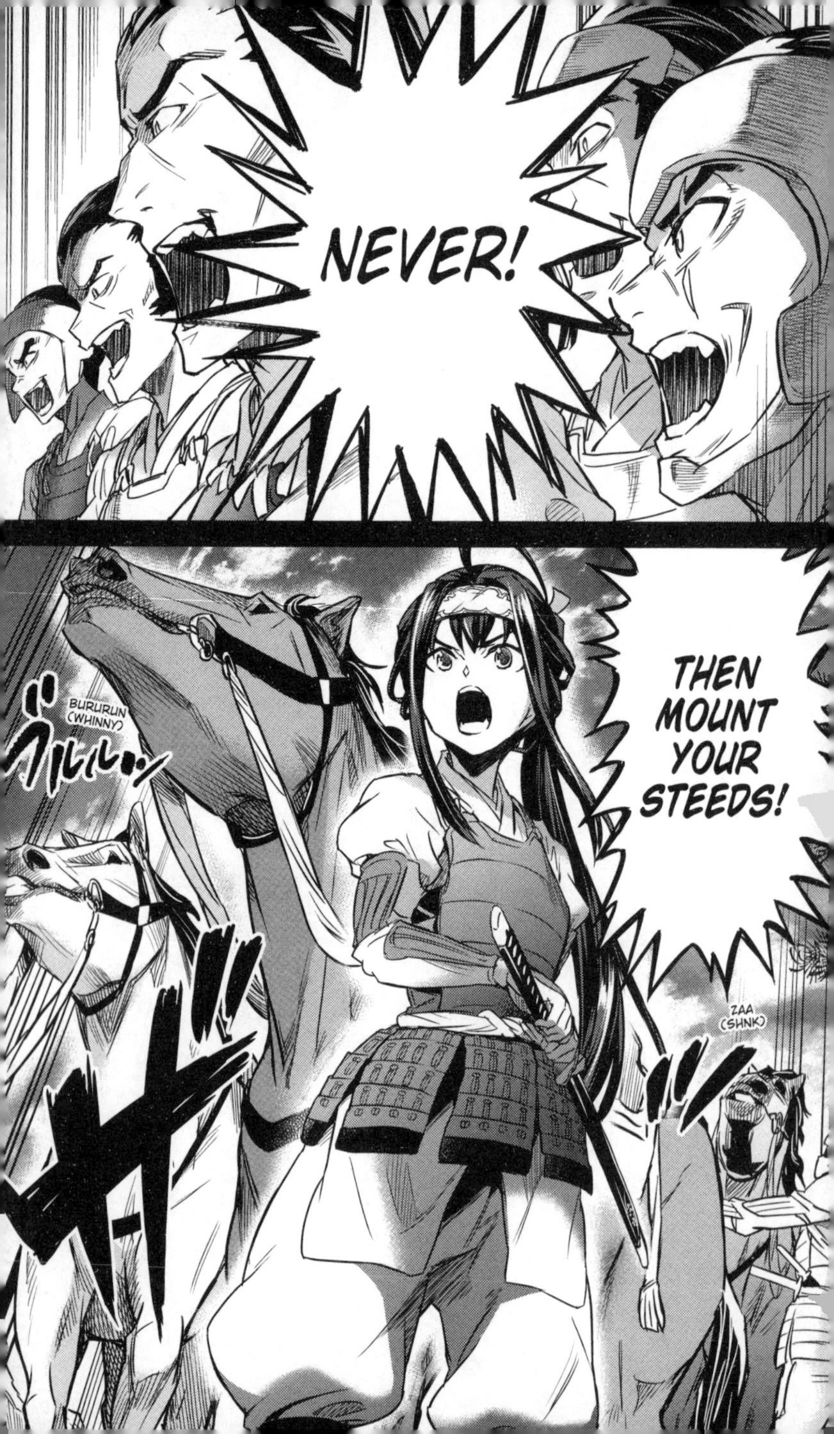
NEVER!
THEN MOUNT YOUR STEEDS!
ZAA (SHNK)
BURURUN (WHINNY)

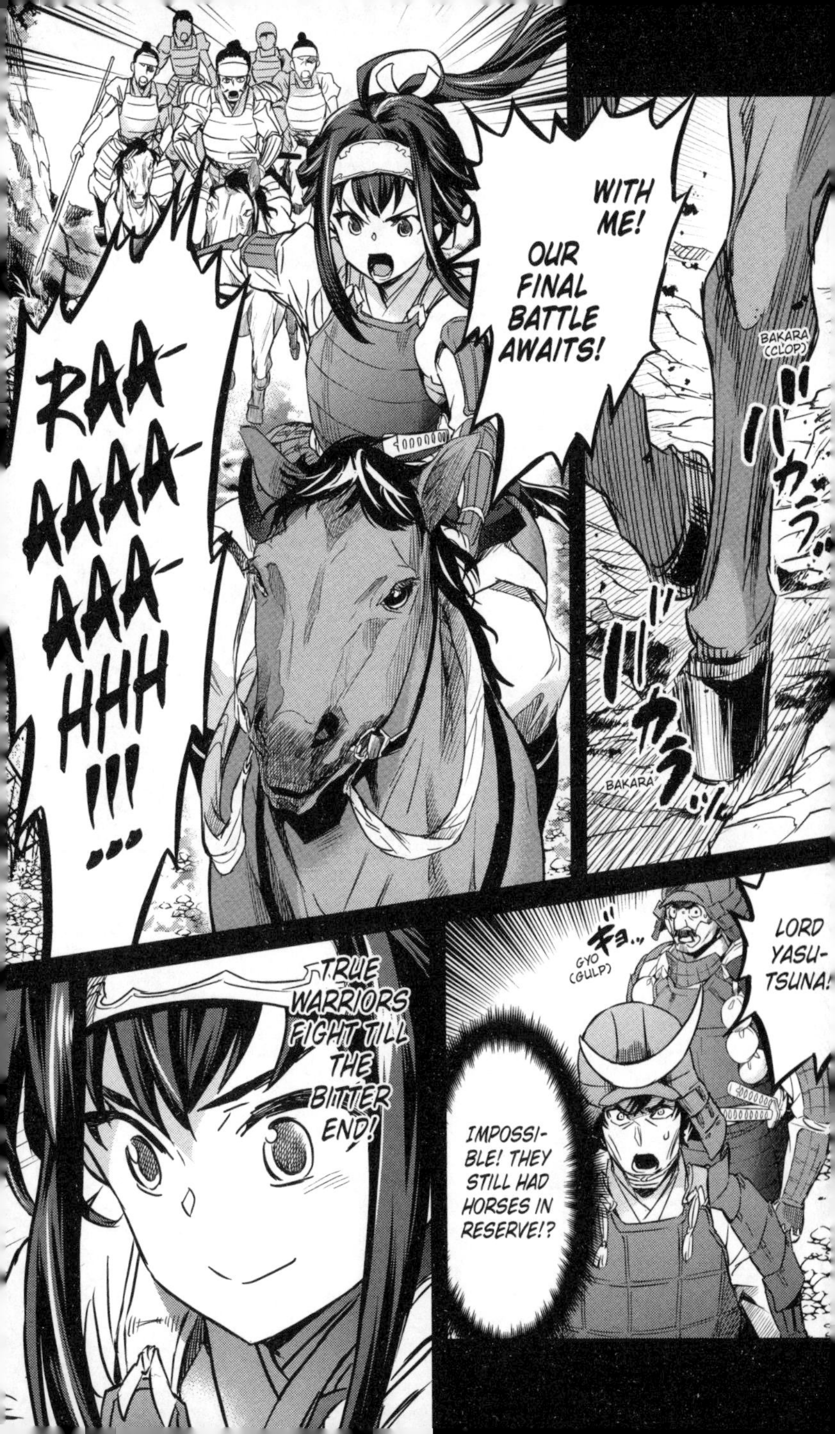

WITH ME! OUR FINAL BATTLE AWAITS!
BAKARA (CLOP)
バカラ..
バカラ..
BAKARA
RAAAAAAAAAHHH!!!...
LORD YASU-TSUNA!
ギョ..
GYO (GULP)
IMPOSSIBLE! THEY STILL HAD HORSES IN RESERVE!?
TRUE WARRIORS FIGHT TILL THE BITTER END!

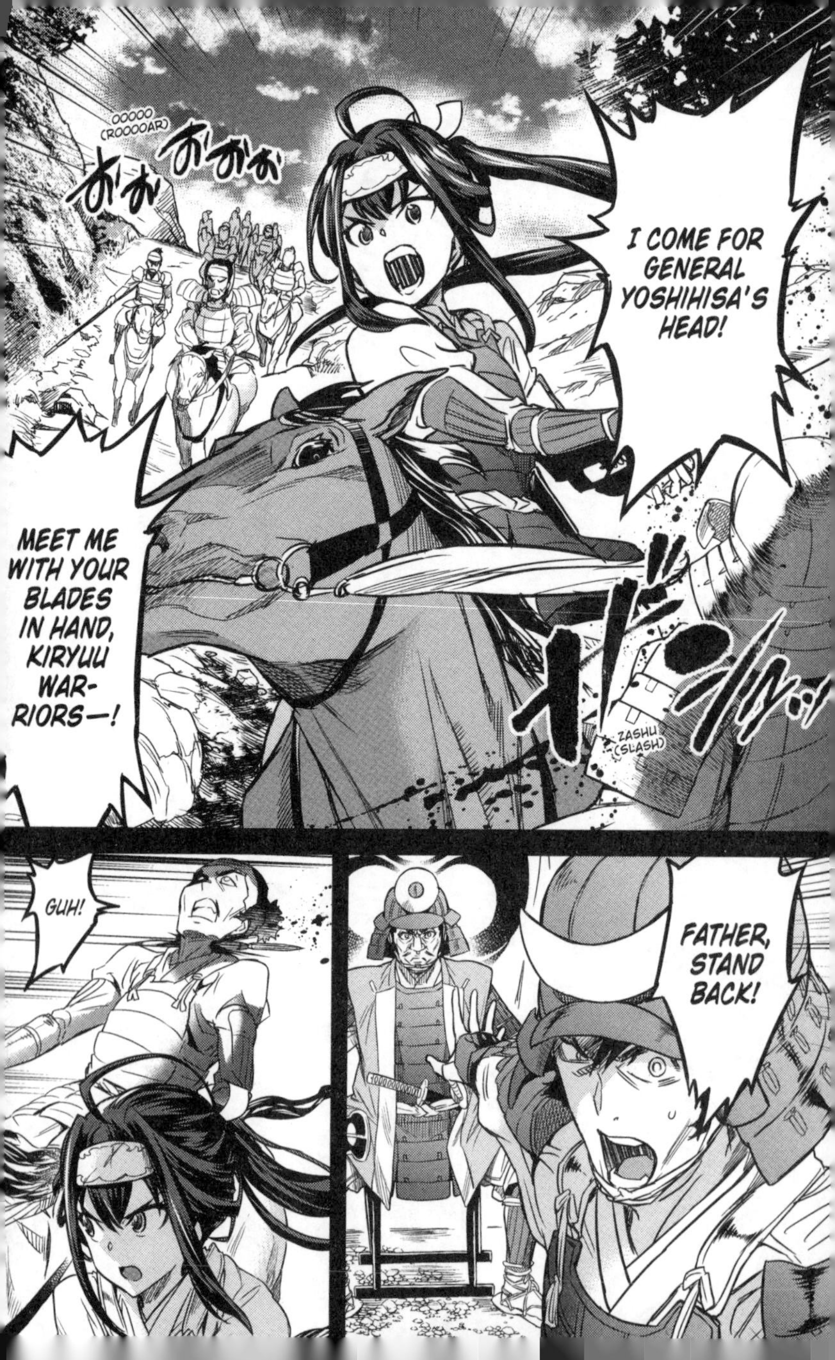
I COME FOR GENERAL YOSHIHISA'S HEAD!
OOOOO (ROOOOAR)
MEET ME WITH YOUR BLADES IN HAND, KIRYUU WAR-RIORS—!
ZASHU (SLASH)
FATHER, STAND BACK!
GUH!

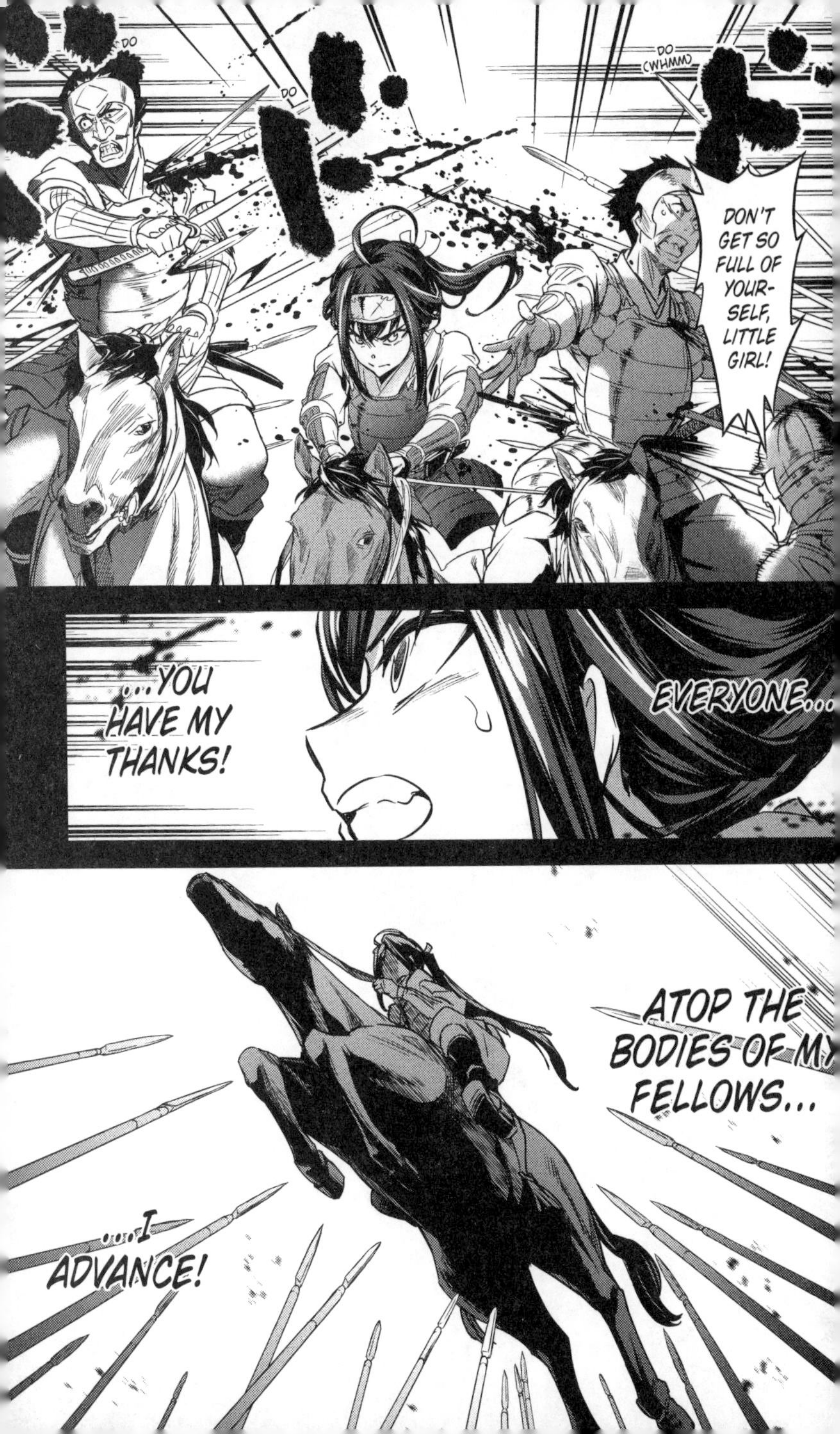
DO
DO (WHMM)
DO
DON'T GET SO FULL OF YOURSELF, LITTLE GIRL!
EVERYONE...
...YOU HAVE MY THANKS!
ATOP THE BODIES OF MY FELLOWS...
...I ADVANCE!

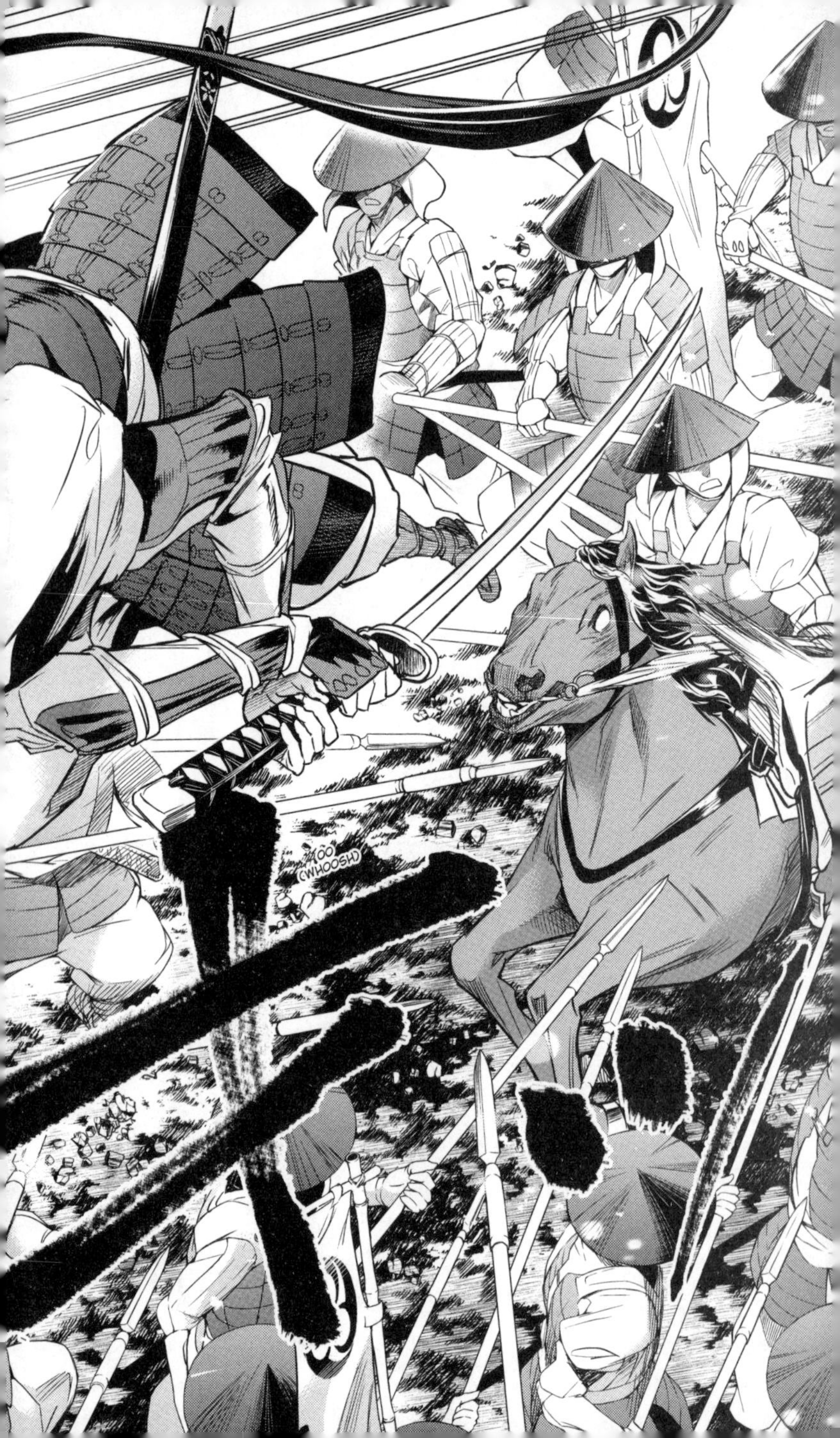
(WHOOSH)

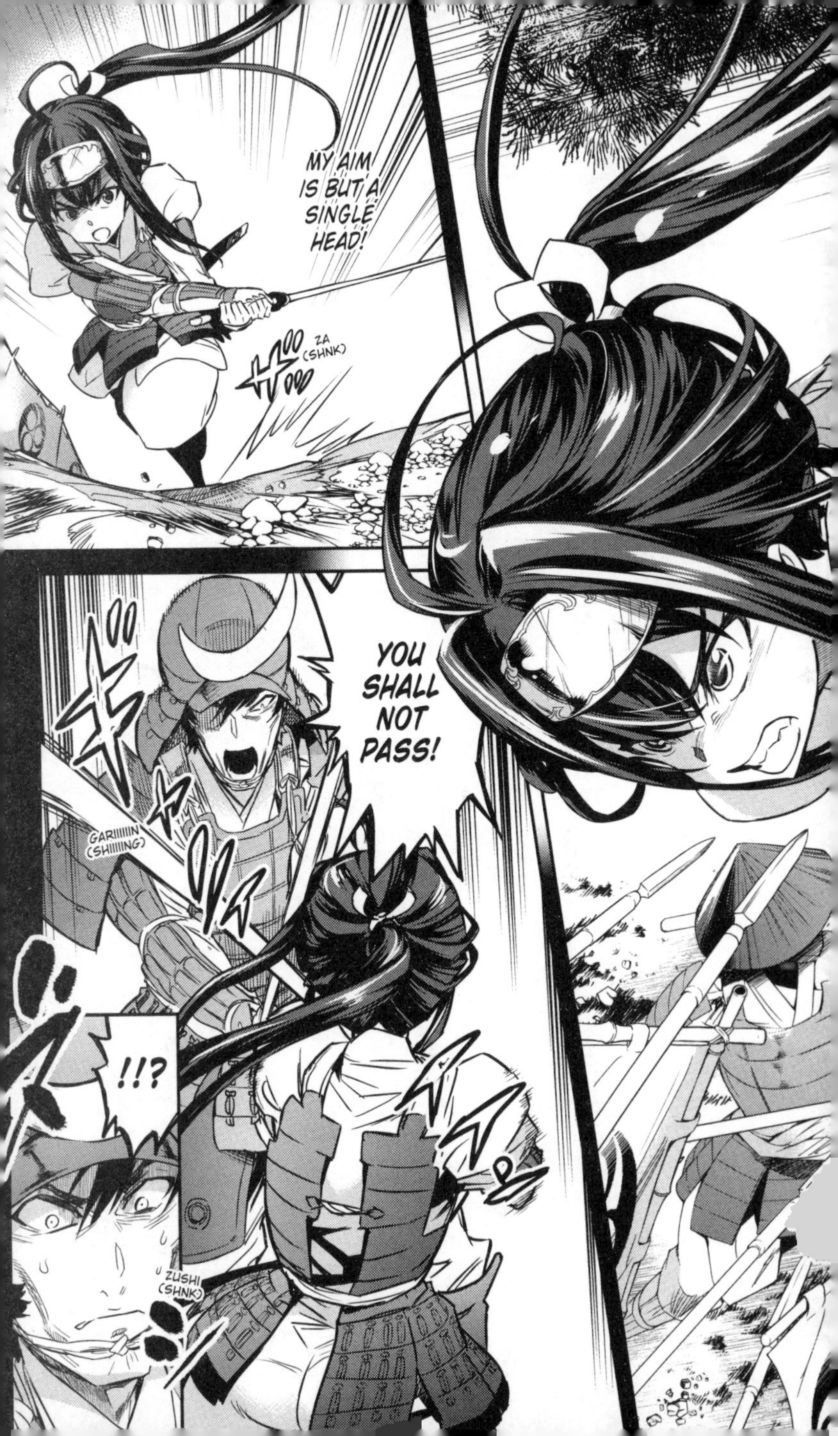
MY AIM IS BUT A SINGLE HEAD!
ZA (SHNK)
YOU SHALL NOT PASS!
GARIIIIIN (SHIIIIING)
!!?
ZUSHI (SHNK)

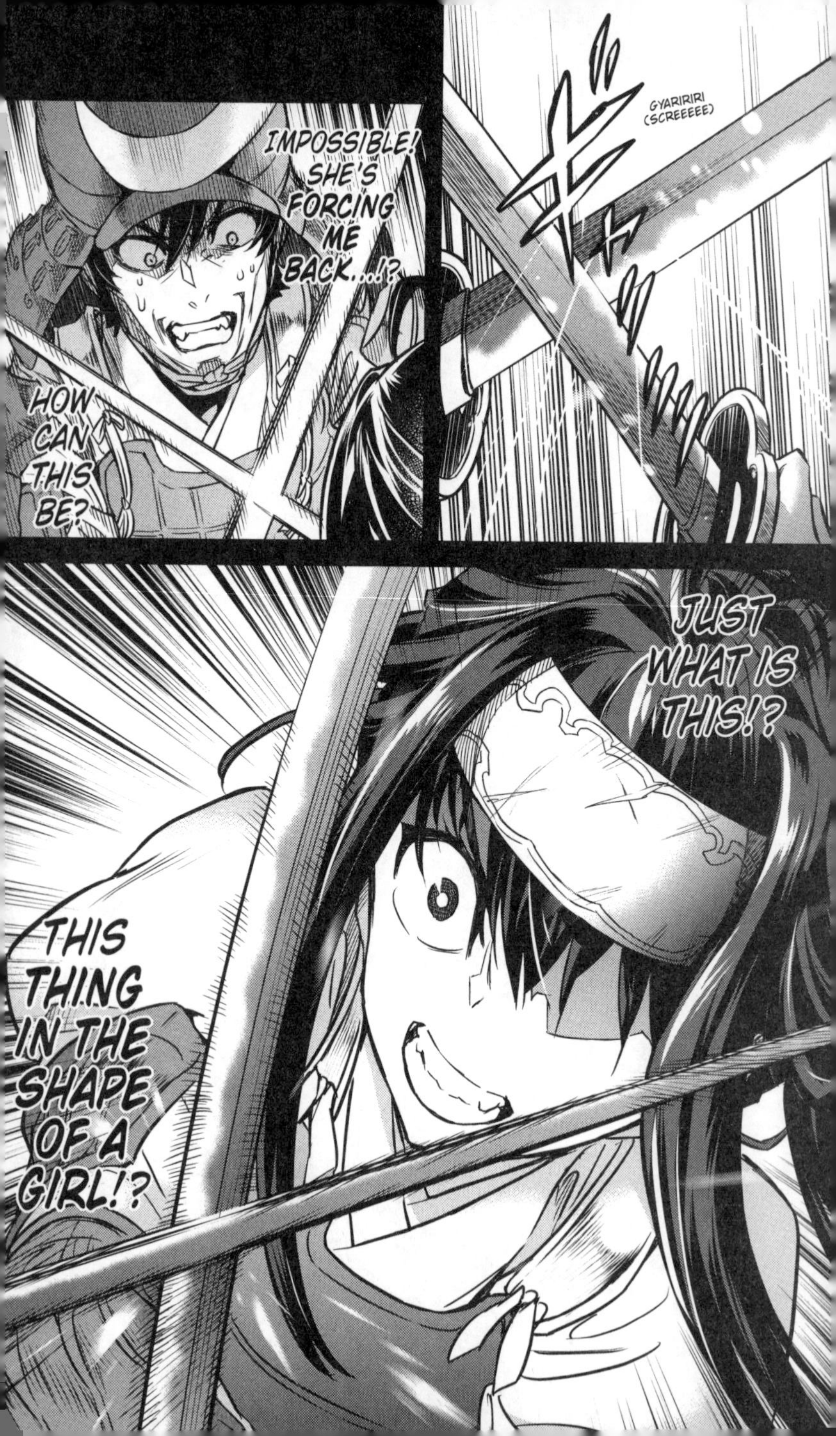
GYARIRIRI (SCREEEEE)
IMPOSSIBLE! SHE'S FORCING ME BACK...!?
HOW CAN THIS BE?
JUST WHAT IS THIS!?
THIS THING IN THE SHAPE OF A GIRL!?

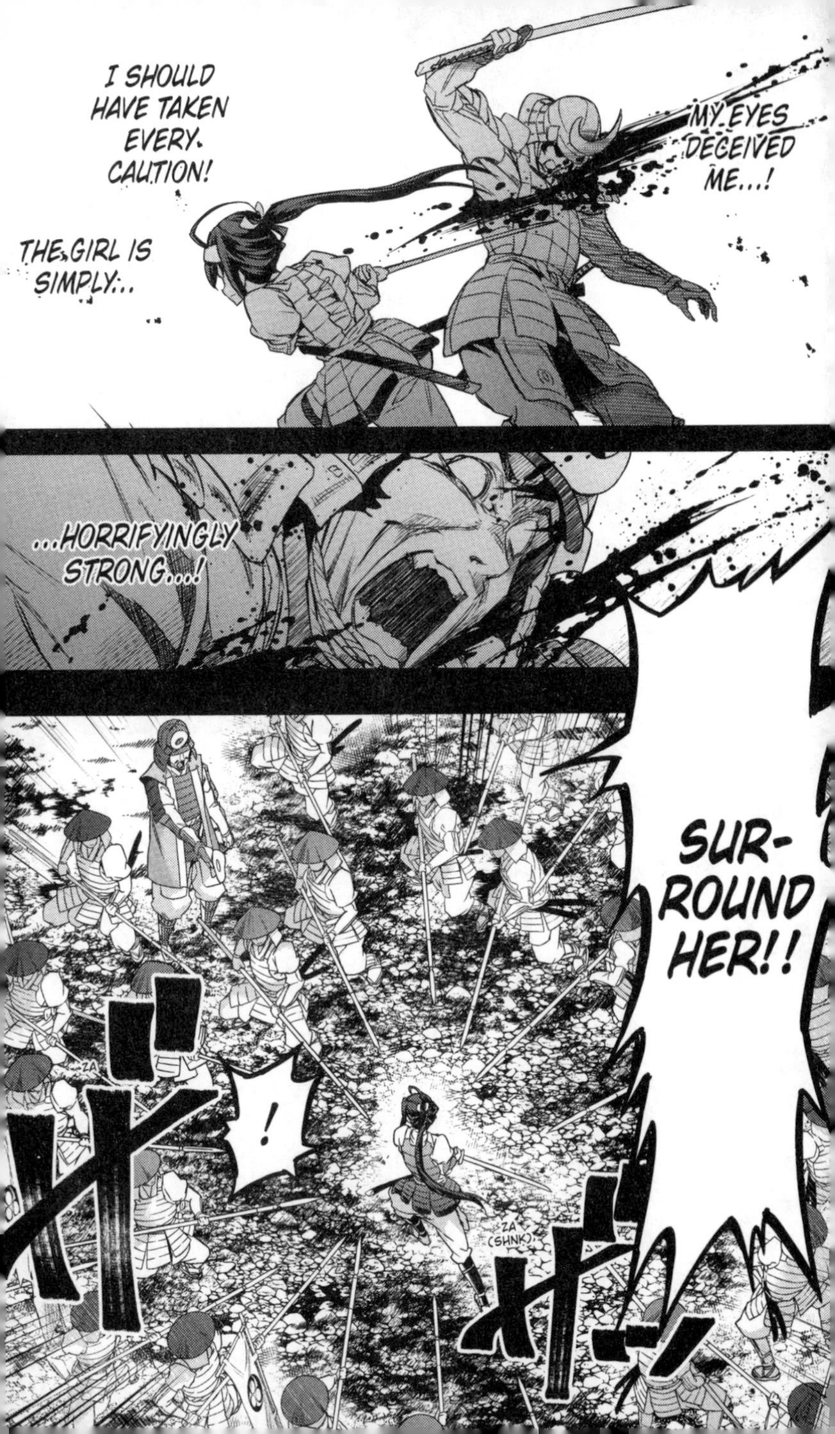
MY EYES DECEIVED ME...!
I SHOULD HAVE TAKEN EVERY CAUTION!
THE GIRL IS SIMPLY...
...HORRIFYINGLY STRONG...!
SUR-ROUND HER!!
ZA (SHNK)
!
ZA

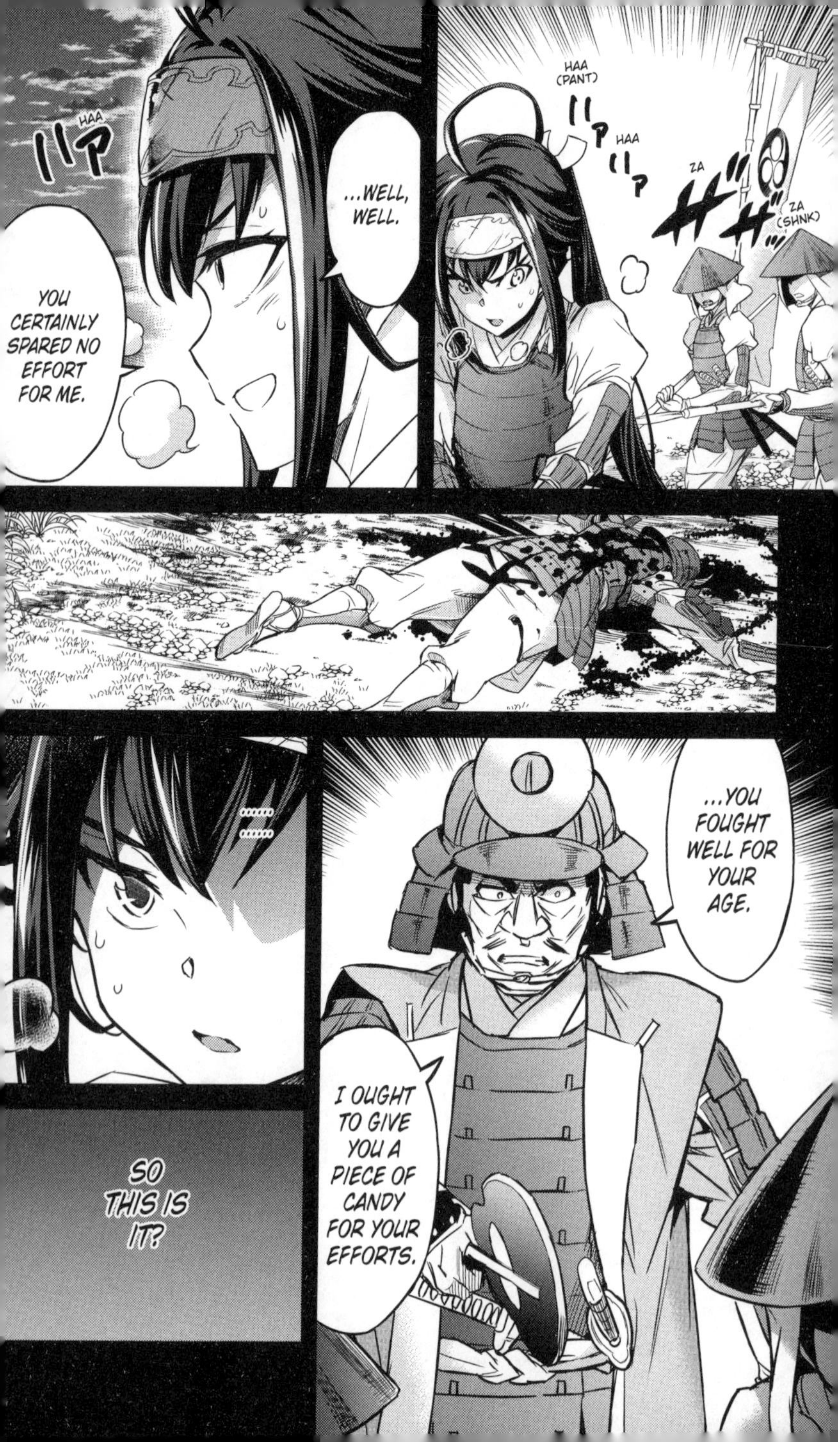
HAA (PANT)
HAA
ZA
ZA (SHNK)
...WELL, WELL.
HAA
YOU CERTAINLY SPARED NO EFFORT FOR ME.
...YOU FOUGHT WELL FOR YOUR AGE.
I OUGHT TO GIVE YOU A PIECE OF CANDY FOR YOUR EFFORTS.
SO THIS IS IT?

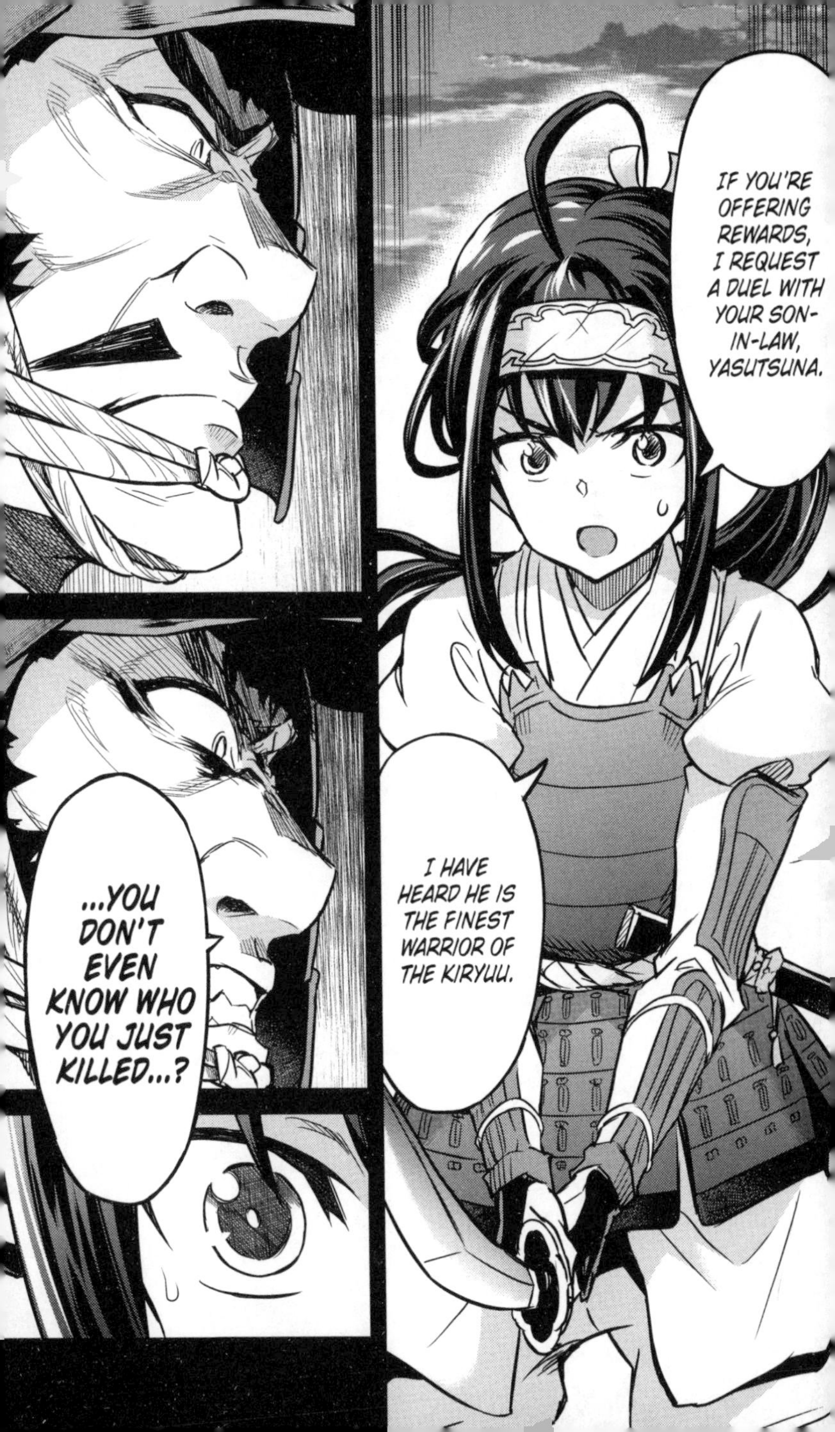
IF YOU'RE OFFERING REWARDS, I REQUEST A DUEL WITH YOUR SON-IN-LAW, YASUTSUNA.
I HAVE HEARD HE IS THE FINEST WARRIOR OF THE KIRYUU.
...YOU DON'T EVEN KNOW WHO YOU JUST KILLED...?

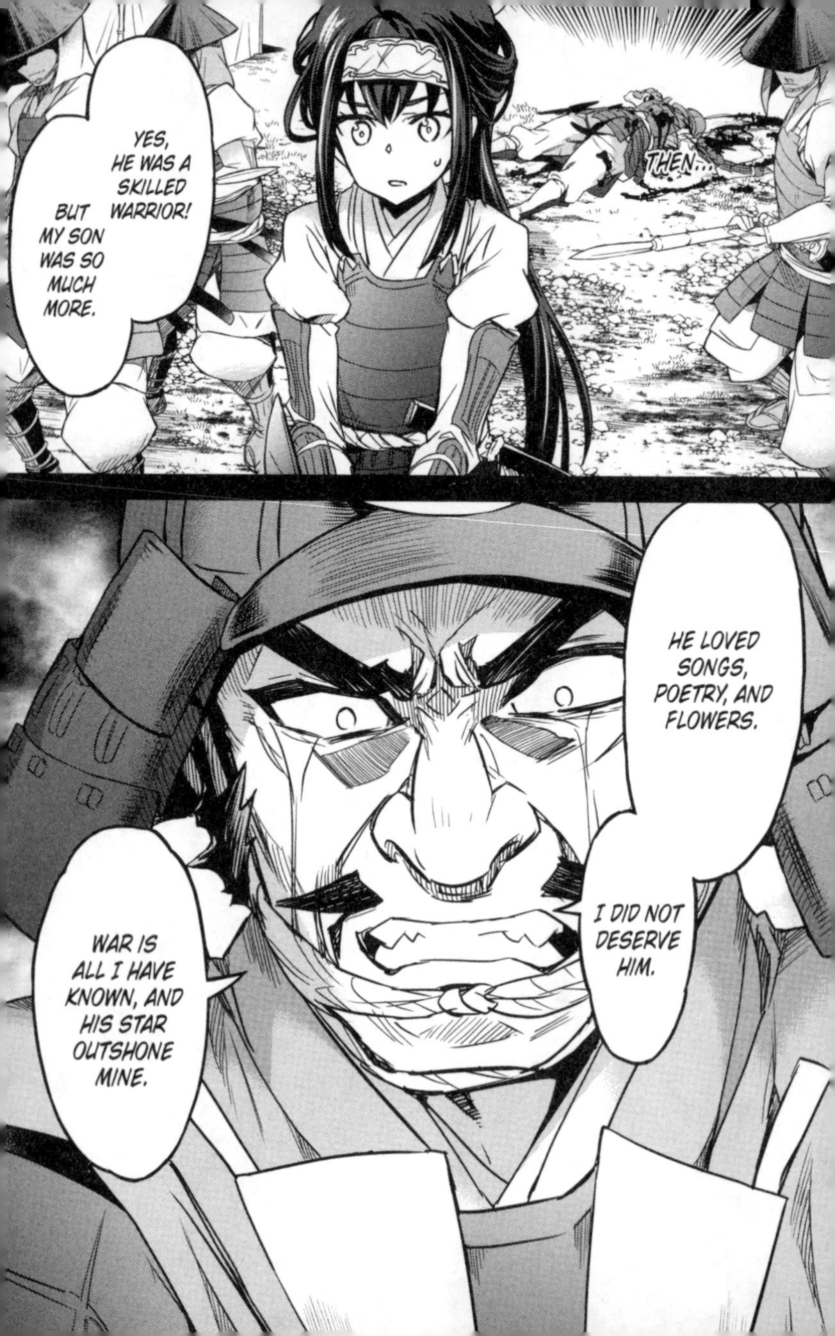
THEN...
YES, HE WAS A SKILLED WARRIOR!
BUT MY SON WAS SO MUCH MORE.
HE LOVED SONGS, POETRY, AND FLOWERS.
I DID NOT DESERVE HIM.
WAR IS ALL I HAVE KNOWN, AND HIS STAR OUTSHONE MINE.

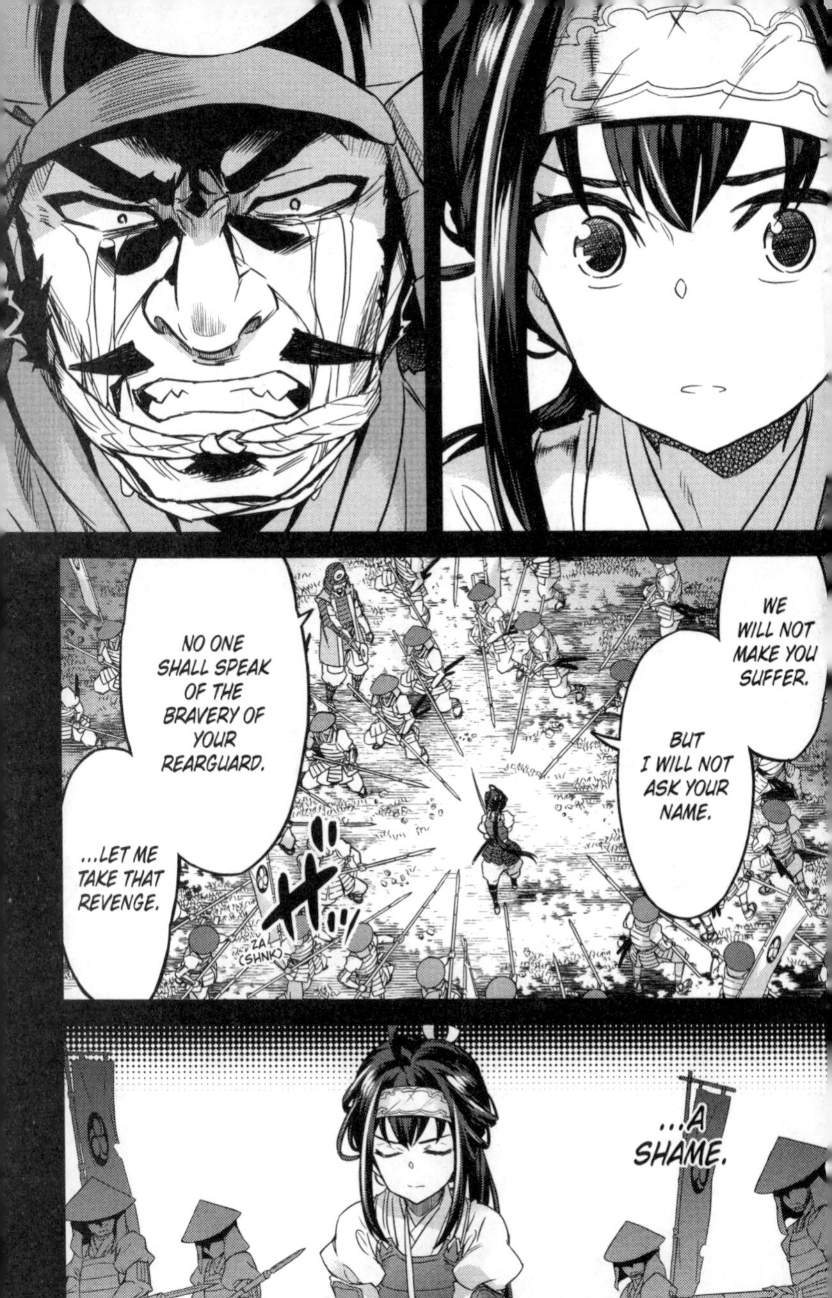
WE WILL NOT MAKE YOU SUFFER.
BUT I WILL NOT ASK YOUR NAME.
NO ONE SHALL SPEAK OF THE BRAVERY OF YOUR REARGUARD.
...LET ME TAKE THAT REVENGE.
ZA (SHNK)
...A SHAME.

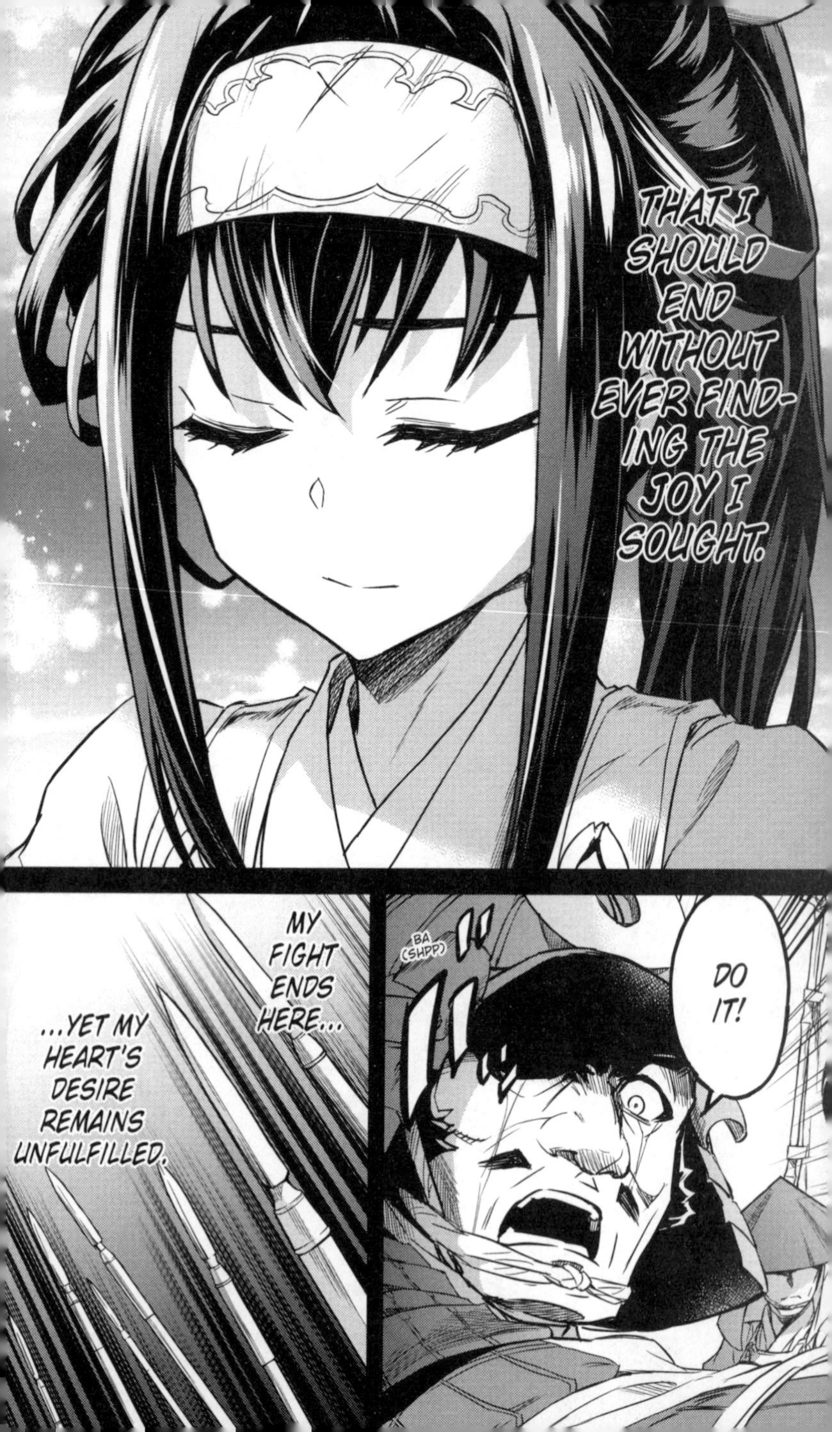
THAT I SHOULD END WITHOUT EVER FINDING THE JOY I SOUGHT.
DO IT!
BA (SHPP)
MY FIGHT ENDS HERE...
...YET MY HEART'S DESIRE REMAINS UNFULFILLED.

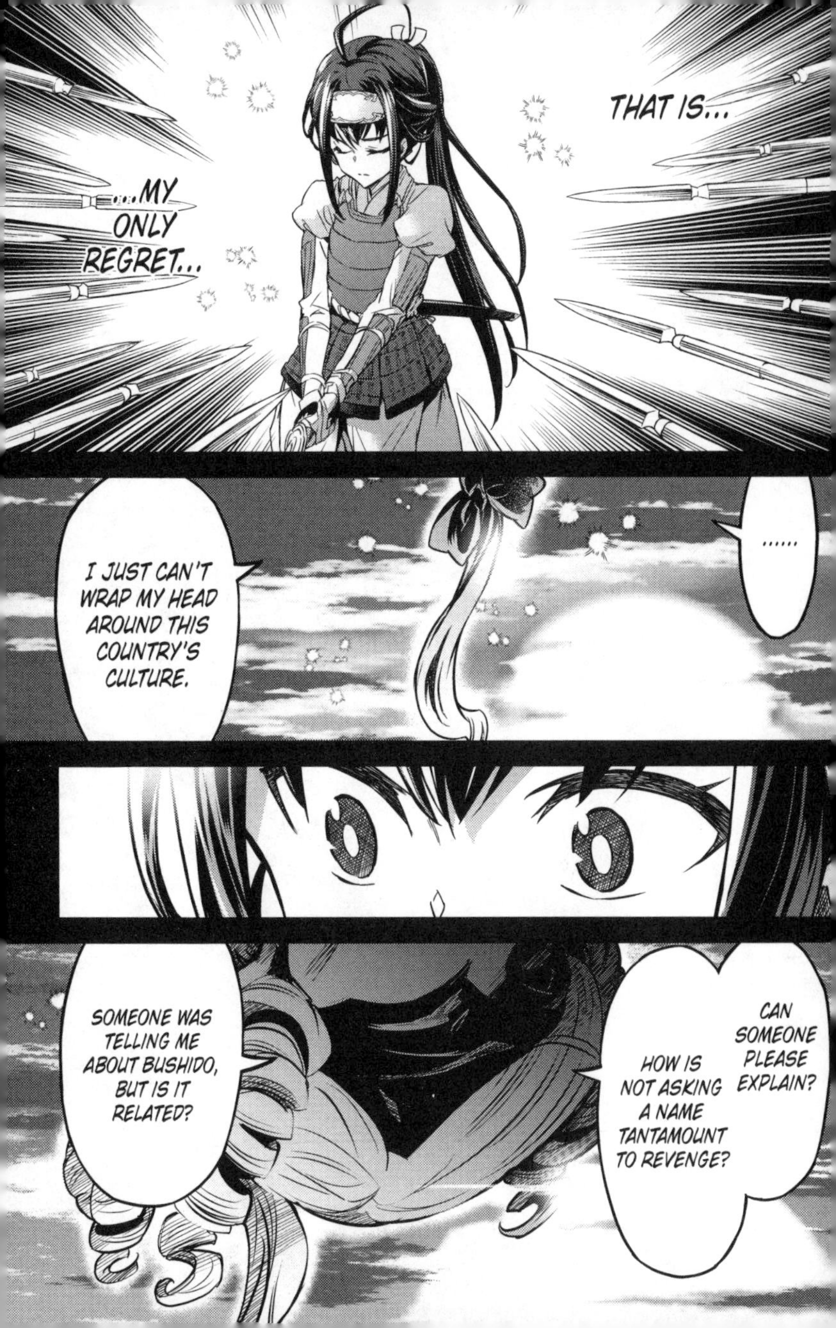
THAT IS...
...MY ONLY REGRET...
......
I JUST CAN'T WRAP MY HEAD AROUND THIS COUNTRY'S CULTURE.
CAN SOMEONE PLEASE EXPLAIN?
HOW IS NOT ASKING A NAME TANTAMOUNT TO REVENGE?
SOMEONE WAS TELLING ME ABOUT BUSHIDO, BUT IS IT RELATED?

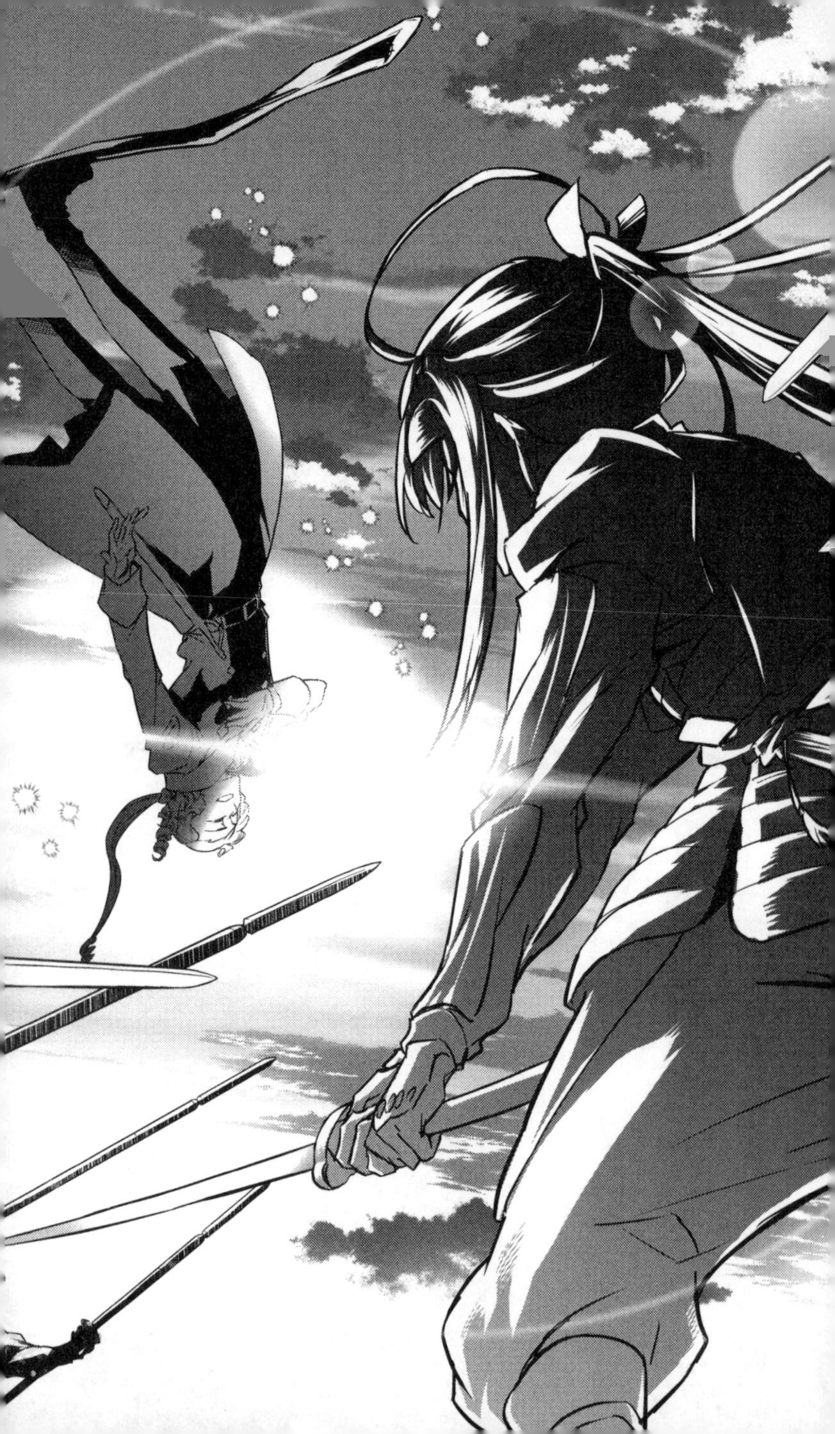

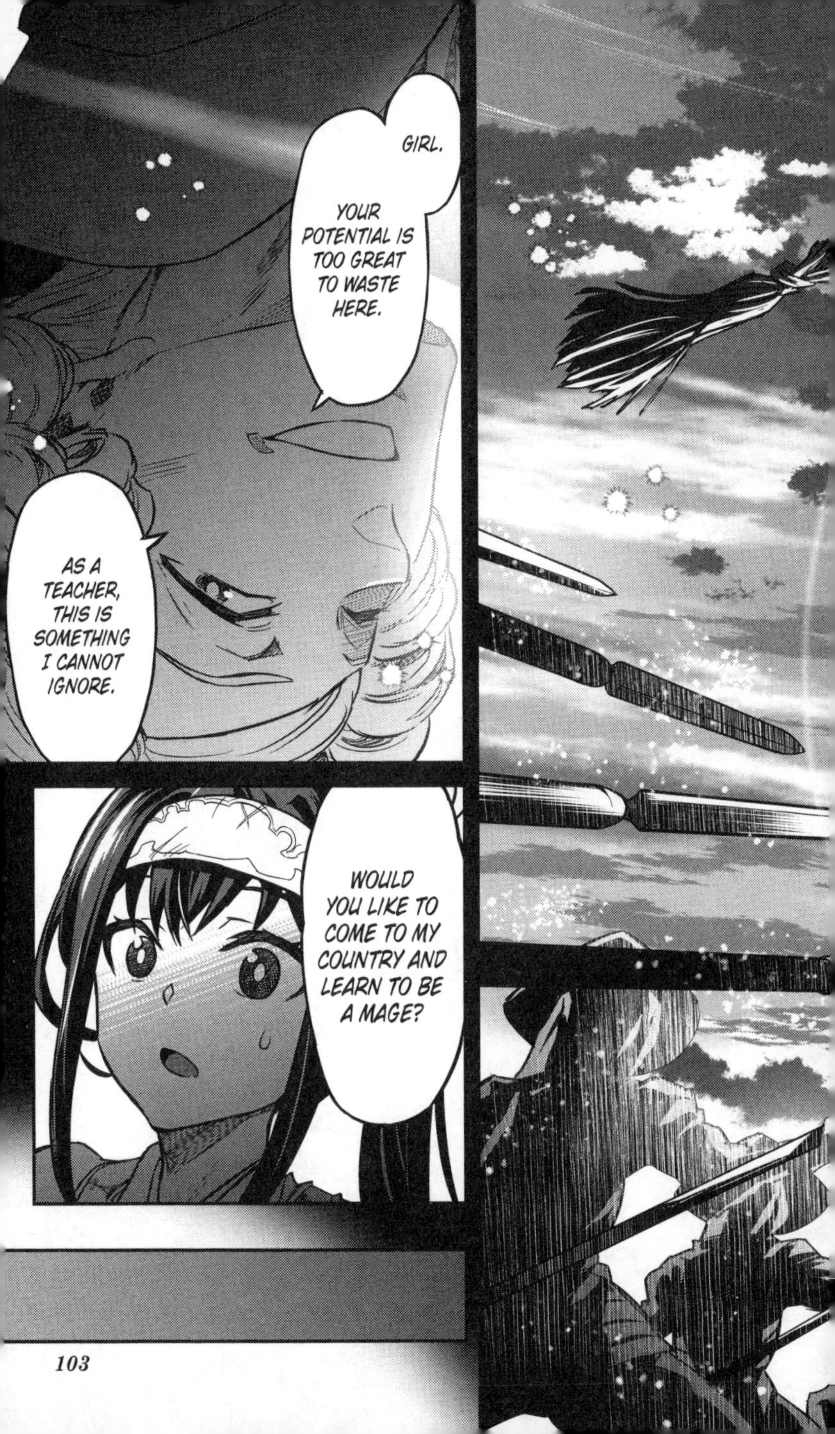
GIRL.
YOUR POTENTIAL IS TOO GREAT TO WASTE HERE.
AS A TEACHER, THIS IS SOMETHING I CANNOT IGNORE.
WOULD YOU LIKE TO COME TO MY COUNTRY AND LEARN TO BE A MAGE?

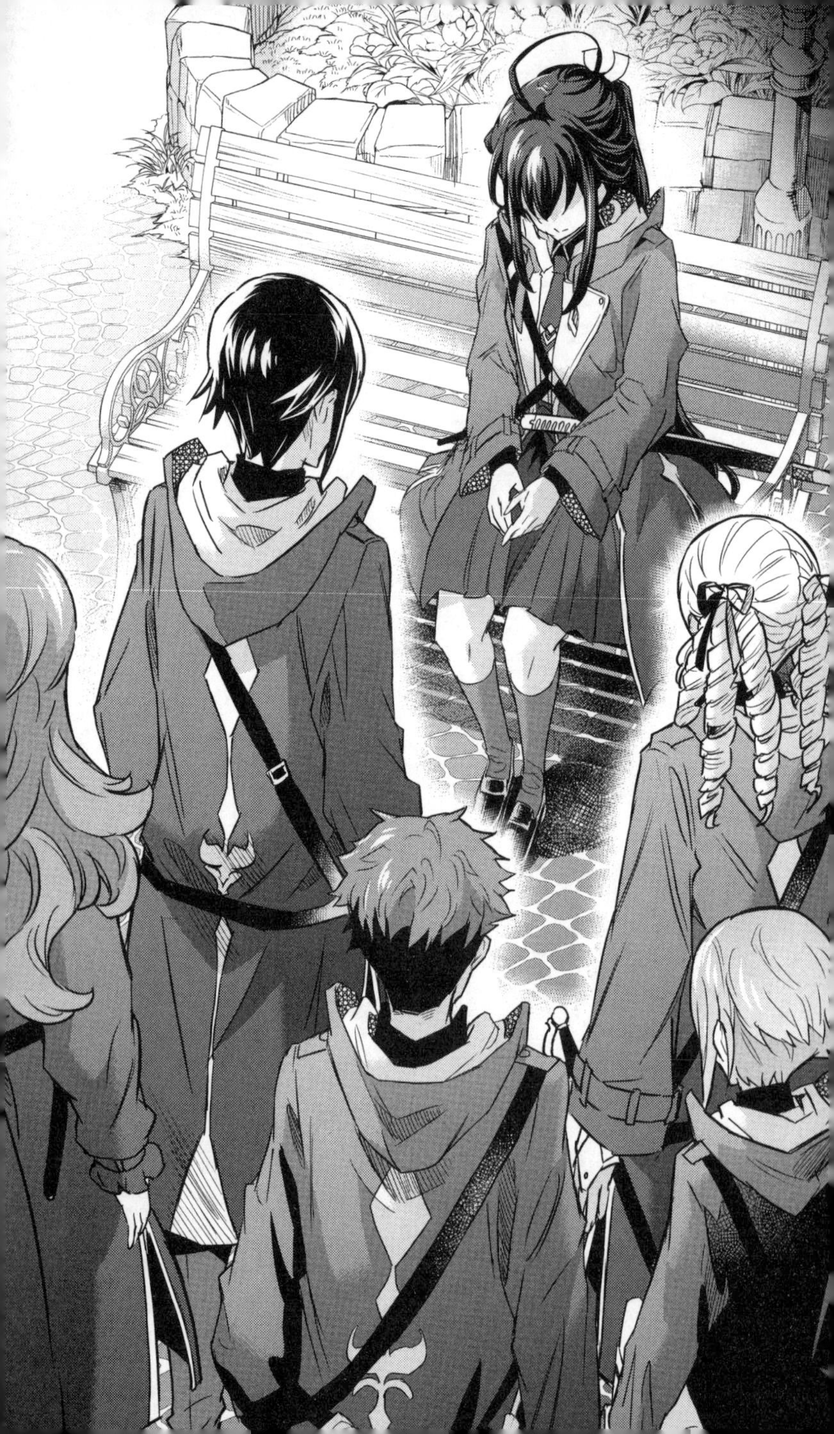

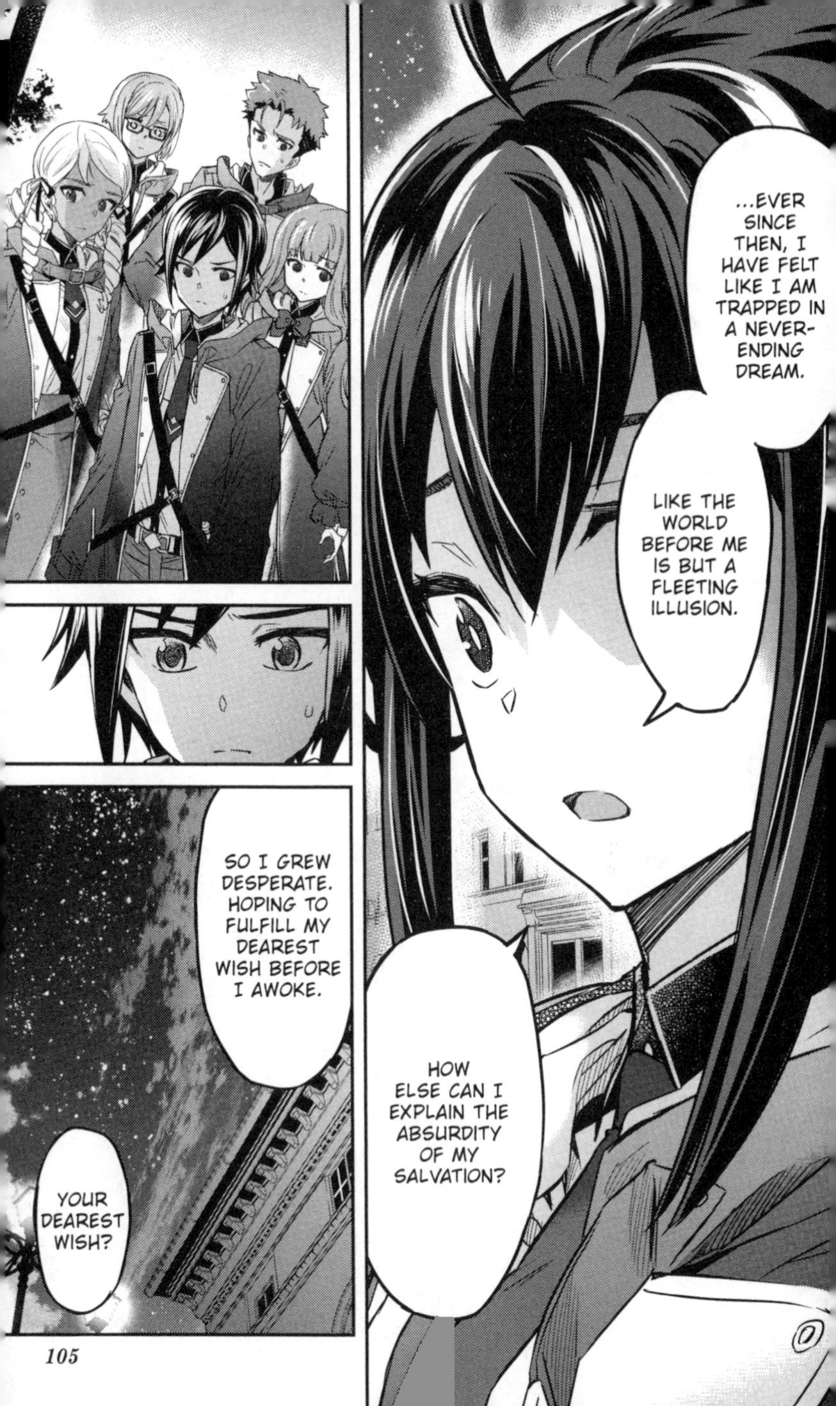
...EVER SINCE THEN, I HAVE FELT LIKE I AM TRAPPED IN A NEVER-ENDING DREAM.
LIKE THE WORLD BEFORE ME IS BUT A FLEETING ILLUSION.
HOW ELSE CAN I EXPLAIN THE ABSURDITY OF MY SALVATION?
SO I GREW DESPERATE. HOPING TO FULFILL MY DEAREST WISH BEFORE I AWOKE.
YOUR DEAREST WISH?

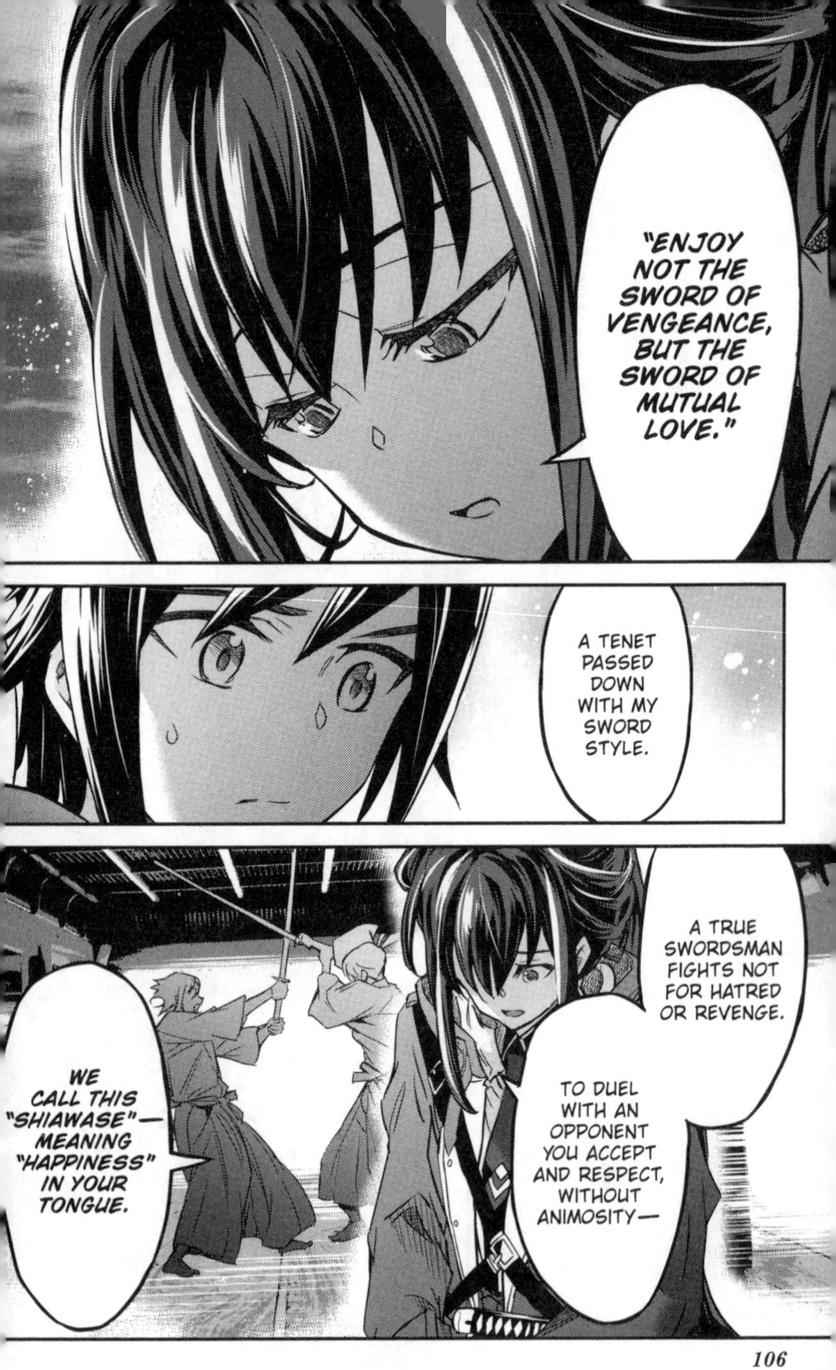
"ENJOY NOT THE SWORD OF VENGEANCE, BUT THE SWORD OF MUTUAL LOVE."
A TENET PASSED DOWN WITH MY SWORD STYLE.
A TRUE SWORDSMAN FIGHTS NOT FOR HATRED OR REVENGE.
TO DUEL WITH AN OPPONENT YOU ACCEPT AND RESPECT, WITHOUT ANIMOSITY—
WE CALL THIS "SHIAWASE"—MEANING "HAPPINESS" IN YOUR TONGUE.

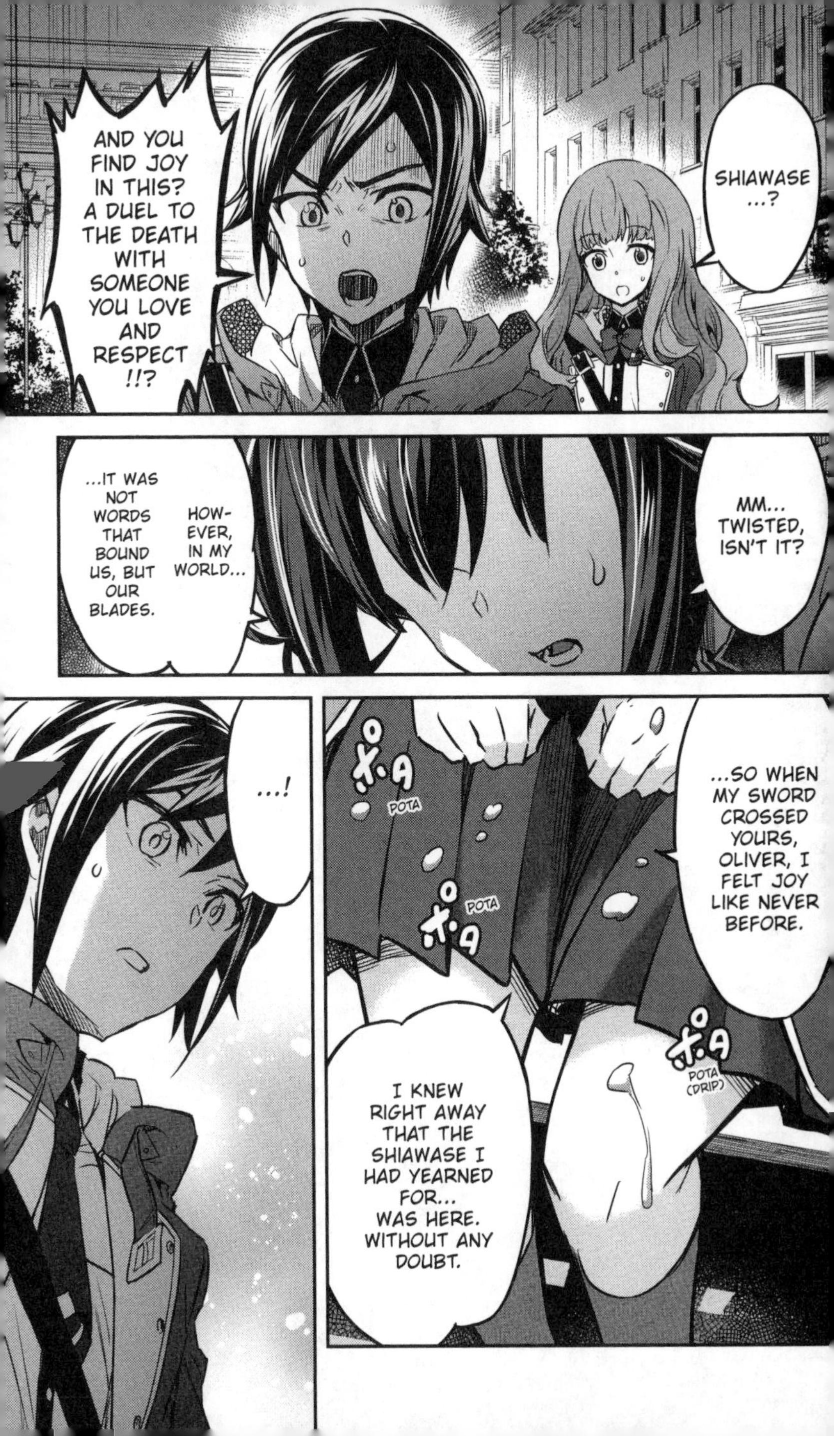
SHIAWASE ...?
AND YOU FIND JOY IN THIS? A DUEL TO THE DEATH WITH SOMEONE YOU LOVE AND RESPECT !!?
MM... TWISTED, ISN'T IT?
HOW-EVER, IN MY WORLD...
...IT WAS NOT WORDS THAT BOUND US, BUT OUR BLADES.
...SO WHEN MY SWORD CROSSED YOURS, OLIVER, I FELT JOY LIKE NEVER BEFORE.
POTA
POTA
POTA (DRIP)
I KNEW RIGHT AWAY THAT THE SHIAWASE I HAD YEARNED FOR... WAS HERE. WITHOUT ANY DOUBT.
...!

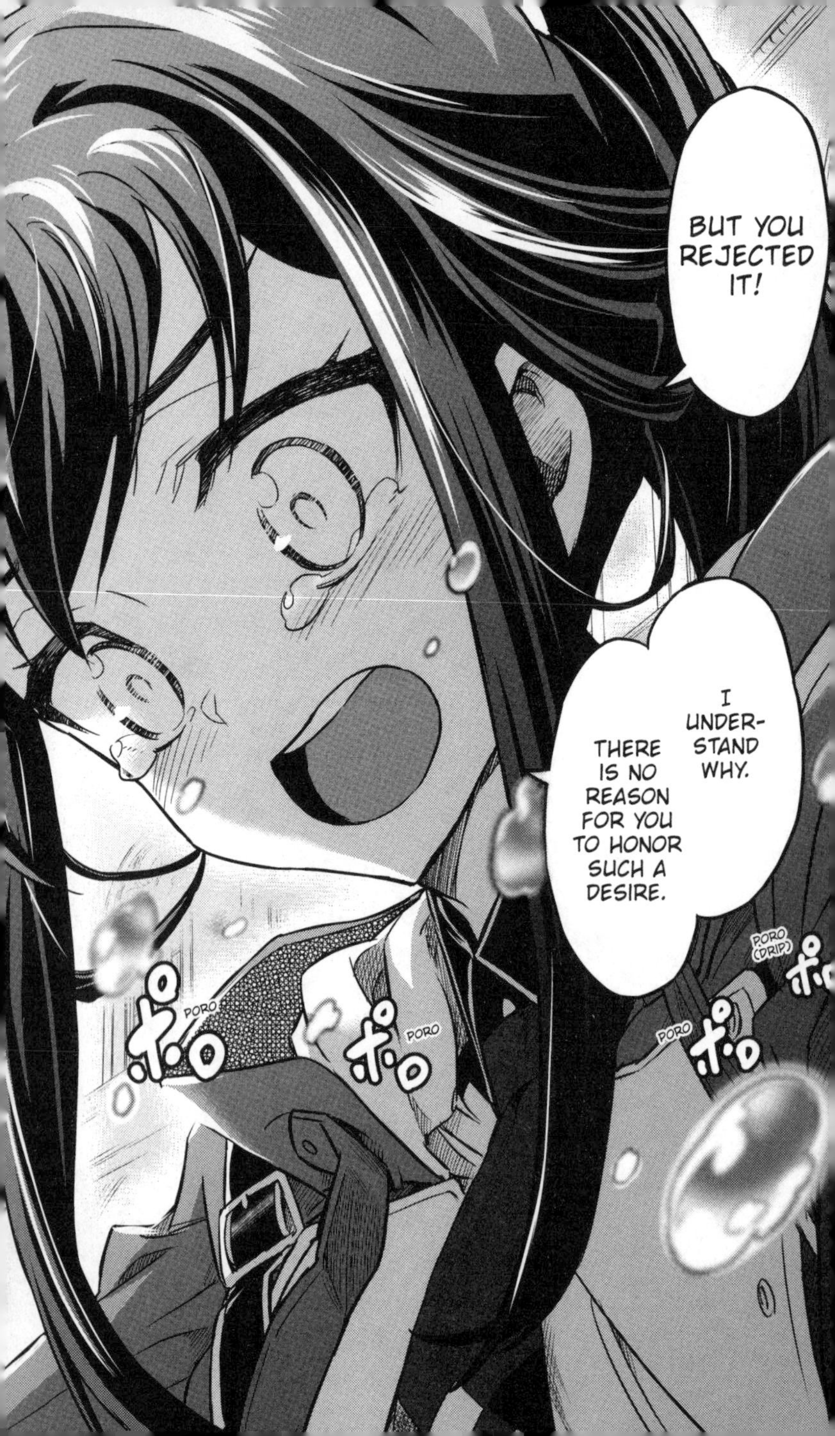
BUT YOU REJECTED IT!
I UNDERSTAND WHY.
THERE IS NO REASON FOR YOU TO HONOR SUCH A DESIRE.
PORO (DRIP)
PORO
PORO
PORO

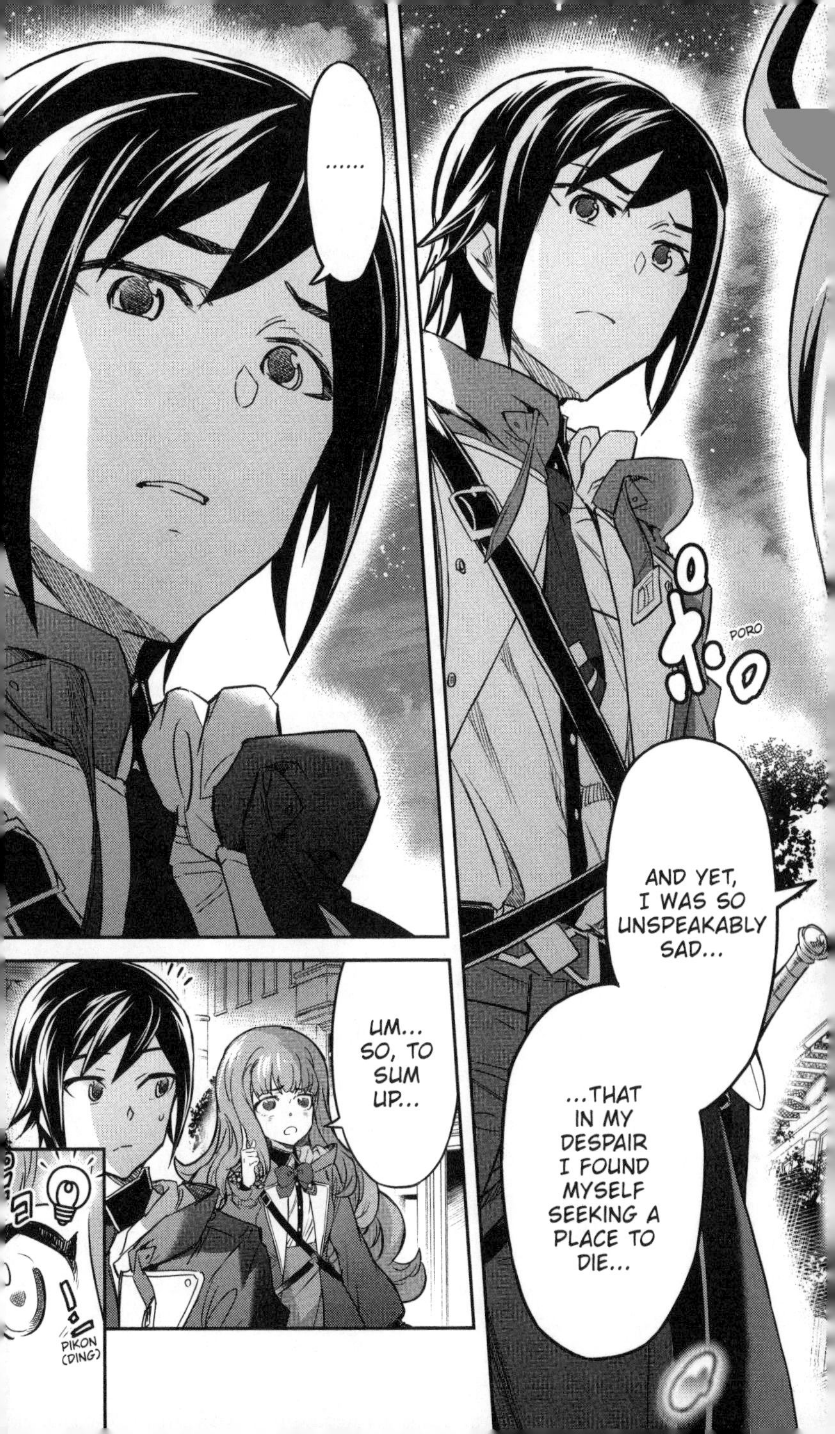
PORO
AND YET, I WAS SO UNSPEAKABLY SAD...
...THAT IN MY DESPAIR I FOUND MYSELF SEEKING A PLACE TO DIE...
......
UM... SO, TO SUM UP...
PIKON (DING)

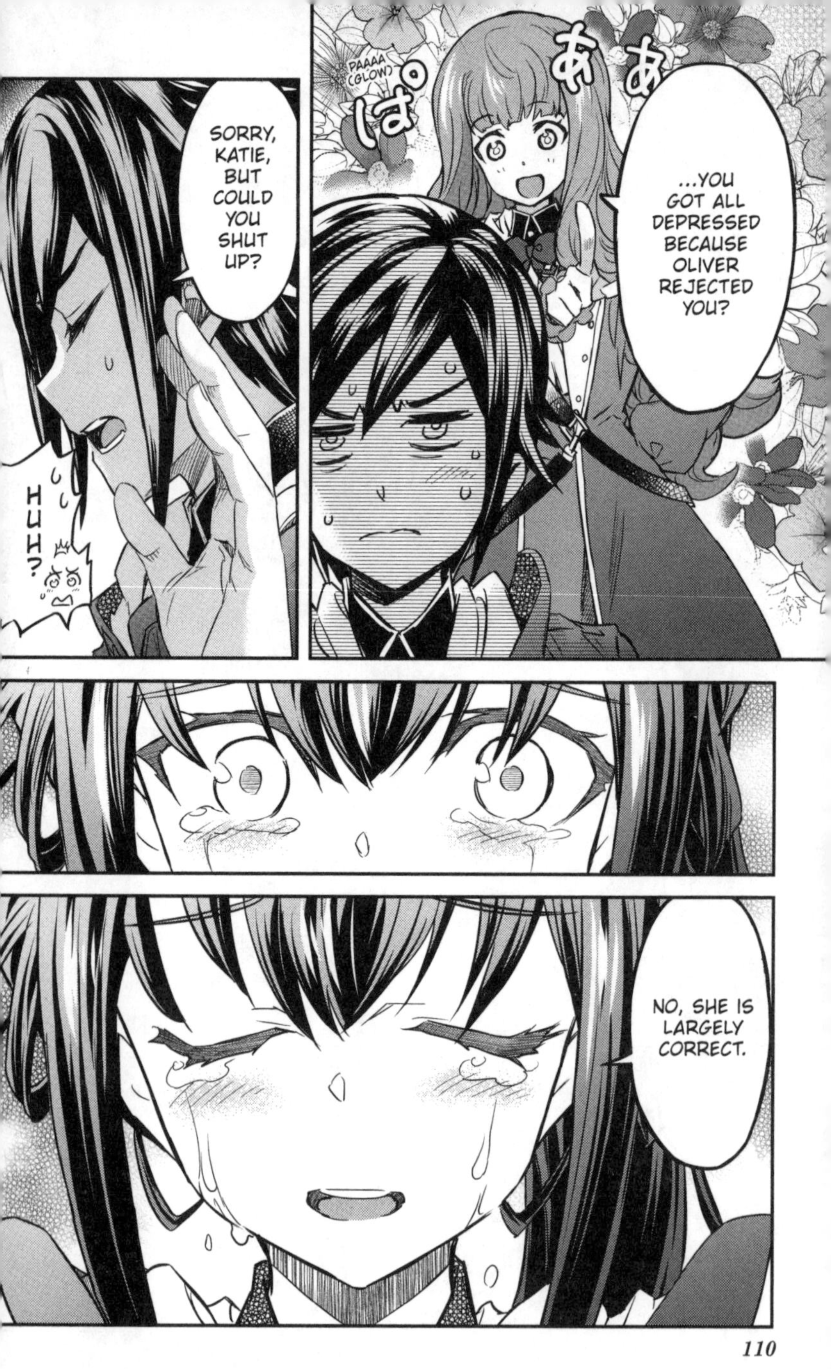
ぱぁぁ
PAAAA (GLOW)
...YOU GOT ALL DEPRESSED BECAUSE OLIVER REJECTED YOU?
SORRY, KATIE, BUT COULD YOU SHUT UP?
HUH?
NO, SHE IS LARGELY CORRECT.

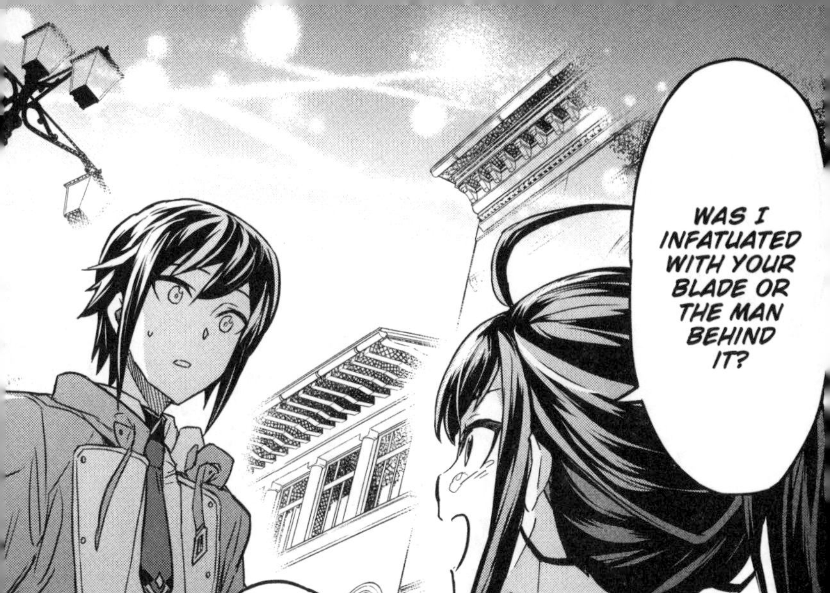
WAS I INFATUATED WITH YOUR BLADE OR THE MAN BEHIND IT?
PERHAPS THERE IS LITTLE DIFFERENCE BETWEEN THE TWO.

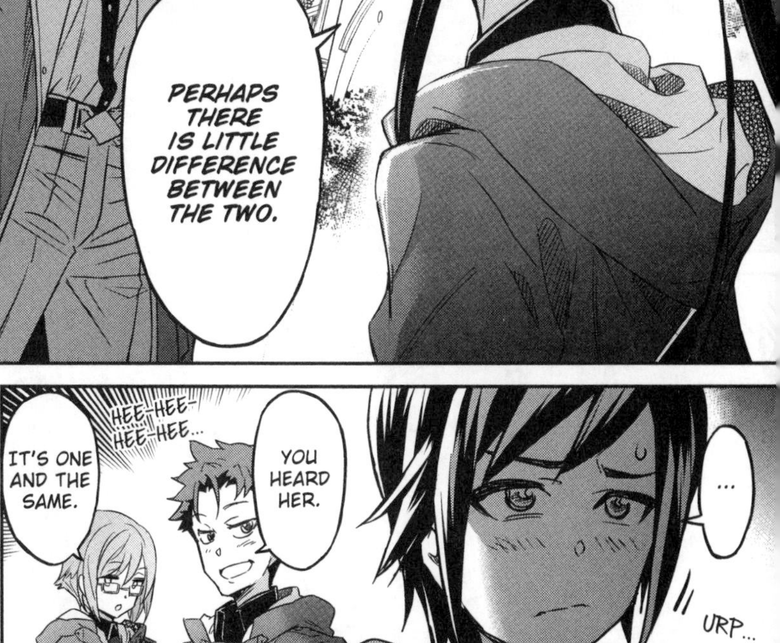
...
URP...
YOU HEARD HER.
HEE-HEE-HEE-HEE...
IT'S ONE AND THE SAME.

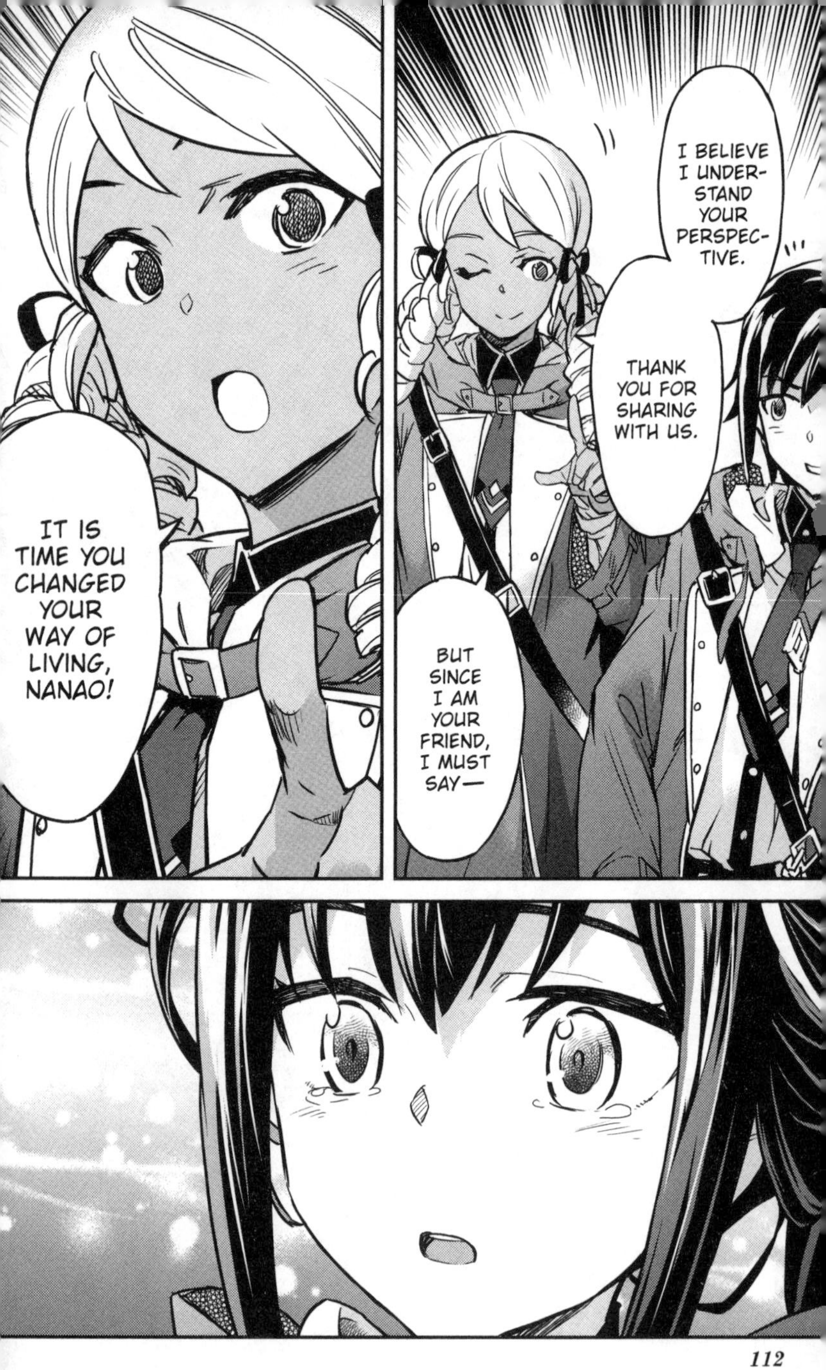
I BELIEVE I UNDER-STAND YOUR PERSPEC-TIVE.
THANK YOU FOR SHARING WITH US.
BUT SINCE I AM YOUR FRIEND, I MUST SAY—
IT IS TIME YOU CHANGED YOUR WAY OF LIVING, NANAO!

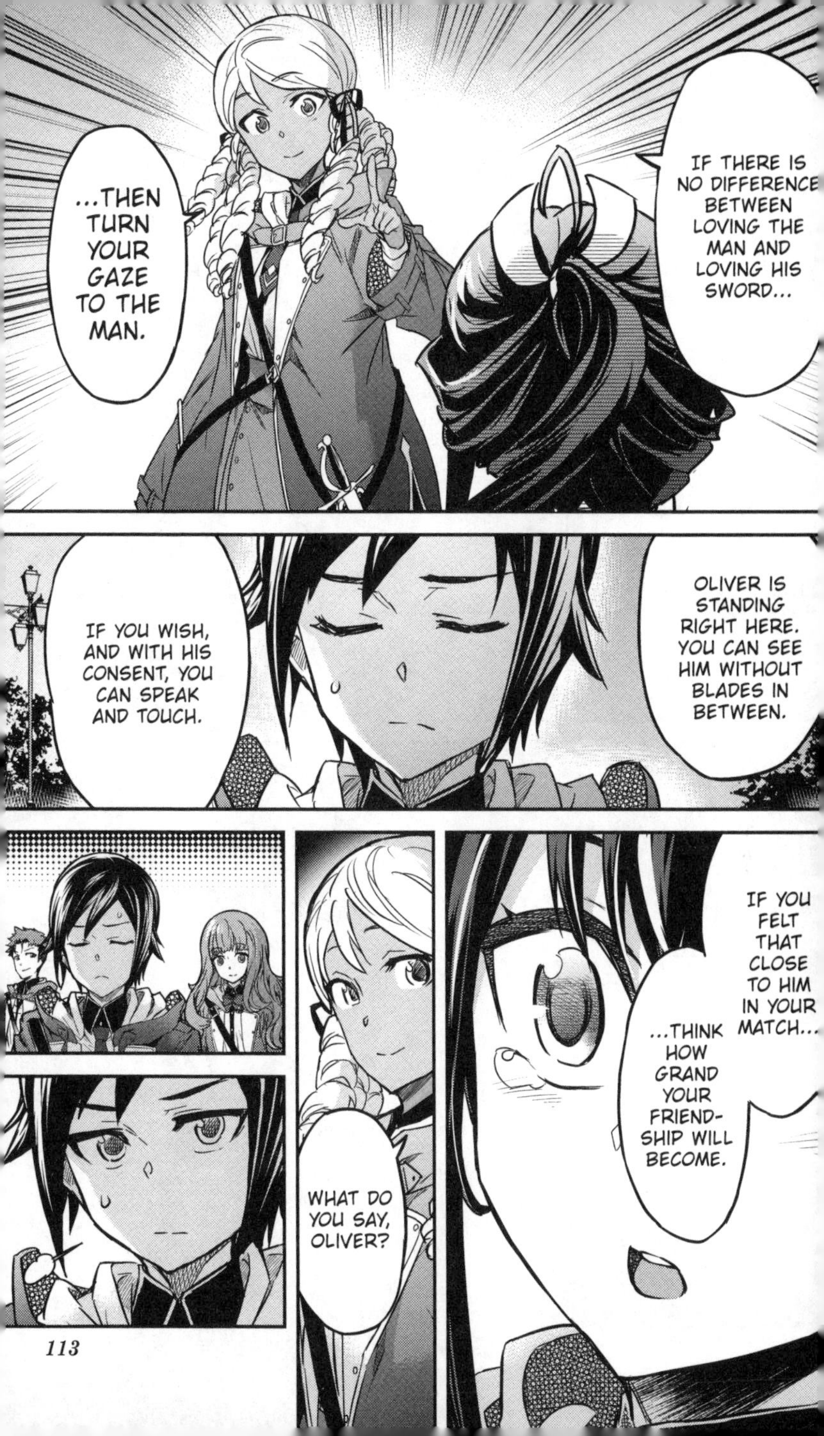
IF THERE IS NO DIFFERENCE BETWEEN LOVING THE MAN AND LOVING HIS SWORD...
...THEN TURN YOUR GAZE TO THE MAN.
OLIVER IS STANDING RIGHT HERE. YOU CAN SEE HIM WITHOUT BLADES IN BETWEEN.
IF YOU WISH, AND WITH HIS CONSENT, YOU CAN SPEAK AND TOUCH.
IF YOU FELT THAT CLOSE TO HIM IN YOUR MATCH...
...THINK HOW GRAND YOUR FRIENDSHIP WILL BECOME.
WHAT DO YOU SAY, OLIVER?

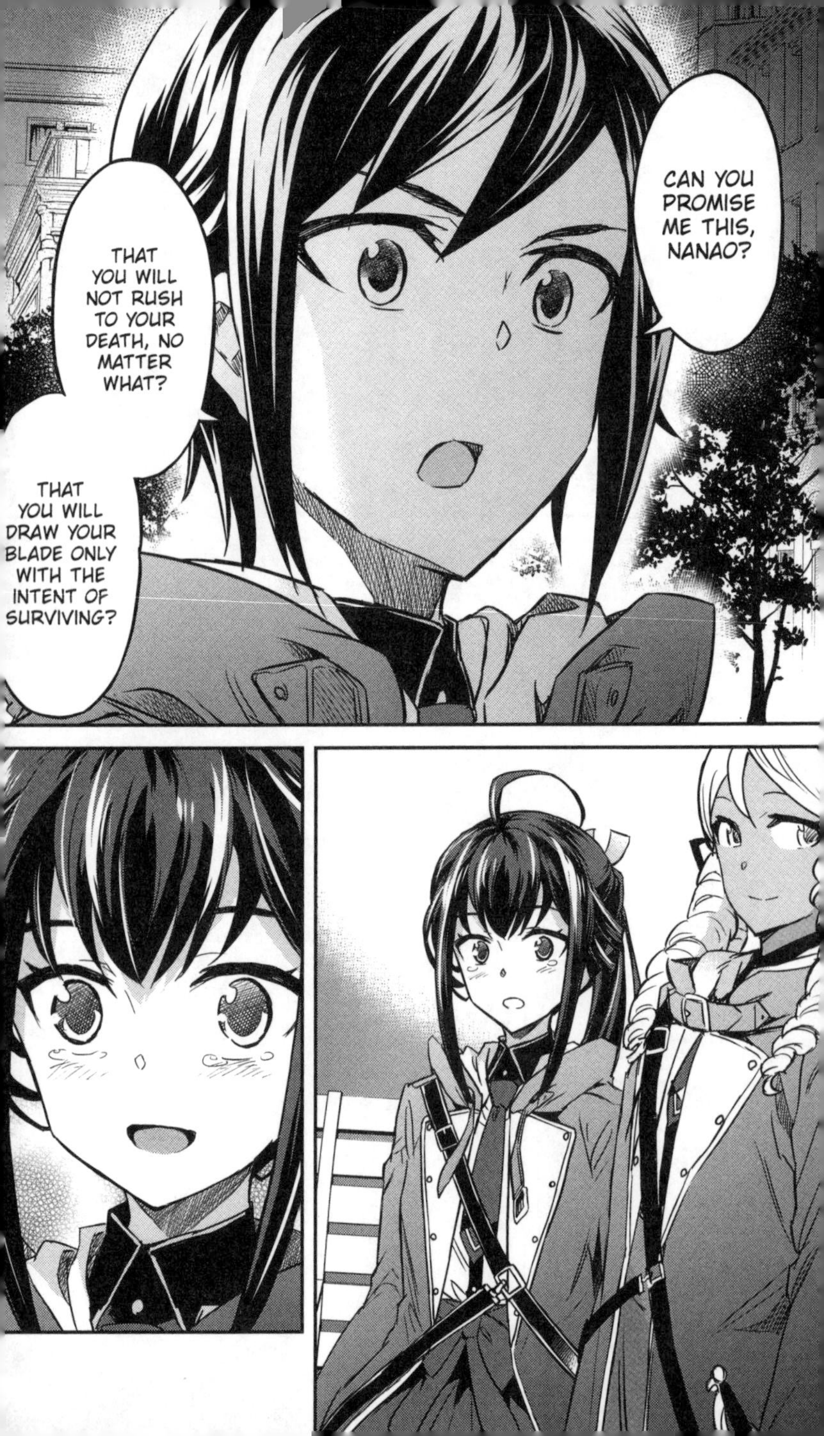
CAN YOU PROMISE ME THIS, NANAO?
THAT YOU WILL NOT RUSH TO YOUR DEATH, NO MATTER WHAT?
THAT YOU WILL DRAW YOUR BLADE ONLY WITH THE INTENT OF SURVIVING?

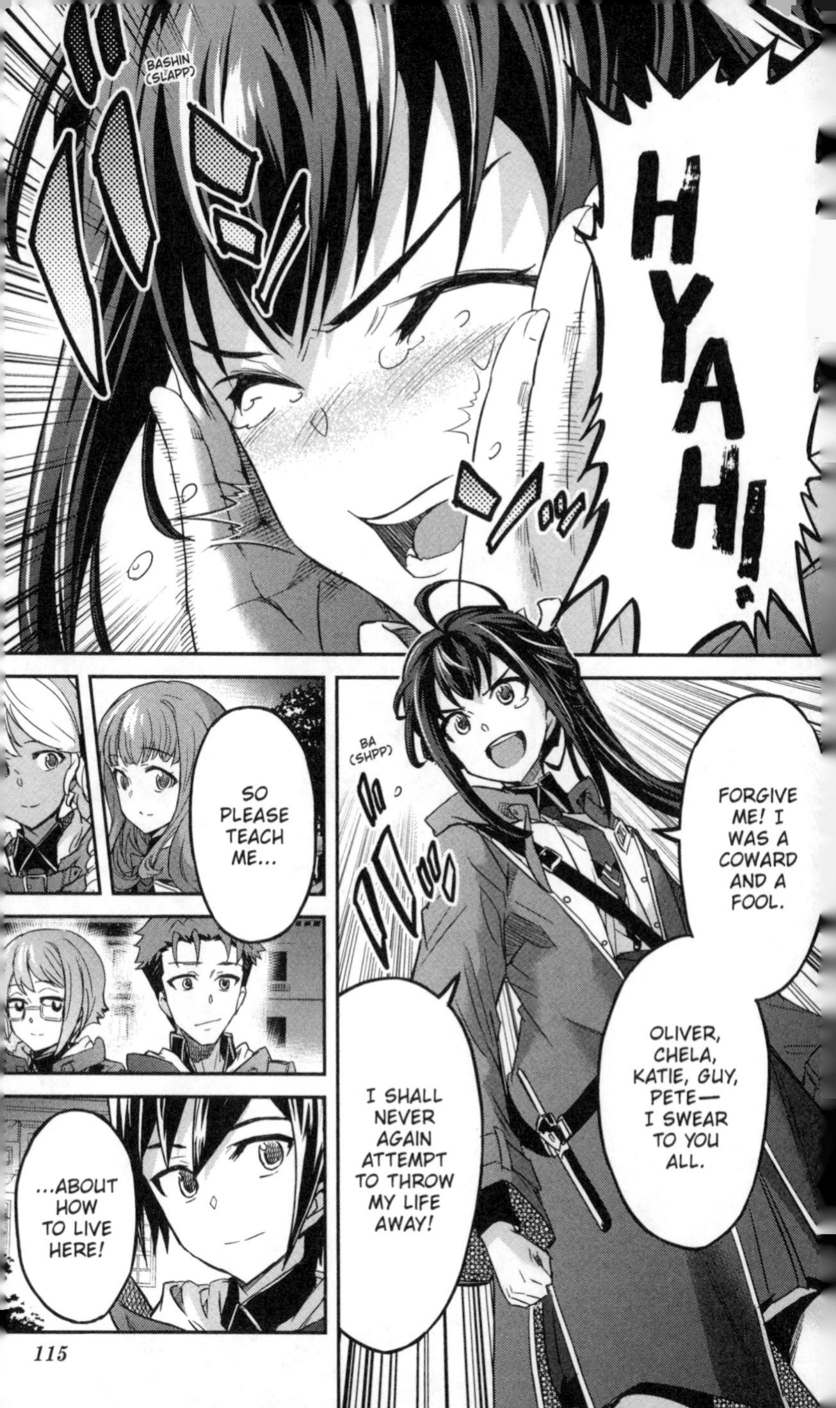
HYAH!
BASHIN (SLAPP)
FORGIVE ME! I WAS A COWARD AND A FOOL.
BA (SHPP)
OLIVER, CHELA, KATIE, GUY, PETE— I SWEAR TO YOU ALL.
I SHALL NEVER AGAIN ATTEMPT TO THROW MY LIFE AWAY!
SO PLEASE TEACH ME...
...ABOUT HOW TO LIVE HERE!

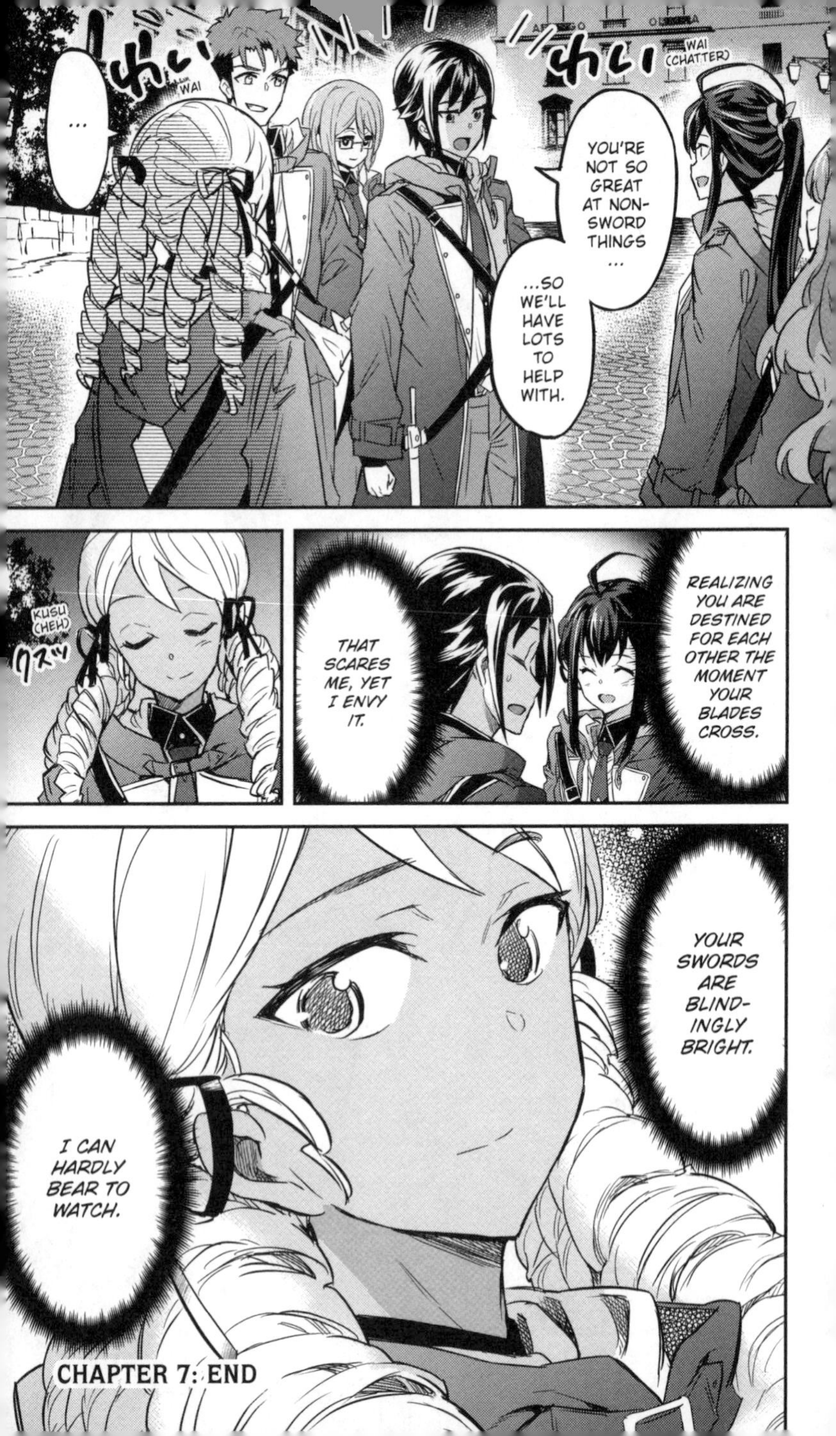
わい
WAI (CHATTER)
YOU'RE NOT SO GREAT AT NON-SWORD THINGS...
...SO WE'LL HAVE LOTS TO HELP WITH.
わい
WAI
...
REALIZING YOU ARE DESTINED FOR EACH OTHER THE MOMENT YOUR BLADES CROSS.
THAT SCARES ME, YET I ENVY IT.
KUSU (HEH)
クスッ
YOUR SWORDS ARE BLINDINGLY BRIGHT.
I CAN HARDLY BEAR TO WATCH.
CHAPTER 7: END

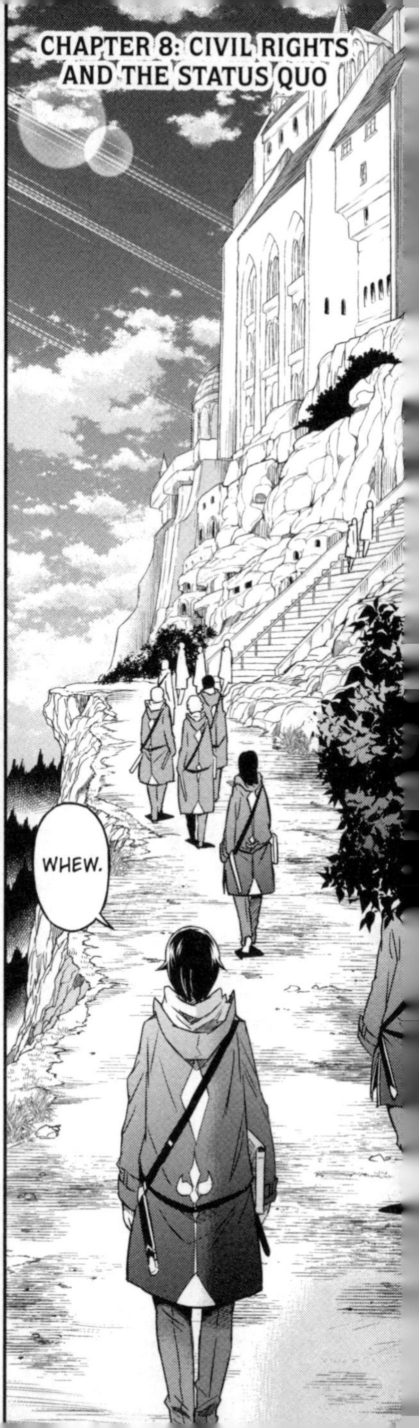
CHAPTER 8: CIVIL RIGHTS AND THE STATUS QUO
WHEW.

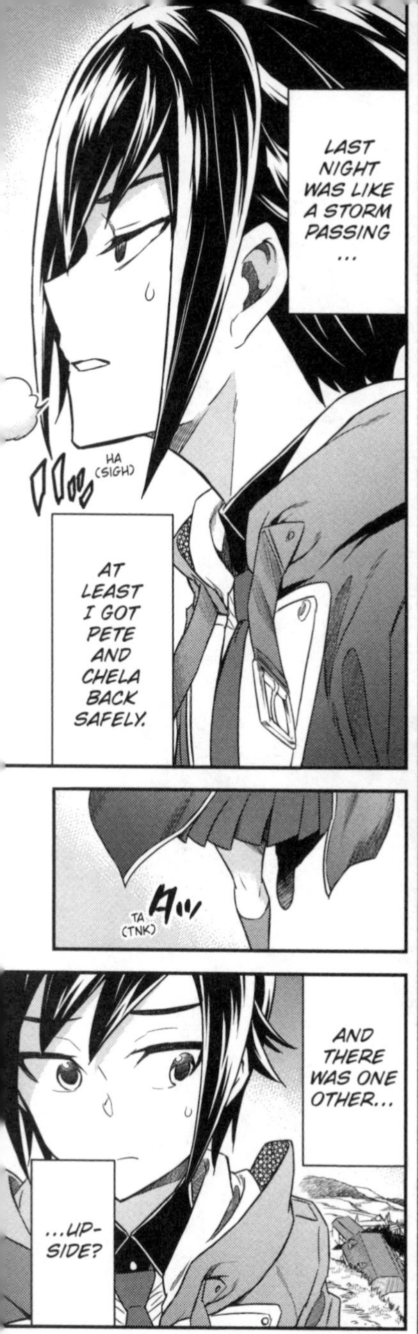
LAST NIGHT WAS LIKE A STORM PASSING ...
HA (SIGH)
AT LEAST I GOT PETE AND CHELA BACK SAFELY.
TA (TNK)
AND THERE WAS ONE OTHER...
...UP-SIDE?

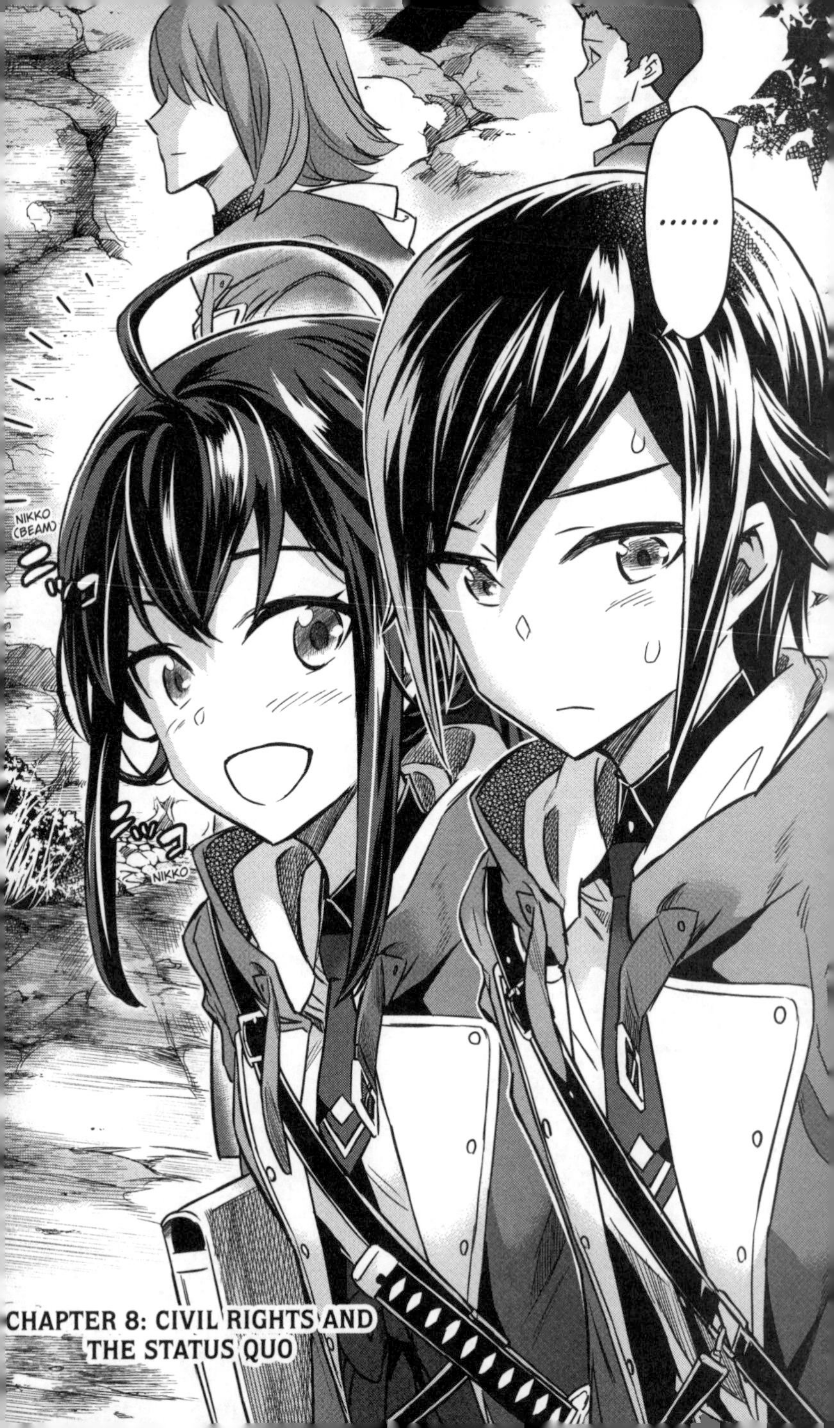
......
NIKKO (BEAM)
NIKKO

CHAPTER 8: CIVIL RIGHTS AND THE STATUS QUO

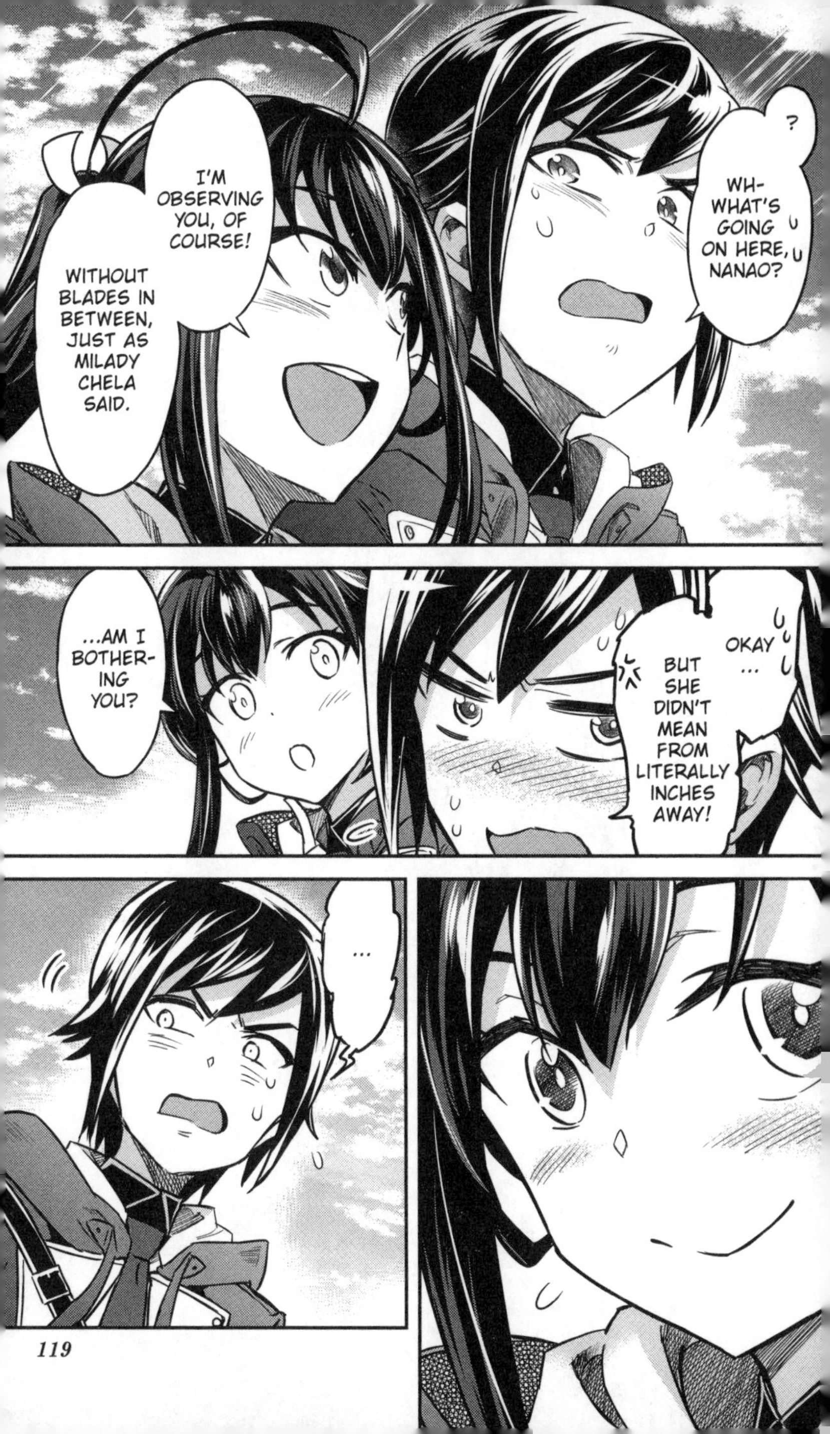
?
WH- WHAT'S GOING ON HERE, NANAO?
I'M OBSERVING YOU, OF COURSE!
WITHOUT BLADES IN BETWEEN, JUST AS MILADY CHELA SAID.
OKAY...
BUT SHE DIDN'T MEAN FROM LITERALLY INCHES AWAY!
...AM I BOTHER-ING YOU?
...

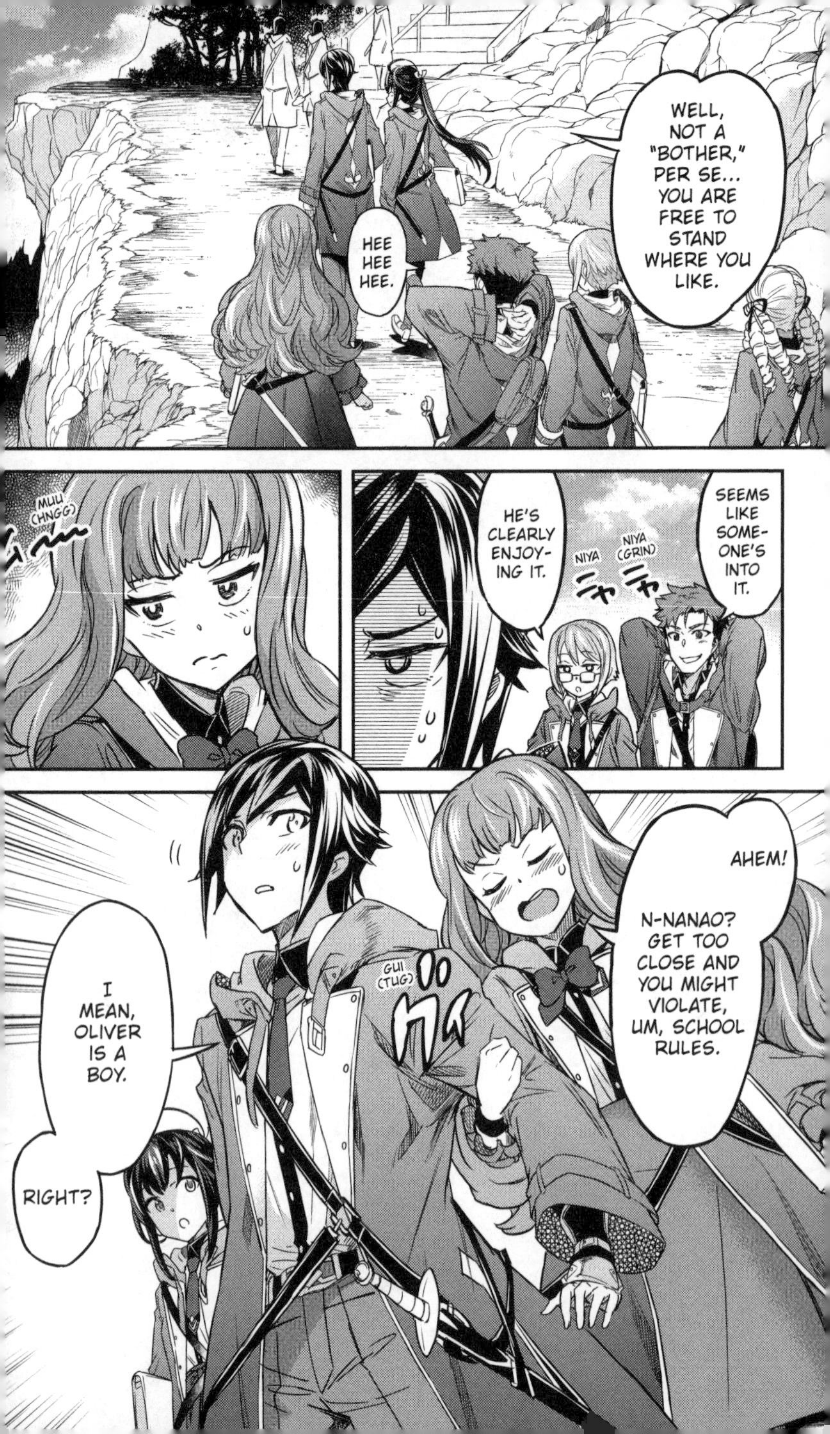
WELL, NOT A "BOTHER," PER SE... YOU ARE FREE TO STAND WHERE YOU LIKE.
HEE HEE HEE.
SEEMS LIKE SOME-ONE'S INTO IT.
NIYA (GRIN)
NIYA
HE'S CLEARLY ENJOY-ING IT.
MUU (HNGG)
AHEM!
N-NANAO? GET TOO CLOSE AND YOU MIGHT VIOLATE, UM, SCHOOL RULES.
GUI (TUG)
I MEAN, OLIVER IS A BOY.
RIGHT?

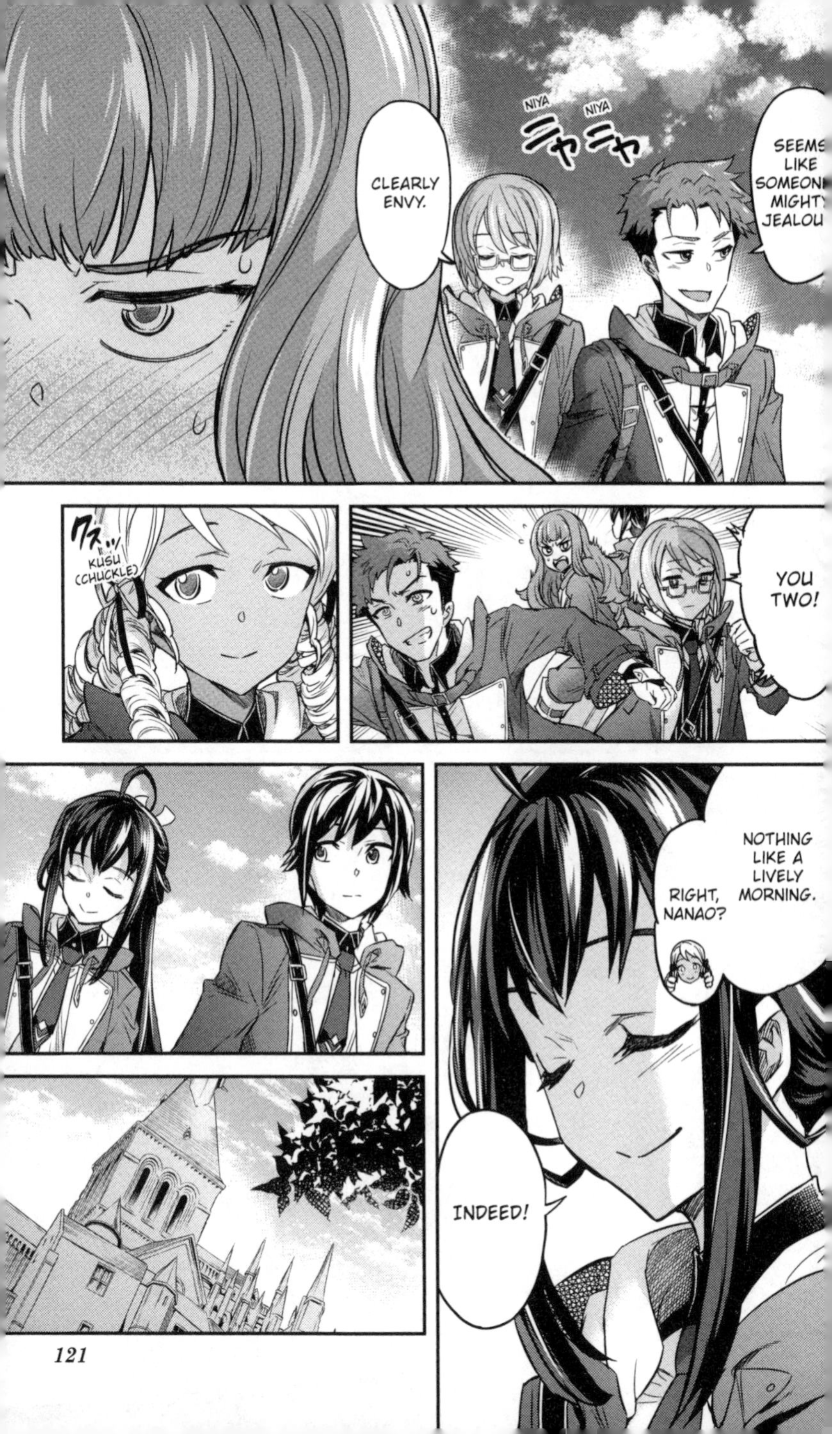
SEEMS LIKE SOMEON MIGHTY JEALOU
NIYA NIYA
ニヤニヤ
CLEARLY ENVY.
YOU TWO!
KUSU (CHUCKLE)
NOTHING LIKE A LIVELY MORNING.
RIGHT, NANAO?
INDEED!

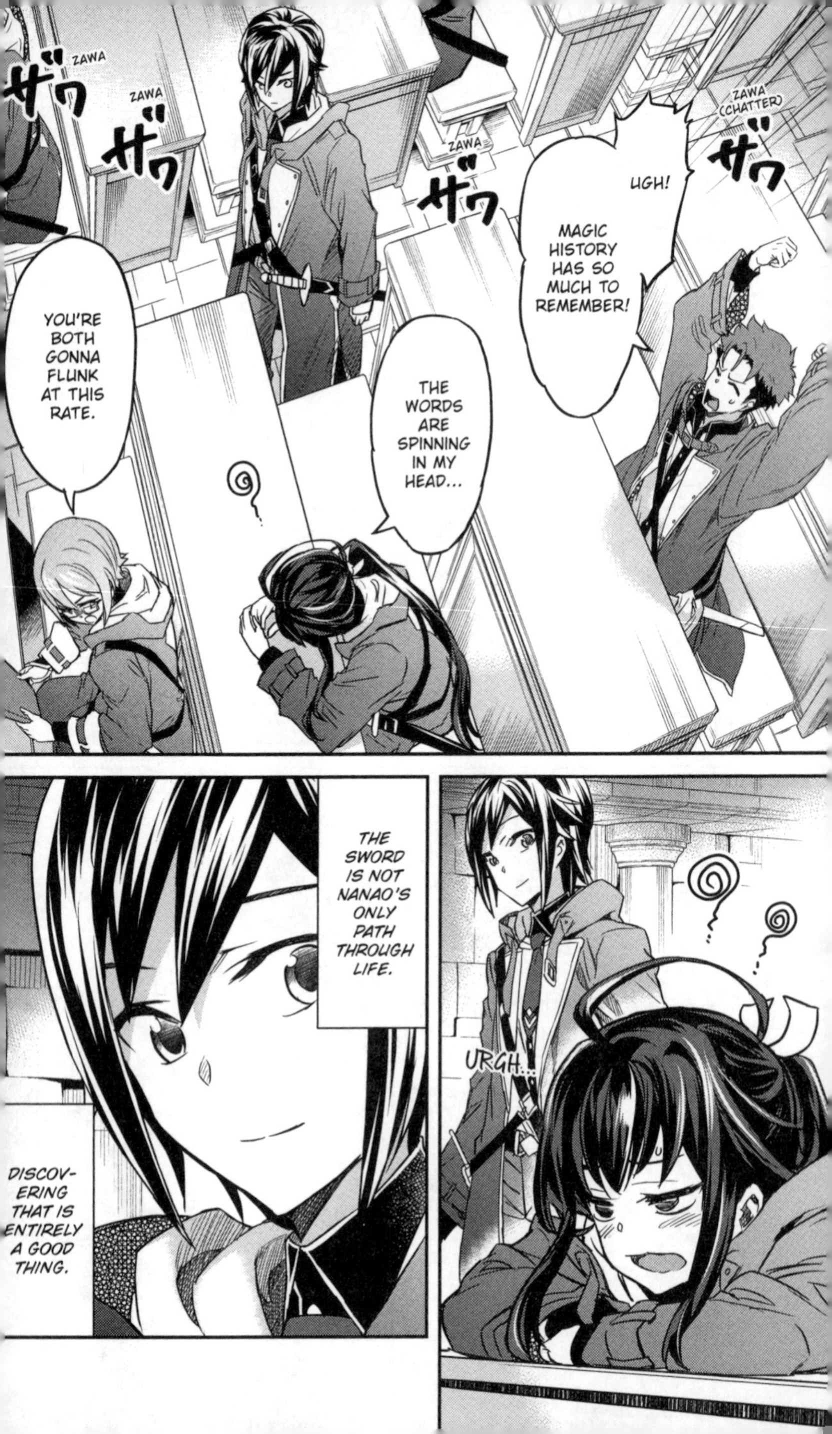
ZAWA (CHATTER)
ザワ
UGH!
MAGIC HISTORY HAS SO MUCH TO REMEMBER!
ZAWA
ザワ
ZAWA
ザワ
ZAWA
ザワ
THE WORDS ARE SPINNING IN MY HEAD...
YOU'RE BOTH GONNA FLUNK AT THIS RATE.
URGH...
THE SWORD IS NOT NANAO'S ONLY PATH THROUGH LIFE.
DISCOV-ERING THAT IS ENTIRELY A GOOD THING.

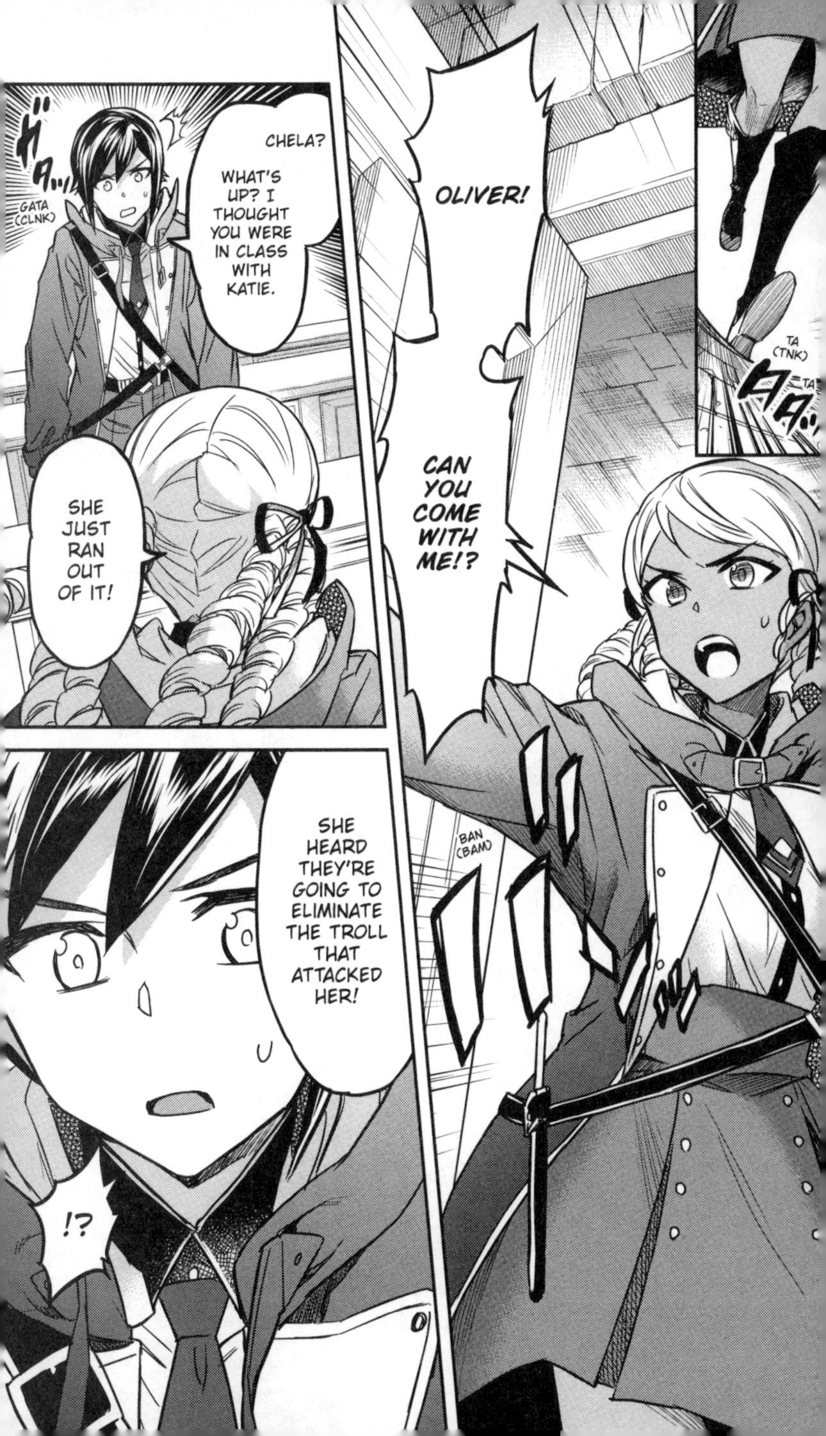
TA (TNK)
TA
OLIVER!
CAN YOU COME WITH ME!?
BAN (BAM)
GATA (CLNK)
CHELA?
WHAT'S UP? I THOUGHT YOU WERE IN CLASS WITH KATIE.
SHE JUST RAN OUT OF IT!
SHE HEARD THEY'RE GOING TO ELIMINATE THE TROLL THAT ATTACKED HER!
!?

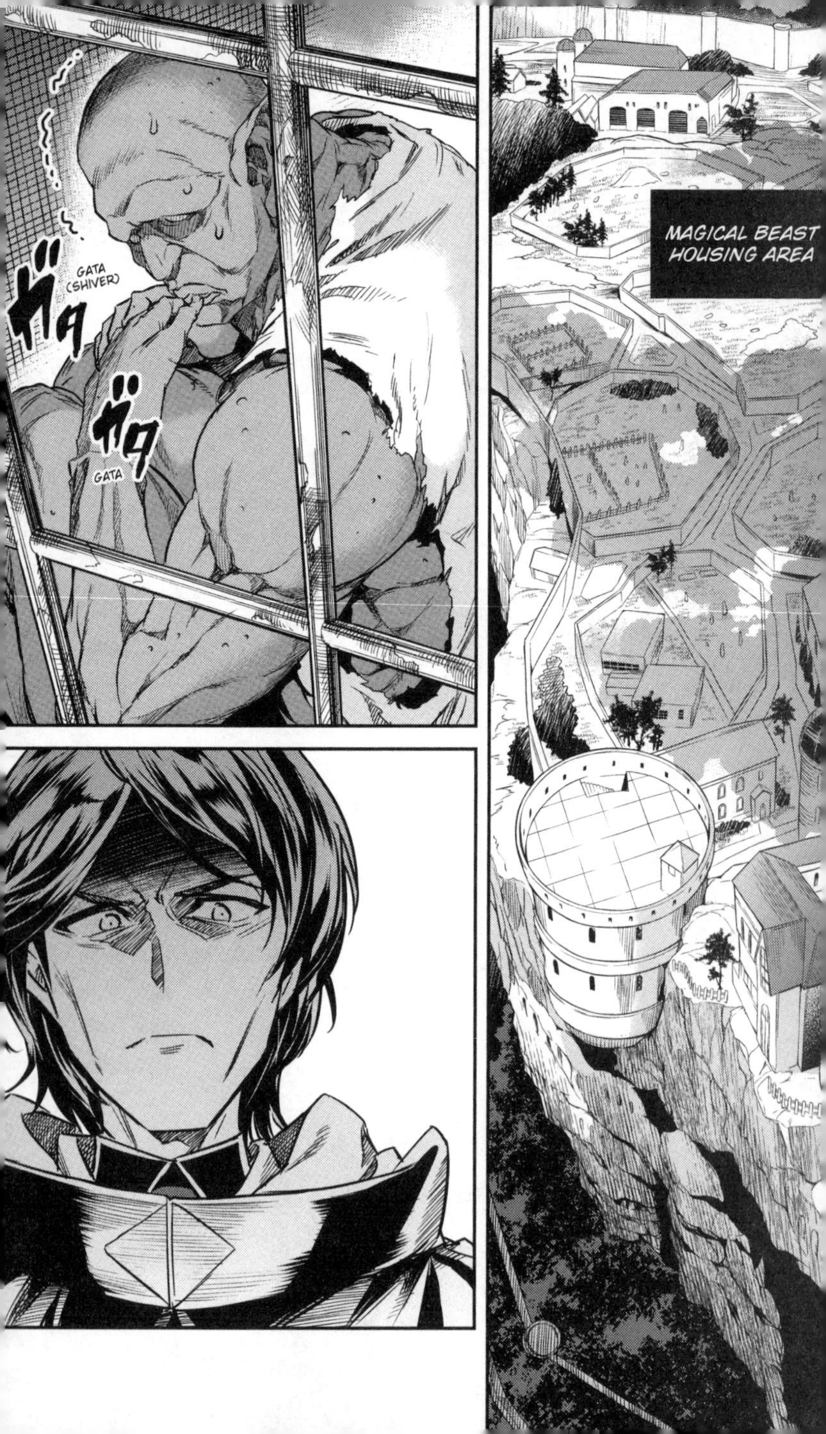
MAGICAL BEAST HOUSING AREA
ガタ
GATA (SHIVER)
ガタ
GATA

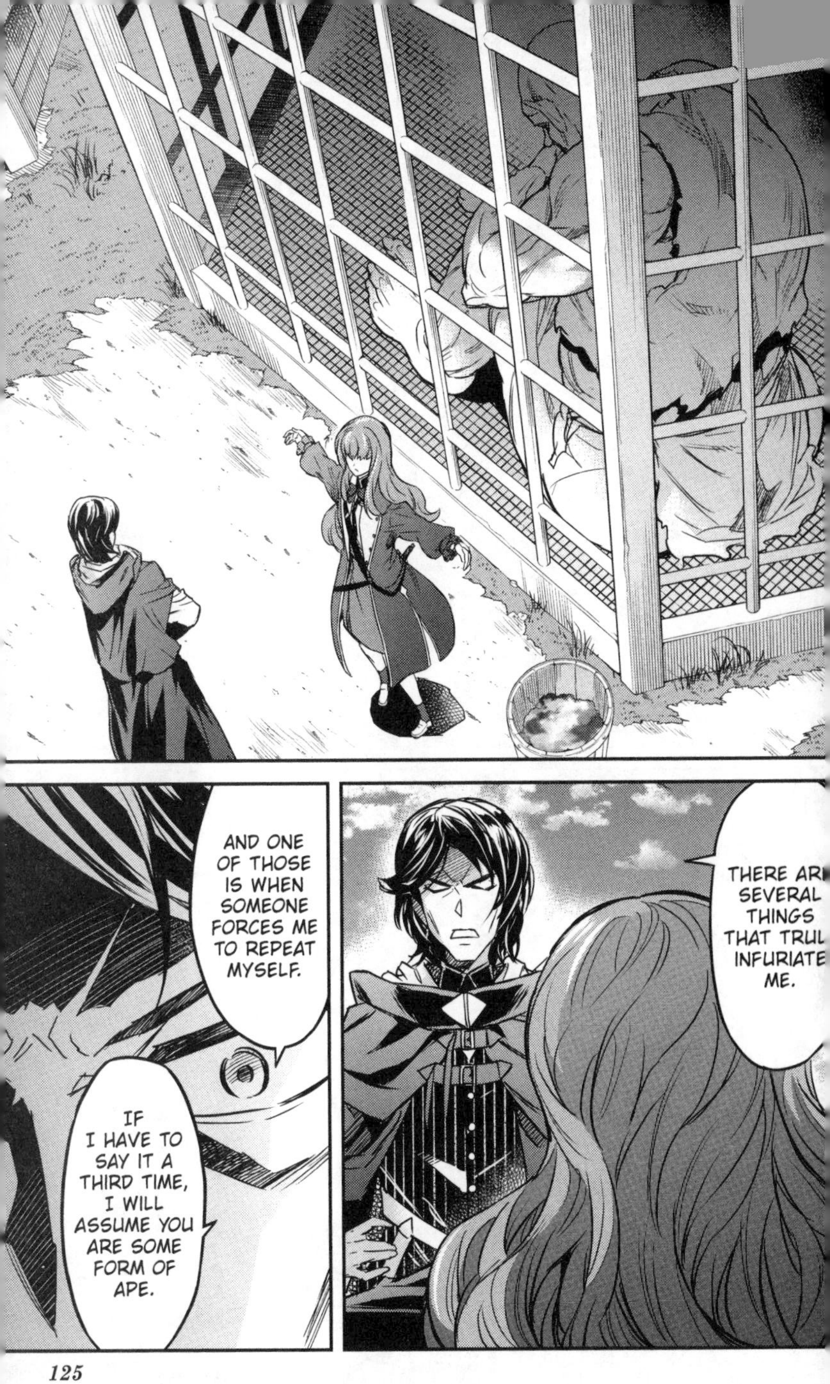
THERE AR SEVERAL THINGS THAT TRUL INFURIATE ME.
AND ONE OF THOSE IS WHEN SOMEONE FORCES ME TO REPEAT MYSELF.
IF I HAVE TO SAY IT A THIRD TIME, I WILL ASSUME YOU ARE SOME FORM OF APE.

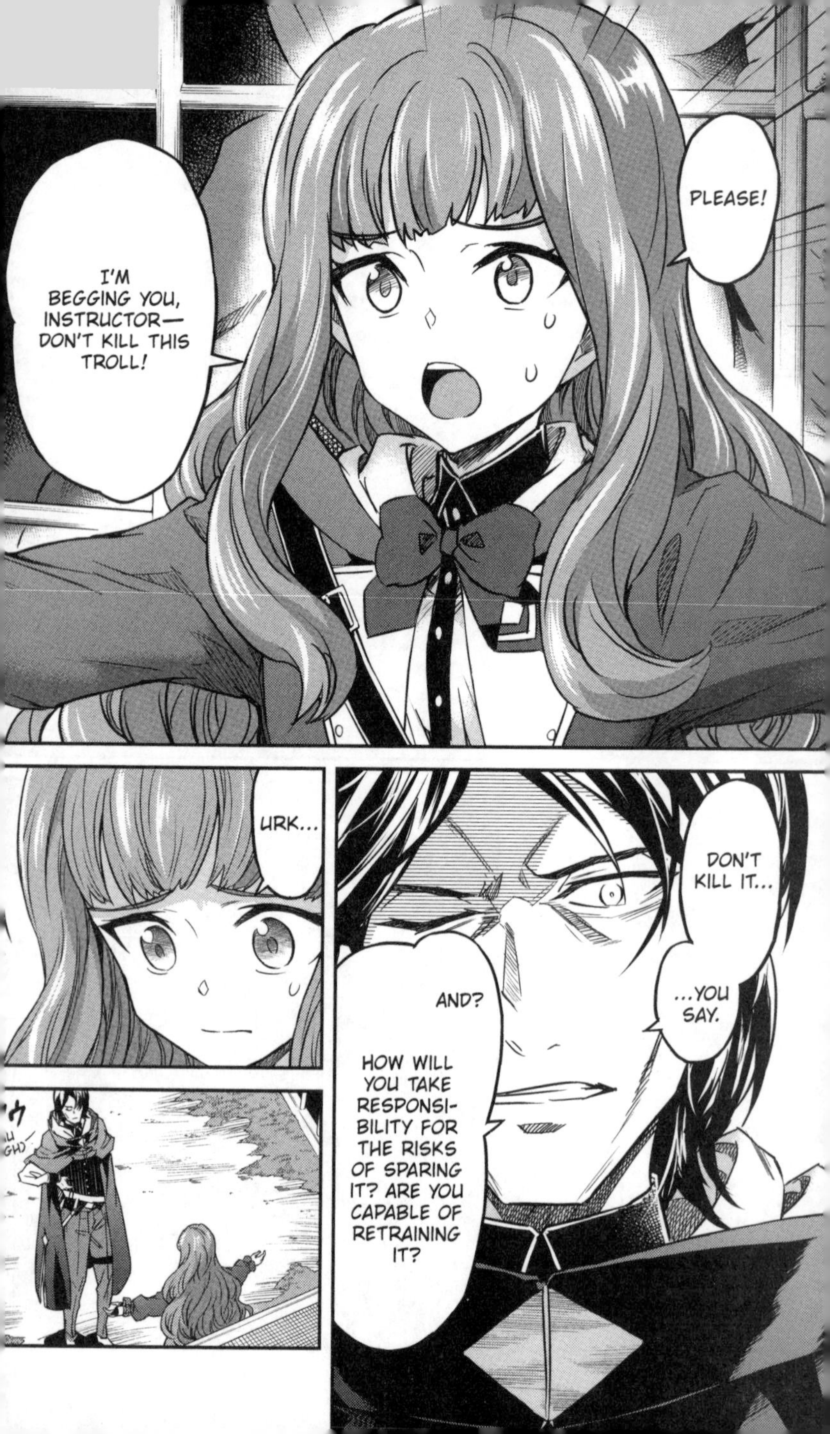
PLEASE!
I'M BEGGING YOU, INSTRUCTOR—DON'T KILL THIS TROLL!
DON'T KILL IT...
...YOU SAY.
AND?
HOW WILL YOU TAKE RESPONSI-BILITY FOR THE RISKS OF SPARING IT? ARE YOU CAPABLE OF RETRAINING IT?
URK...

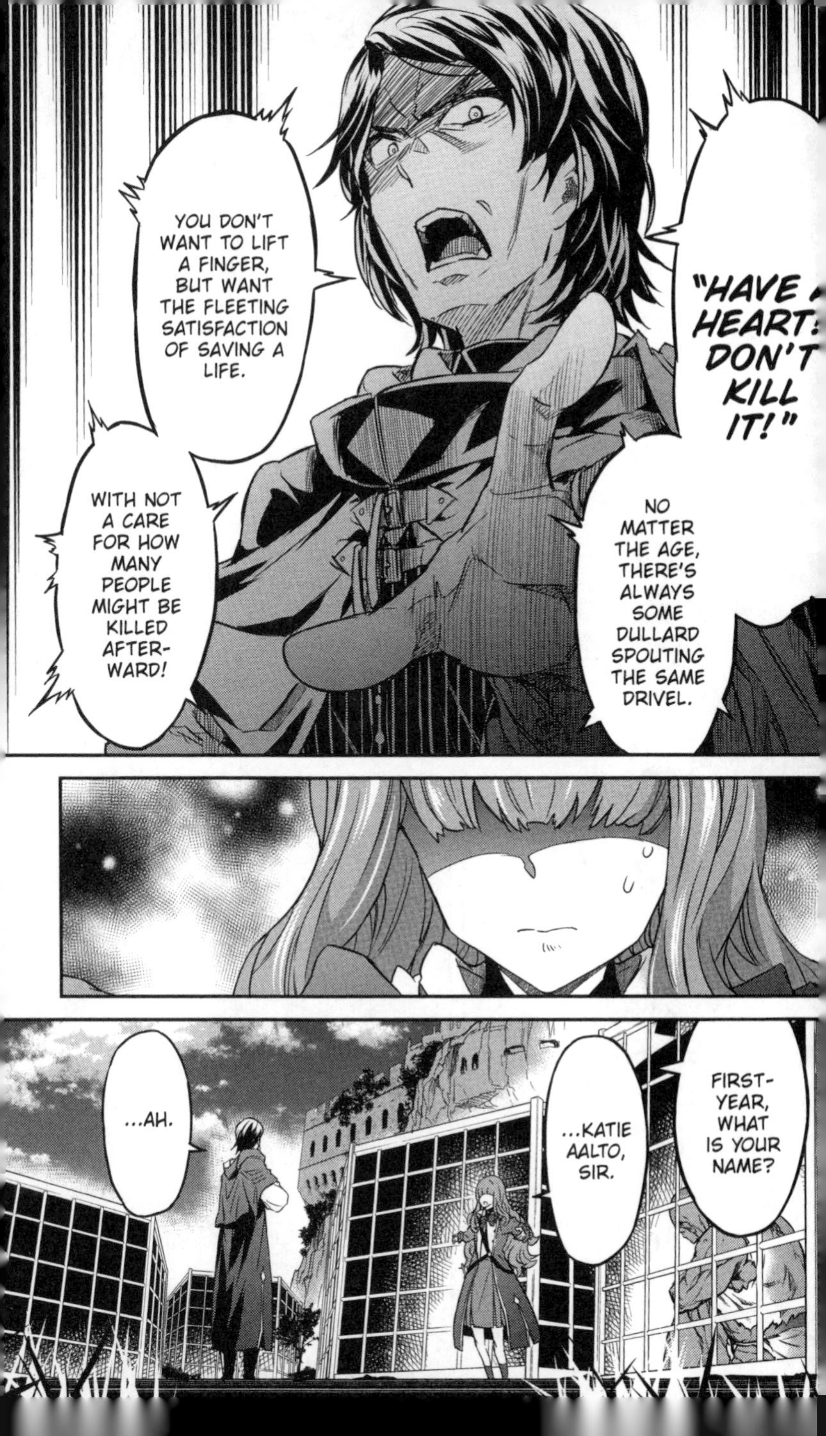
"HAVE A HEART! DON'T KILL IT!"
NO MATTER THE AGE, THERE'S ALWAYS SOME DULLARD SPOUTING THE SAME DRIVEL.
YOU DON'T WANT TO LIFT A FINGER, BUT WANT THE FLEETING SATISFACTION OF SAVING A LIFE.
WITH NOT A CARE FOR HOW MANY PEOPLE MIGHT BE KILLED AFTER-WARD!
FIRST-YEAR, WHAT IS YOUR NAME?
...KATIE AALTO, SIR.
...AH.

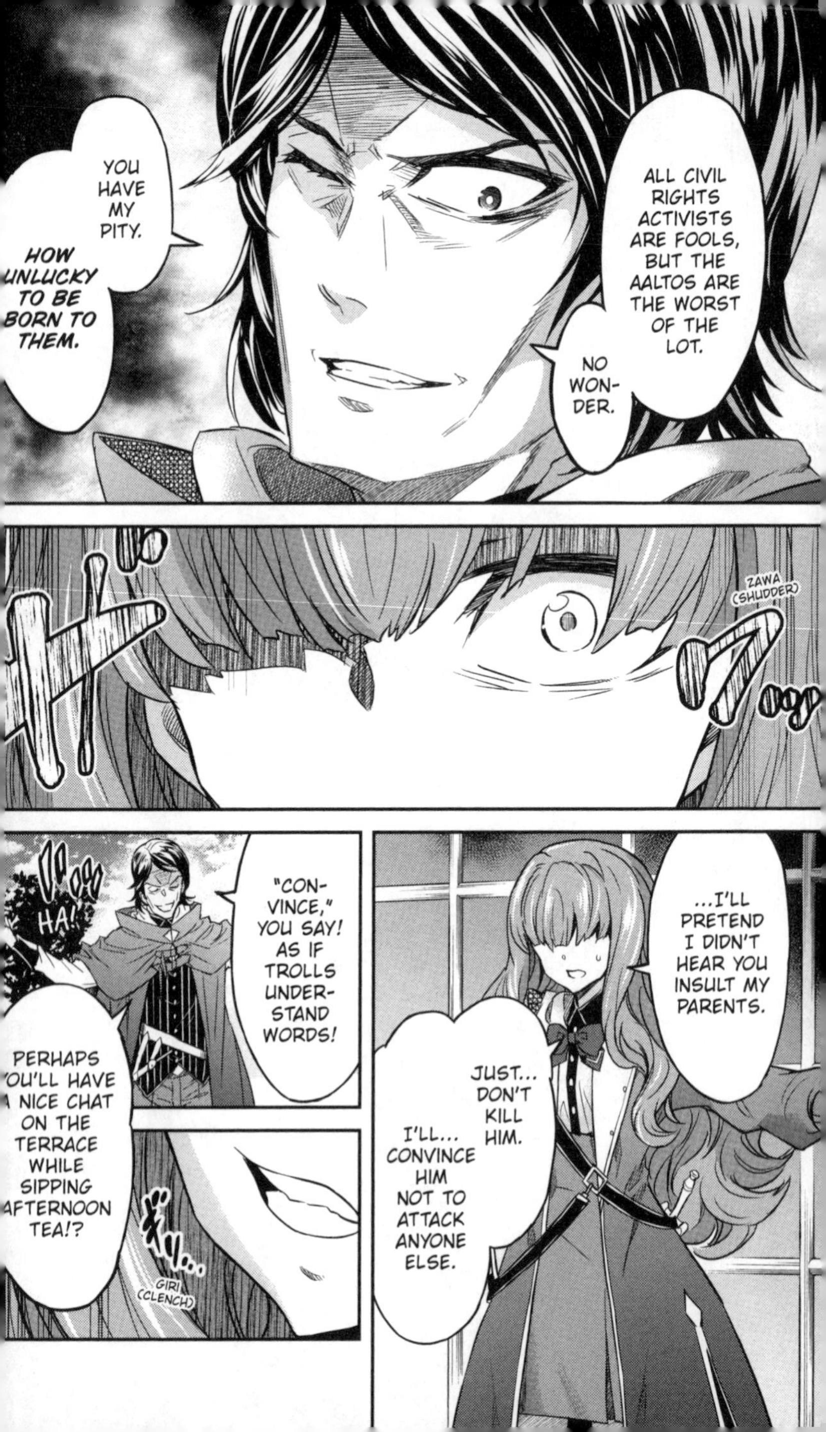
ALL CIVIL RIGHTS ACTIVISTS ARE FOOLS, BUT THE AALTOS ARE THE WORST OF THE LOT.
NO WONDER.
YOU HAVE MY PITY.
HOW UNLUCKY TO BE BORN TO THEM.
ZAWA (SHUDDER)
...I'LL PRETEND I DIDN'T HEAR YOU INSULT MY PARENTS.
JUST... DON'T KILL HIM.
I'LL... CONVINCE HIM NOT TO ATTACK ANYONE ELSE.
HA!
"CON-VINCE," YOU SAY! AS IF TROLLS UNDER-STAND WORDS!
PERHAPS YOU'LL HAVE NICE CHAT ON THE TERRACE WHILE SIPPING AFTERNOON TEA!?
GIRI (CLENCH)

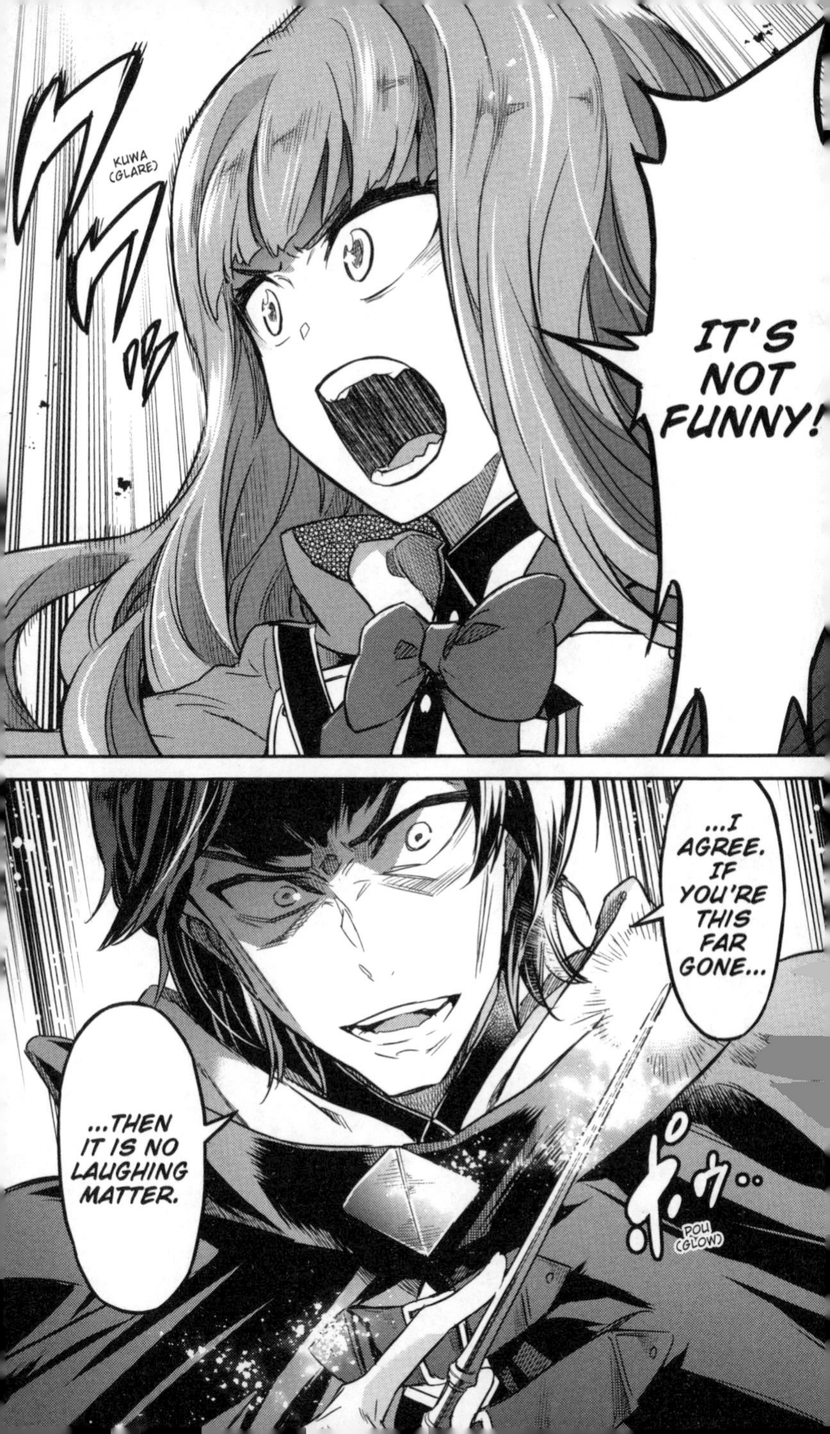
KUWA (GLARE)
IT'S NOT FUNNY!
...I AGREE. IF YOU'RE THIS FAR GONE...
...THEN IT IS NO LAUGHING MATTER.
POU (GLOW)

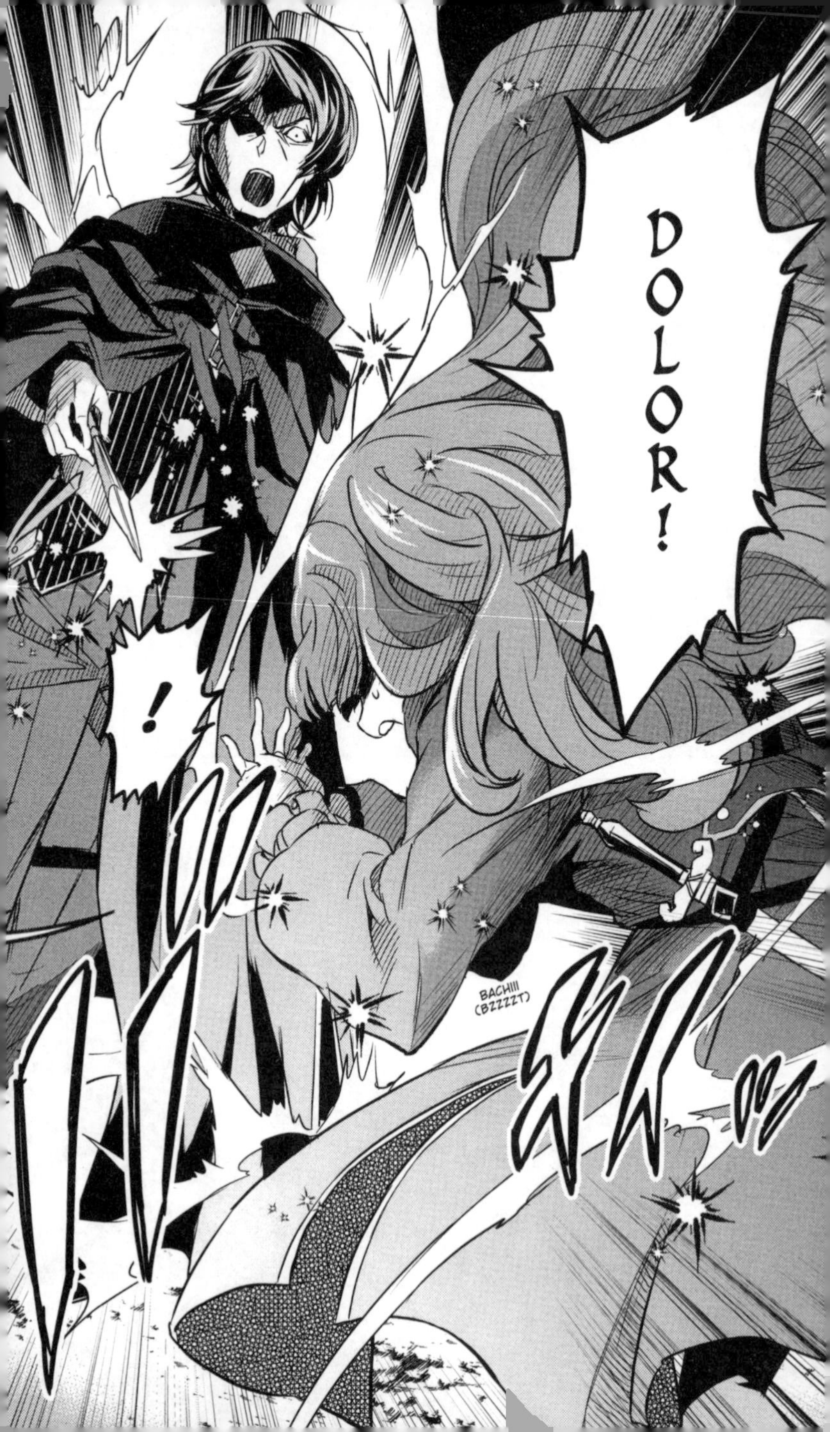
DOLOR!
!
BACHIII
(BZZZZT)

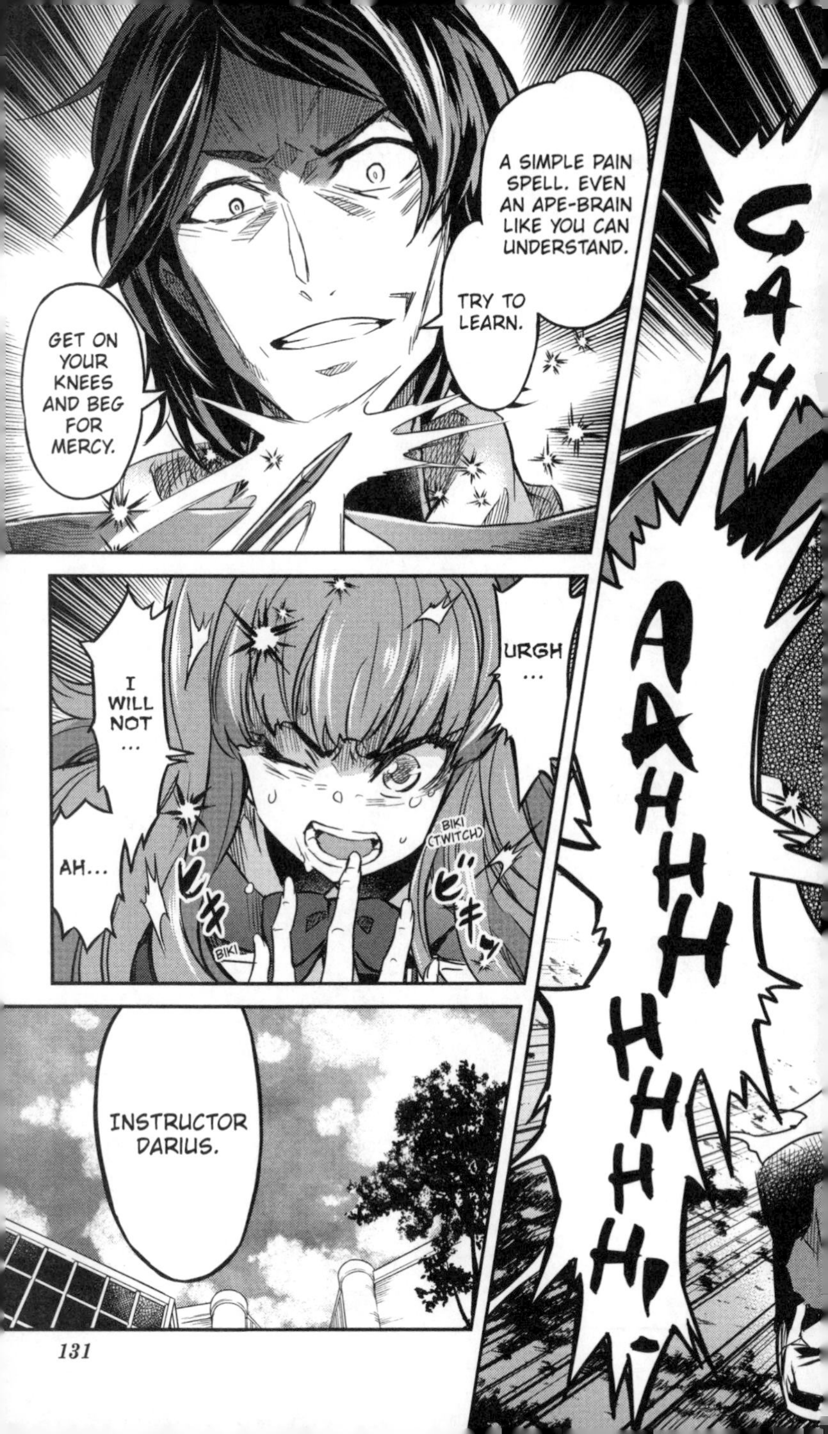

GAH
AAHHHHHHH!!
A SIMPLE PAIN SPELL. EVEN AN APE-BRAIN LIKE YOU CAN UNDERSTAND.
TRY TO LEARN.
GET ON YOUR KNEES AND BEG FOR MERCY.
URGH...
I WILL NOT...
BIKI (TWITCH)
ビキッ
ビキ
BIKI
AH...
INSTRUCTOR DARIUS.

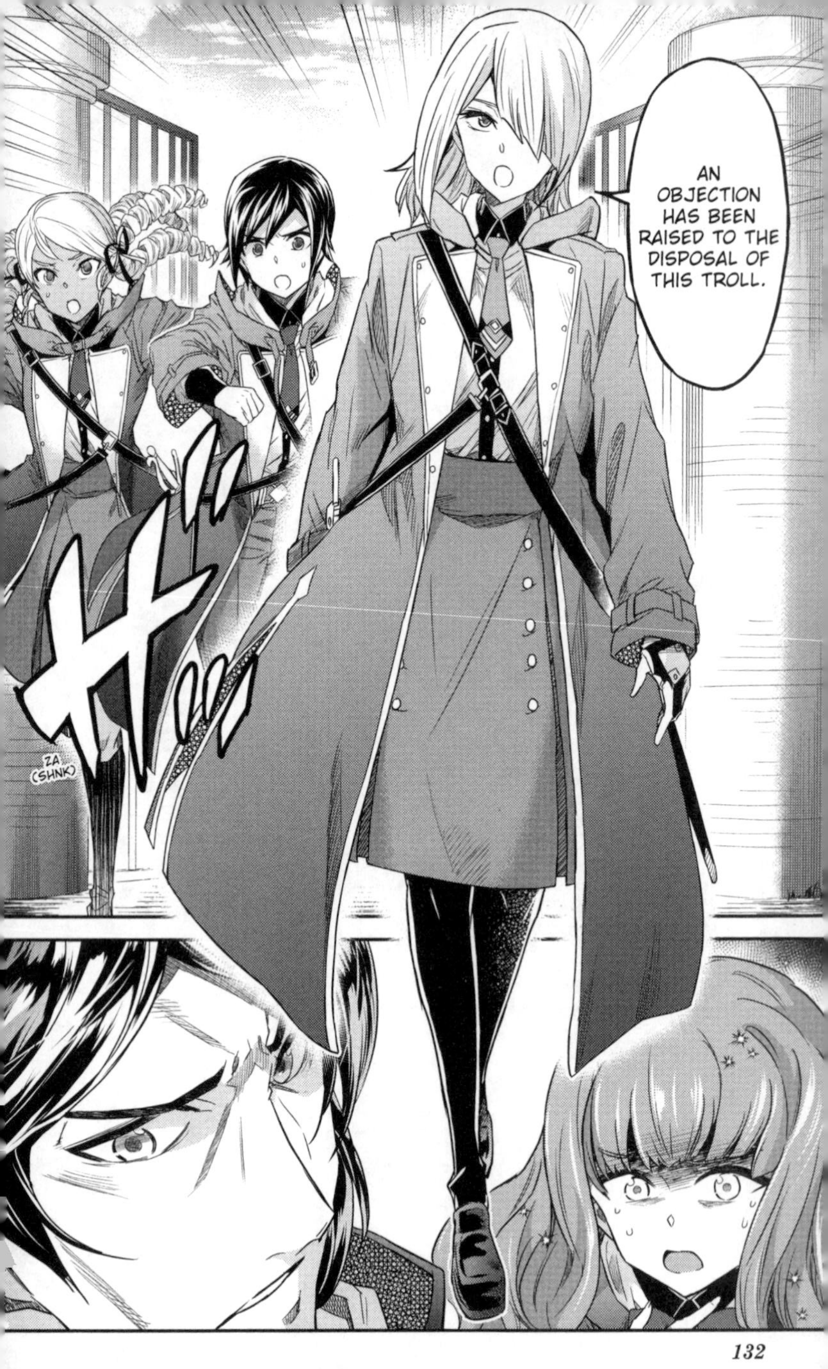
AN OBJECTION HAS BEEN RAISED TO THE DISPOSAL OF THIS TROLL.
ZA (SHNK)

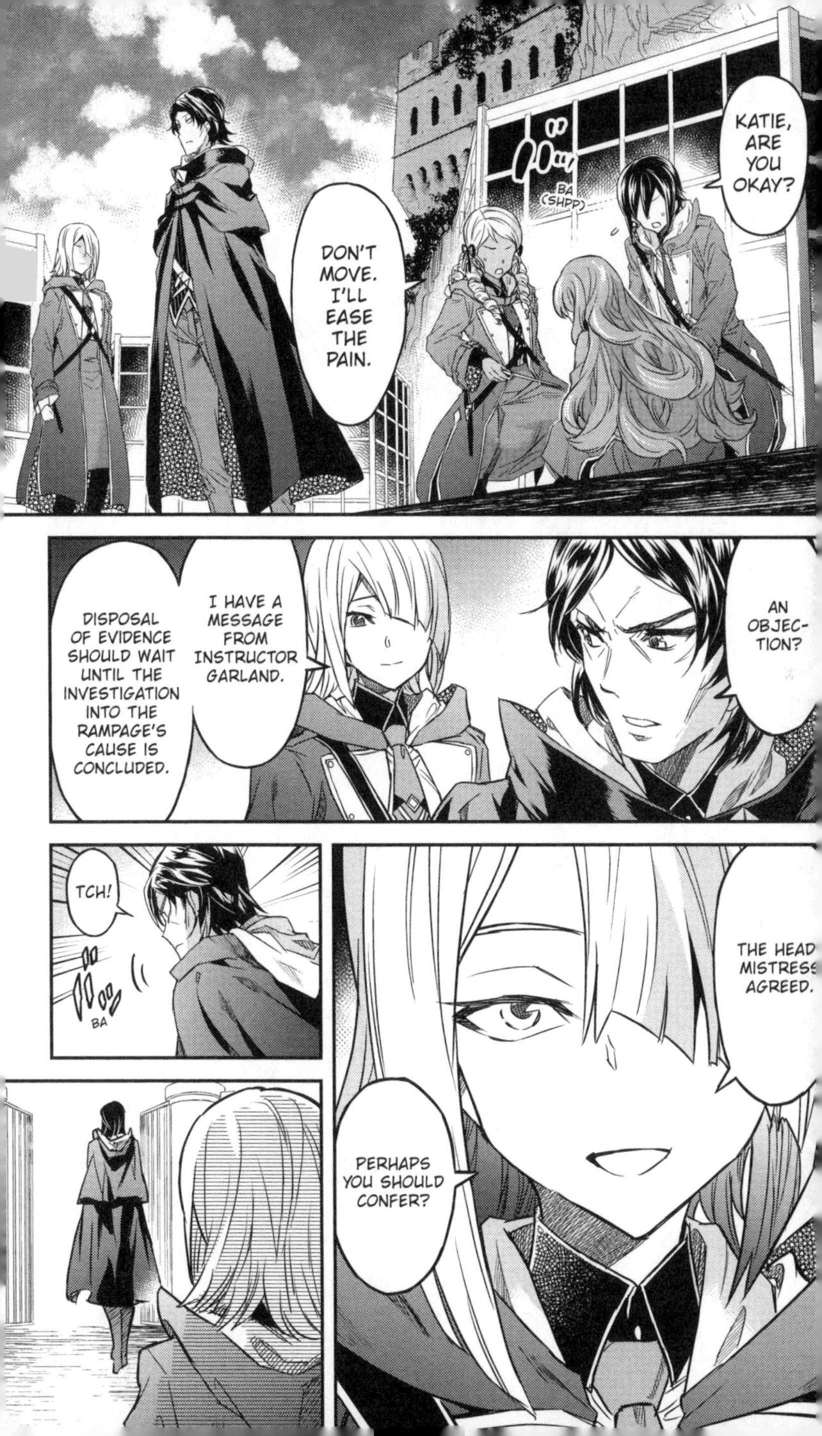
KATIE, ARE YOU OKAY?
BA (SHPP)
DON'T MOVE. I'LL EASE THE PAIN.
AN OBJECTION?
I HAVE A MESSAGE FROM INSTRUCTOR GARLAND.
DISPOSAL OF EVIDENCE SHOULD WAIT UNTIL THE INVESTIGATION INTO THE RAMPAGE'S CAUSE IS CONCLUDED.
THE HEADMISTRESS AGREED.
PERHAPS YOU SHOULD CONFER?
TCH!
BA

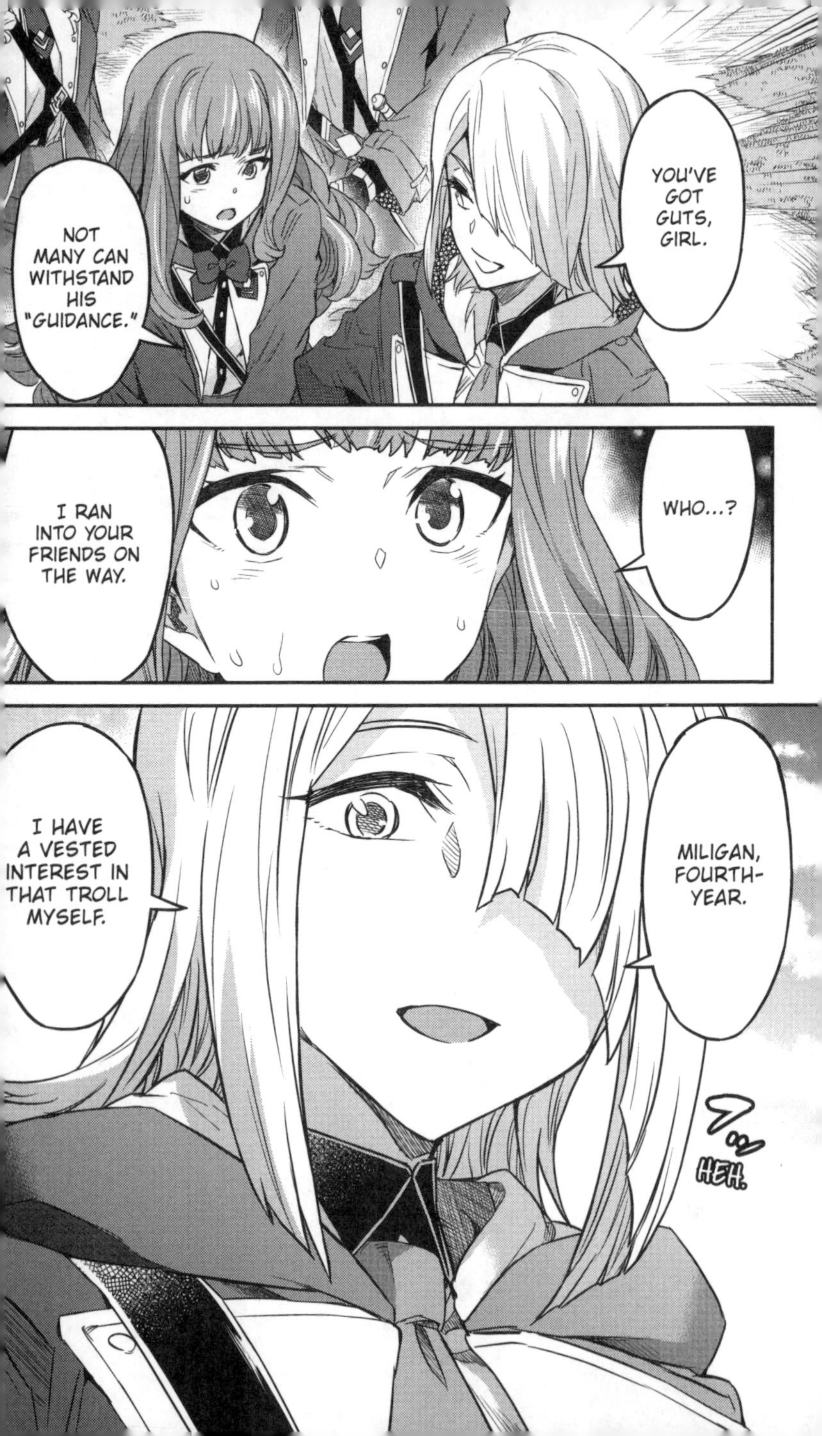
YOU'VE GOT GUTS, GIRL.
NOT MANY CAN WITHSTAND HIS "GUIDANCE."
WHO...?
I RAN INTO YOUR FRIENDS ON THE WAY.
MILIGAN, FOURTH-YEAR.
I HAVE A VESTED INTEREST IN THAT TROLL MYSELF.
HEH.

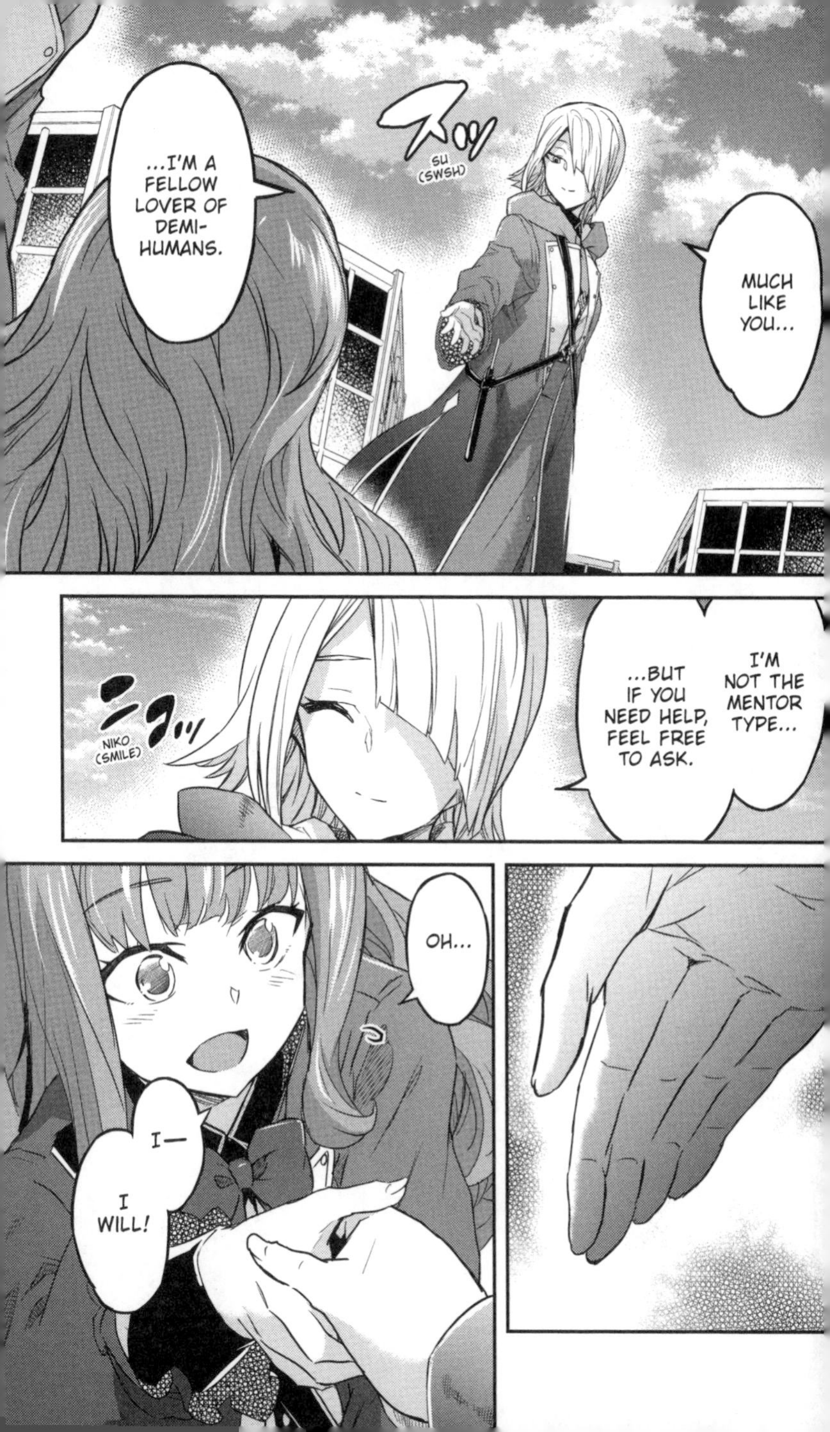
SU (SWSH)
MUCH LIKE YOU…
…I'M A FELLOW LOVER OF DEMI-HUMANS.
I'M NOT THE MENTOR TYPE…
…BUT IF YOU NEED HELP, FEEL FREE TO ASK.
NIKO (SMILE)
OH…
I—
I WILL!

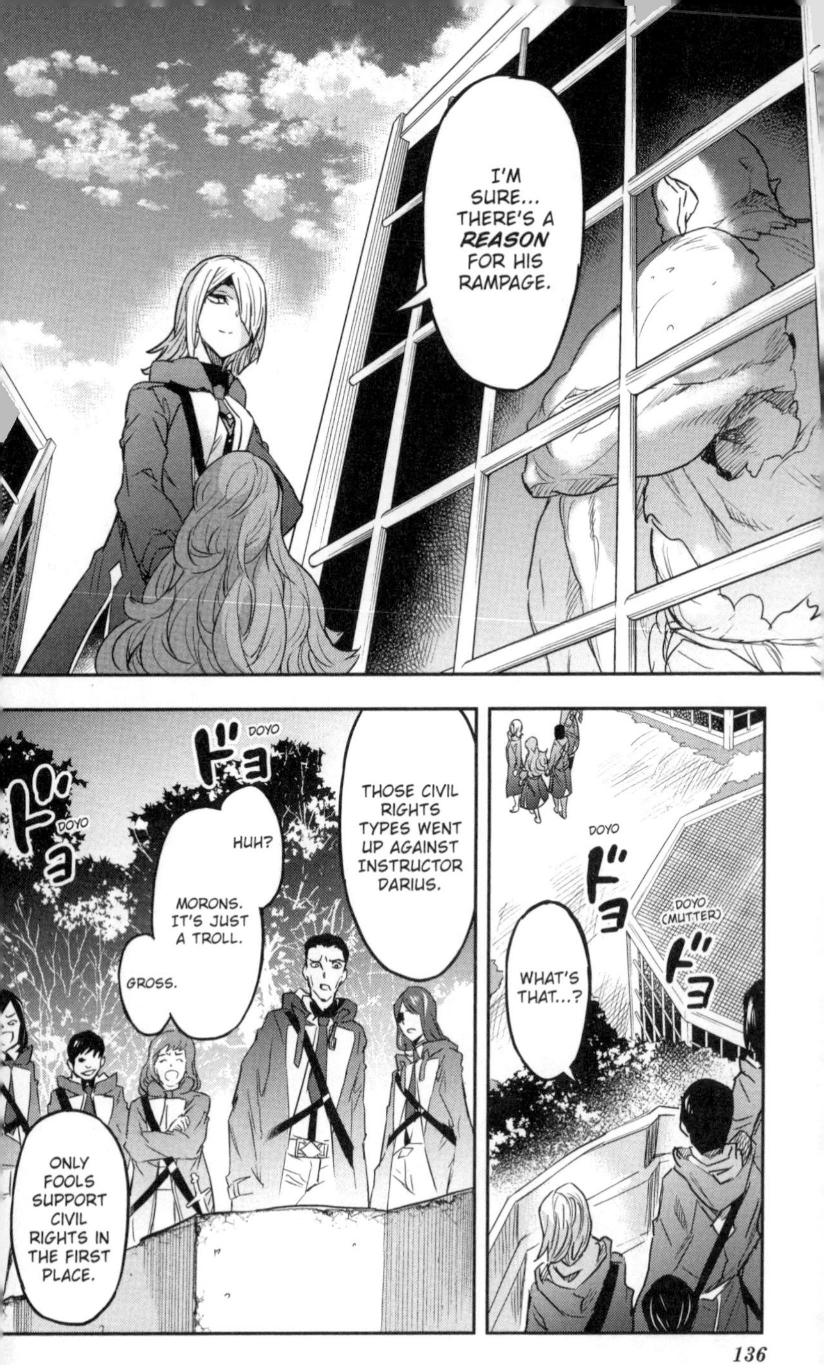
I'M SURE... THERE'S A REASON FOR HIS RAMPAGE.
DOYO
ドヨ
DOYO (MUTTER)
ドヨ
WHAT'S THAT...?
THOSE CIVIL RIGHTS TYPES WENT UP AGAINST INSTRUCTOR DARIUS.
DOYO
ドヨ
DOYO
ドヨ
HUH?
MORONS. IT'S JUST A TROLL.
GROSS.
ONLY FOOLS SUPPORT CIVIL RIGHTS IN THE FIRST PLACE.

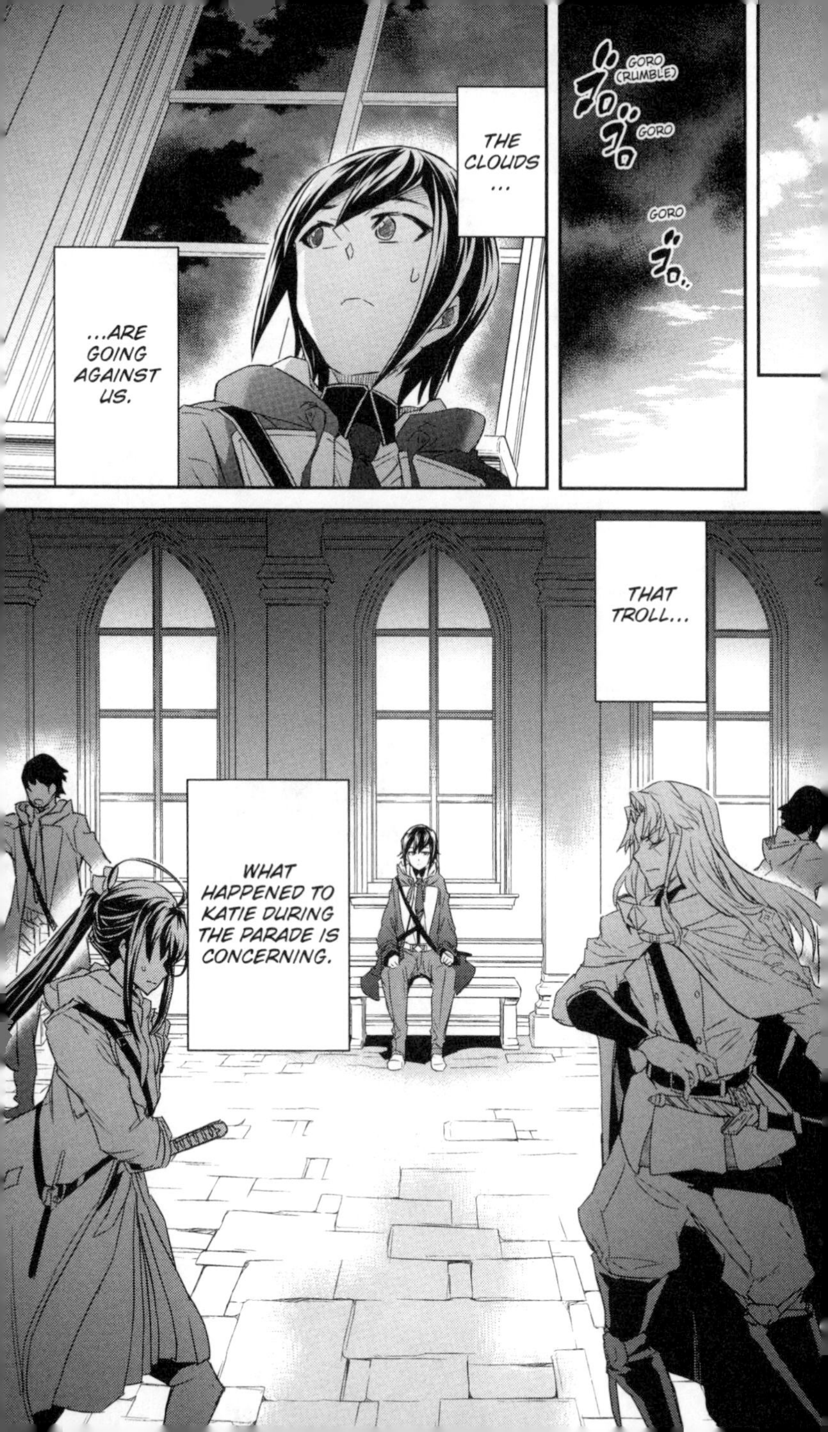
GORO (RUMBLE)
ゴロゴロ
GORO
GORO
ゴロ..
THE CLOUDS ...
...ARE GOING AGAINST US.
THAT TROLL...
WHAT HAPPENED TO KATIE DURING THE PARADE IS CONCERNING.

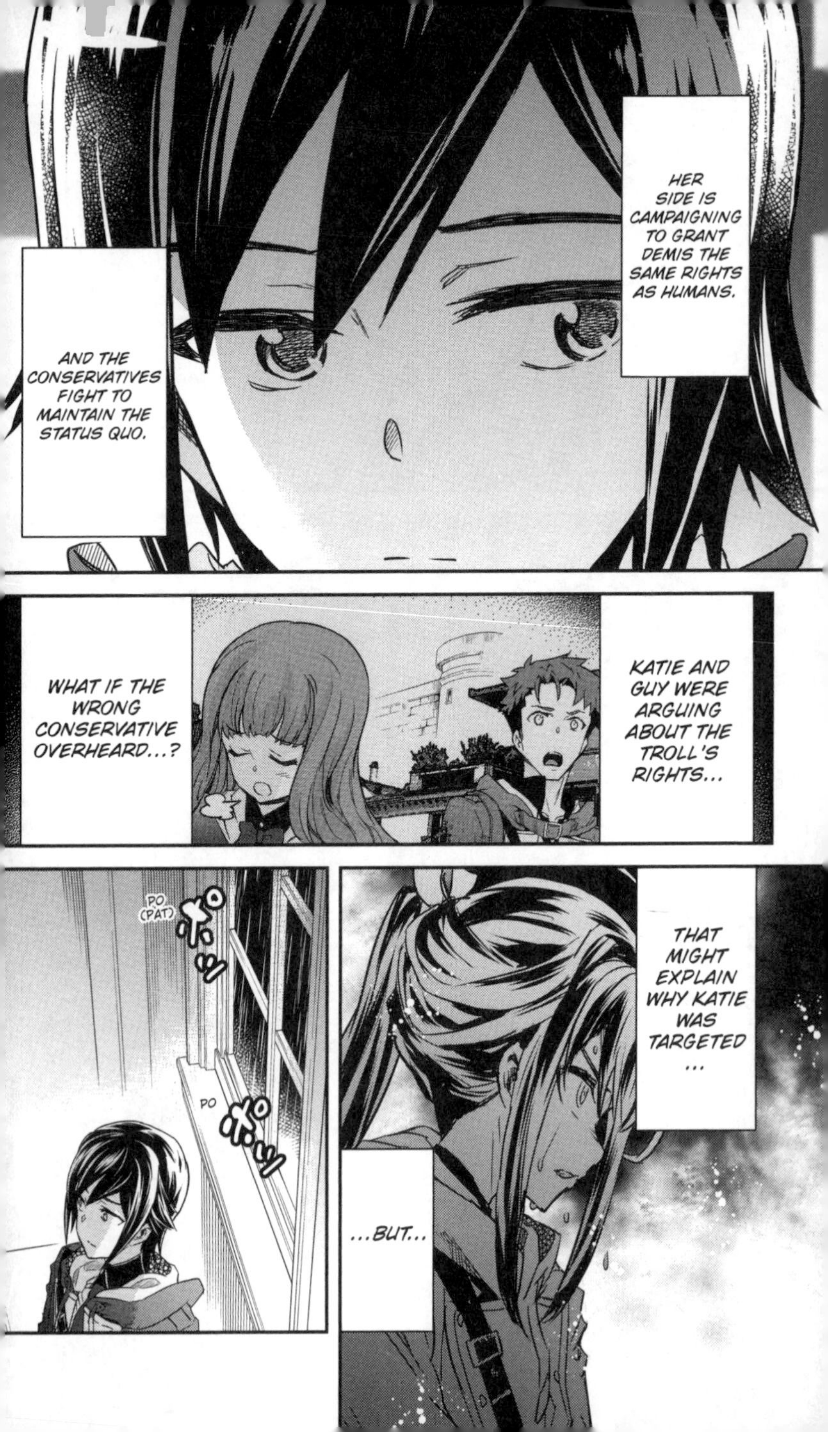
HER SIDE IS CAMPAIGNING TO GRANT DEMIS THE SAME RIGHTS AS HUMANS.
AND THE CONSERVATIVES FIGHT TO MAINTAIN THE STATUS QUO.
KATIE AND GUY WERE ARGUING ABOUT THE TROLL'S RIGHTS...
WHAT IF THE WRONG CONSERVATIVE OVERHEARD...?
THAT MIGHT EXPLAIN WHY KATIE WAS TARGETED ...
...BUT...
PO (PAT)
PO

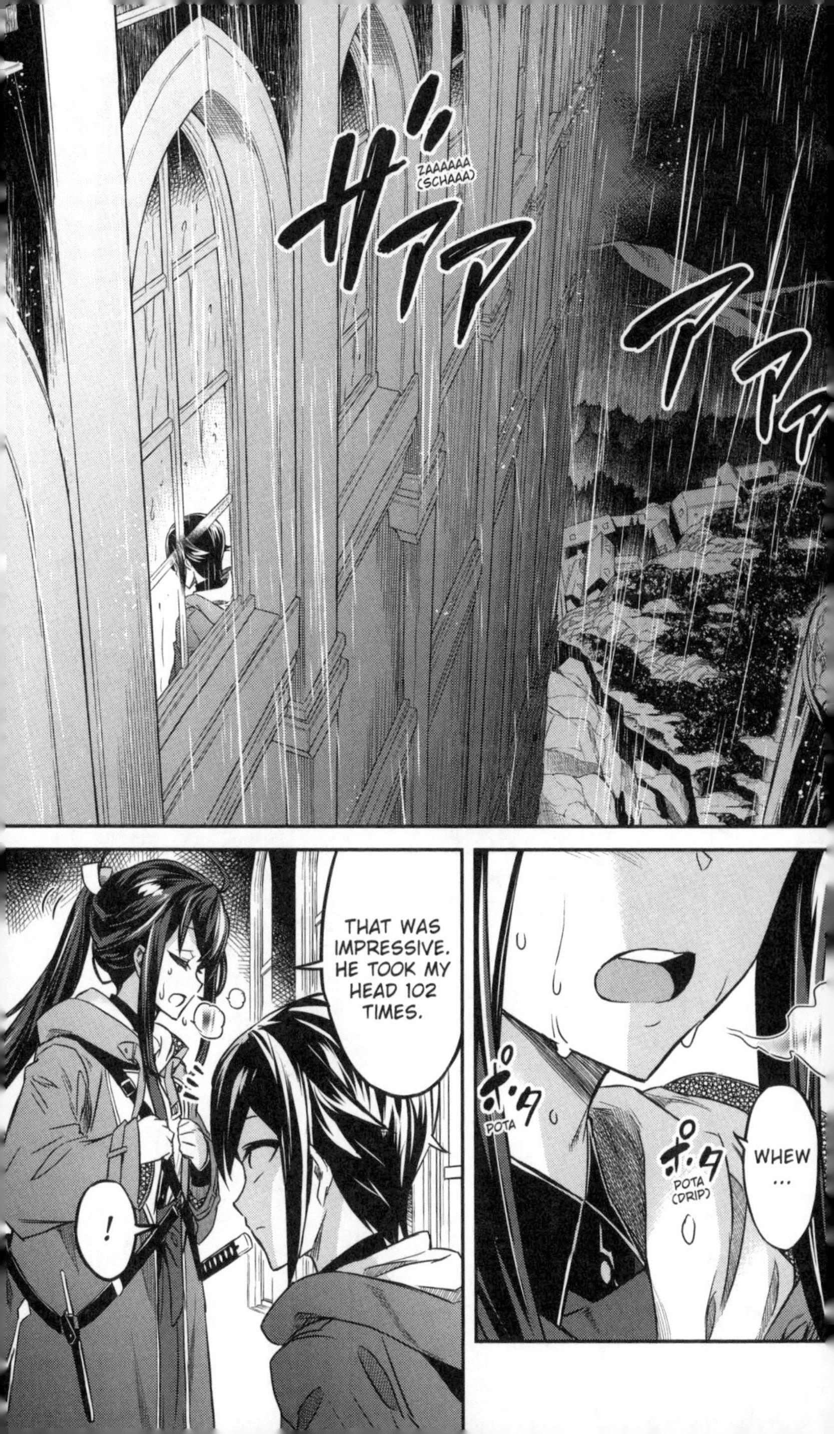
ZAAAAAA (SCHAAA)
WHEW ...
POTA (DRIP)
POTA
THAT WAS IMPRESSIVE. HE TOOK MY HEAD 102 TIMES.
!

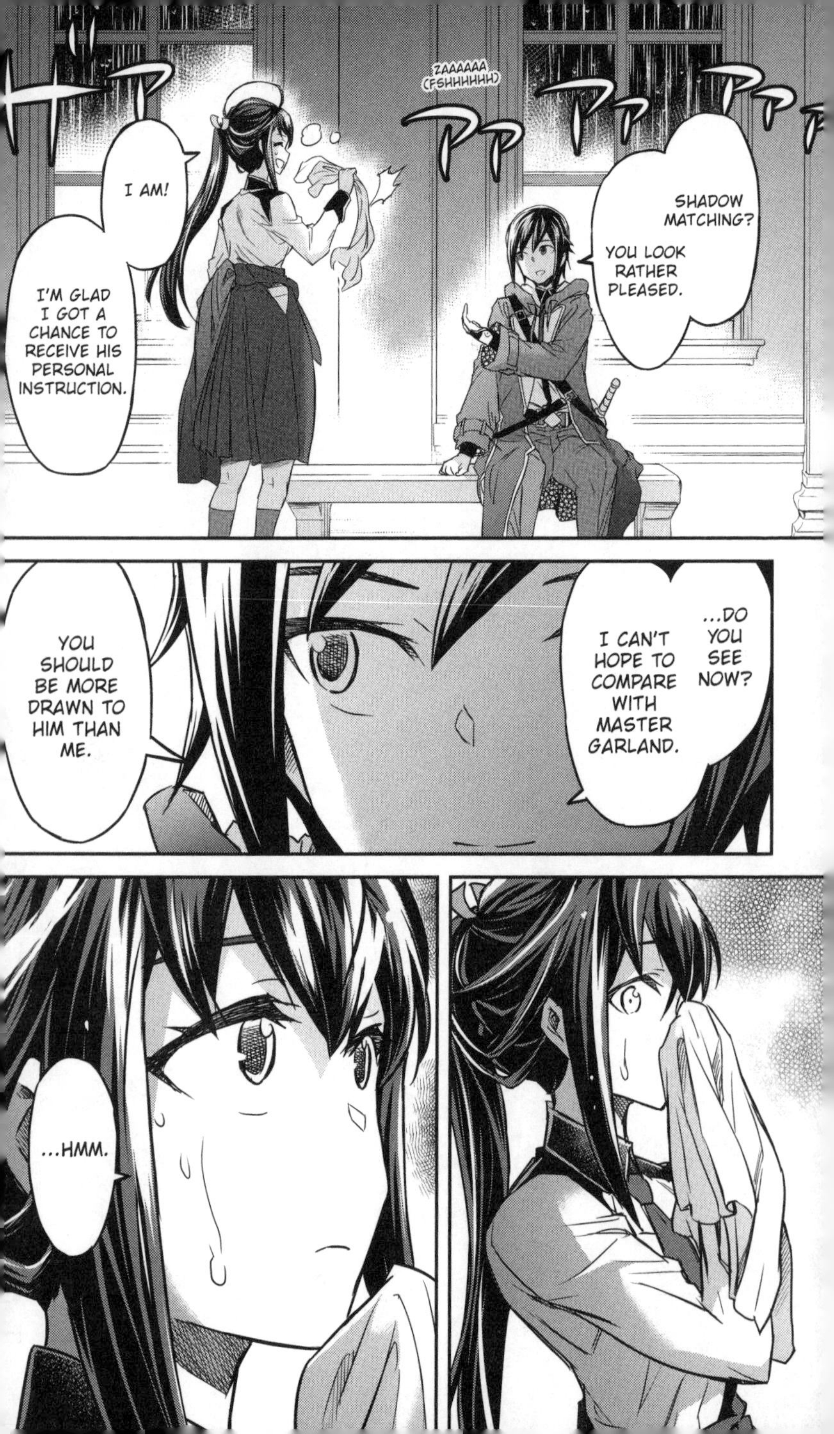
ZAAAAAA (FSHHHHHH)
SHADOW MATCHING?
YOU LOOK RATHER PLEASED.
I AM!
I'M GLAD I GOT A CHANCE TO RECEIVE HIS PERSONAL INSTRUCTION.
...DO YOU SEE NOW?
I CAN'T HOPE TO COMPARE WITH MASTER GARLAND.
YOU SHOULD BE MORE DRAWN TO HIM THAN ME.
...HMM.

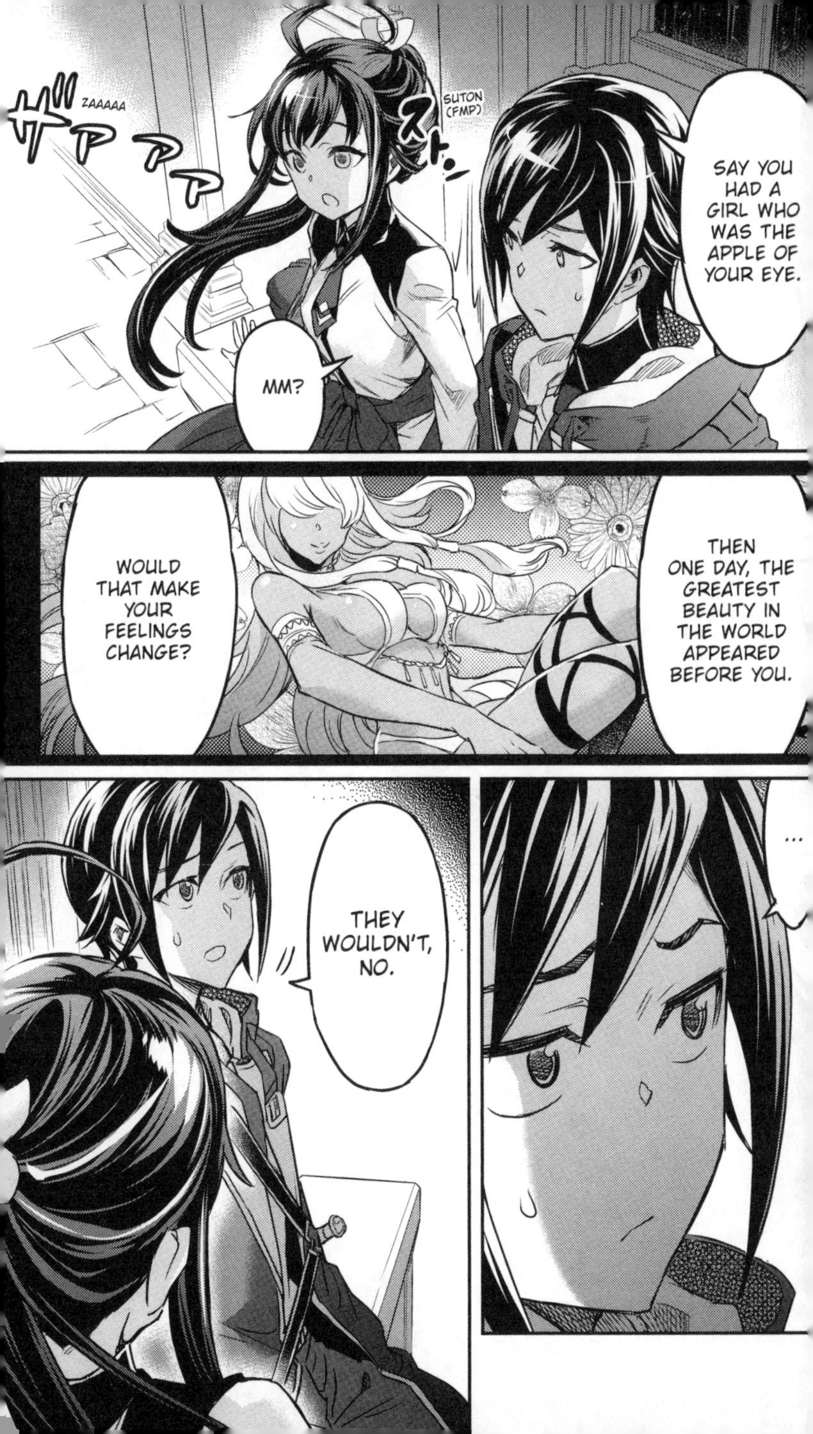
SAY YOU HAD A GIRL WHO WAS THE APPLE OF YOUR EYE.
SUTON (FMP)
ZAAAAA
MM?
THEN ONE DAY, THE GREATEST BEAUTY IN THE WORLD APPEARED BEFORE YOU.
WOULD THAT MAKE YOUR FEELINGS CHANGE?
...
THEY WOULDN'T, NO.

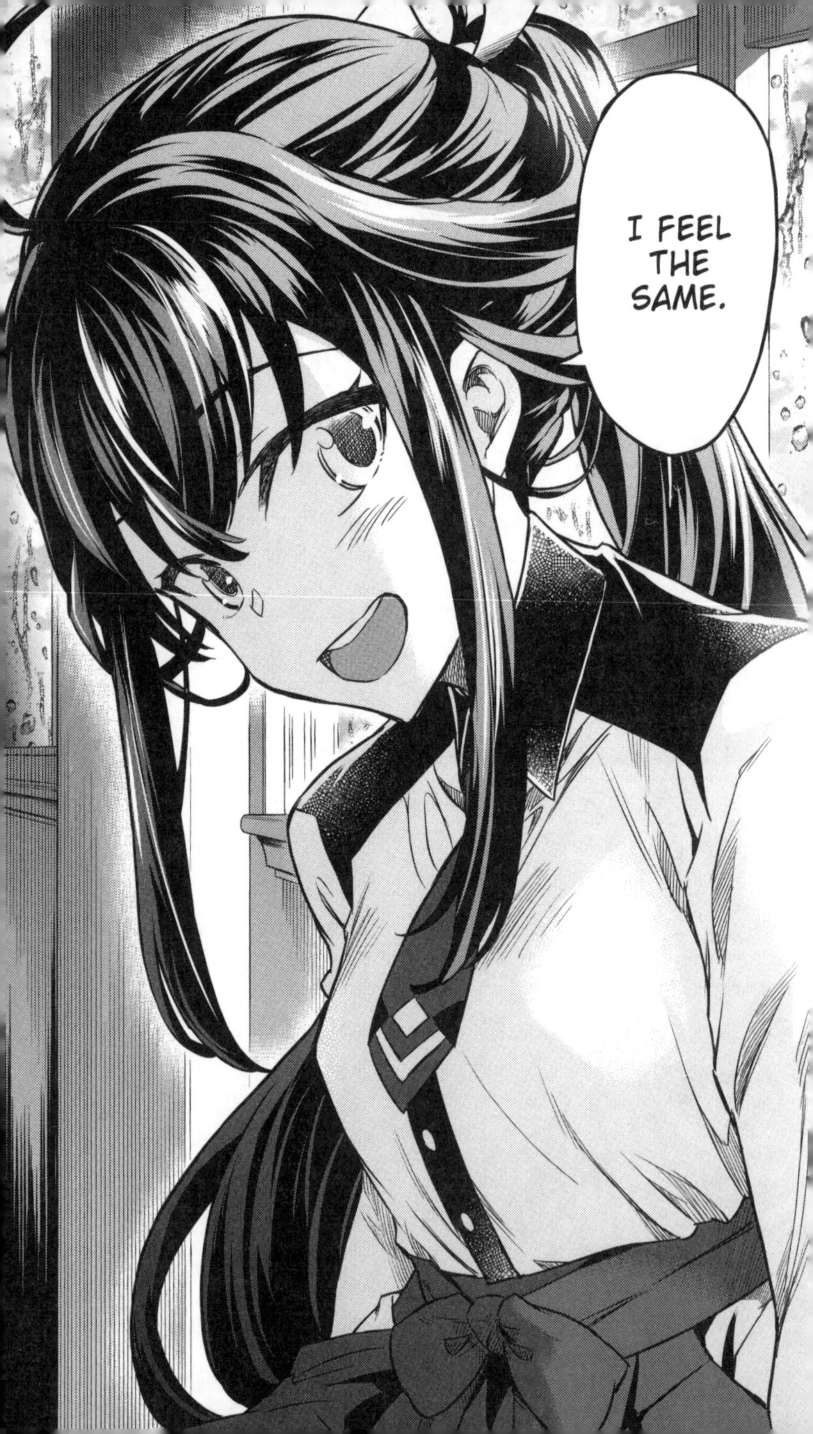
I FEEL THE SAME.

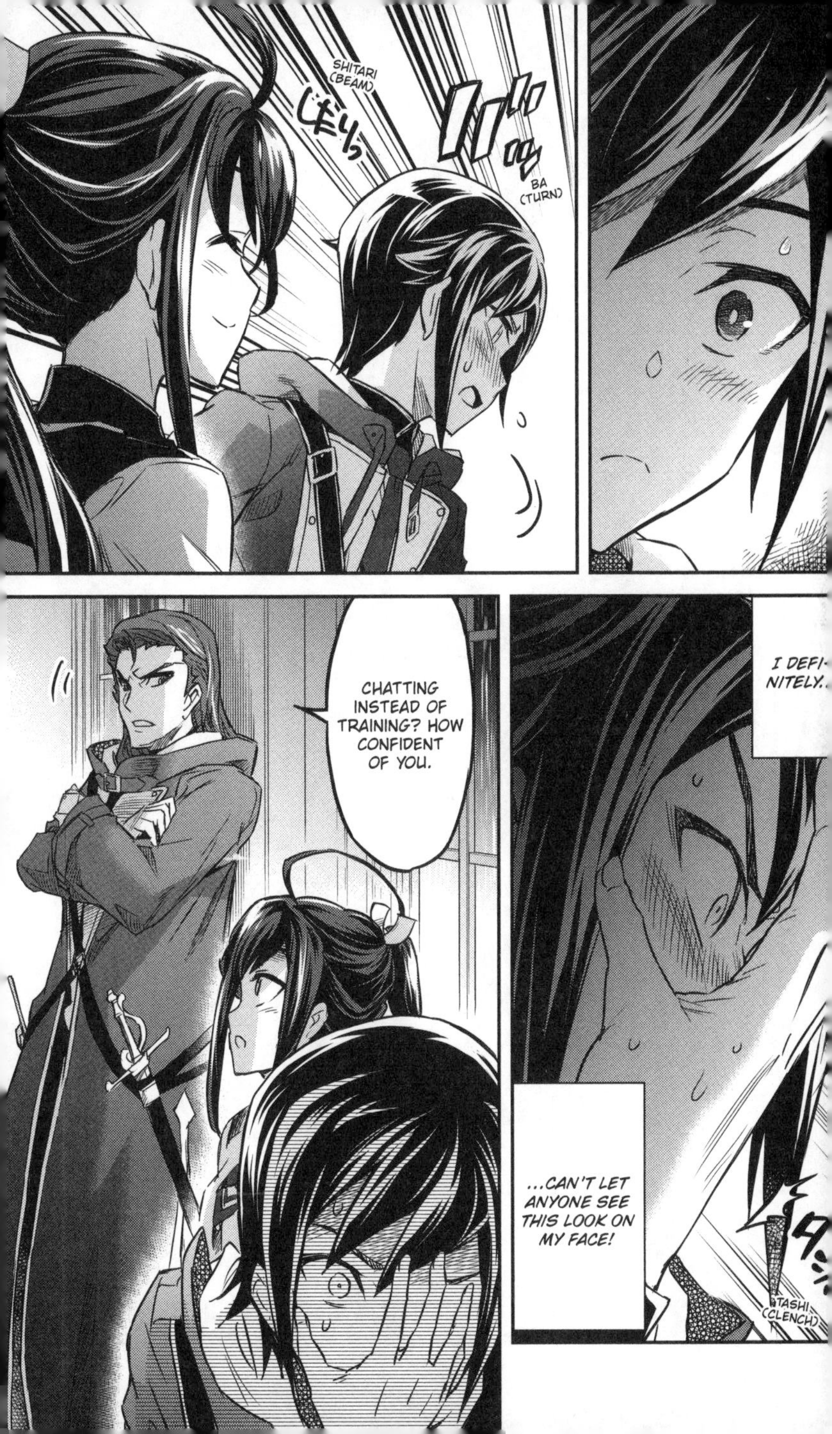
SHITARI (BEAM)
BA (TURN)
I DEFI-NITELY...
...CAN'T LET ANYONE SEE THIS LOOK ON MY FACE!
TASHI (CLENCH)
CHATTING INSTEAD OF TRAINING? HOW CONFIDENT OF YOU.

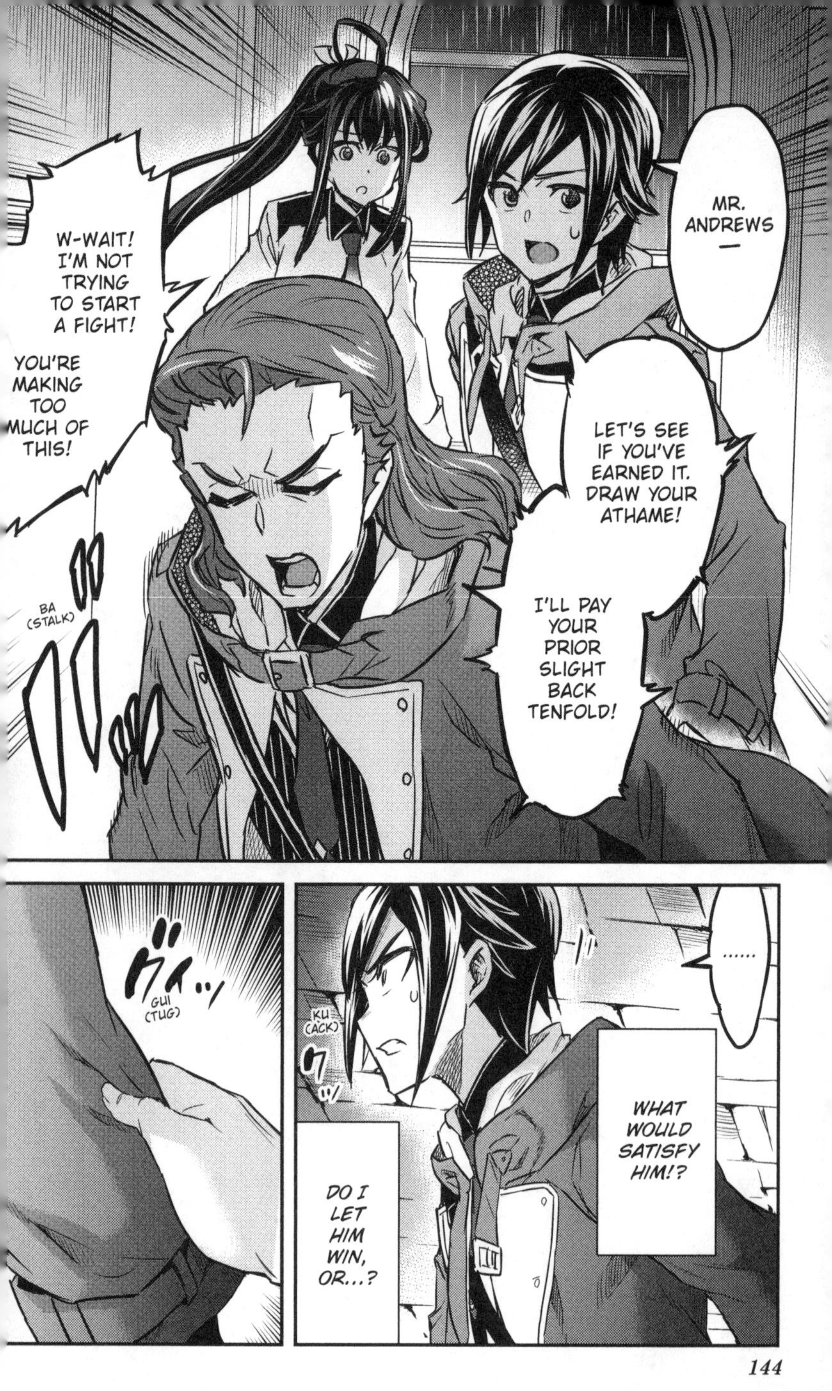
MR. ANDREWS —
LET'S SEE IF YOU'VE EARNED IT. DRAW YOUR ATHAME!
I'LL PAY YOUR PRIOR SLIGHT BACK TENFOLD!
W-WAIT! I'M NOT TRYING TO START A FIGHT!
YOU'RE MAKING TOO MUCH OF THIS!
BA (STALK)
......
KU (ACK)
WHAT WOULD SATISFY HIM!?
DO I LET HIM WIN, OR...?
GUI (TUG)

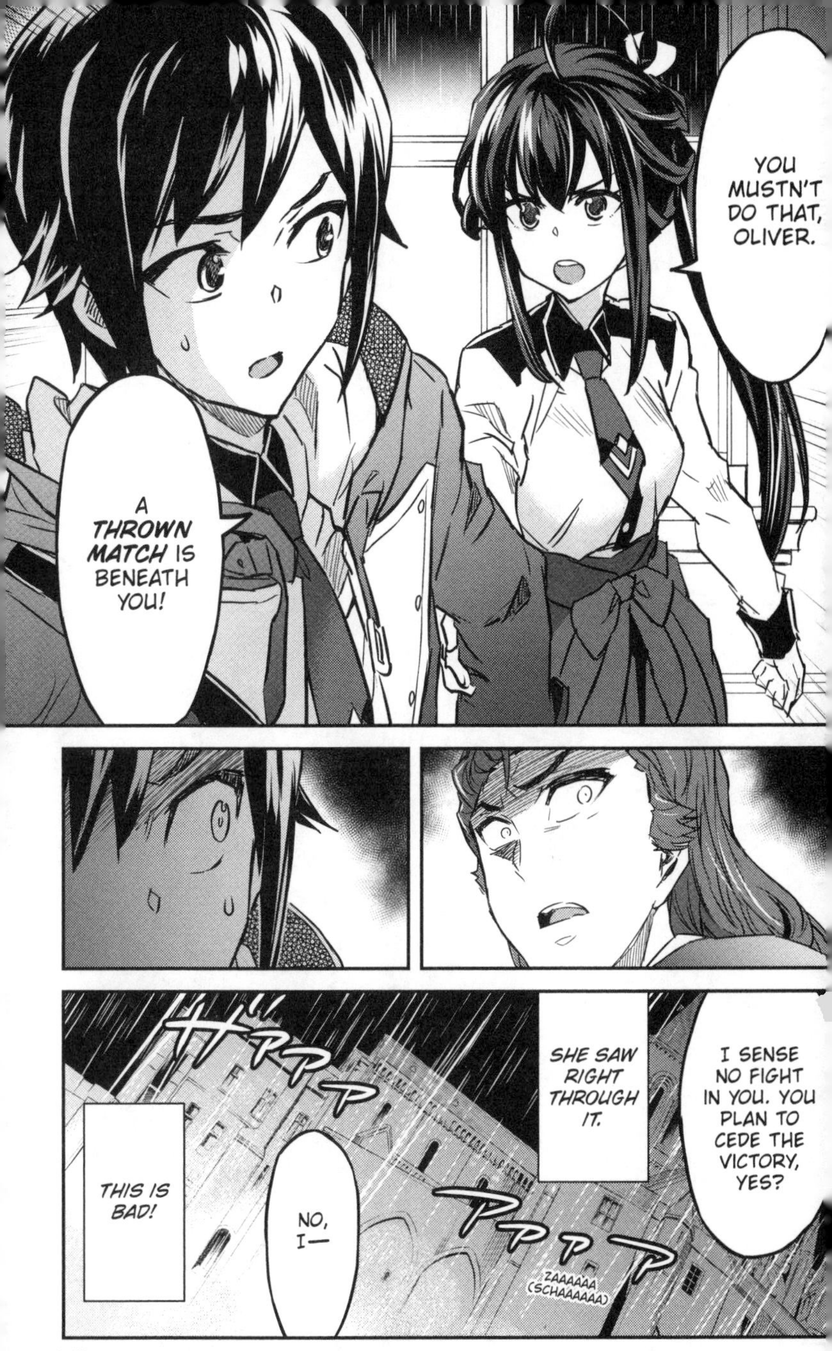
YOU MUSTN'T DO THAT, OLIVER.
A *THROWN MATCH* IS BENEATH YOU!
I SENSE NO FIGHT IN YOU. YOU PLAN TO CEDE THE VICTORY, YES?
SHE SAW RIGHT THROUGH IT.
ZAAAAAA (SCHAAAAAAA)
NO, I—
THIS IS BAD!

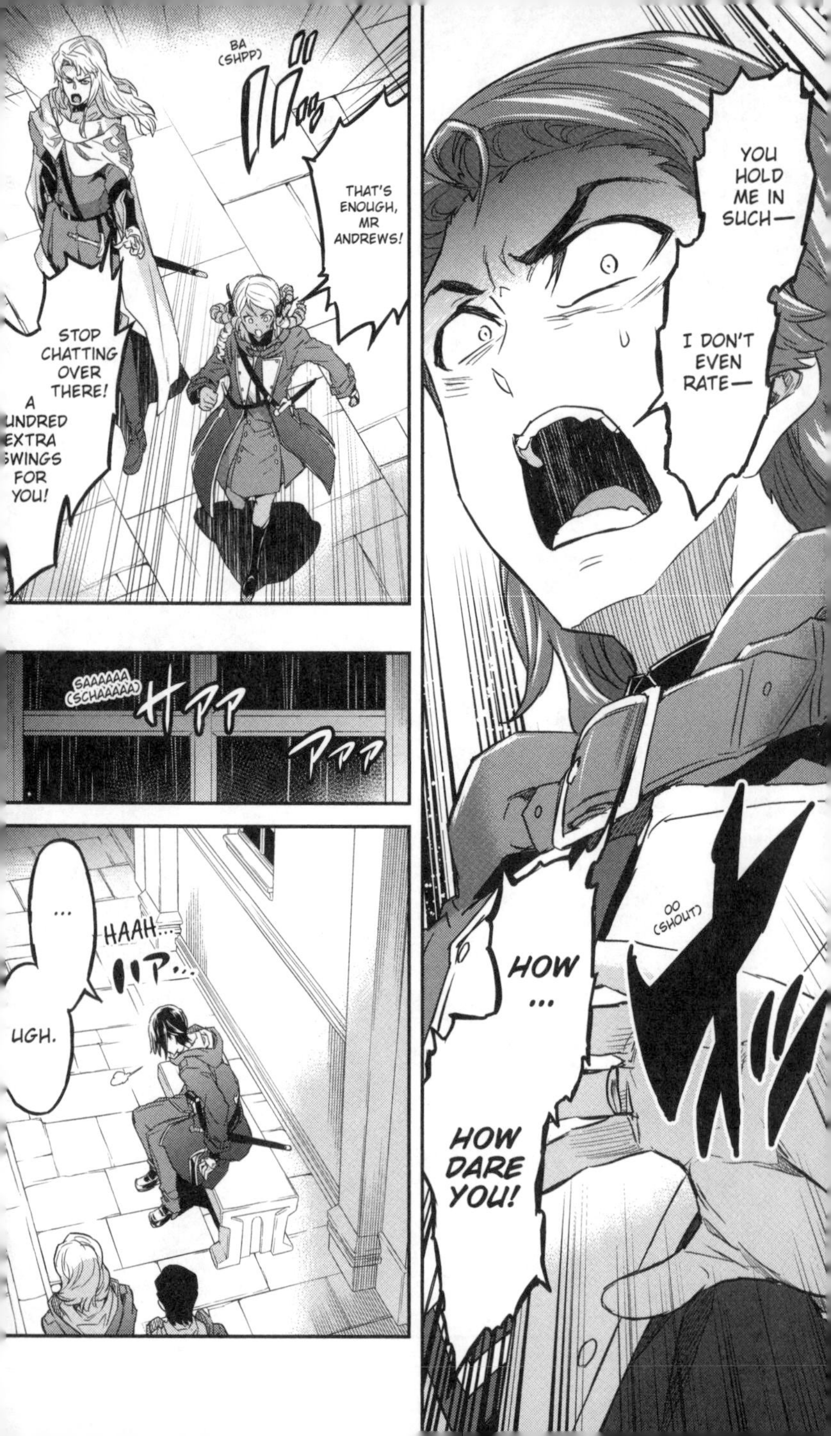
YOU HOLD ME IN SUCH—
I DON'T EVEN RATE—
OO (SHOUT)
HOW ...
HOW DARE YOU!
BA (SHPP)
THAT'S ENOUGH, MR ANDREWS!
STOP CHATTING OVER THERE!
A UNDRED EXTRA SWINGS FOR YOU!
SAAAAAA (SCHAAAAA)
...
HAAH...
UGH.

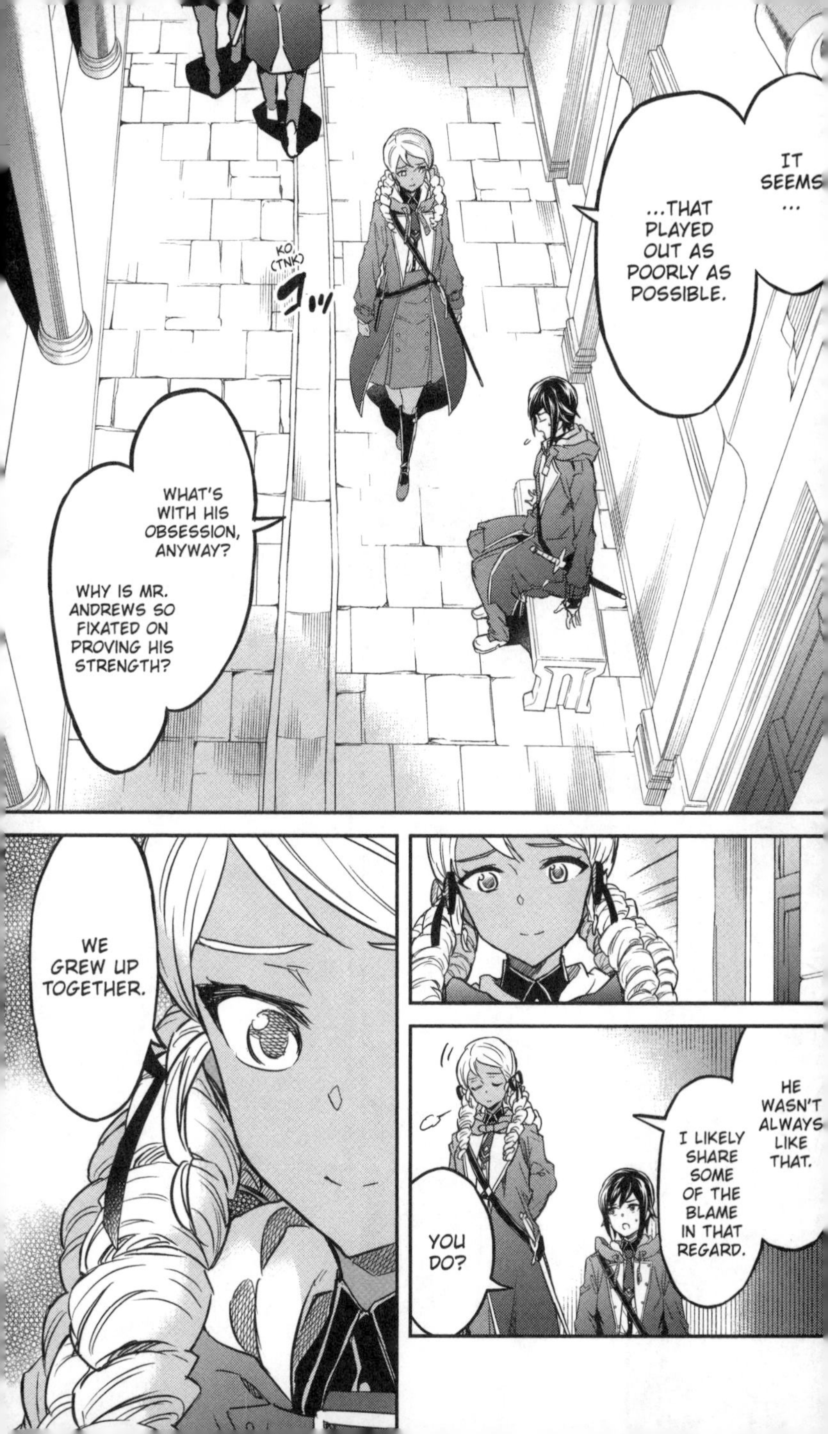
IT SEEMS...
...THAT PLAYED OUT AS POORLY AS POSSIBLE.
KO, (TNK)
ゴッ
WHAT'S WITH HIS OBSESSION, ANYWAY?
WHY IS MR. ANDREWS SO FIXATED ON PROVING HIS STRENGTH?
HE WASN'T ALWAYS LIKE THAT.
I LIKELY SHARE SOME OF THE BLAME IN THAT REGARD.
YOU DO?
WE GREW UP TOGETHER.

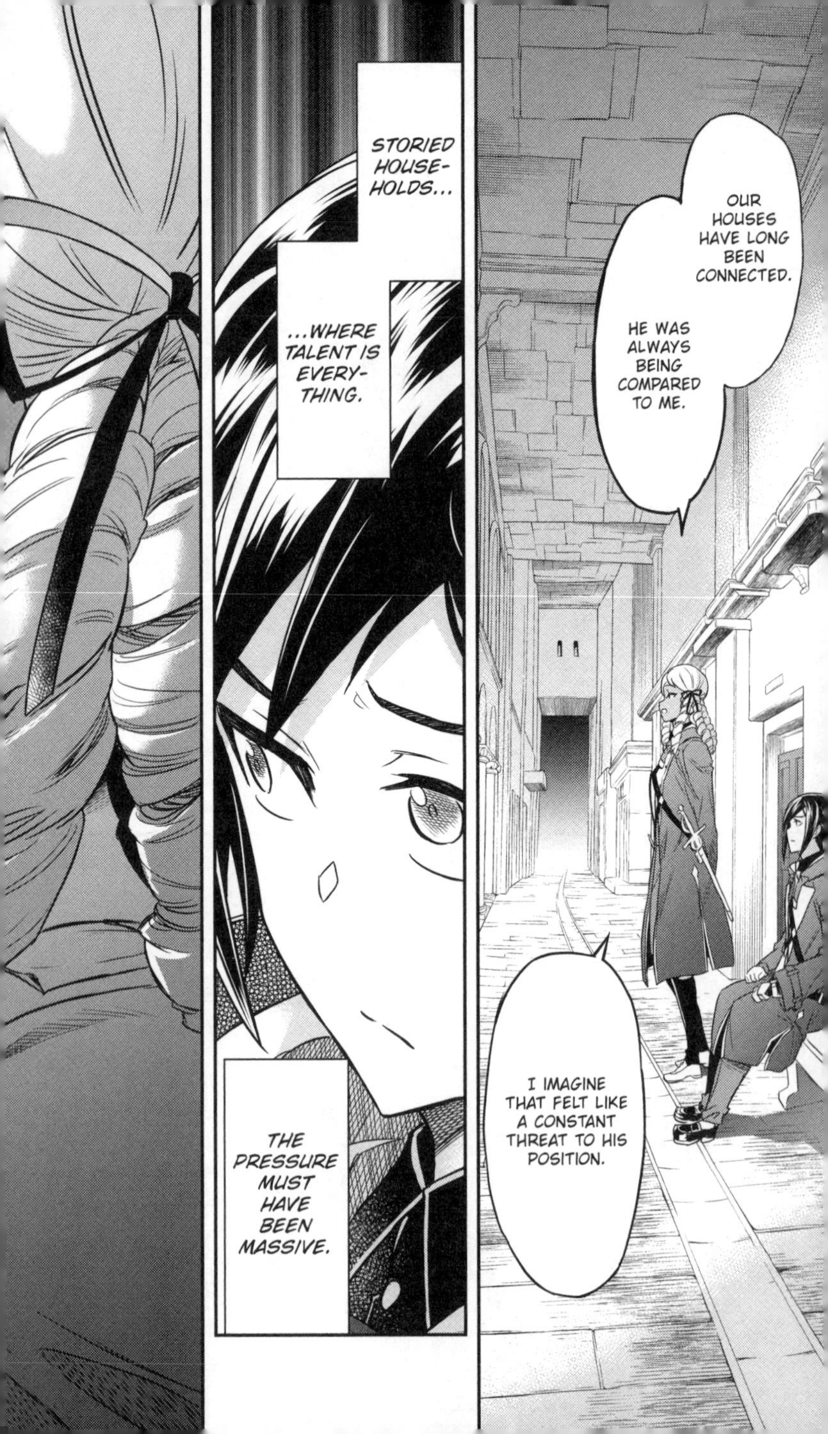
OUR HOUSES HAVE LONG BEEN CONNECTED.
HE WAS ALWAYS BEING COMPARED TO ME.
I IMAGINE THAT FELT LIKE A CONSTANT THREAT TO HIS POSITION.
STORIED HOUSE-HOLDS...
...WHERE TALENT IS EVERY-THING.
THE PRESSURE MUST HAVE BEEN MASSIVE.

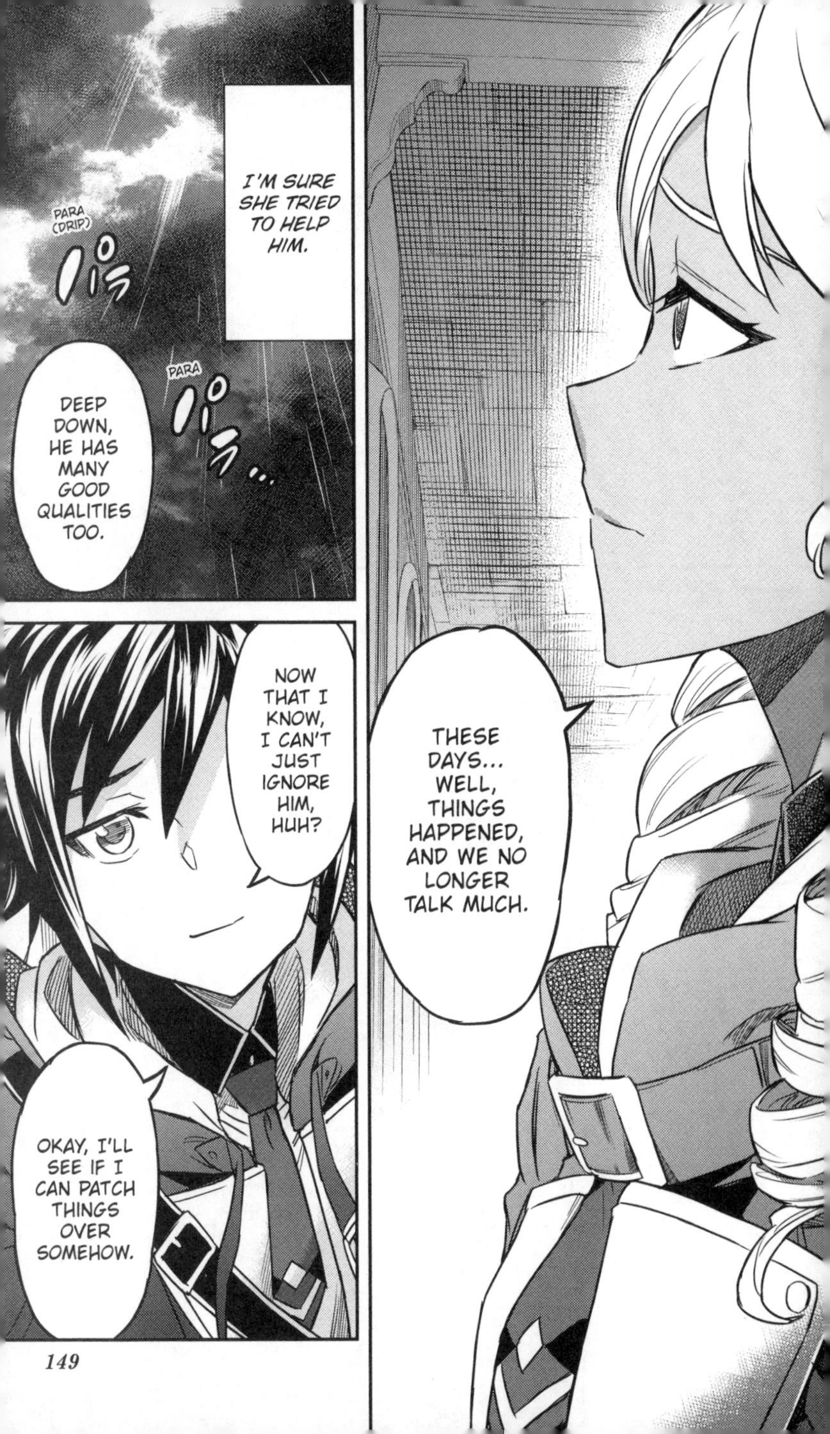
THESE DAYS... WELL, THINGS HAPPENED, AND WE NO LONGER TALK MUCH.
I'M SURE SHE TRIED TO HELP HIM.
PARA (DRIP)
パラ
PARA
パラ...
DEEP DOWN, HE HAS MANY GOOD QUALITIES TOO.
NOW THAT I KNOW, I CAN'T JUST IGNORE HIM, HUH?
OKAY, I'LL SEE IF I CAN PATCH THINGS OVER SOMEHOW.

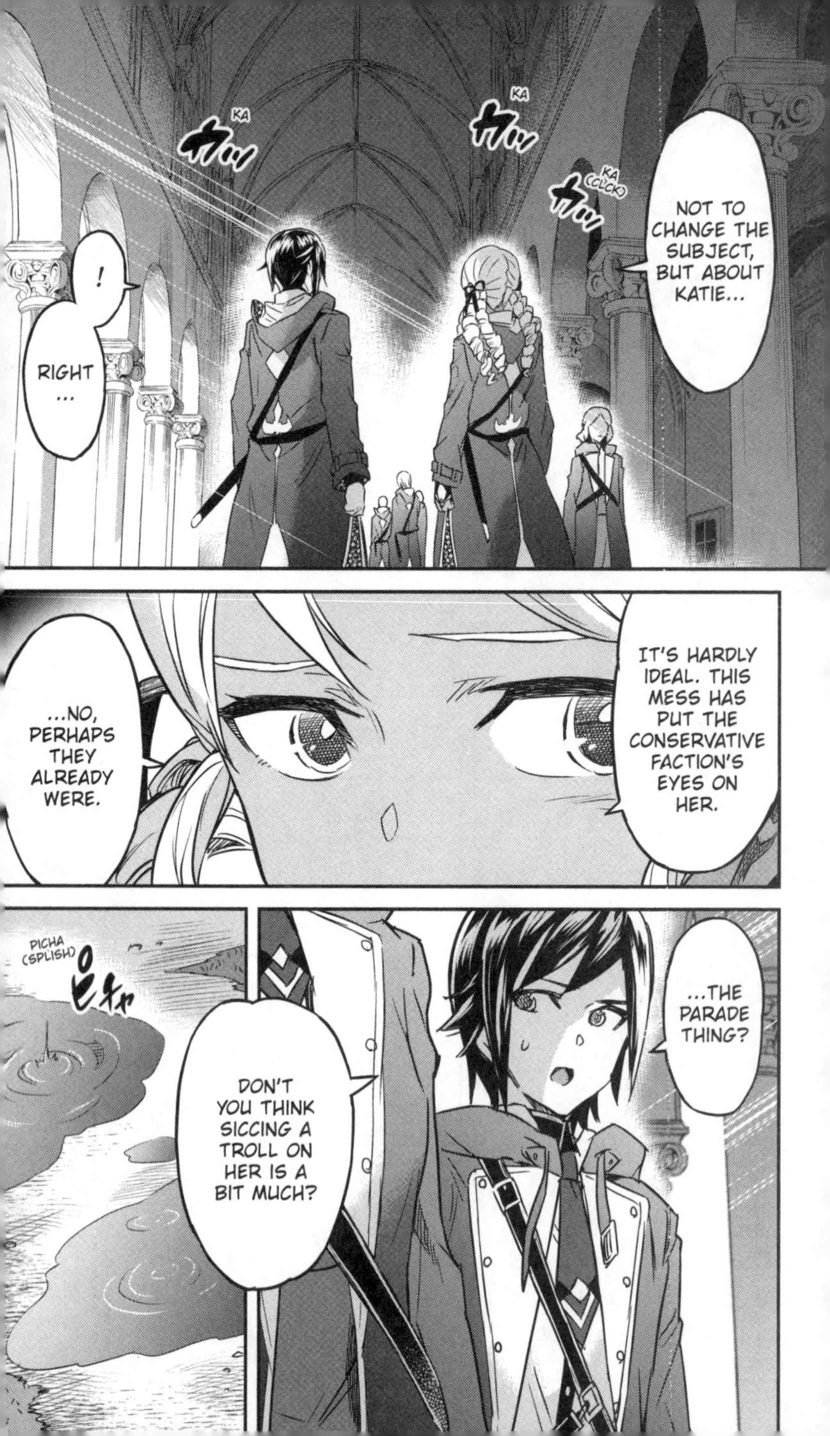
KA
KA (CLICK)
NOT TO CHANGE THE SUBJECT, BUT ABOUT KATIE...
KA
!
RIGHT ...
IT'S HARDLY IDEAL. THIS MESS HAS PUT THE CONSERVATIVE FACTION'S EYES ON HER.
...NO, PERHAPS THEY ALREADY WERE.
...THE PARADE THING?
DON'T YOU THINK SICCING A TROLL ON HER IS A BIT MUCH?
PICHA (SPLISH)

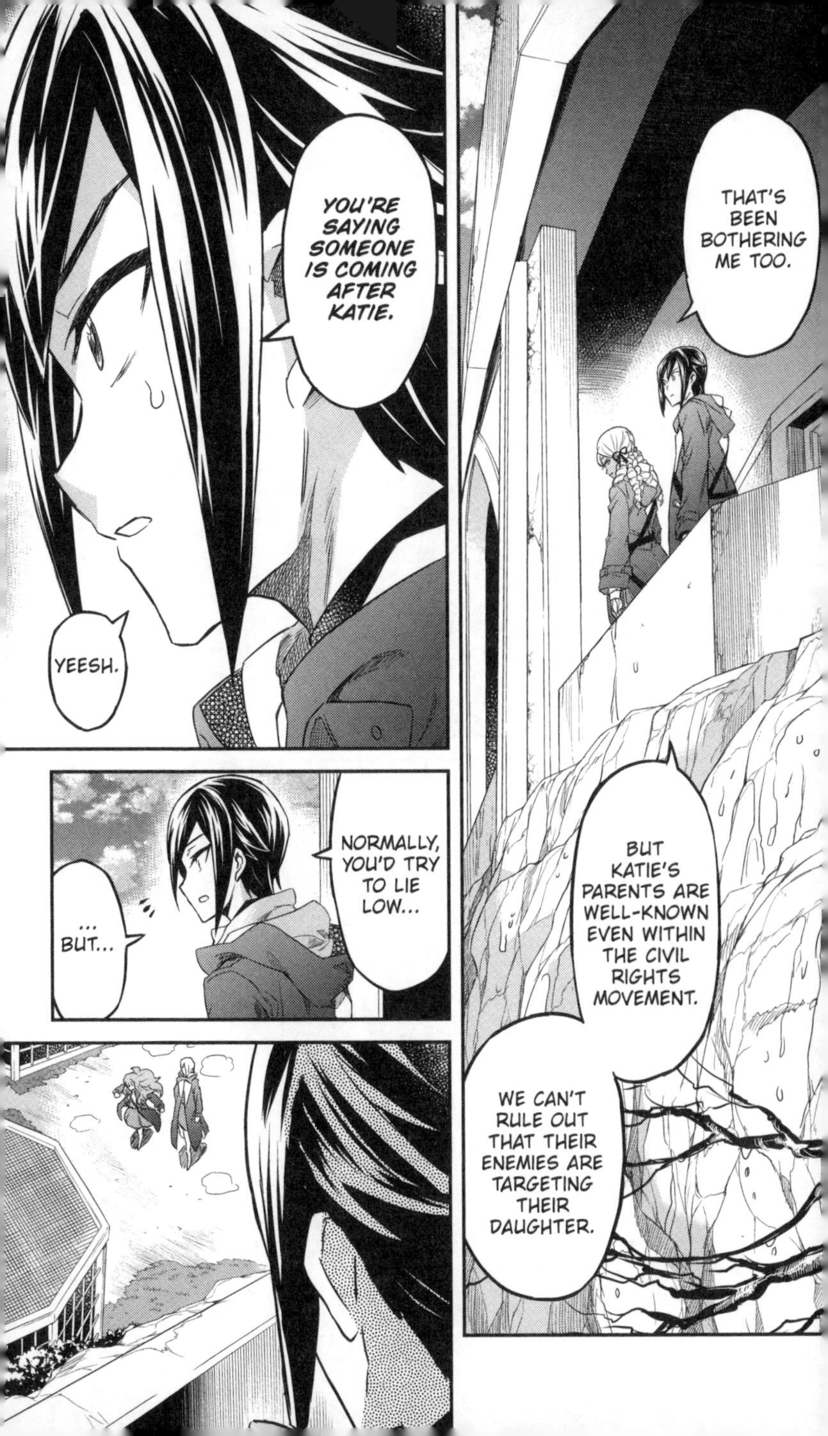
THAT'S BEEN BOTHERING ME TOO.
BUT KATIE'S PARENTS ARE WELL-KNOWN EVEN WITHIN THE CIVIL RIGHTS MOVEMENT.
WE CAN'T RULE OUT THAT THEIR ENEMIES ARE TARGETING THEIR DAUGHTER.
YOU'RE SAYING SOMEONE IS COMING AFTER KATIE.
YEESH.
NORMALLY, YOU'D TRY TO LIE LOW...
... BUT...

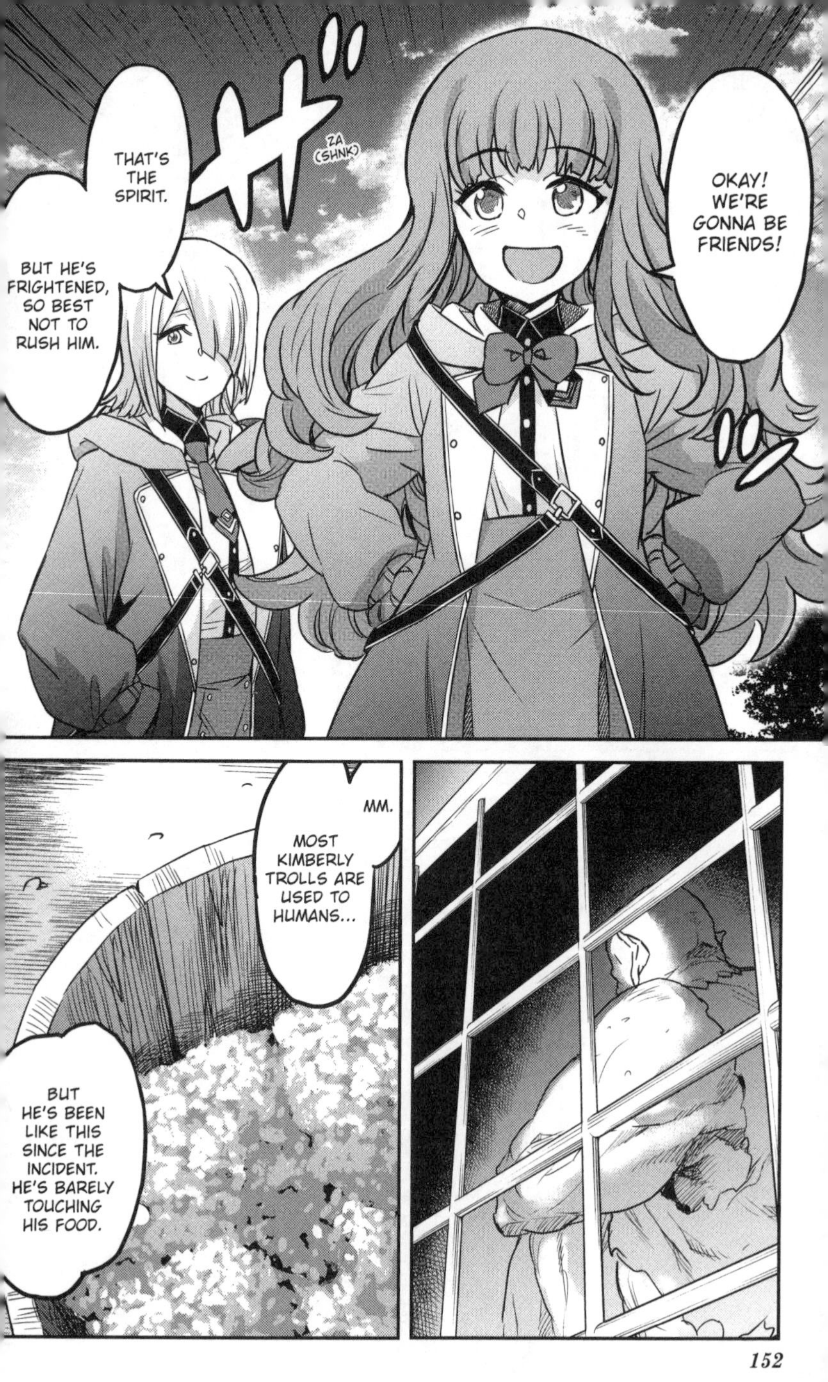
OKAY! WE'RE GONNA BE FRIENDS!
ZA (SHNK)
THAT'S THE SPIRIT.
BUT HE'S FRIGHTENED, SO BEST NOT TO RUSH HIM.
MM.
MOST KIMBERLY TROLLS ARE USED TO HUMANS...
BUT HE'S BEEN LIKE THIS SINCE THE INCIDENT. HE'S BARELY TOUCHING HIS FOOD.

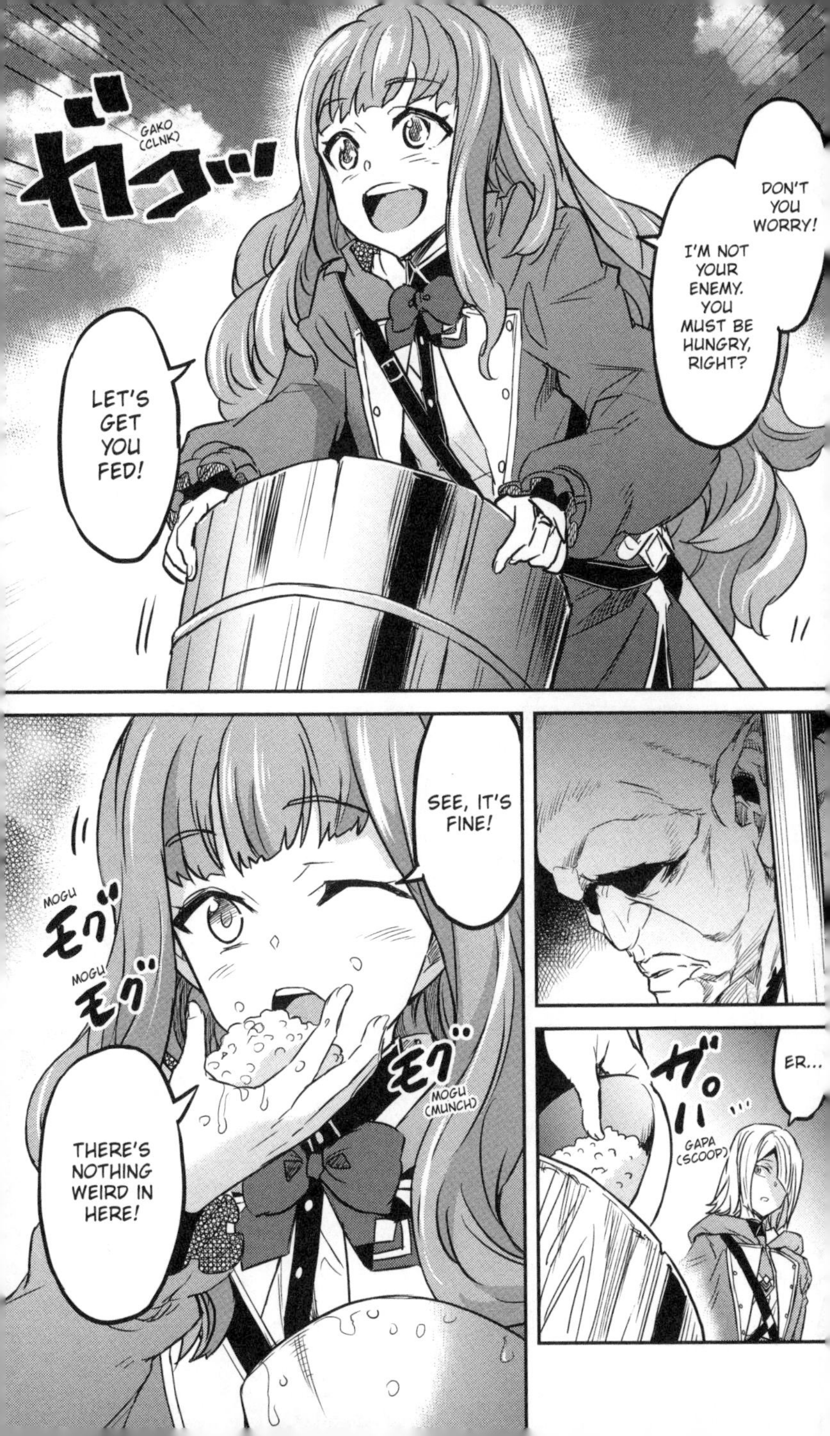
DON'T YOU WORRY!
I'M NOT YOUR ENEMY. YOU MUST BE HUNGRY, RIGHT?
ガコッ
GAKO (CLNK)
LET'S GET YOU FED!
ER...
ガパッ
GAPA (SCOOP)
SEE, IT'S FINE!
モグ
MOGU
モグ
MOGU
モグ
MOGU (MUNCH)
THERE'S NOTHING WEIRD IN HERE!

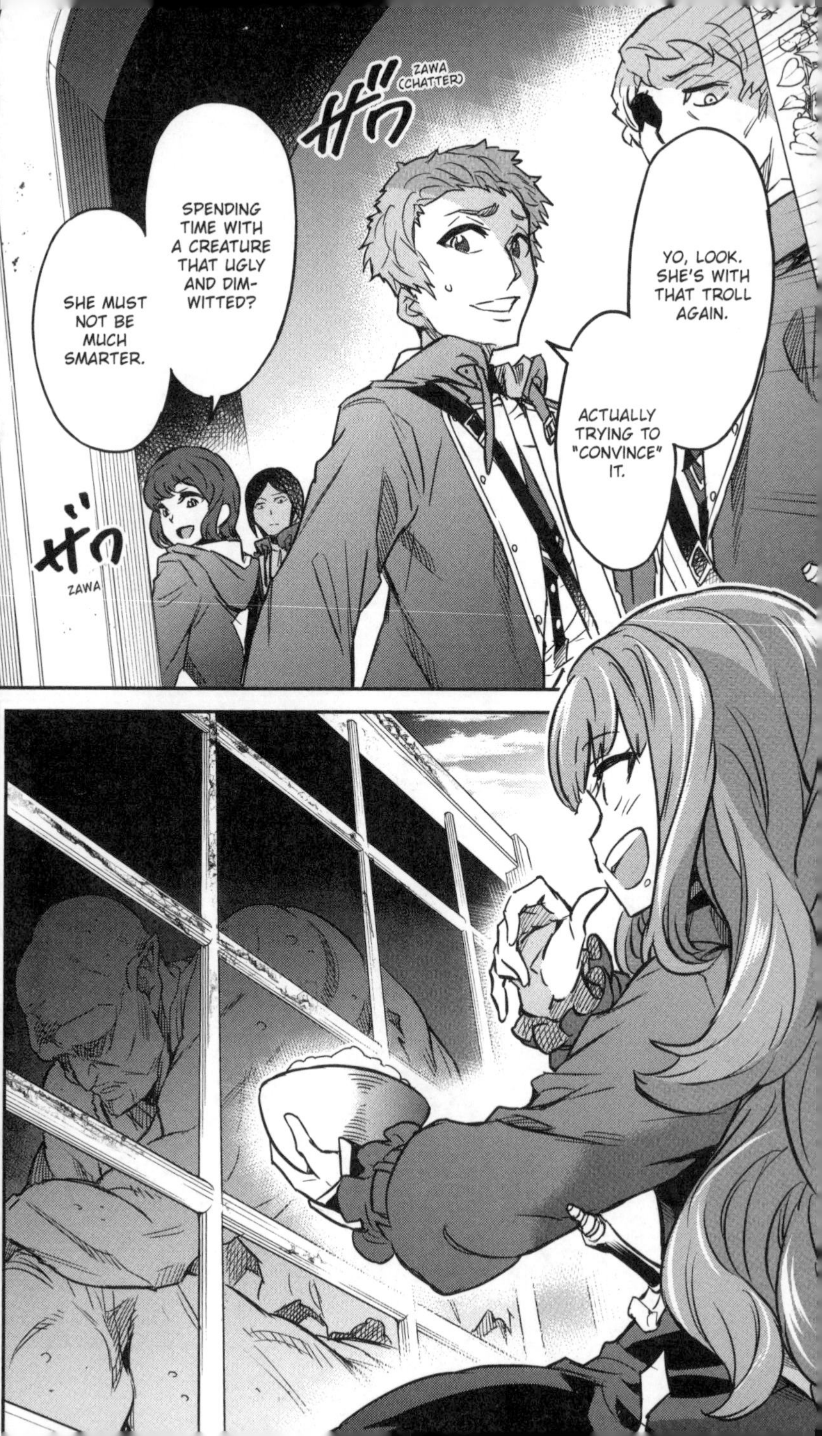
ZAWA (CHATTER)
YO, LOOK. SHE'S WITH THAT TROLL AGAIN.
ACTUALLY TRYING TO "CONVINCE" IT.
SPENDING TIME WITH A CREATURE THAT UGLY AND DIM-WITTED?
SHE MUST NOT BE MUCH SMARTER.
ZAWA

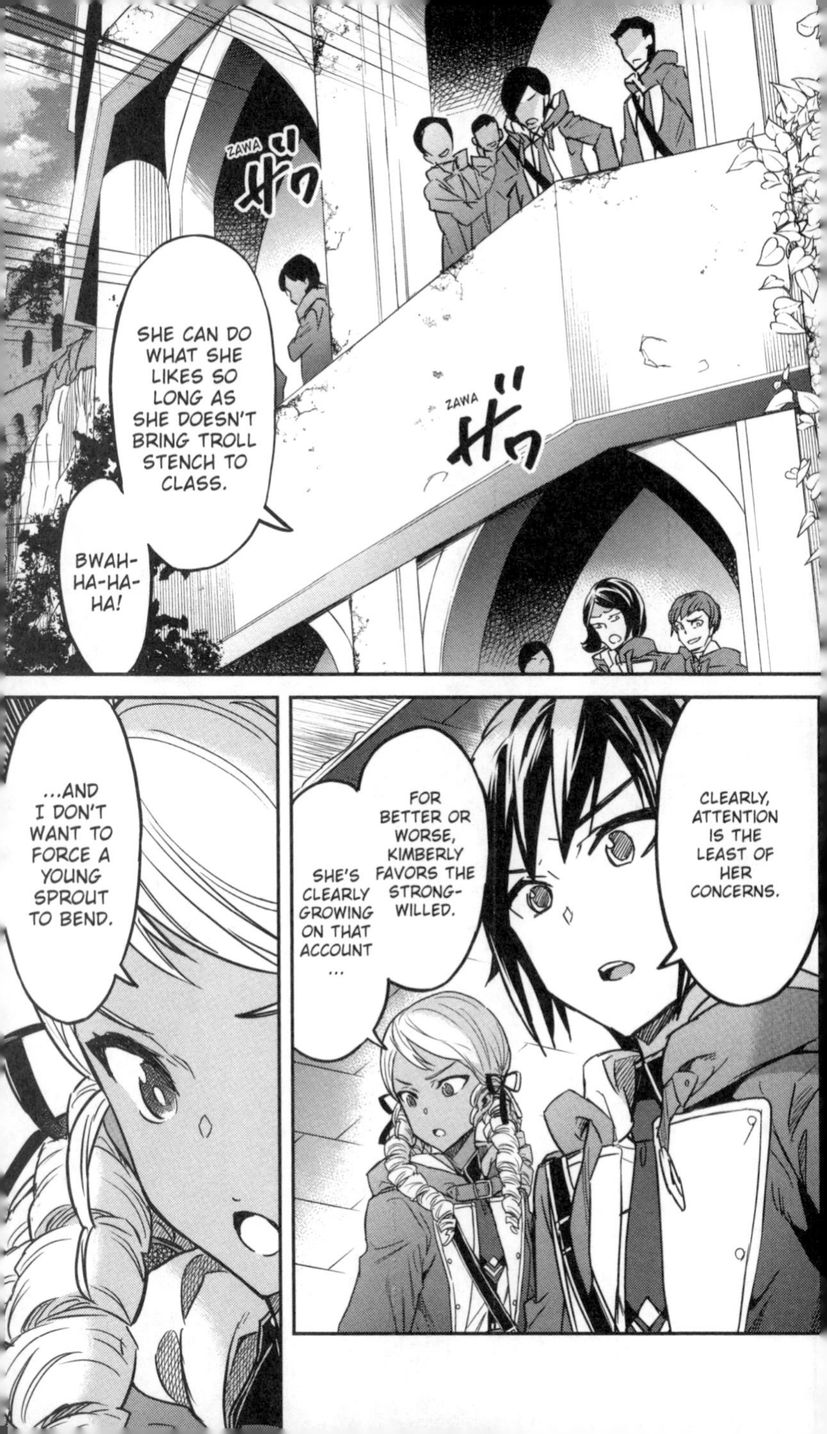
ZAWA ザワ
SHE CAN DO WHAT SHE LIKES SO LONG AS SHE DOESN'T BRING TROLL STENCH TO CLASS.
ZAWA ザワ
BWAH-HA-HA-HA!
CLEARLY, ATTENTION IS THE LEAST OF HER CONCERNS.
FOR BETTER OR WORSE, KIMBERLY FAVORS THE STRONG-WILLED.
SHE'S CLEARLY GROWING ON THAT ACCOUNT...
...AND I DON'T WANT TO FORCE A YOUNG SPROUT TO BEND.

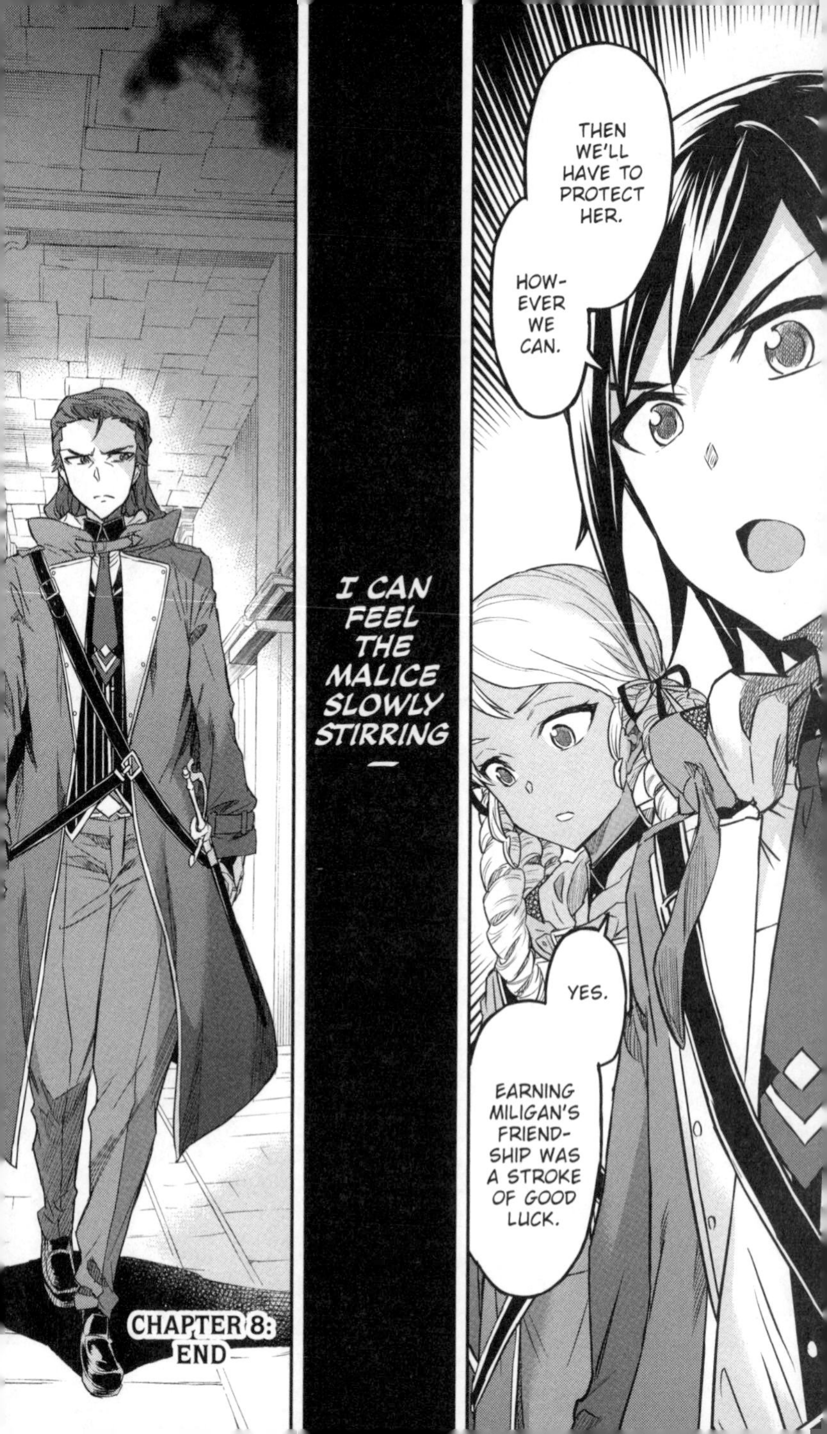
THEN WE'LL HAVE TO PROTECT HER.
HOW-EVER WE CAN.
YES.
EARNING MILIGAN'S FRIEND-SHIP WAS A STROKE OF GOOD LUCK.
I CAN FEEL THE MALICE SLOWLY STIRRING—
CHAPTER 8: END

CHAPTER 9: COLOSSEUM

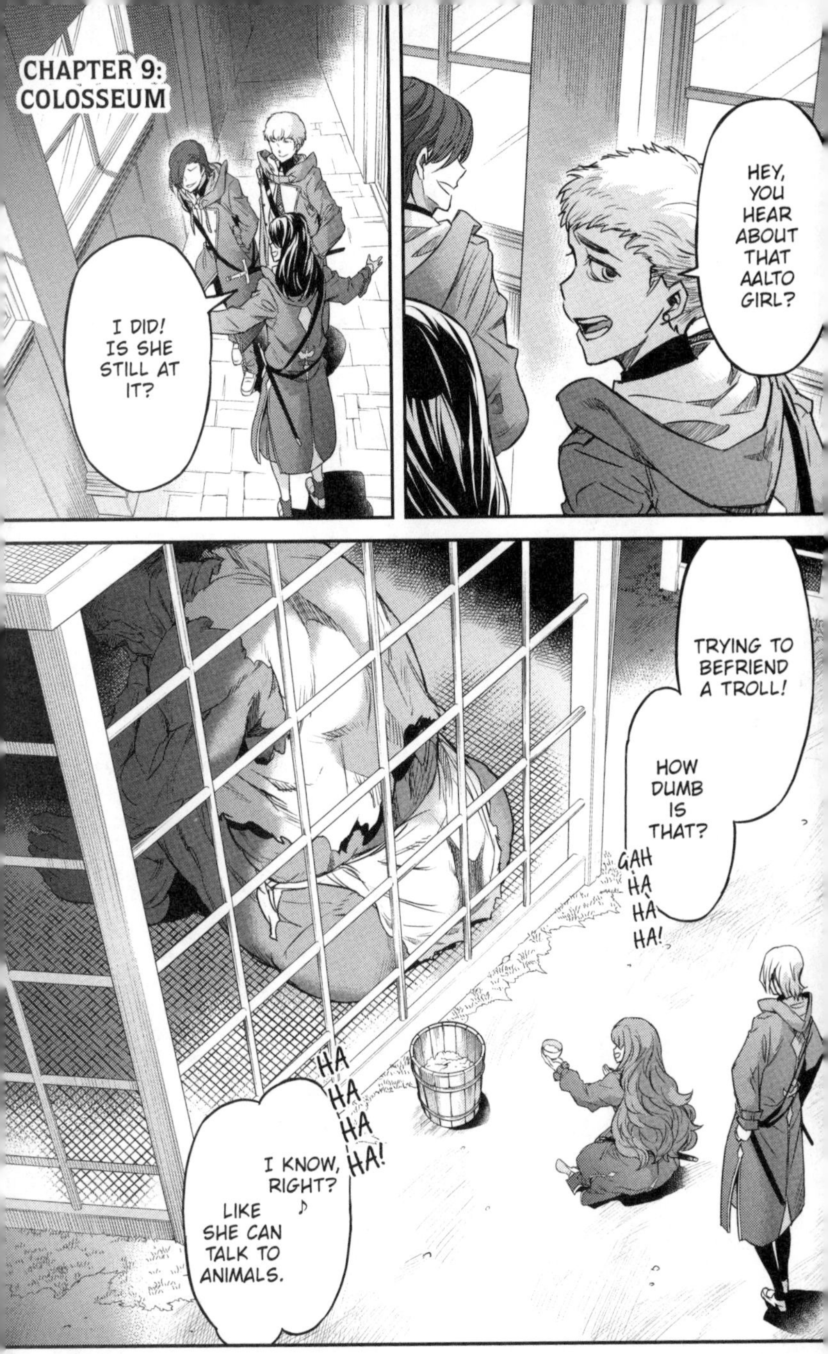
HEY, YOU HEAR ABOUT THAT AALTO GIRL?
I DID! IS SHE STILL AT IT?
TRYING TO BEFRIEND A TROLL!
HOW DUMB IS THAT?
GAH HA HA HA!
HA HA HA HA!
I KNOW, RIGHT? ♪
LIKE SHE CAN TALK TO ANIMALS.

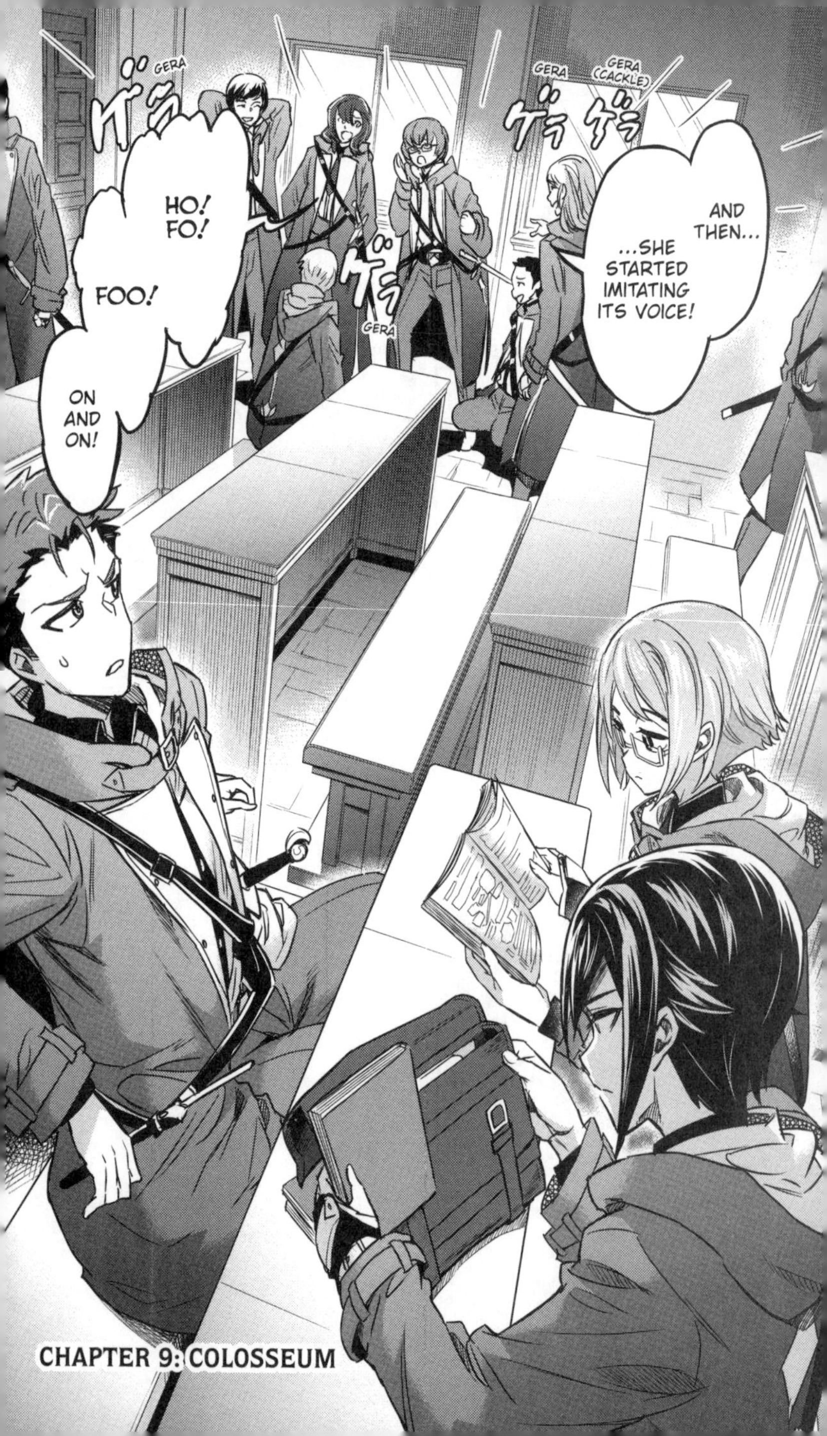
GERA GERA (CACKLE)
AND THEN... ...SHE STARTED IMITATING ITS VOICE!
GERA
HO! FO! FOO! ON AND ON!
GERA
CHAPTER 9: COLOSSEUM

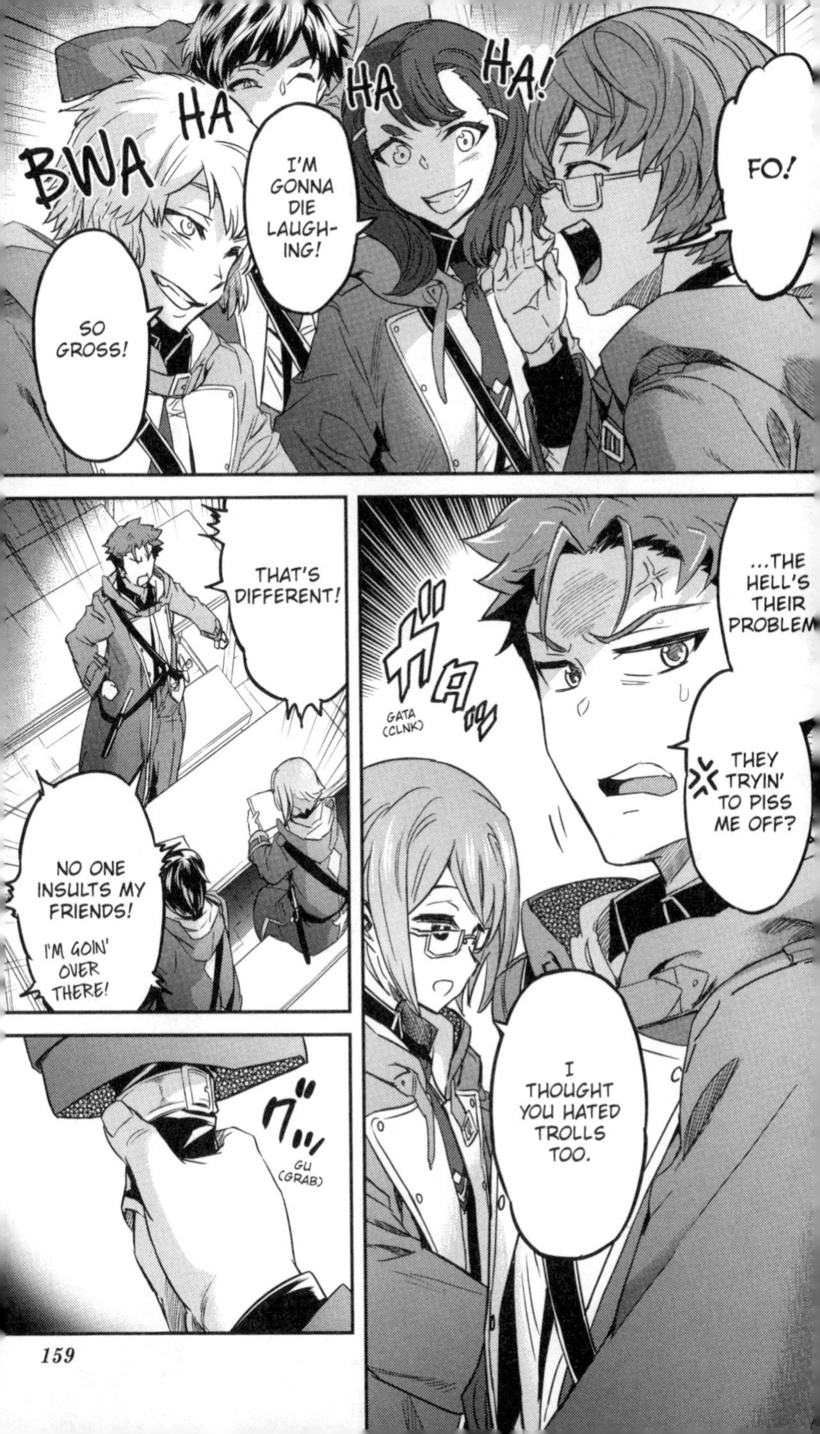
FO!
BWA HA HA HA!
I'M GONNA DIE LAUGHING!
SO GROSS!
...THE HELL'S THEIR PROBLEM
THEY TRYIN' TO PISS ME OFF?
GATA (CLNK)
I THOUGHT YOU HATED TROLLS TOO.
THAT'S DIFFERENT!
NO ONE INSULTS MY FRIENDS!
I'M GOIN' OVER THERE!
GU (GRAB)

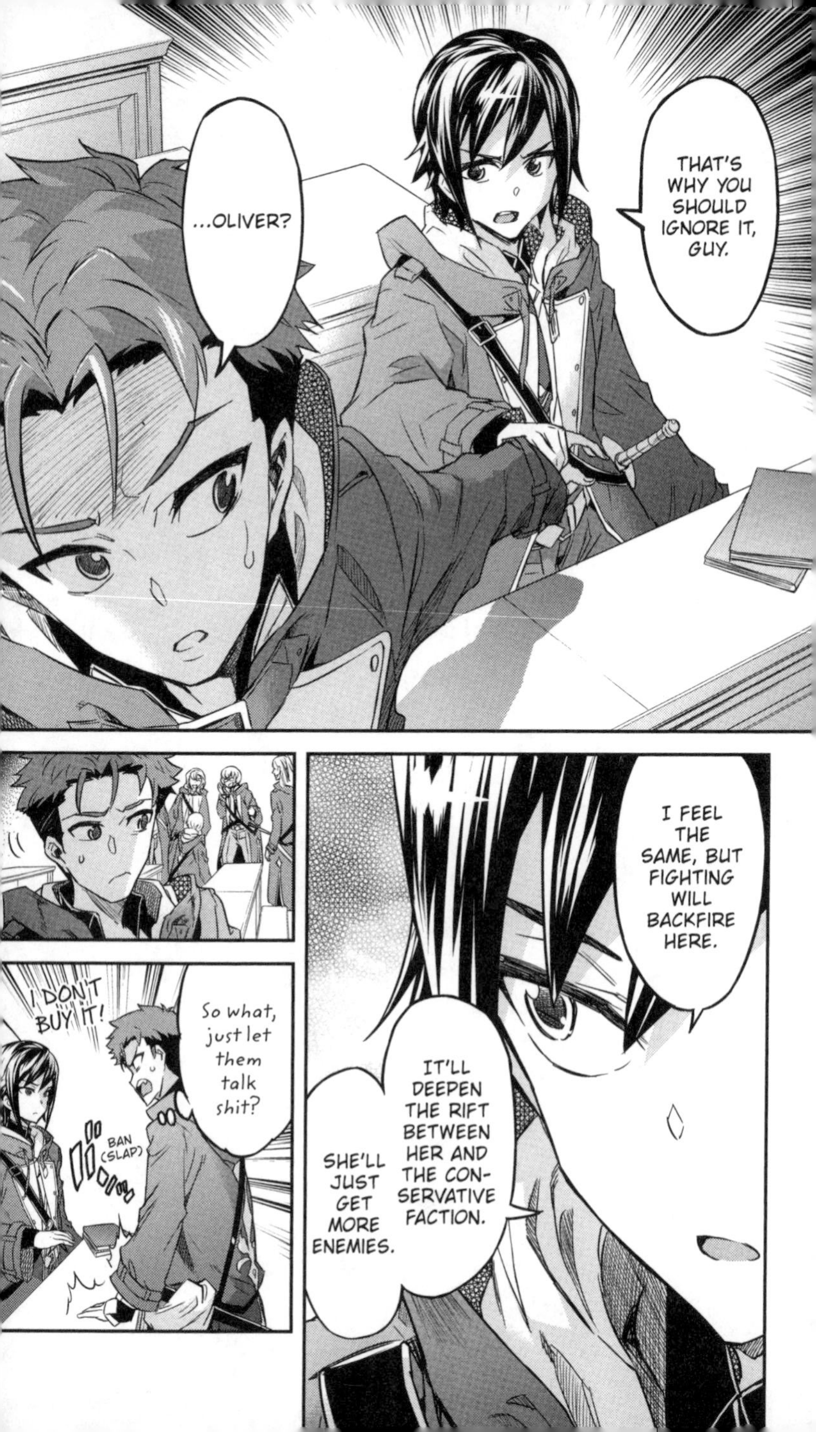
THAT'S WHY YOU SHOULD IGNORE IT, GUY.
...OLIVER?
I FEEL THE SAME, BUT FIGHTING WILL BACKFIRE HERE.
IT'LL DEEPEN THE RIFT BETWEEN HER AND THE CON-SERVATIVE FACTION.
SHE'LL JUST GET MORE ENEMIES.
So what, just let them talk shit?
I DON'T BUY IT!
BAN (SLAP)

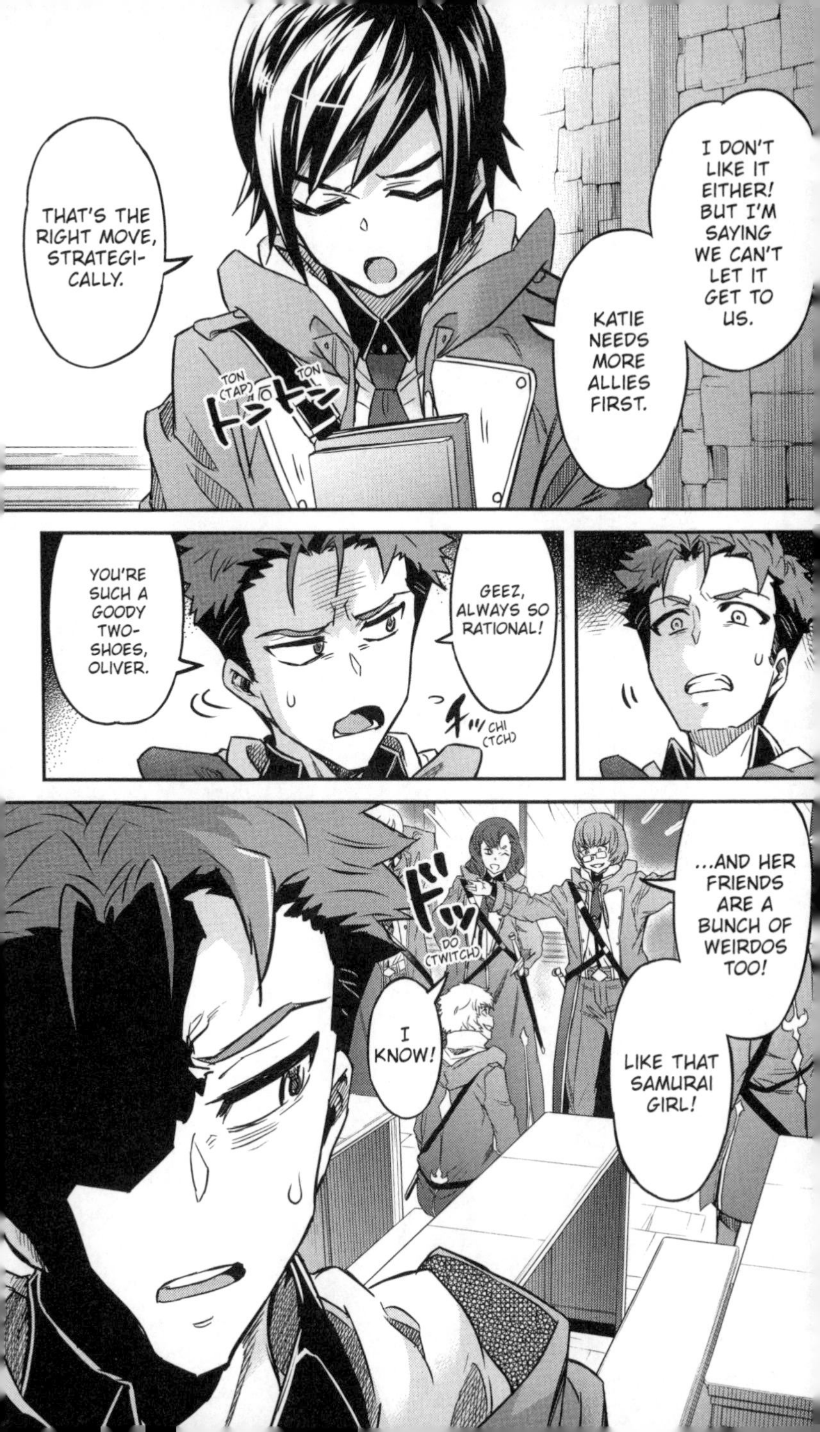
I DON'T LIKE IT EITHER! BUT I'M SAYING WE CAN'T LET IT GET TO US.
KATIE NEEDS MORE ALLIES FIRST.
TON TON (TAP)
THAT'S THE RIGHT MOVE, STRATEGI-CALLY.
GEEZ, ALWAYS SO RATIONAL!
CHI (TCH)
YOU'RE SUCH A GOODY TWO-SHOES, OLIVER.
...AND HER FRIENDS ARE A BUNCH OF WEIRDOS TOO!
LIKE THAT SAMURAI GIRL!
DO (TWITCH)
I KNOW!

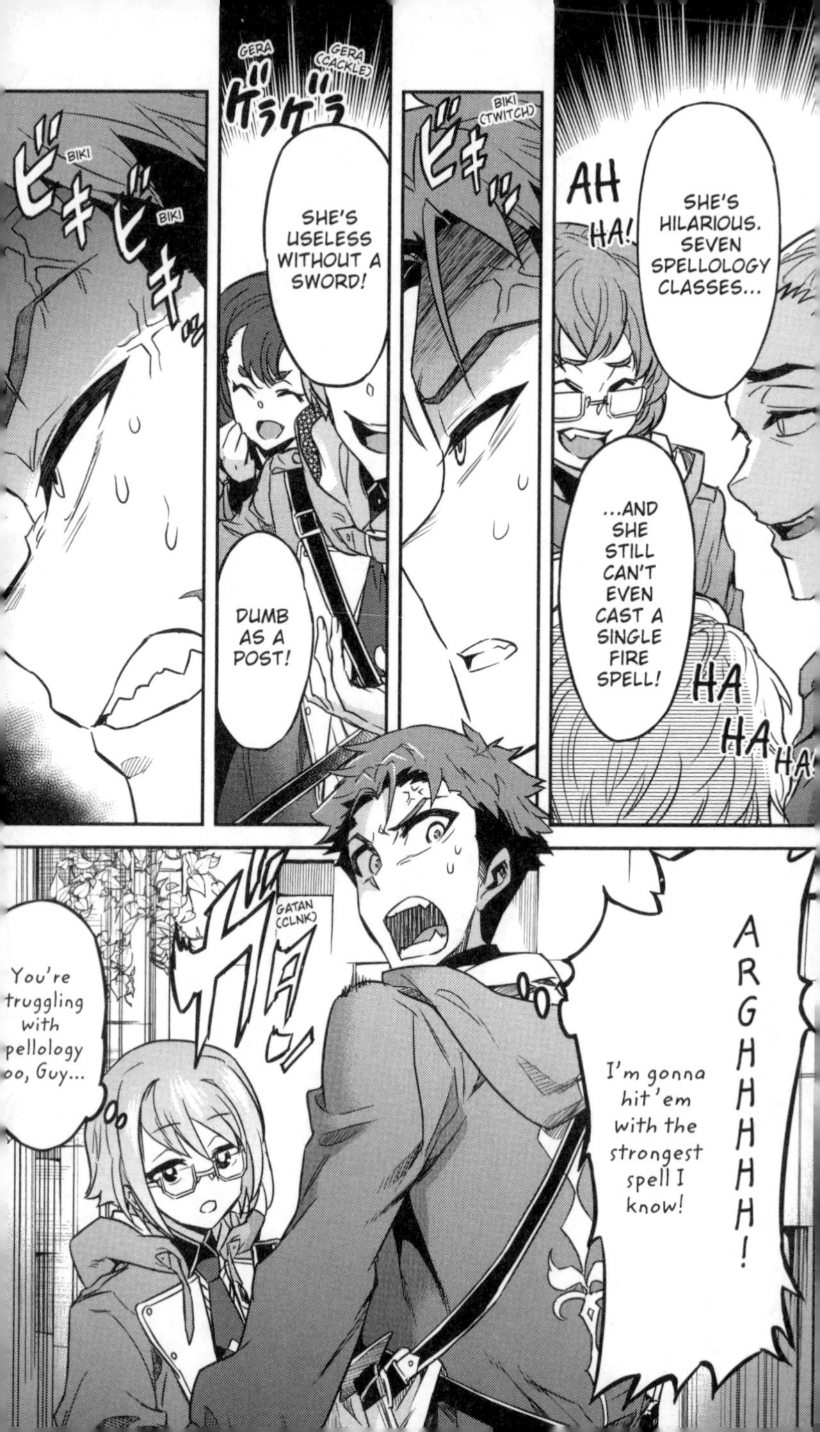
AH HA!
SHE'S HILARIOUS. SEVEN SPELLOLOGY CLASSES...
...AND SHE STILL CAN'T EVEN CAST A SINGLE FIRE SPELL!
HA HA HA
BIKI (TWITCH)
GERA GERA (CACKLE)
SHE'S USELESS WITHOUT A SWORD!
DUMB AS A POST!
BIKI
BIKI
ARGHHHHHH!
I'm gonna hit 'em with the strongest spell I know!
GATAN (CLNK)
You're truggling with pellology oo, Guy...

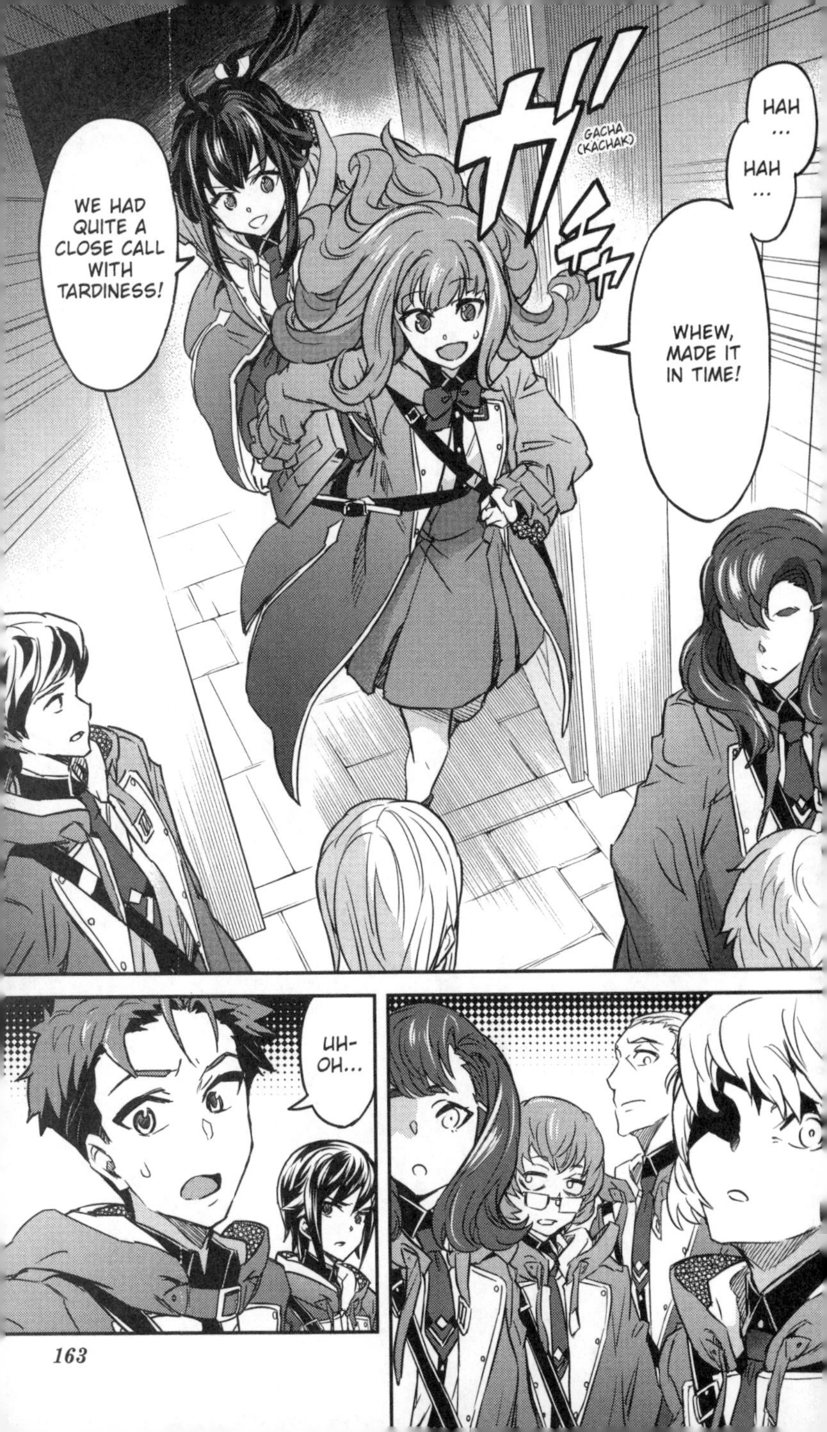
HAH... HAH...
WHEW, MADE IT IN TIME!
GACHA (KACHAK)
WE HAD QUITE A CLOSE CALL WITH TARDINESS!
UH-OH...

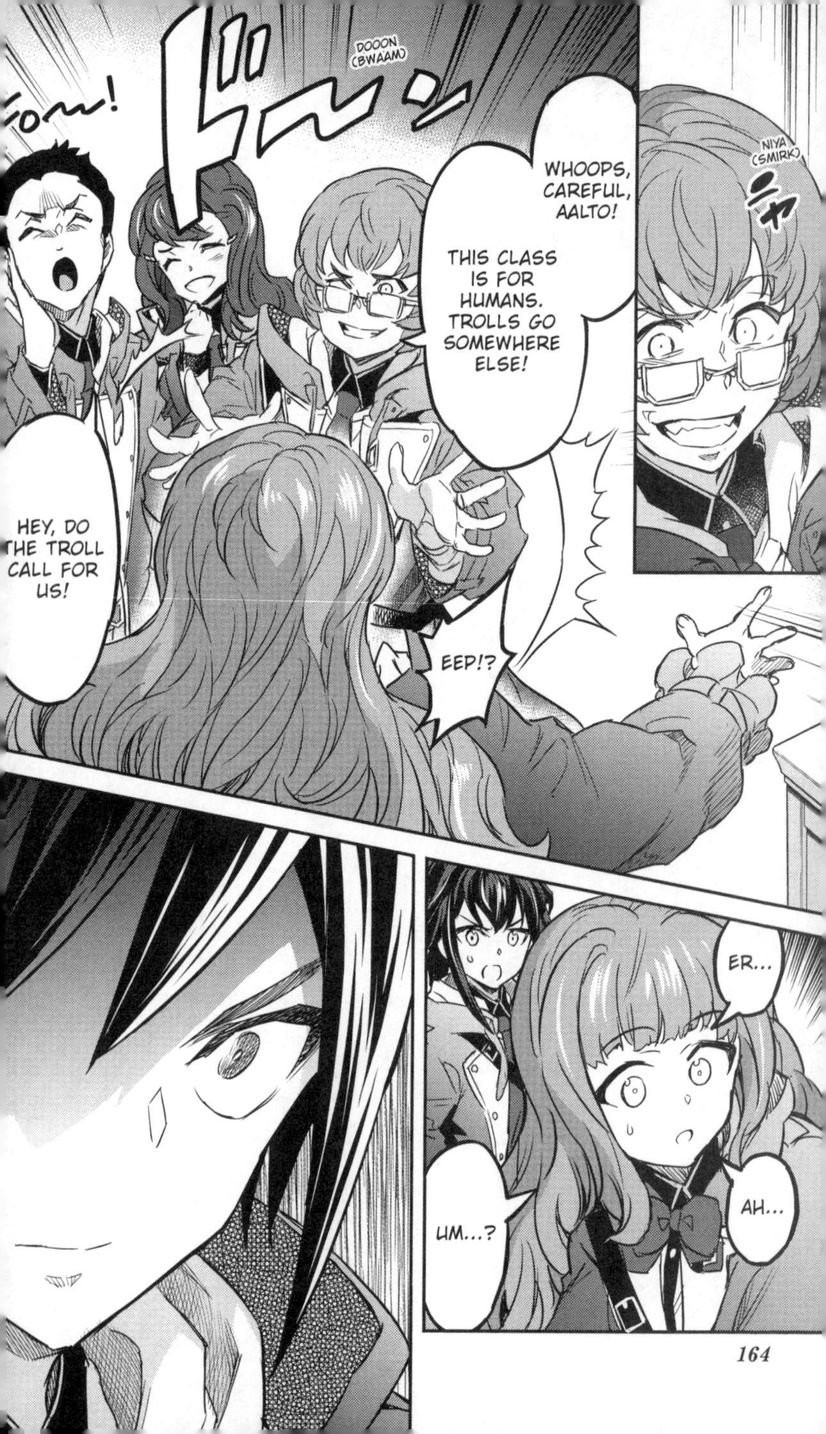
NIYA (SMIRK)
ニヤ
WHOOPS, CAREFUL, AALTO!
THIS CLASS IS FOR HUMANS. TROLLS GO SOMEWHERE ELSE!
DOOON (BWAAM)
HEY, DO THE TROLL CALL FOR US!
EEP!?
ER...
AH...
UM...?

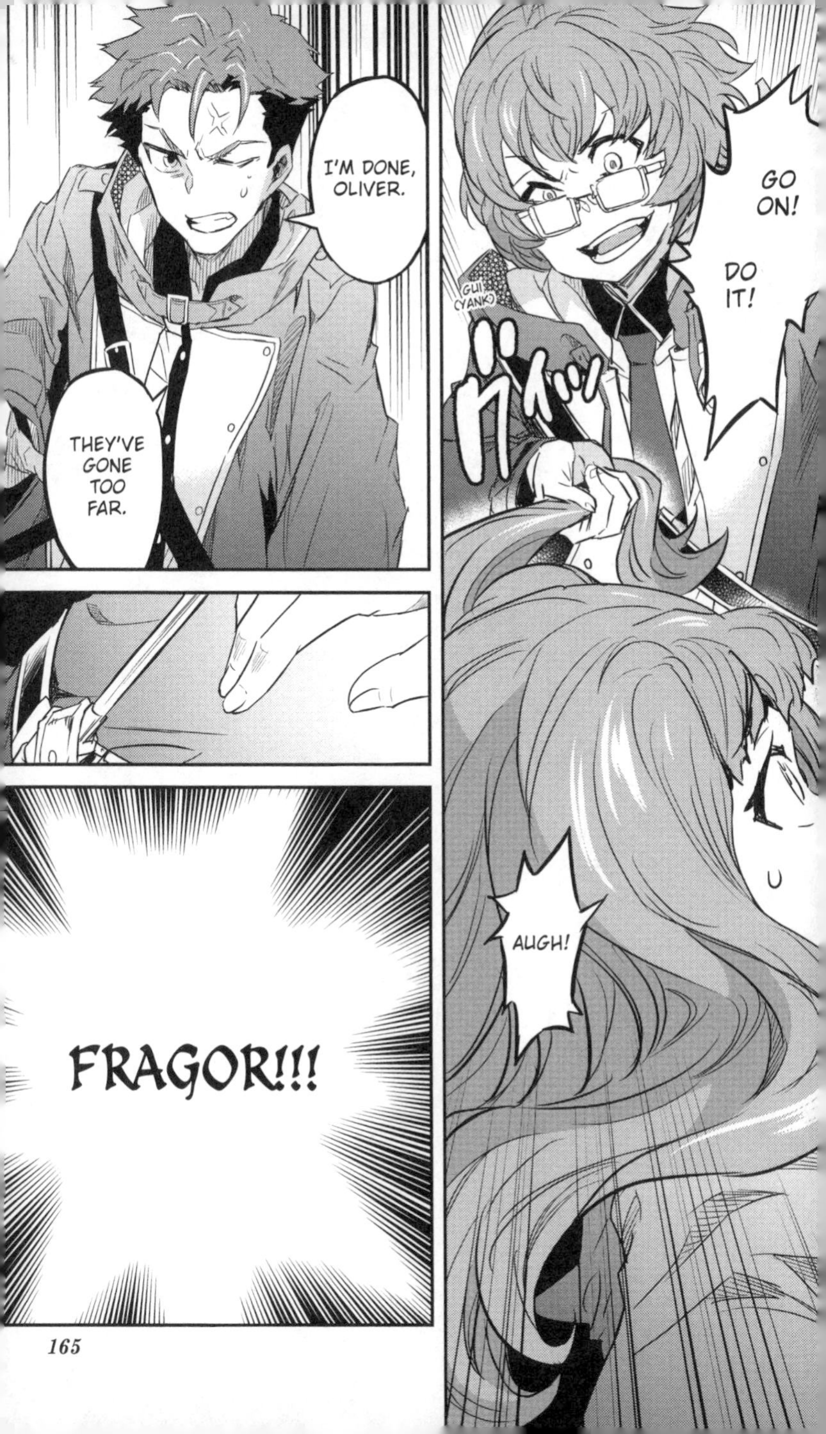
GO ON!
DO IT!
GUI (YANK)
AUGH!
I'M DONE, OLIVER.
THEY'VE GONE TOO FAR.
FRAGOR!!!

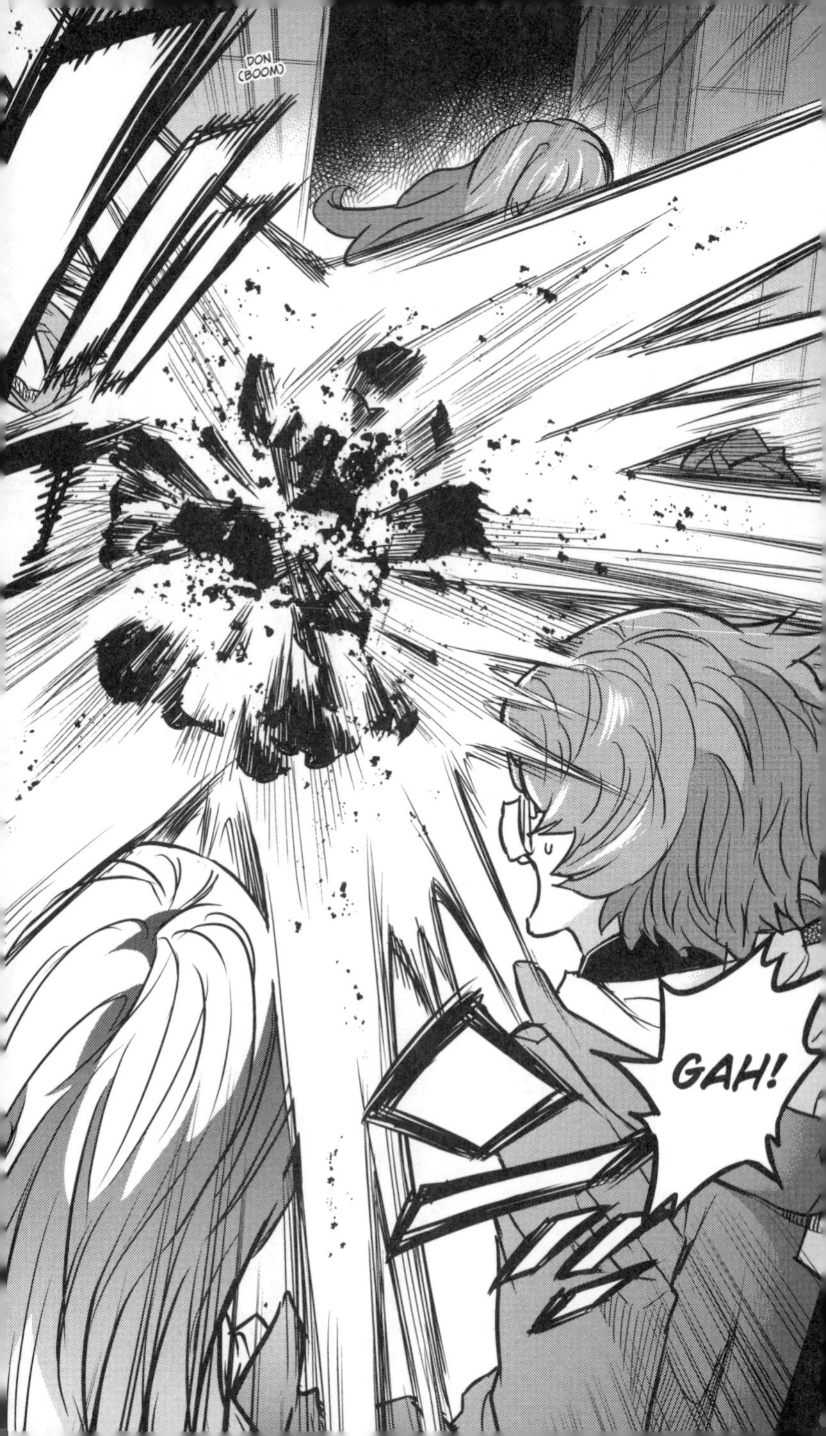
DON
(BOOM)
GAH!

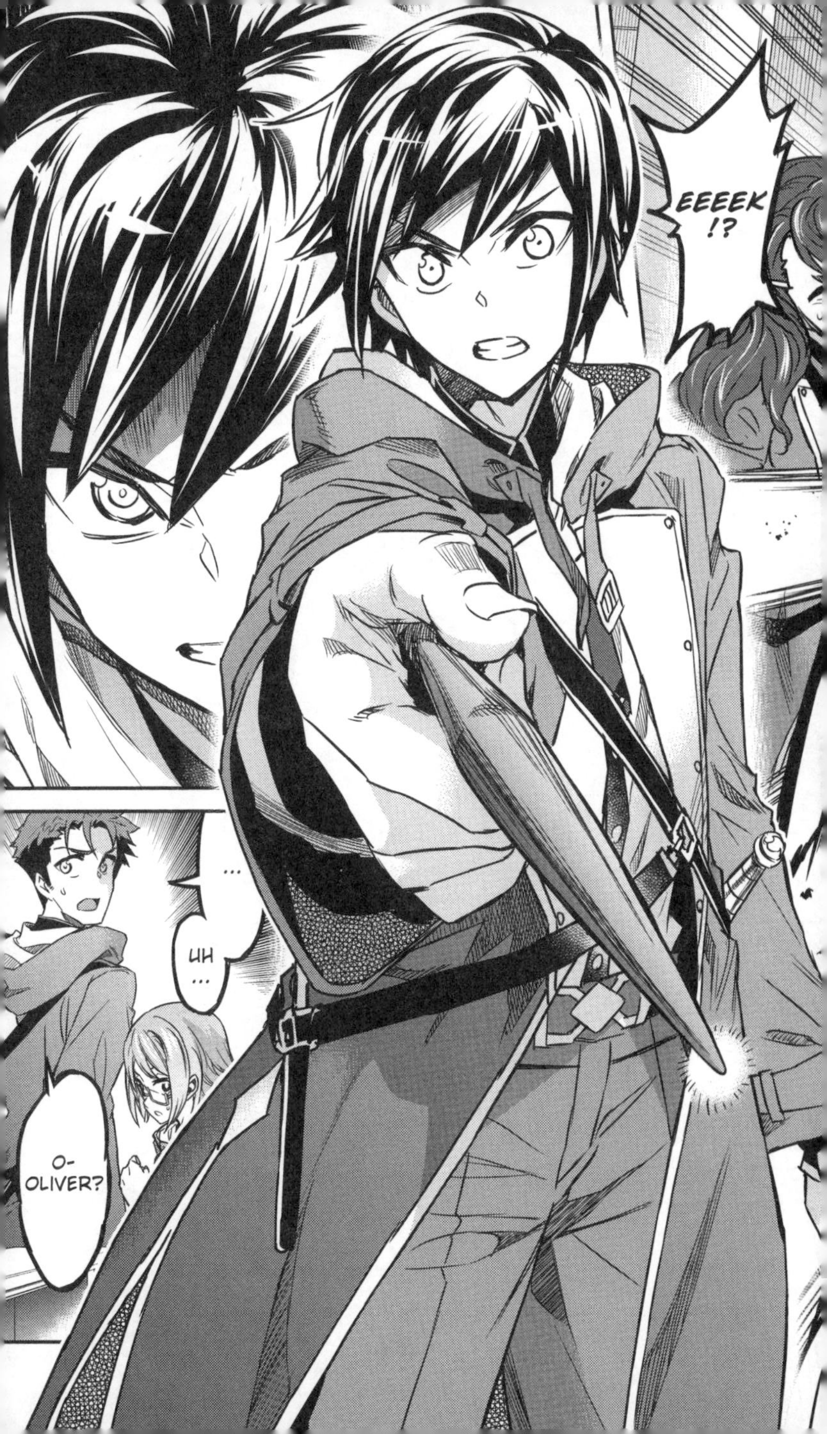
EEEEK !?
...
UH ...
O- OLIVER?

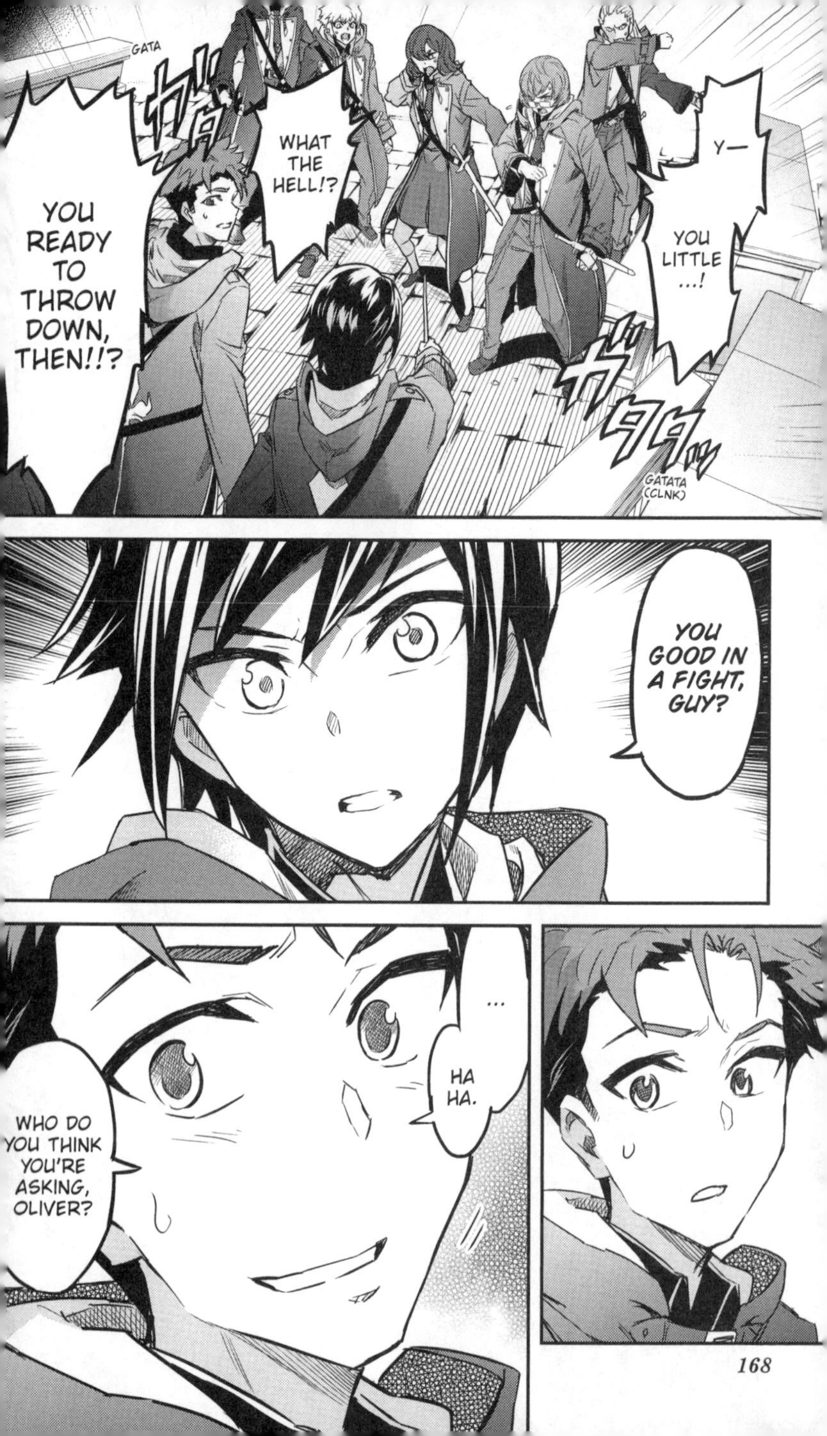
Y—
YOU LITTLE ...!
WHAT THE HELL!?
GATA
YOU READY TO THROW DOWN, THEN!!?
GATATA (CLNK)
YOU GOOD IN A FIGHT, GUY?
...
HA HA.
WHO DO YOU THINK YOU'RE ASKING, OLIVER?

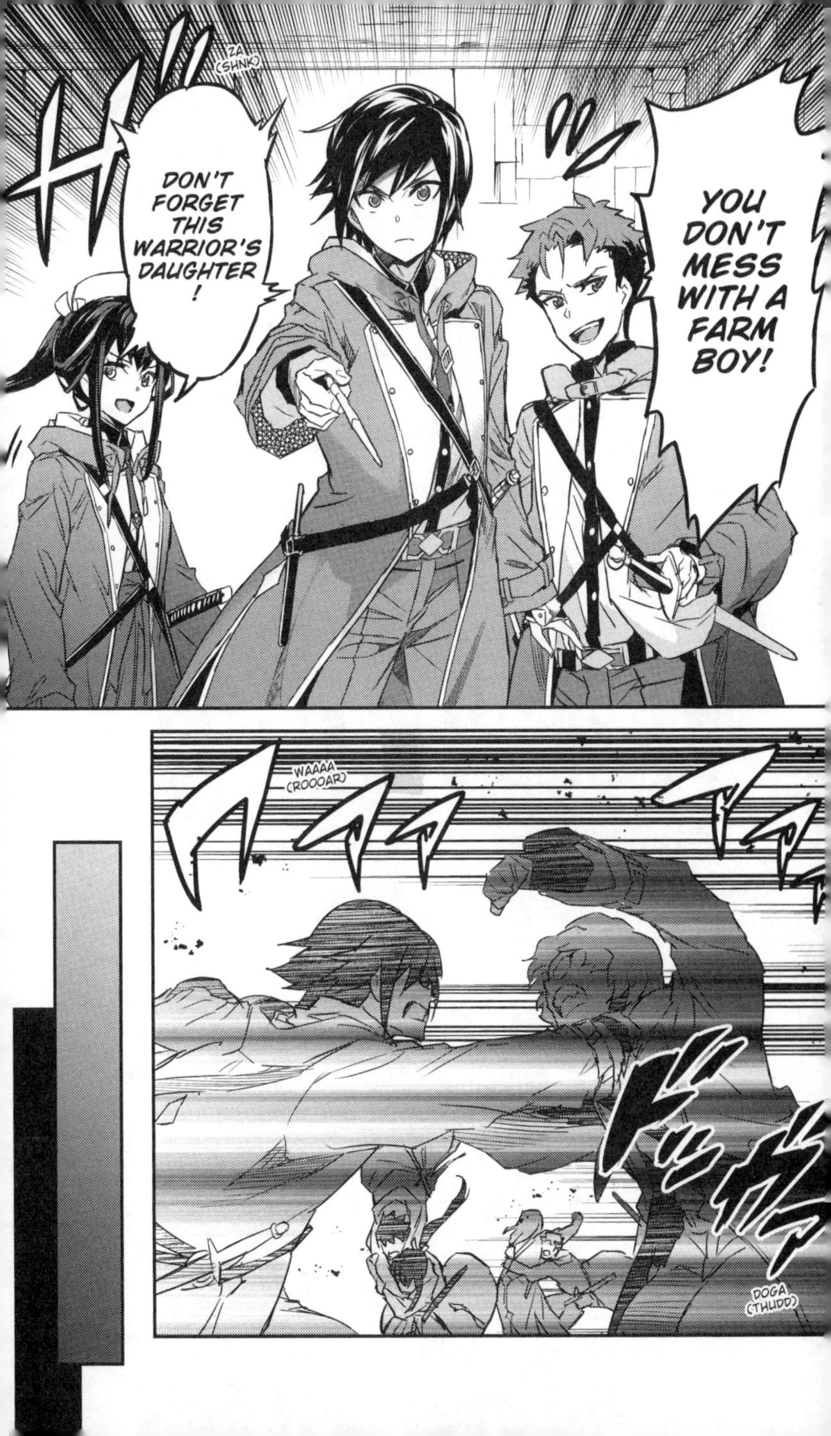

YOU DON'T MESS WITH A FARM BOY!
ZA (SHNK)
DON'T FORGET THIS WARRIOR'S DAUGHTER!
WAAAA (ROOOAR)
DOGA (THUDD)

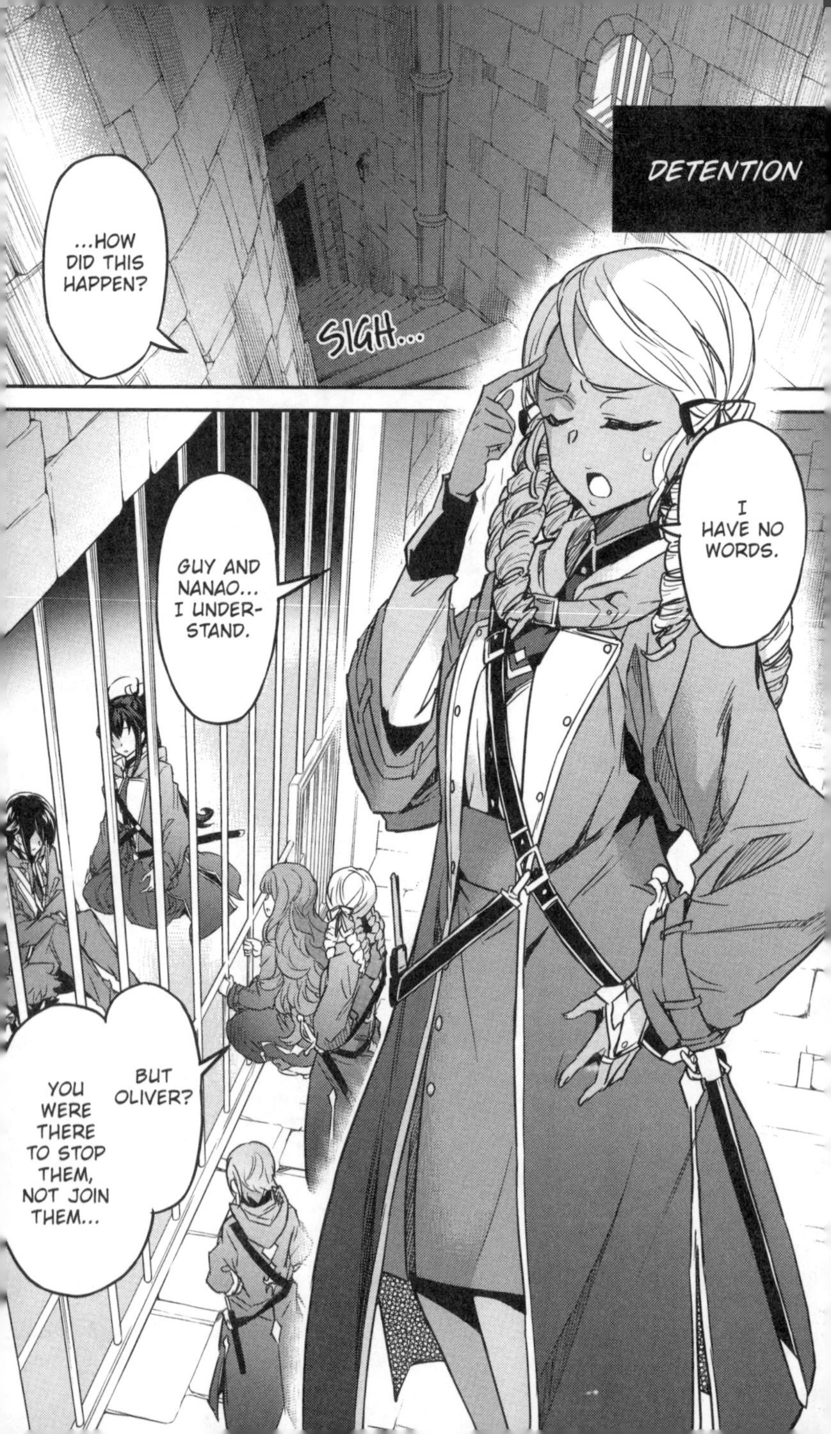
DETENTION
...HOW DID THIS HAPPEN?
SIGH...
I HAVE NO WORDS.
GUY AND NANAO... I UNDERSTAND.
BUT OLIVER?
YOU WERE THERE TO STOP THEM, NOT JOIN THEM...

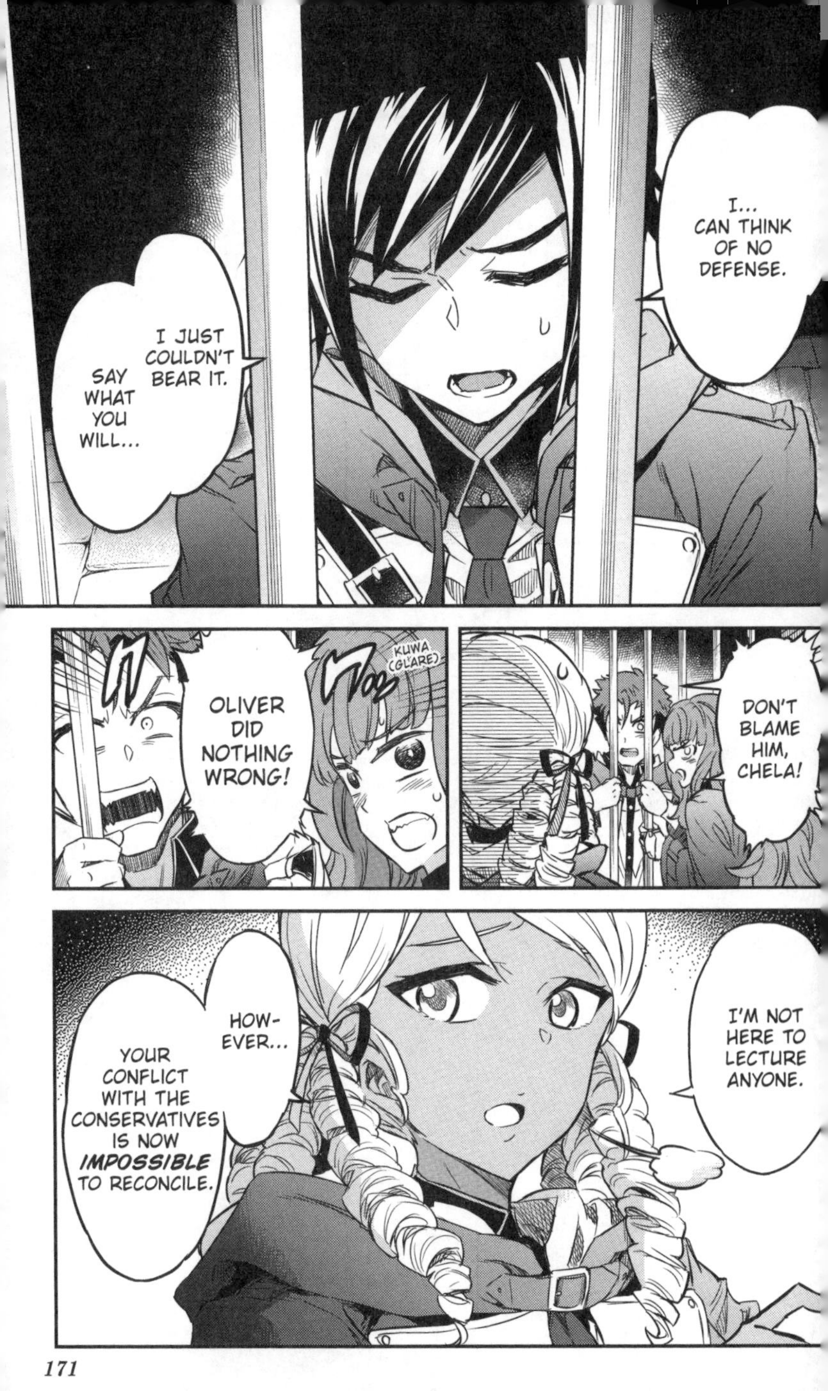
I... CAN THINK OF NO DEFENSE.
I JUST COULDN'T BEAR IT.
SAY WHAT YOU WILL...
DON'T BLAME HIM, CHELA!
KUWA (GLARE)
OLIVER DID NOTHING WRONG!
I'M NOT HERE TO LECTURE ANYONE.
HOW-EVER...
YOUR CONFLICT WITH THE CONSERVATIVES IS NOW *IMPOSSIBLE* TO RECONCILE.

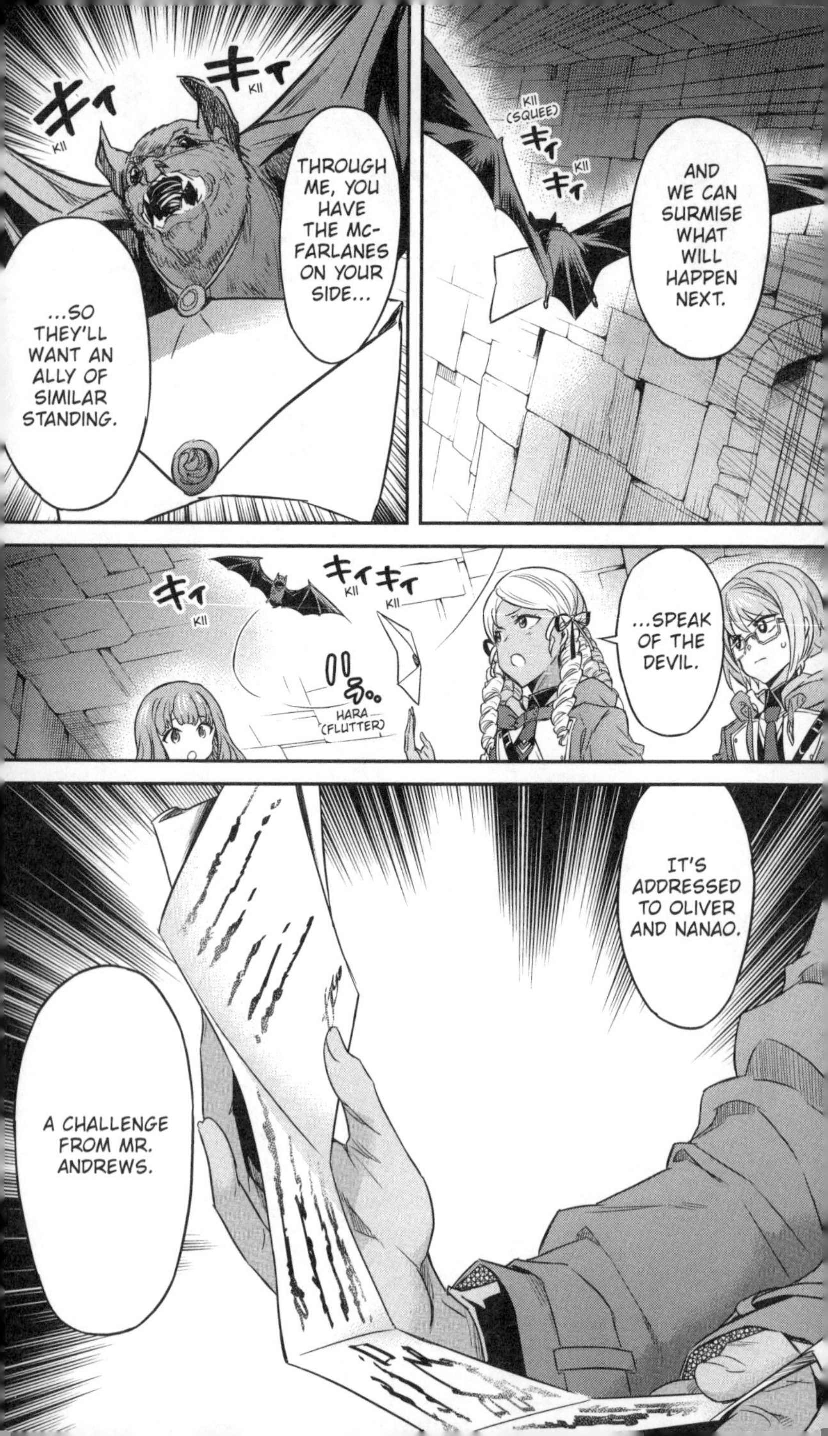
KII (SQUEE)
キィ
KII
キィ
AND WE CAN SURMISE WHAT WILL HAPPEN NEXT.
キィ
KII
キィ
KII
THROUGH ME, YOU HAVE THE MC-FARLANES ON YOUR SIDE...
...SO THEY'LL WANT AN ALLY OF SIMILAR STANDING.
...SPEAK OF THE DEVIL.
キィキィ
KII KII
HARA (FLUTTER)
キィ
KII
IT'S ADDRESSED TO OLIVER AND NANAO.
A CHALLENGE FROM MR. ANDREWS.

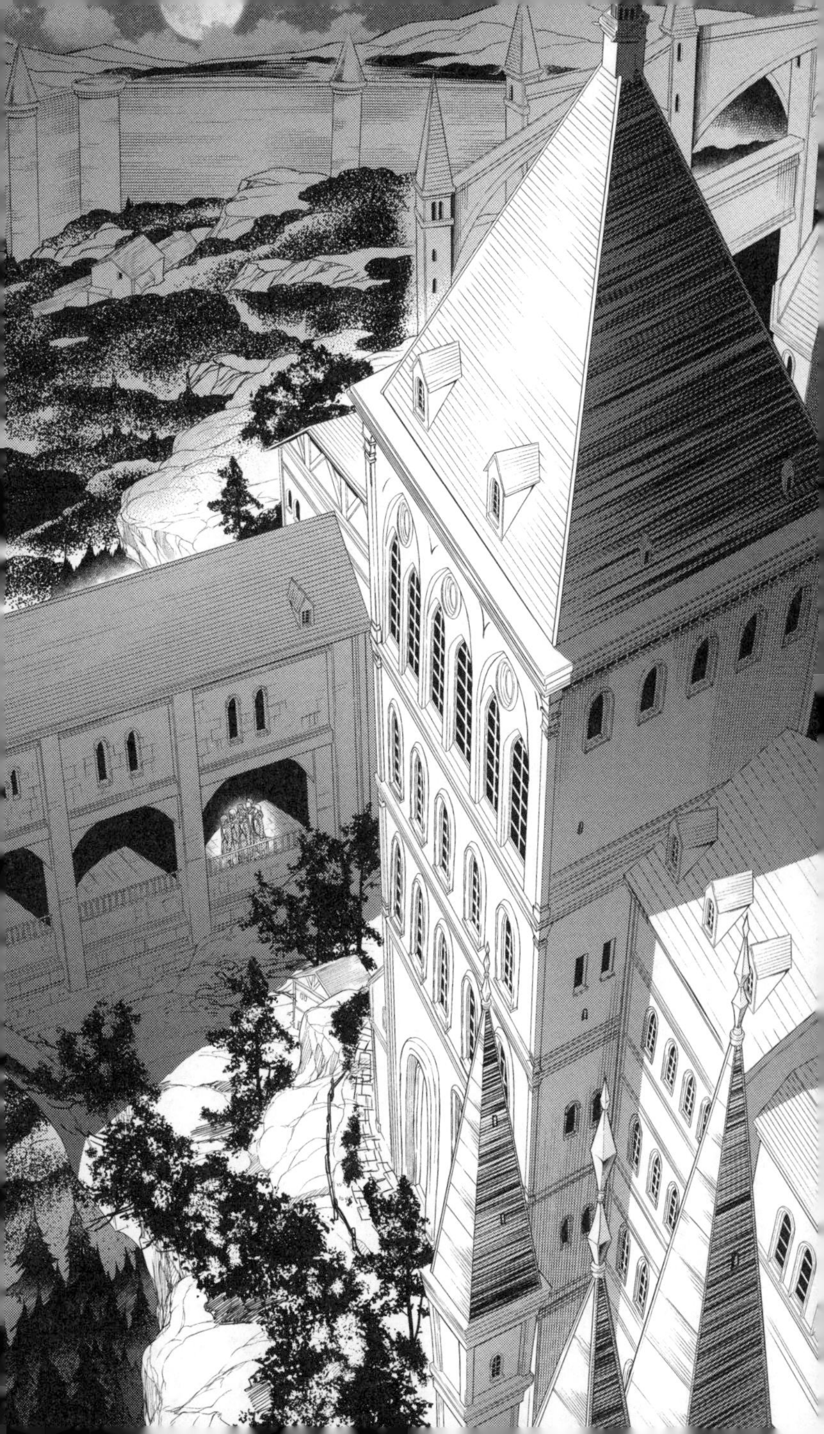

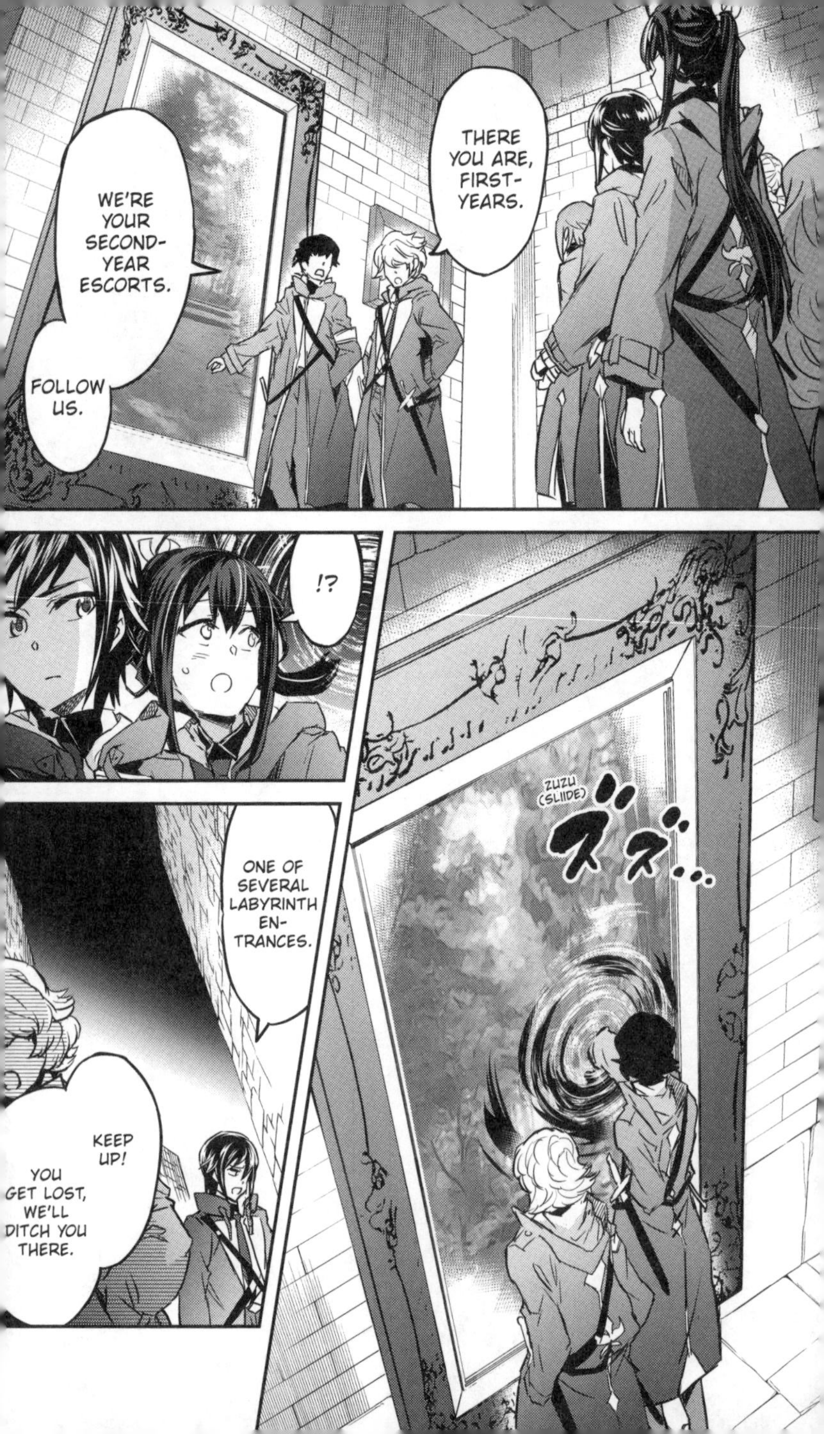
THERE YOU ARE, FIRST-YEARS.
WE'RE YOUR SECOND-YEAR ESCORTS.
FOLLOW US.
ZUZU (SLIIDE)
ズズ...
!?
ONE OF SEVERAL LABYRINTH EN-TRANCES.
KEEP UP!
YOU GET LOST, WE'LL DITCH YOU THERE.

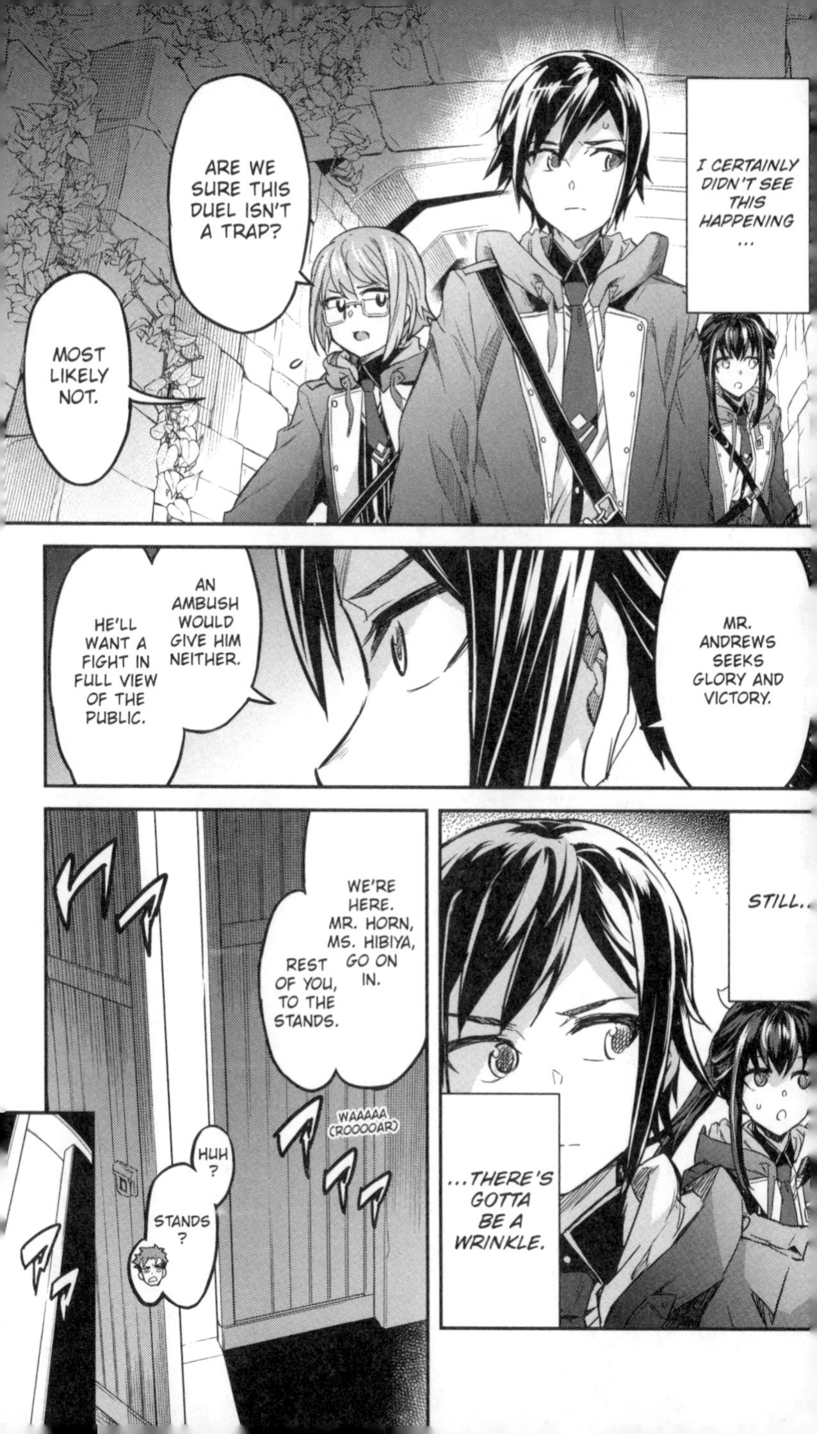
I CERTAINLY DIDN'T SEE THIS HAPPENING...
ARE WE SURE THIS DUEL ISN'T A TRAP?
MOST LIKELY NOT.
MR. ANDREWS SEEKS GLORY AND VICTORY.
AN AMBUSH WOULD GIVE HIM NEITHER.
HE'LL WANT A FIGHT IN FULL VIEW OF THE PUBLIC.
STILL...
...THERE'S GOTTA BE A WRINKLE.
WE'RE HERE. MR. HORN, MS. HIBIYA, GO ON IN.
REST OF YOU, TO THE STANDS.
WAAAAA (ROOOOAR)
HUH?
STANDS?

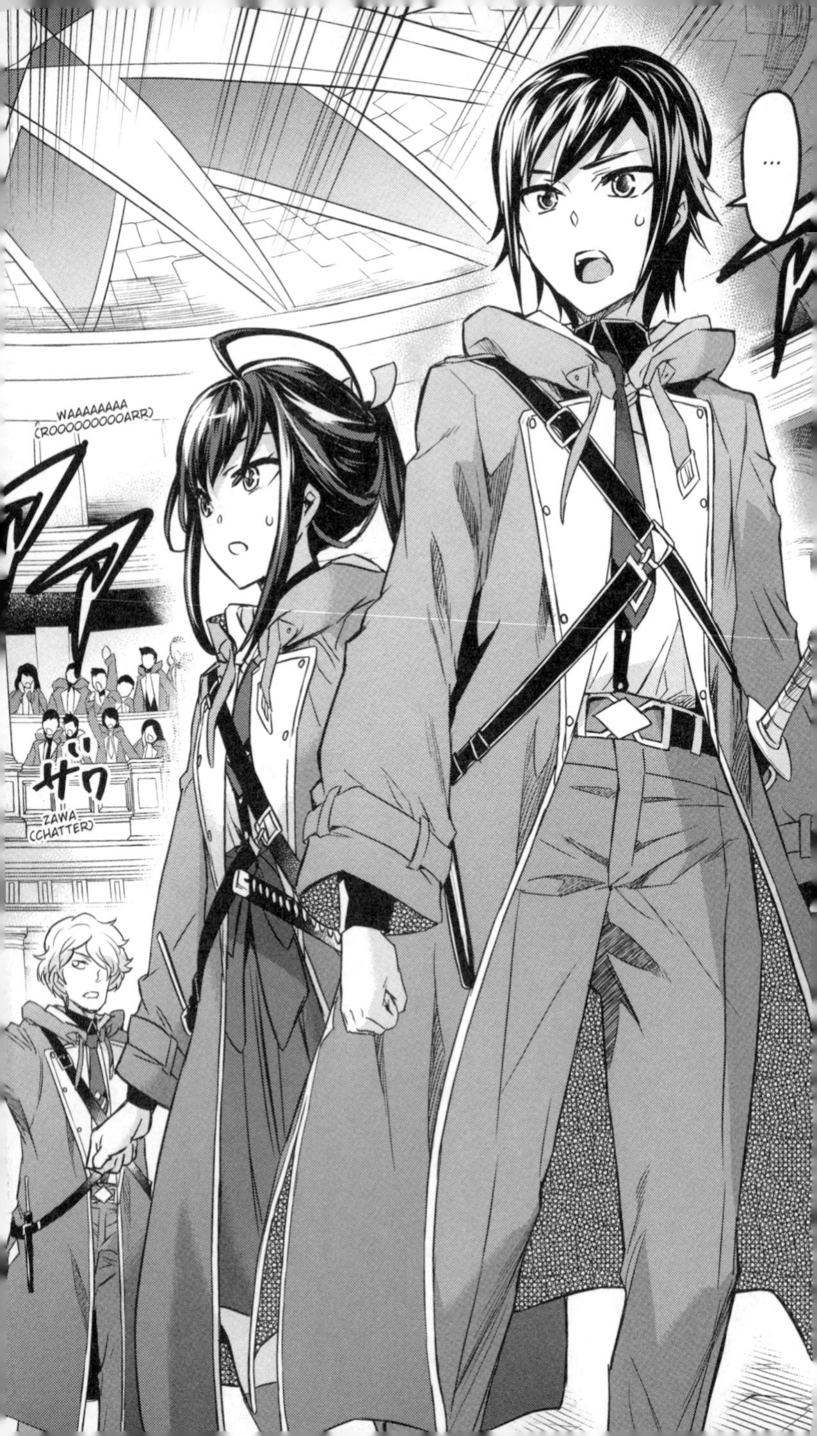
...
WAAAAAAAA
(ROOOOOOOOOARR)
ZAWA
(CHATTER)

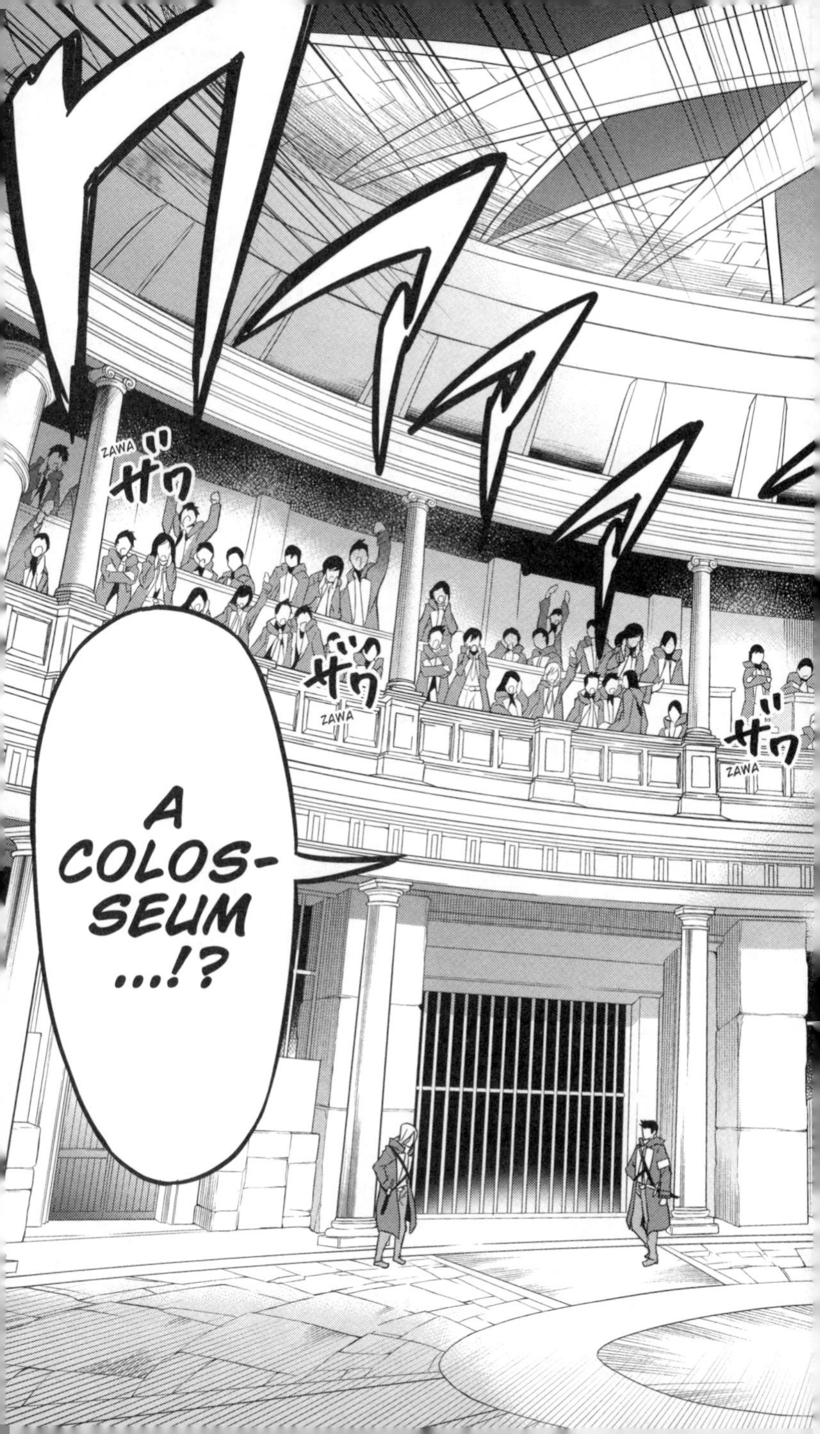
ZAWA ザワ
ZAWA ザワ
ZAWA ザワ
A COLOSSEUM...!?

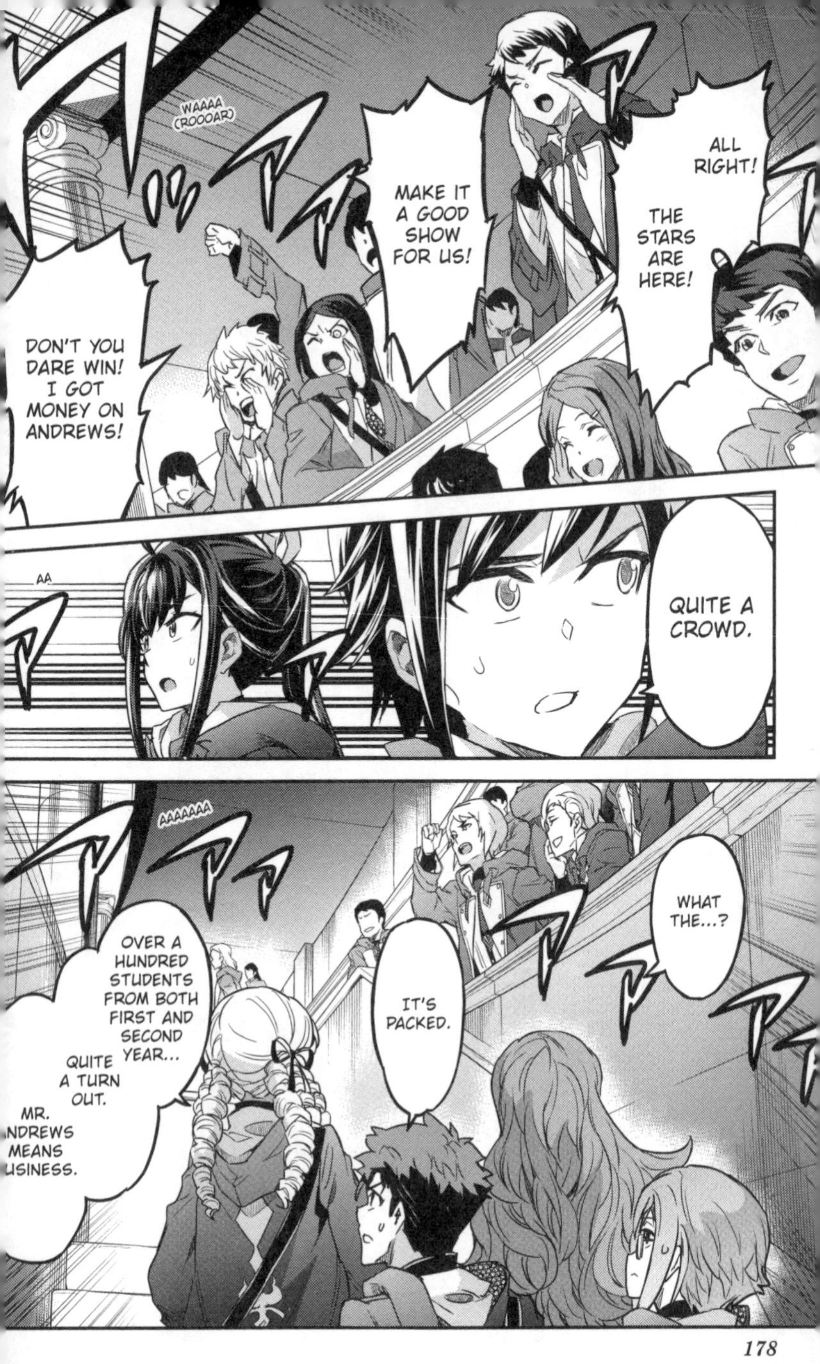
ALL RIGHT!
THE STARS ARE HERE!
MAKE IT A GOOD SHOW FOR US!
WAAAA (ROOOAR)
DON'T YOU DARE WIN! I GOT MONEY ON ANDREWS!
QUITE A CROWD.
AA
AAAAAAA
WHAT THE...?
IT'S PACKED.
OVER A HUNDRED STUDENTS FROM BOTH FIRST AND SECOND YEAR...
QUITE A TURN OUT.
MR. NDREWS MEANS USINESS.

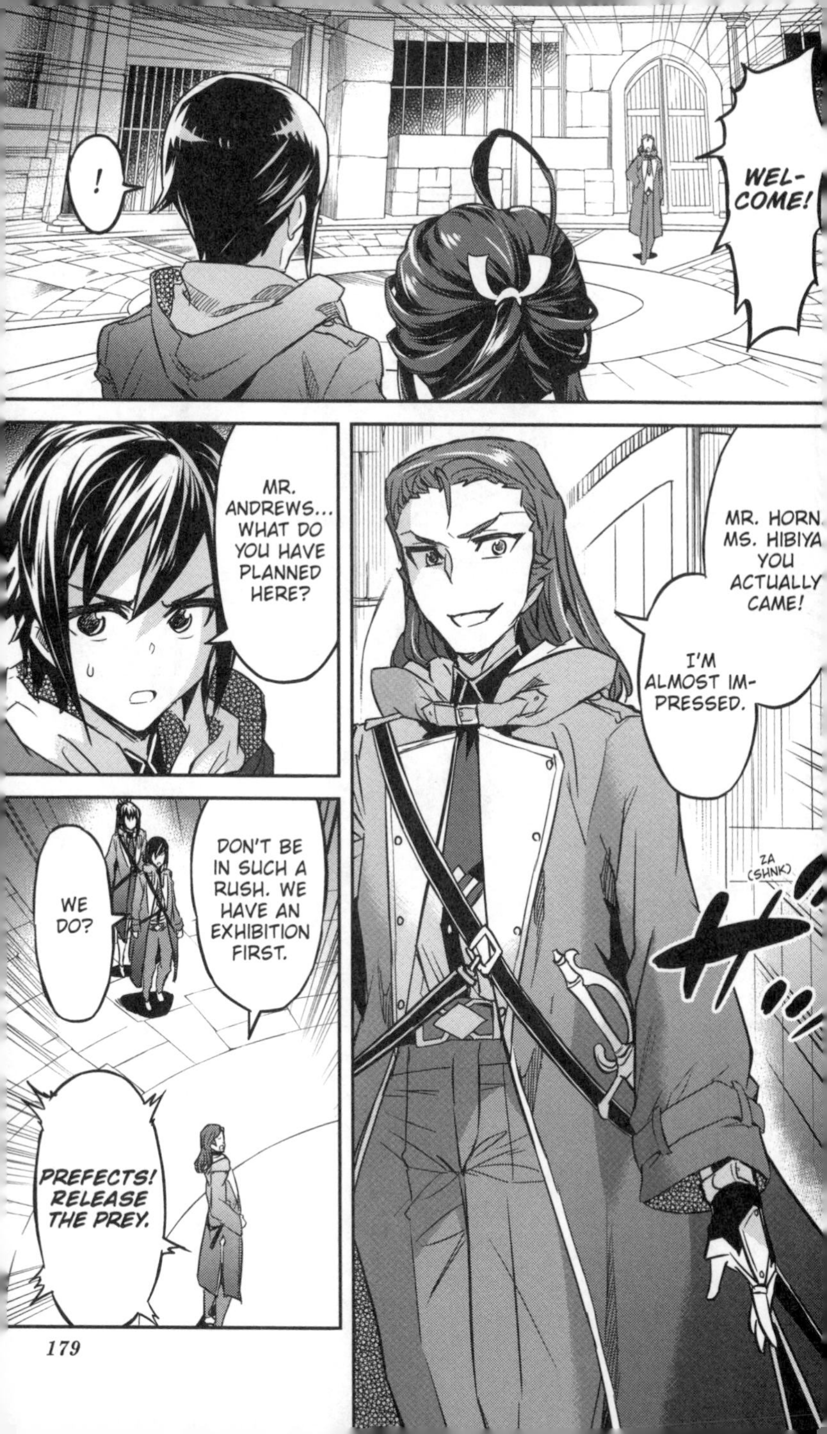
WEL-
COME!
!
MR. HORN. MS. HIBIYA YOU ACTUALLY CAME!
I'M ALMOST IM-
PRESSED.
ZA (SHNK)
MR. ANDREWS... WHAT DO YOU HAVE PLANNED HERE?
DON'T BE IN SUCH A RUSH. WE HAVE AN EXHIBITION FIRST.
WE DO?
PREFECTS! RELEASE THE PREY.

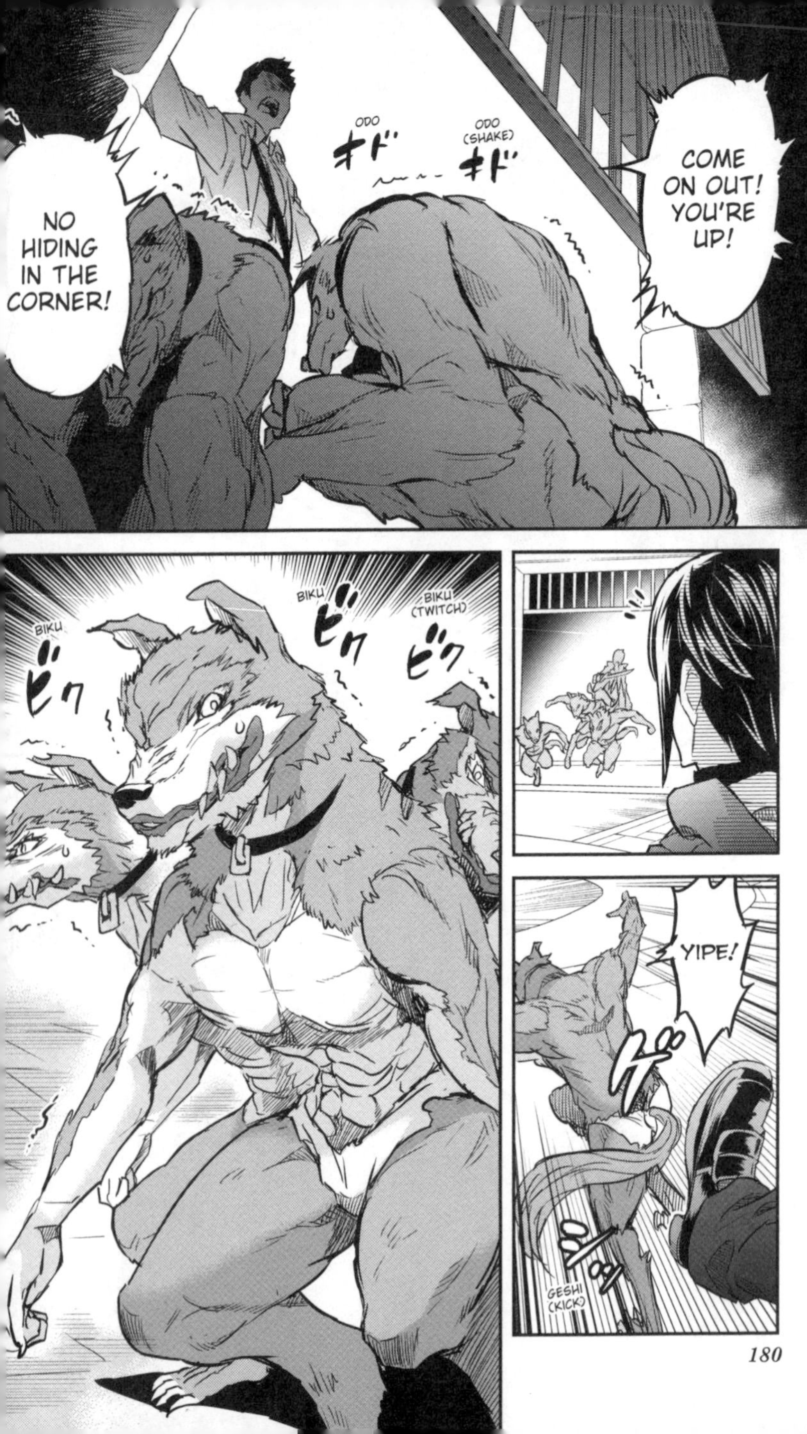
COME ON OUT! YOU'RE UP!
ODO (SHAKE)
ODO
NO HIDING IN THE CORNER!
YIPE!
GESHI (KICK)
BIKU (TWITCH)
BIKU
BIKU

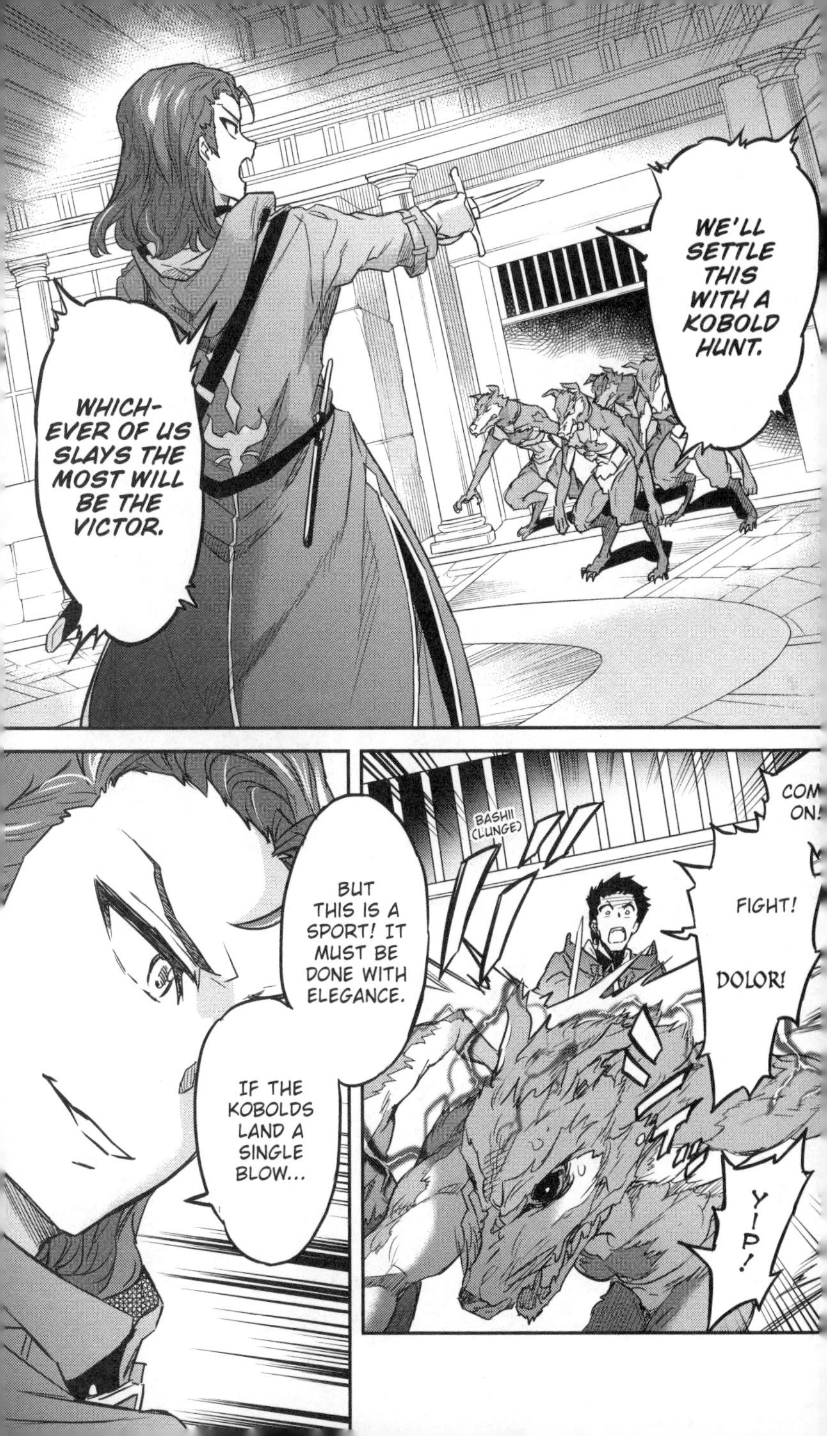
WE'LL SETTLE THIS WITH A KOBOLD HUNT.
WHICH-EVER OF US SLAYS THE MOST WILL BE THE VICTOR.
COM ON!
FIGHT!
DOLOR!
BASHII (LUNGE)
YIP!
BUT THIS IS A SPORT! IT MUST BE DONE WITH ELEGANCE.
IF THE KOBOLDS LAND A SINGLE BLOW...

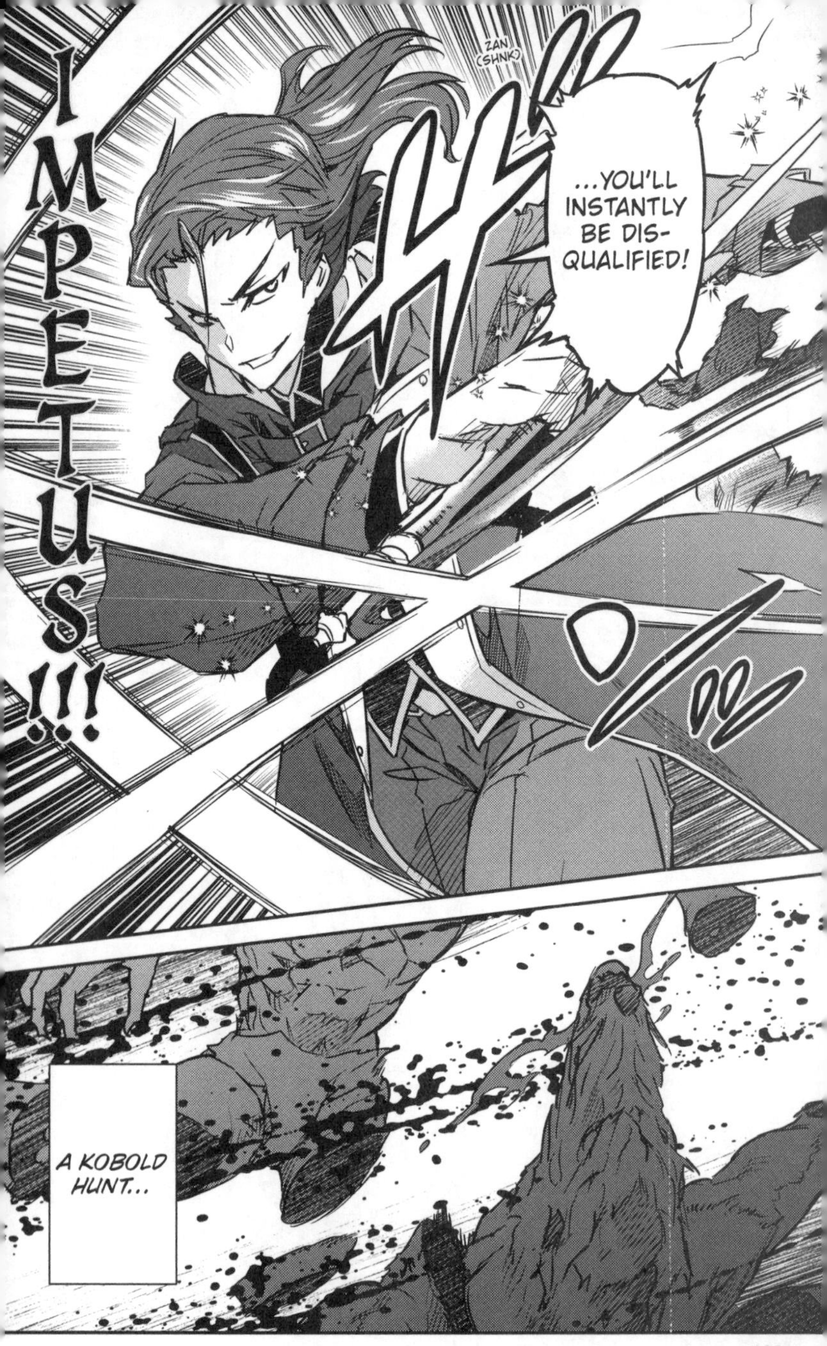
...YOU'LL INSTANTLY BE DIS-QUALIFIED!
ZAN (SHNK)
IMPETUS!!!
A KOBOLD HUNT...

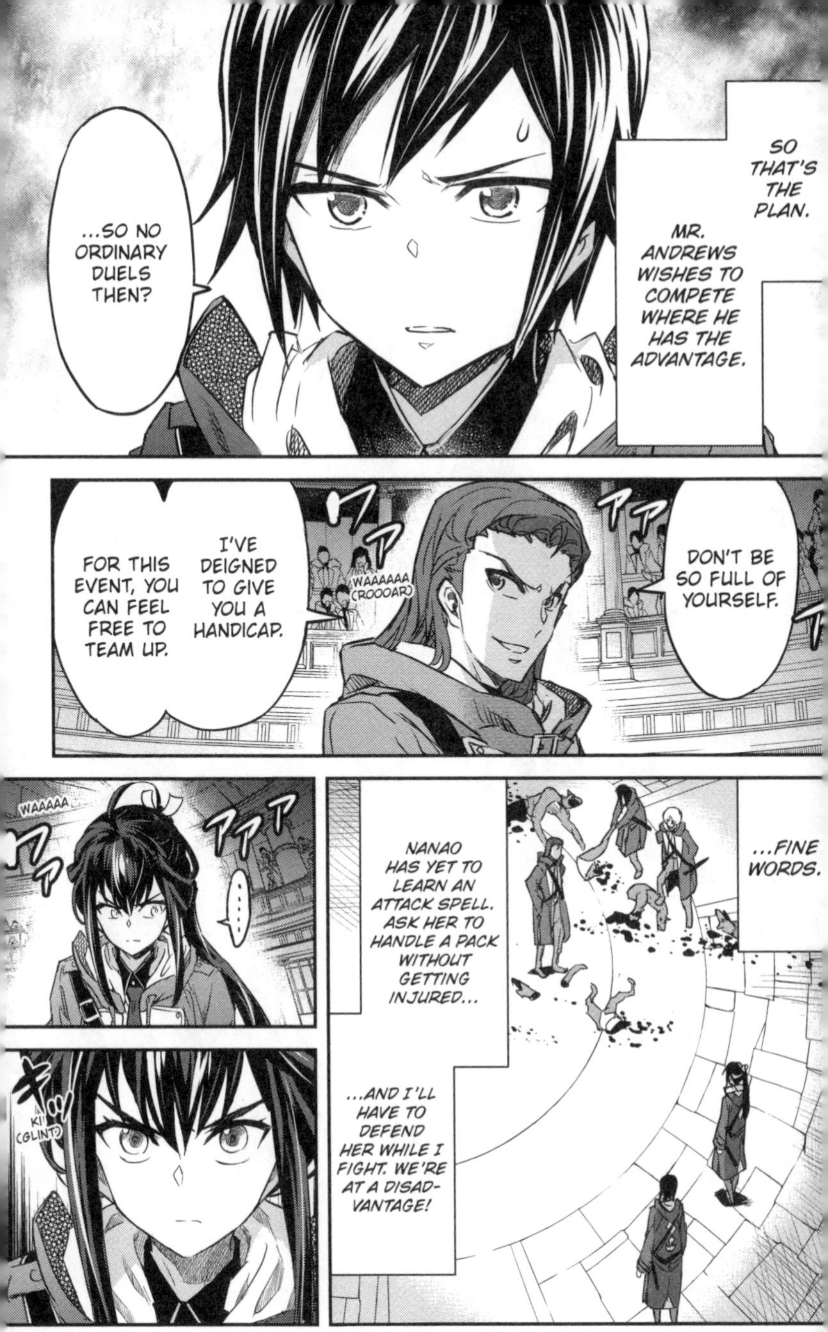
SO THAT'S THE PLAN.
MR. ANDREWS WISHES TO COMPETE WHERE HE HAS THE ADVANTAGE.
...SO NO ORDINARY DUELS THEN?
DON'T BE SO FULL OF YOURSELF.
WAAAAAA (ROOOAR)
I'VE DEIGNED TO GIVE YOU A HANDICAP.
FOR THIS EVENT, YOU CAN FEEL FREE TO TEAM UP.
...FINE WORDS.
NANAO HAS YET TO LEARN AN ATTACK SPELL. ASK HER TO HANDLE A PACK WITHOUT GETTING INJURED...
...AND I'LL HAVE TO DEFEND HER WHILE I FIGHT. WE'RE AT A DISAD-VANTAGE!
WAAAAA
......
KI' (GLINT)

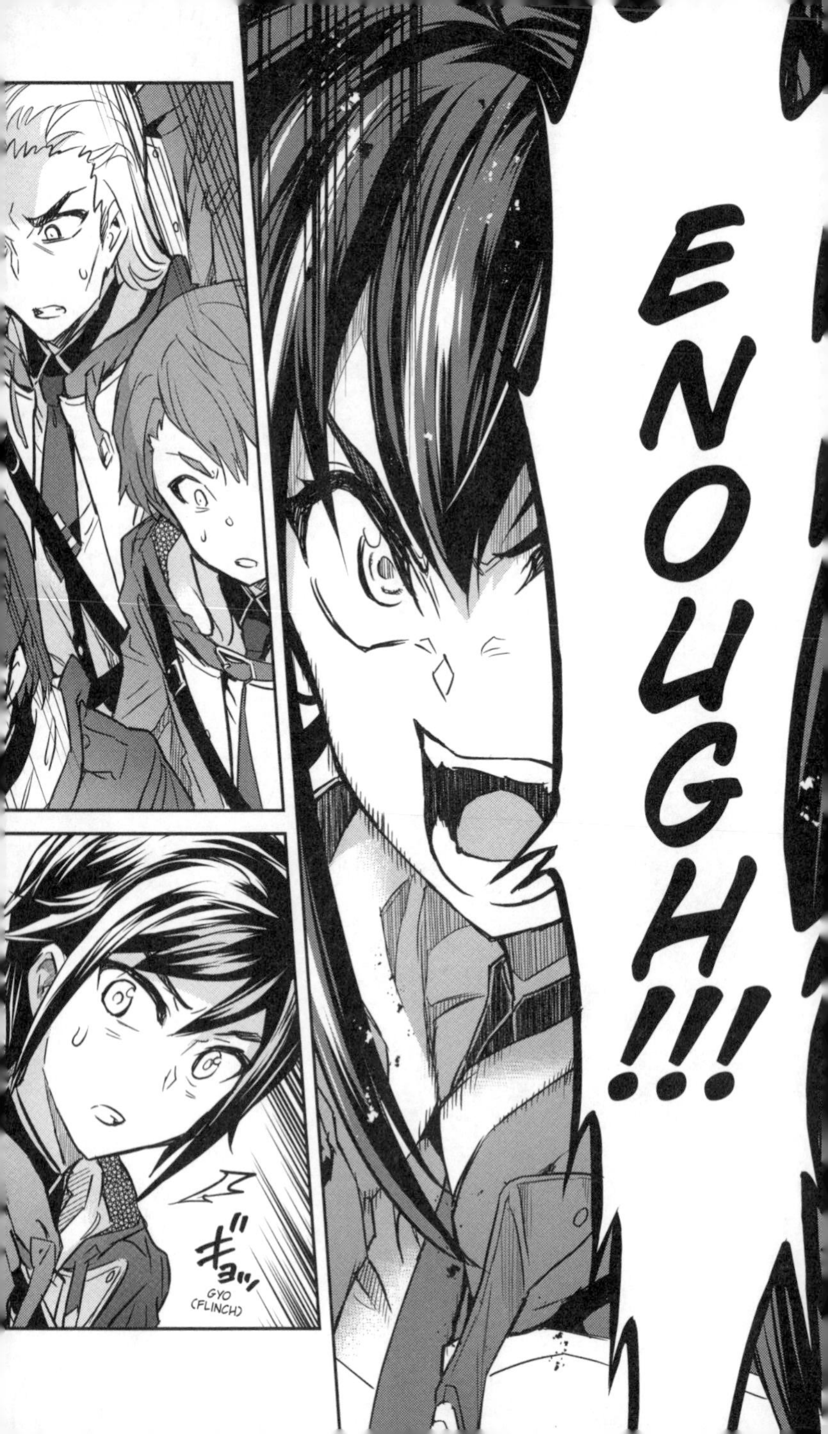
ENOUGH!!!
ギョッ
GYO (FLINCH)

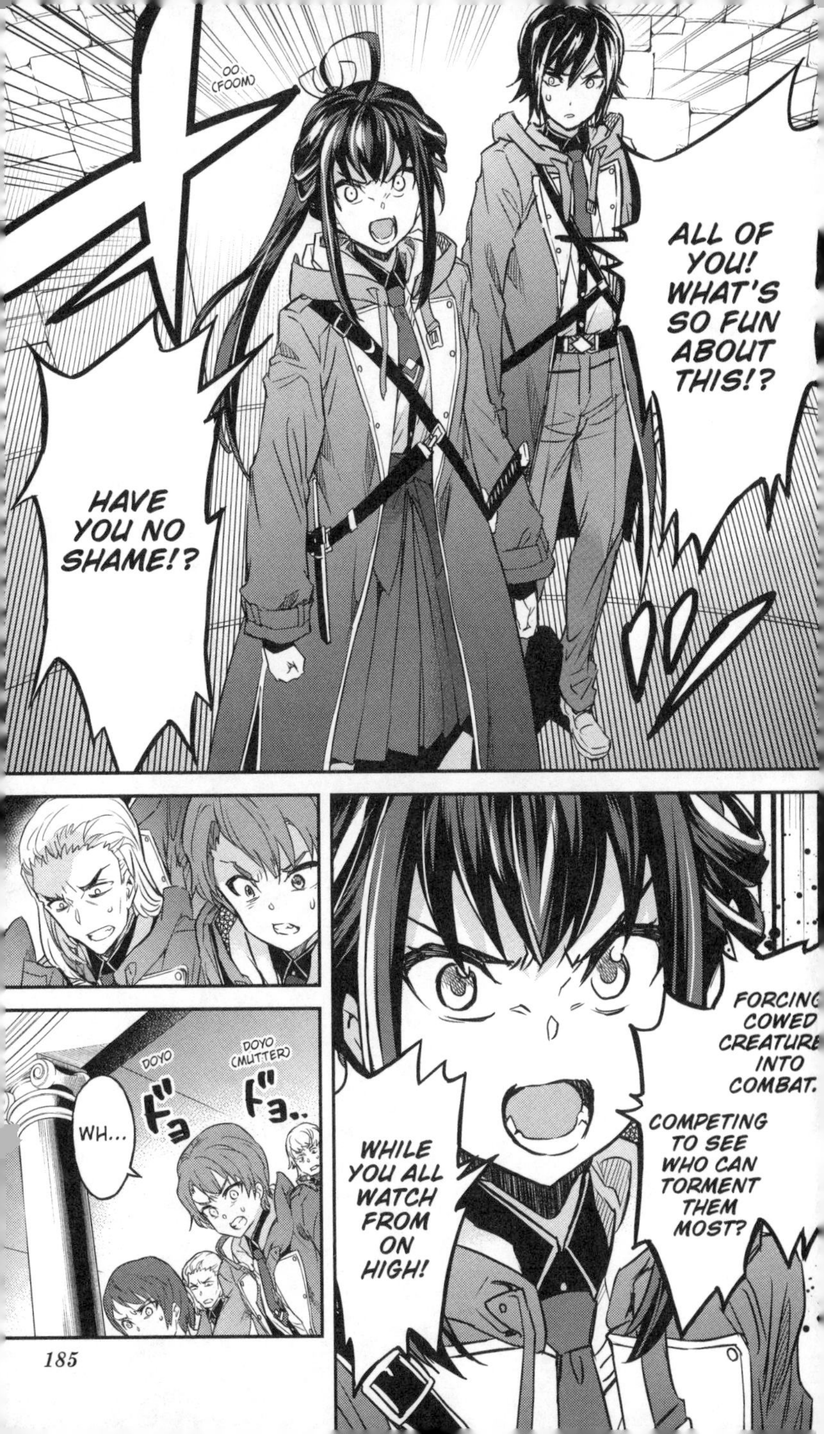
OO (FOOM)
ALL OF YOU! WHAT'S SO FUN ABOUT THIS!?
HAVE YOU NO SHAME!?
FORCING COWED CREATURE INTO COMBAT.
COMPETING TO SEE WHO CAN TORMENT THEM MOST?
WHILE YOU ALL WATCH FROM ON HIGH!
DOYO (MUTTER)
ドョ..
DOYO
ドョ
WH...

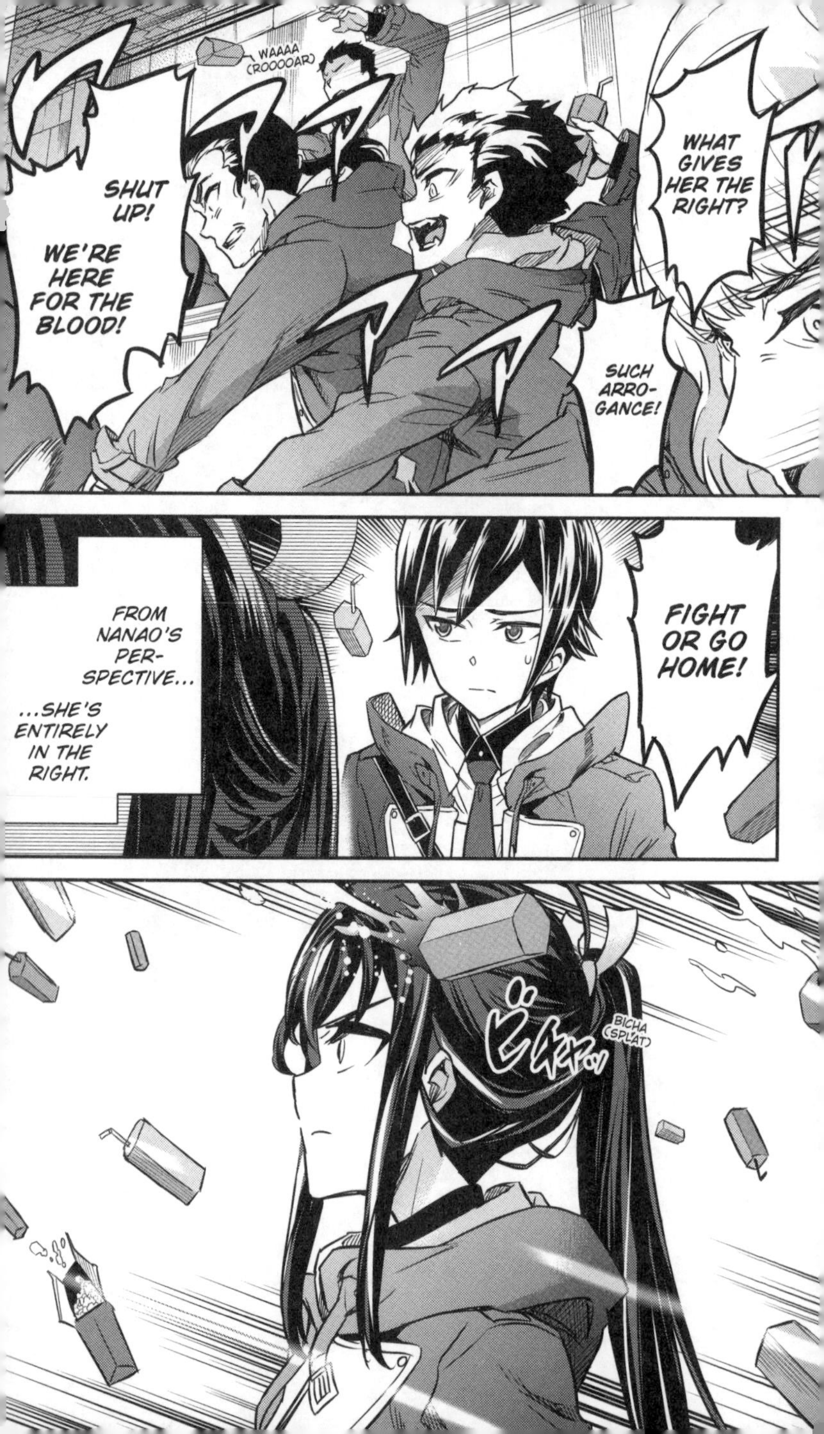
WHAT GIVES HER THE RIGHT?
WAAAA (ROOOOAR)
SUCH ARRO-GANCE!
SHUT UP!
WE'RE HERE FOR THE BLOOD!
FIGHT OR GO HOME!
FROM NANAO'S PER-SPECTIVE...
...SHE'S ENTIRELY IN THE RIGHT.
BICHA (SPLAT)

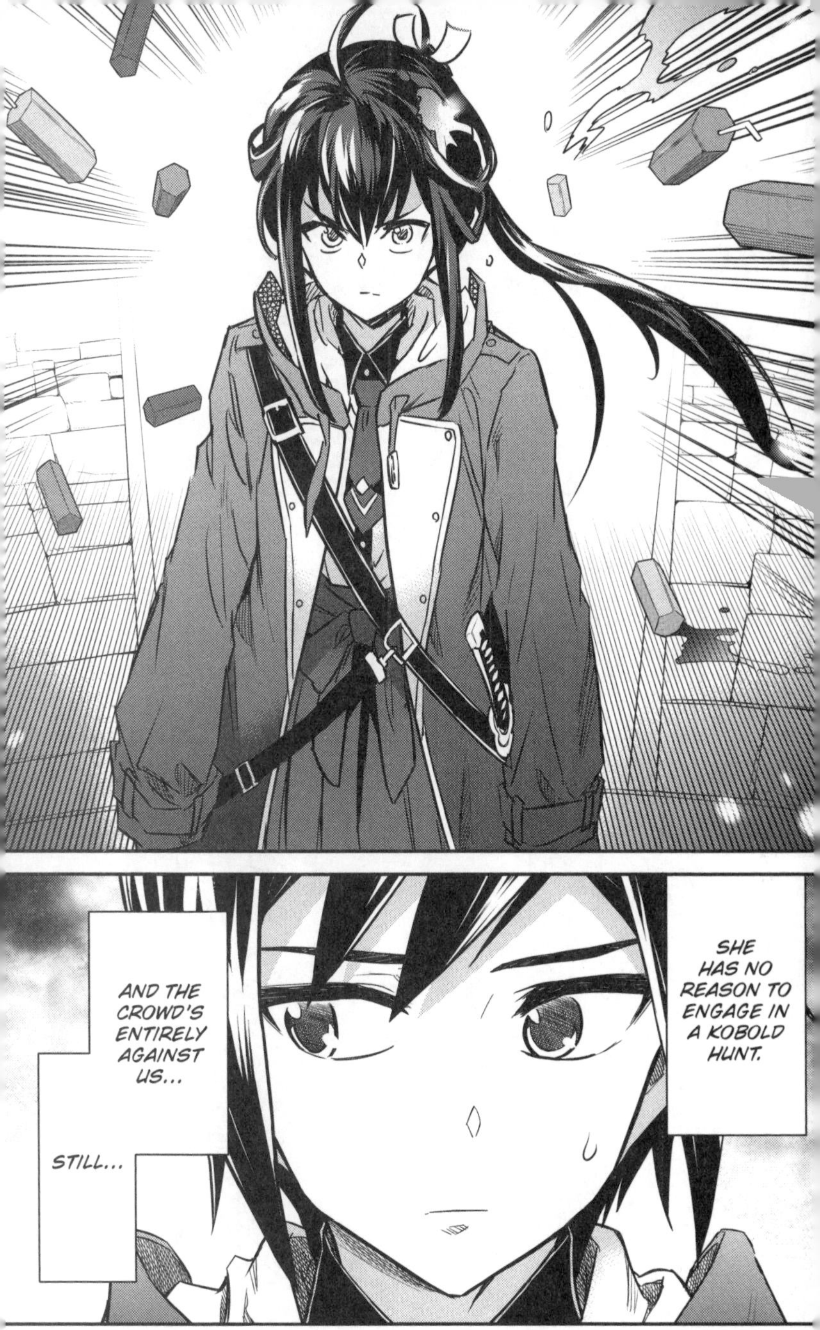
SHE HAS NO REASON TO ENGAGE IN A KOBOLD HUNT.
AND THE CROWD'S ENTIRELY AGAINST US...
STILL...

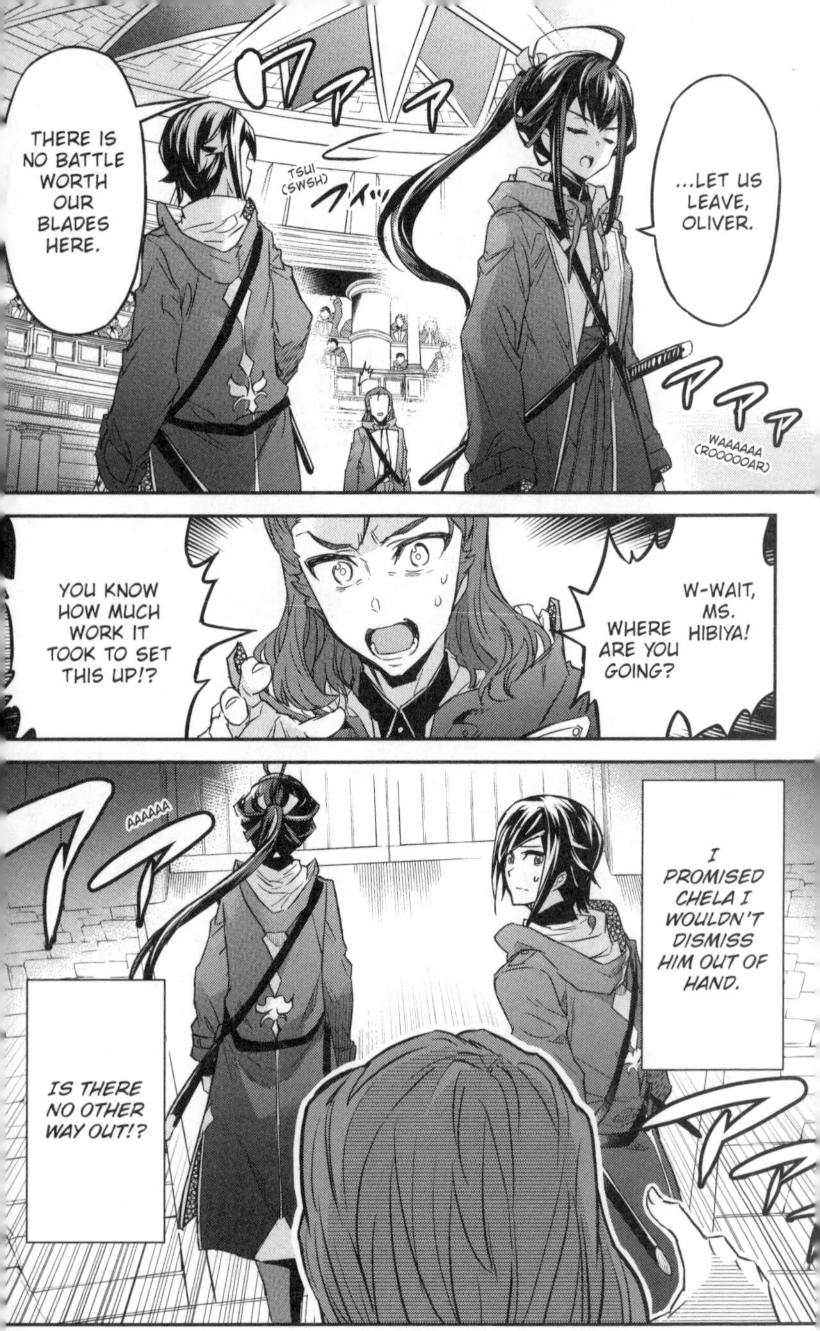

...LET US LEAVE, OLIVER.
TSUI (SWSH)
THERE IS NO BATTLE WORTH OUR BLADES HERE.
WAAAAAAA (ROOOOOAR)
W-WAIT, MS. HIBIYA!
WHERE ARE YOU GOING?
YOU KNOW HOW MUCH WORK IT TOOK TO SET THIS UP!?
I PROMISED CHELA I WOULDN'T DISMISS HIM OUT OF HAND.
AAAAAA
IS THERE NO OTHER WAY OUT!?

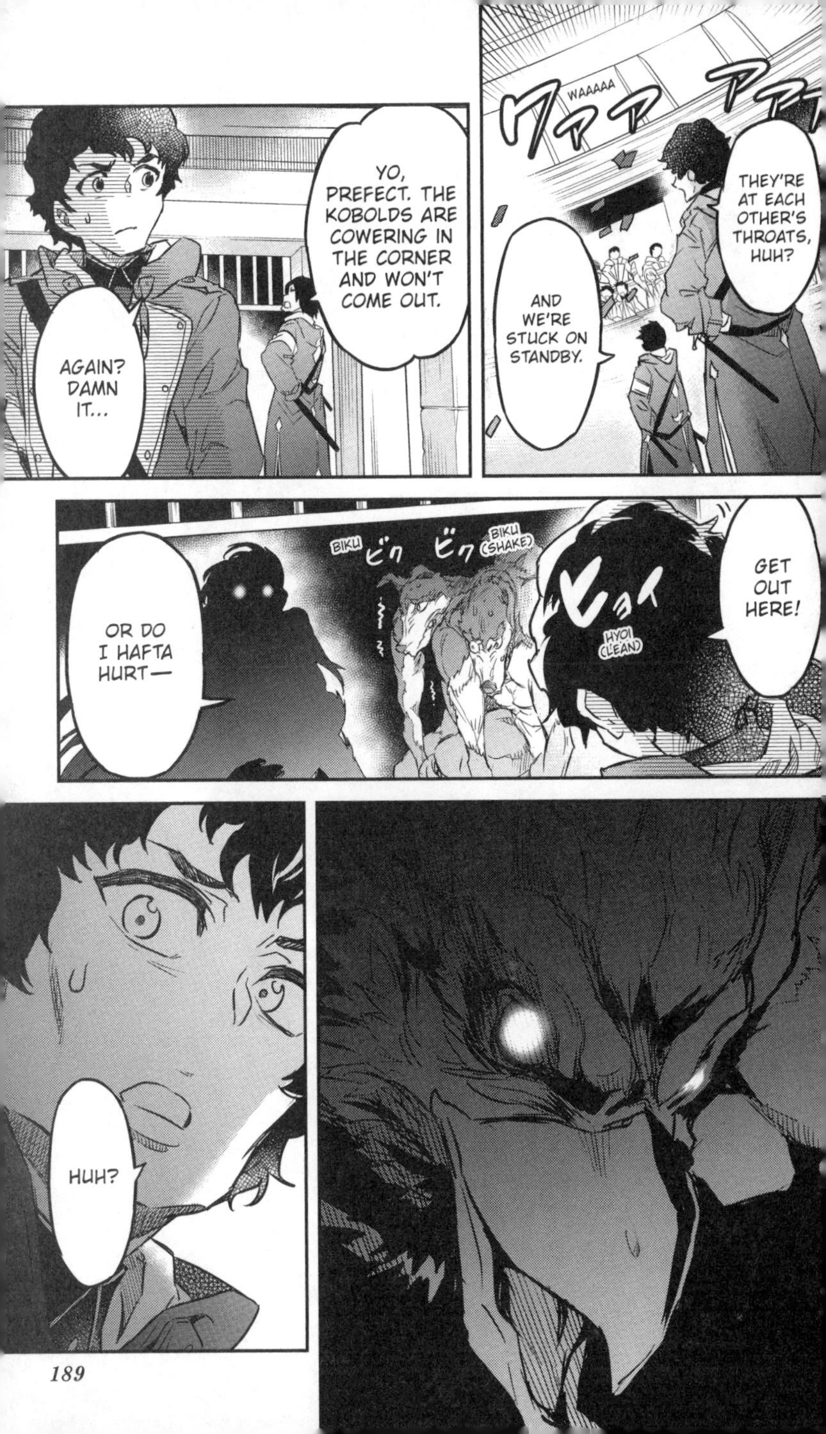
WAAAAA
THEY'RE AT EACH OTHER'S THROATS, HUH?
AND WE'RE STUCK ON STANDBY.
YO, PREFECT. THE KOBOLDS ARE COWERING IN THE CORNER AND WON'T COME OUT.
AGAIN? DAMN IT...
GET OUT HERE!
HYOI (LEAN)
BIKU (SHAKE)
BIKU
OR DO I HAFTA HURT—
HUH?

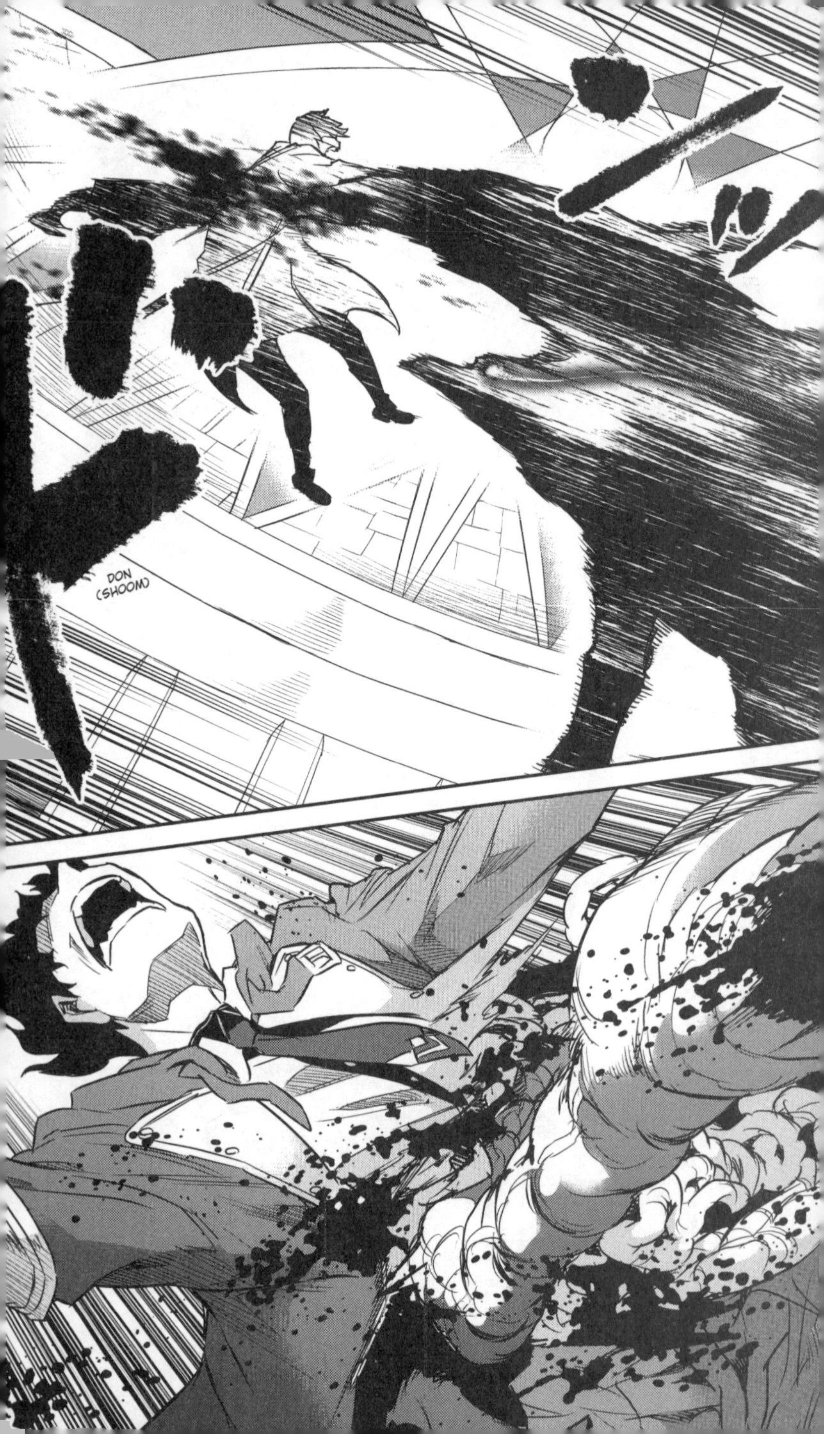
DON
(SHOOM)

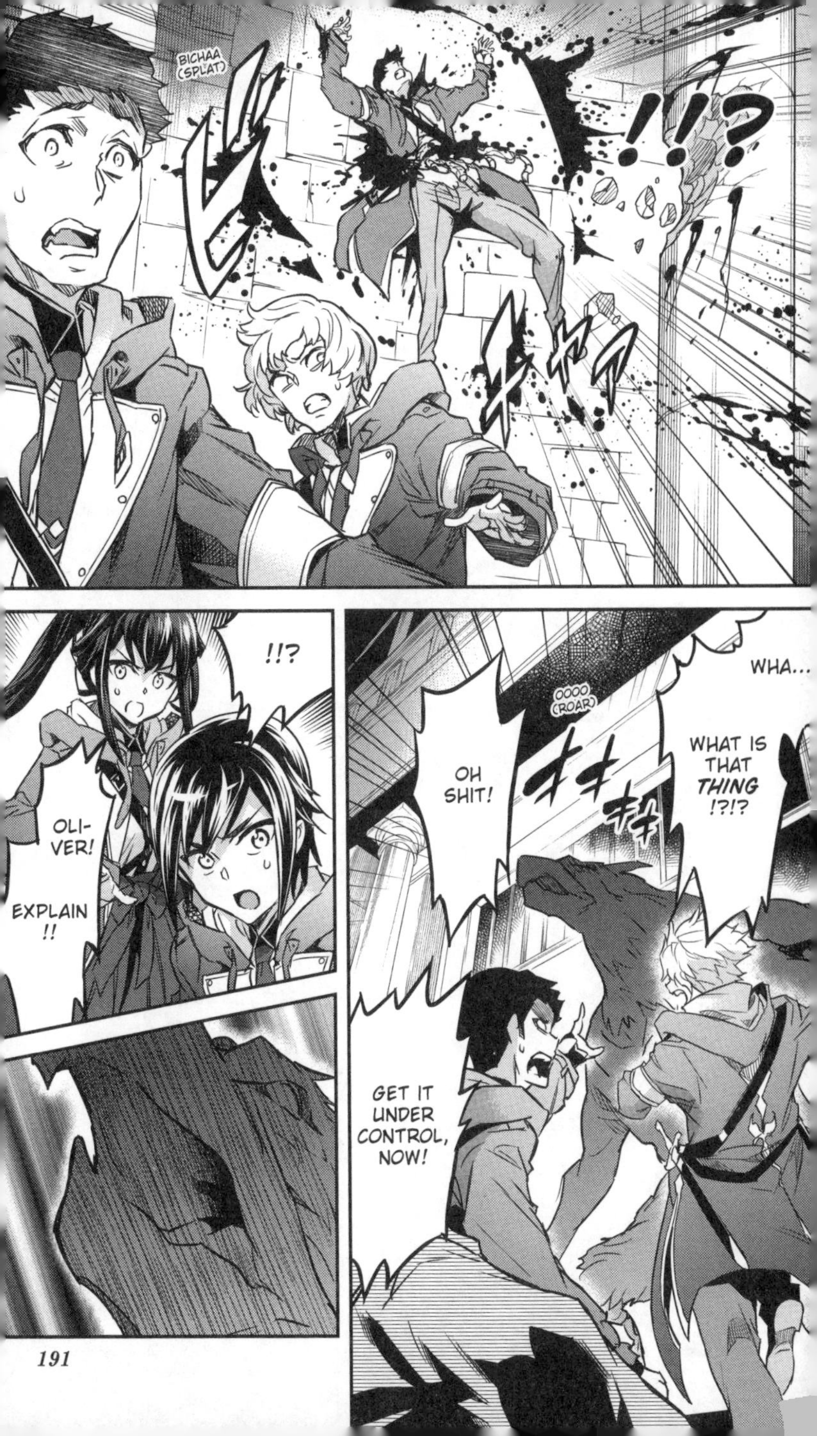
!!?
BICHAA (SPLAT)
WHA...
WHAT IS THAT THING !?!?
OOOO (ROAR)
OH SHIT!
GET IT UNDER CONTROL, NOW!
!!?
OLI-VER!
EXPLAIN !!

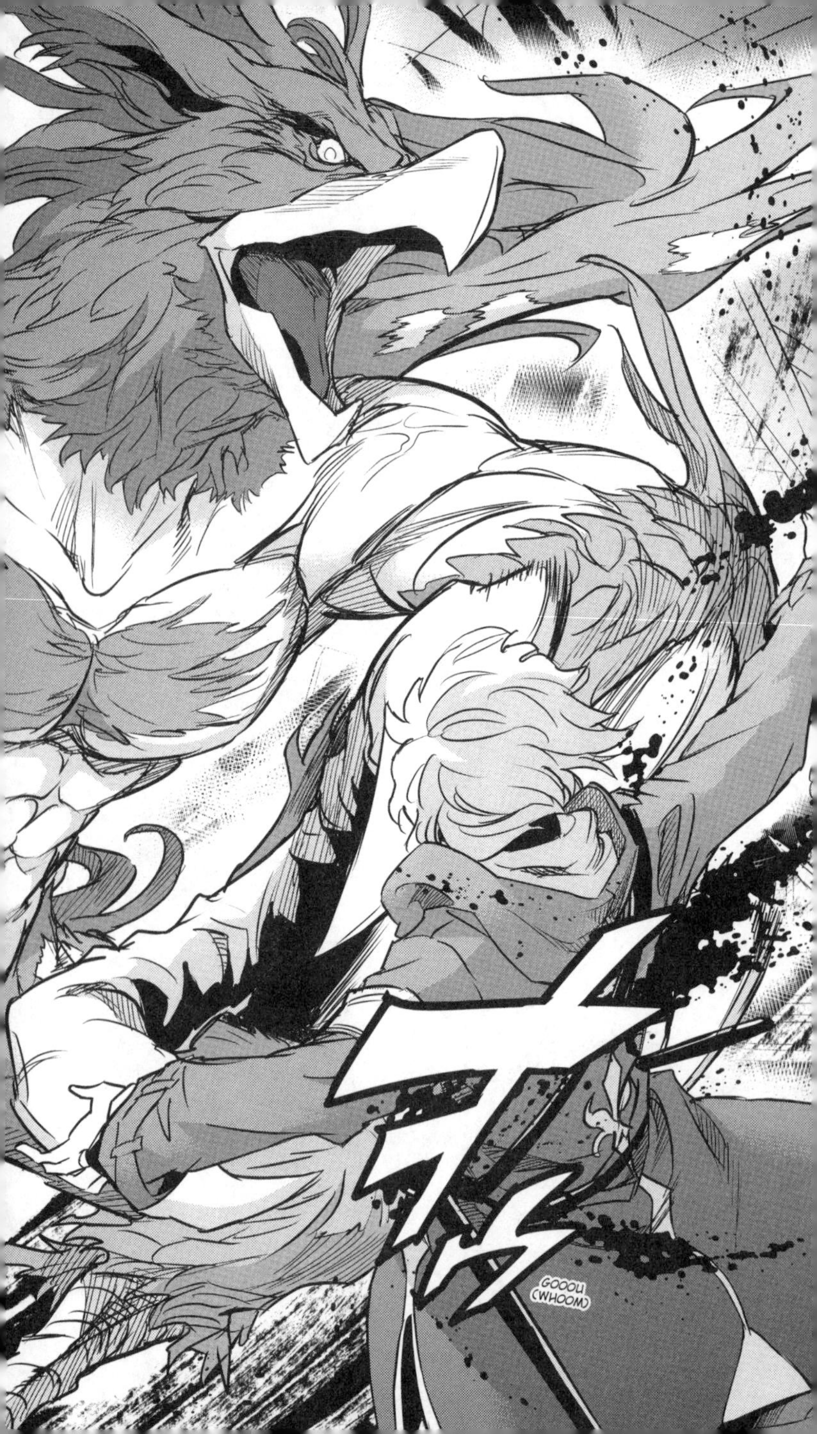
GOOOU
(WHOOM)